My Weakness
for
His Strength

VOLUME 2

My Weakness
for
His Strength

VOLUME 2

MICHAEL WELLS

Abiding Life Press

© 2017 by Michael Wells
Published by Abiding Life Press
A division of Abiding Life Ministries International
P.O. Box 620998, Littleton, CO 80162

Printed in the United States of America
ISBN: 978-0-9819546-5-3

Translations used for Bible quotations are most often New American Standard Bible. When noted, The Holy Bible, New International Version or The Amplified Bible.

Cover designed by Bob Fuller of Fuller Creative.

To my God
who loves and gives everything.

Contents

Contents

Contents

Contents

Contents

Contents

Contents

Contents

Contents

Contents

Contents

Foreword

It is November, 2016, and I have just finished cleaning up the manuscript for this second devotional book of Michael Wells. When he graduated to heaven in October, 2011, I had to hit the ground running with the demands of Abiding Life Ministries International, which he had founded and directed since 1989. Many other projects came along to elbow out my being able to work on this book, so by the time this gets published, it will be nearly six years since the first *My Weakness for His Strength* devotional came out, just around the time of his departure for heaven. I present this book now, though, without apology for tardiness, because my dear Lord has impressed on me for so long and in various ways that His timing is perfect. His timing is perfect. He is on the throne, He is working out His will among us, everything is going to turn out great in the end, and He is never late.

I have never tired of editing through Mike's work, because I am once again discipled by the Lord's revelations that pour out through the writing. Mike would be the first to say he learned much from the teachings of Andrew Murray, Arthur Burt, Watchman Nee, F.J. Huegel, and countless others. As Mike also said, once revelation moves from head to heart, where the Lord seals it in as part of oneself, it is no longer truth someone else said but truth received, owned, and inseparable from a person. That is the beauty of how truth circulates through the Body of Christ to feed and bring life to all the members, not just a special gifted few. God shows no partiality. This book, then, as hopefully you will note in every article, was written to glorify God, not man.

At times as I read through an article it seemed meaningless to me, and I might have presumptuously discarded it except for the knowledge that though it may not speak to me, someone somewhere will find the article to be exactly what the Holy Spirit arranged for him or her to read that day in order to speak revelation into the person's soul and spirit. That person might be me the next time I read it! Michael was a prolific writer as well as a wonderfully warm and engaging speaker, counselor, friend, and pastor, with the wherewithal to travel consistently—his favorite places being to the remote villages around the world—to bring the message of Christ in us, the hope of glory to as many as would listen and take it to heart. This book is one small part of what he left behind for us to enjoy in the presence of the Lord until we can all meet together in heaven to be immersed in Truth by the presence of the Lord forever.

—Betty Wells

Introduction

While sitting in an old man's house discussing various theological topics, I turned and said, "Tell me what you think!"

His response humbled me, "Oh, I wouldn't think of saying anything. I have never before met anyone who knew all there is to know about God." He put me in my place. Who knows all there is to know about God?

Many of the articles in this second volume of *My Weakness for His Strength* came from discussions I had in a discipleship setting. They deal with a variety of issues facing believers today. Not every article applies to every believer. As you read, there will be times when your spirit leaps within you and gives a divine amen! Yet at other times you will finish an article scratching your head, thinking, *That just cannot be right*, the reason being that it probably is not right! In every pastor and teacher, I believe, God leaves glaring flaws everyone can see but the teacher himself. It keeps believers safe from following fallible man and focused instead on following the infallible God. For this reason, along with the fact that, like all believers, I am in process myself, growing into what I have always been, there will be errors in the articles. Please do not throw out everything between these pages because of some obviously wrong things that may be found. Let the peace of God rule in your heart. One constant I say is absolutely true and right, "There is nothing His nearness will not cure!"

An agent was telling me how they trained people to recognize the difference between fake and real $100 bills. They would have people hold and examine the nearly perfect fake bills for weeks. Soon those bills became the norm. Eventually they would insert a real $100 note, and immediately everyone recognized what was just a little strange about the bill. By handling the fake for so long, the real was obvious, and at first it was assumed that the real bill was a fake. We deal in fake Christianity for so many years that it becomes the norm, and then, when the real thing comes before us, the first thought is, *What I am hearing and seeing must be a fake, because there is something just a little different about it.* Reality is that the fake has been lived in for so long that the real appears to be false. It is obvious something is different, and so we question. Well, in the fake everything comes ahead of Jesus, and in the real, Jesus comes ahead of everything else.

—Michael Wells

My Weakness
for
His Strength
VOLUME 2

DAY 1 — DAY 367

DAY 1
A Note to Fathers

*And our fathers were unwilling to be obedient
to him [Moses], but repudiated him and
in their hearts turned back to Egypt.*

—ACTS 7:39

The Bible refers to fathers as those who are responsible for leadership in the marriage, family, and country. Leadership is an interesting thing. Some men are born leaders, some are made leaders by others, and then there are those who make themselves leaders. Yet in the family, every man is called to be a leader. There are no excuses, for God will give everything needed to accomplish whatever tasks He calls a man to do. Men abiding in Christ are to lead. In order to lead, a father must recognize that leading is its own reward, simply because not all will follow. Success in leading cannot be measured by the number of people who follow. If we judge our obedience by the obedience of others, we will always be dissatisfied. A father must have firm resolve as he goes about leading in obedience to God, and he must trust in God's hands the results. A basic problem with obedience is when we believe others are to be obedient to make us happy! Consequently, too much energy is exerted in trying to force others to be obedient, and all this adds up to is frustration. The measure of success for a father is not in who listens and follows, but in whether the father has been obedient to God and fulfilled his own responsibility.

Everyone in the family has a free will. Therefore, the Bible does not say that a father is responsible for every action of the wife and children. The father's obedience may contrast with the disobedience of others.

Do not give up as a father because others do not follow; rather, continue to be leaven in the whole family. I have met many fathers completely disillusioned by the lack of regard for their leadership in the family, since their every decision is questioned and avoided, not respected. In the end, they begin to wonder what they are even doing there, supposing their main role in the family is a paycheck, believing they would never be missed, and entering midlife crisis. But fathers should not give in to the enemy, who links success with the numbers that follow; this is why he believes he was made a success by the few who followed him out of heaven into hell.

Let God give us a proper definition of success: simply being obedient! When we are obedient though we see nothing—standing fast and waiting for the fruit—we will be counted with the "others" of Hebrews 11.

DAY 2
A Wiped Memory

If we confess our sins, He is faithful and righteous to forgive us our sins and to cleanse us from all unrighteousness.

—I JOHN 1:9

I talked to a fellow who had attended a party crashed by some pseudo-gang members. The poor fellow was caught unaware and beaten unconscious with a bat. He woke up several days later with his jaw wired shut, fortunate to be alive. When the details of the event were related, one could barely keep from becoming enraged at the stupidity and injustice of someone's nearly being killed for absolutely no reason. To compound the situation, no one was charged with the brutal beating. Yet what amazed me most was the lack of hostility in the wronged person. On three different occasions I talked to him about the event, and he showed no anger, desire for vengeance, or frustration. Why? The explanation is simply that he could not remember the event. Because of the physiological trauma, his memory was wiped clean from two weeks leading up to the beating through the initial days in the hospital. He was of no use to the police in the case, for he could not pick the criminals out of a lineup. Since he had a wiped memory, he might even help his attackers if he saw them in need, put his arm around them, and buy them a cup of coffee. I realized that without the memory of an offense, it would be impossible to be vengeful. When the memory is erased concerning a wrong, the desire for vengeance is also removed.

We may not believe it, but God is clear on this point: He is in the business of wiping the memory of our offenses. All it takes from us is a simple acknowledgment of the failure, and the following morning He would not pick us out of a lineup to be condemned, but He will help us in time of need, put His arm around us, and fellowship with us. Does this sound too good to be true? Isn't all of Christianity too good to be true? The fact that there can be no vengeance where there is no memory of an offense brings confession into its proper perspective. Have we failed? Is our failure now the focus of our life? If so, it is due simply to our belief that God remembers and ponders it. But He does not! With confession comes the wiping of the remembrance of the offense and a renewed fellowship beginning the moment of repentance. We are no longer to let lying emotions keep us from His presence. The truth of who He is will set us free, the truth of the depth of forgiveness will give confidence, and the truth of His love and desire for us will bring the revelation that sin simply does not fit a believer.

DAY 3
Absolute Truth

Jesus said to him, "I am the Way, and the Truth, and the Life; no one comes to the Father but through Me."

—JOHN 14:6

How often we hear this type of questioning from unbelievers: "How can you Christians say that you are the only ones going to heaven? How can you say that you have the only way? All rivers lead to the ocean; therefore, all religions lead to God! How can Christians be so fortunate as to be the only people on the planet with an answer?"

First, for the world there is an inherent difficulty in Christianity, the same difficulty that made Christ intolerable: His claim to absolute truth. He even went so far as to claim that He was the Truth. This claim to absoluteness has been the cause of countless martyrdoms. Nevertheless, this is where we stand as believers. Never shrink from the absoluteness of Christ; rather, make full use of it. When I debate the absoluteness of Christ with an unbeliever, I know that absoluteness is on my side. No matter how full the person says life is, no matter how confidently he presents his belief system and proclaims that it gives peace and contentment, no matter how eloquently he defends his alternate lifestyle, the Lord's absoluteness is on my side.

Let me explain. Truth is judged by two things, results and consequences. A simple illustration is gravity. It is a law. Abide by it and reap the results; disobey and experience the consequences. The consequences are out of our control, since we relinquished control when we disobeyed the law.

Absolute spiritual truth is the same. To date I have experienced no consequences for shrugging off, neglecting, and disobeying the teachings of Islam, Buddhism, Confucianism, Hinduism, Jehovah's Witnesses, Mormons, New Age, Materialism, and a multitude of other false religions. What does this tell us? If there are no consequences from being disobedient to what man calls truth, then it is not truth at all. Are there results from following The Truth (Christ), and are there consequences from not following The Truth? History can provide thousands of examples proving the validity of His absoluteness. Those who forsake His call to high morals and commands to love, who reject forgiveness as a way of life, who feed the desire of the flesh, and who adjust law to fit self-centered desire never seem to improve. Gandhi, when asked what Christians could do to reach souls in India, responded, "Practice the teaching of Christ without diluting it!" He recognized the absoluteness of Christ without ever accepting Him.

Remember, no matter what any say in their defense, if they are living by another truth, they are going against the grain of the whole universe, and consequently their lives are not full, abundant, satisfied, or happy. When Jehovah's Witnesses come to my door, my response has become, "If what you say is true, why are you so unfulfilled?" It is interesting to see the response. At first there is denial and then, in the end, justification for their unhappiness. There has to be a contrast between their ideas of truth and absolute Truth.

Second, the idea that all rivers run to the ocean or that all spokes support the same hub does not apply to absolute Truth. I often ask someone, "What if a terrorist group were holding a hundred people in one building and your loved one in another, and you were asked to make the decision either to allow the terrorists to kill your loved one or all one hundred people? There are no other options. The hundred would be set free if your loved one were killed. What would you choose?" Of course, the person would have to pick the death of his loved one. "Now imagine how you would feel after the death if someone were to come up to you and proclaim that there actually had been a thousand ways the situation could have been resolved without the necessity of the death of your loved one. How would you feel, knowing that there truly had been no other options? I would say insulted, at the very least! Likewise, it is an insult to say there are a thousand ways to find God, Who sacrificed His Loved One, His only begotten Son, to make the only Way to save mankind."

Third, imagine how a couple would feel if their child had been murdered and regarding the apprehended murderer the judge proclaimed, "Let him go! There need not be any other consequences. After all, he is a pretty good fellow overall." The couple would have no respect for the judge who would not grant justice. Often in marriage counseling each spouse makes a defense for his/her behavior and condemns the other's actions; both want justice. If God is holy and just, then He must render judgment; however, He is also love. Once again we see the genius of God in judging the Son for our sin that we might be the recipients of His love. He is both judgment and love. Amazing! All He requires is faith in Him, yet seemingly for many this is too much.

Fourth, man needs a working religion. Christianity is doable in that Jesus does the work in us. Like the life of a vine flows into the branch, His life that has done and can do all moves through us. No other religion is doable. In fact, no other religion is readable, judging by Hindu, Buddhist, or Mormon writings; I immediately develop a mental hernia. They are confusing and filled with cartoons, though Hinduism, developed by the rich to suppress the poor, is now being accepted in America in the form of New Age teaching. Ask anyone to read Matthew 5, 6, and 7. Is there anything that causes offense? Is there anything that cannot be understood? Not only that, but if Christ's life is resident within, any feeble attempt from a person to respond to the Lord's desires in these directives will produce results. Yes, the life of The Truth, Jesus, is absolute.

DAY 4
Acknowledged Intelligence and Creativity Is The End Of Intelligence and Creativity!

> *Do not deceive yourselves. If any one of you thinks he is wise by the standards of this age, he should become a "fool" so that he may become wise.*
>  —I CORINTHIANS 3:18 [NIV]

I must admit that I love the way God works. There is the world and there is God. There is my perception, from my "earth" suit, and then there is His. I probably enjoy this the most in my own life from being an "international speaker." Can you imagine such folly on the part of God? Michael Wells, a published author! What a joke. That very thought to those who knew me growing up (probably until age 30) would have evoked a justifiable laugh. Add to the mix that it is the support team that makes it possible for me to be like the donkey on which Jesus rode into Jerusalem as I travel from country to country (the singing and palm leaves were not for the donkey). Actually, the donkey has it over me on many counts not worth mentioning. You know me and I see no difference between the believer who published a book and the one who did not, or between the preacher of a "mega church" and the one with five worshippers attending his meetings. This much, despite my stupidity, I have gotten right. What happens is not about man; it is about Jesus. I just wanted to make a point to my friends. I have a witness, and the witness is that I have seen God witness THROUGH me to something He has spent years bringing to the forefront in a believer's life. I have witnessed the life-changing impact of a witness to the witness of the Holy Spirit. As far as I know, I have not believed that I created anything but merely witnessed to it. The point is that much has been done in the lives of believers that, when looking back, we realize we had very little to do with; we were merely a witness to what God was doing. We know that if He gets all the glory then He does all the work.

However, here is what I often see: Recognized creativity and intelligence in one's self is the end of creativity and intelligence in one's self, for God is only Creative to the one who does not know what to do and gives wisdom to the foolish. If we truly want to remain wise and creative in our lives, we must constantly acknowledge to Him our lack of wisdom and creativity and that we need His. I promise this will change life, marriage, parenting skills, work ethics, and more. When boasting that WE had a revelation, that WE were wise, and that WE watched lives turned around, WE are done! Period! It is a spiritual absolute. When I see men take credit and copyright a revelation of God, it is the last one they will have; they have proven they are not to be trusted with the talents that are given. They bury their talent.

God does give revelation to man, but I must repeat, GOD gives revelation to man, and if that revelation helped you with your family, do not make a program around yourself. Let me expand on this. Let us say that you are talking to someone who KNOWS about the government, he KNOWS everything that is happening. He KNOWS about the news media and KNOWS about what the world leaders are up to. He KNOWS all about abortion, gay rights, people's thinking, and more. He KNOWS. Well, how would you have a conversation with someone who KNOWS? I would like to know how he KNOWS so much about things that are hidden from the rest of us. Then based on the "absolute" of what he KNOWS, he has a solution. This is really amazing to watch. Here is a statement at which I really marvel: "It is KNOWN that Christians are a people of hatred and bigotry." My, someone needs to double up on the pink pills the doctor gave him. He KNOWS that Christians are a people of hate? When believers in the U.S. alone gave 500 billion dollars in aid around the world, when believers fight against slavery, when believers fight oppression, or when believers want the best for a pregnant fourteen-year-old in Haiti? I could go on, but why? The someone's of the world "KNOW." Then when they happen to get trapped in a corner because of the illogic of what they "KNOW," they really do not KNOW, and my statement is that they have been driveling all along if they do not really KNOW but have been telling me all along how they really FEEL. Jesus KNEW, and I would sit at His feet, but for all these people who KNOW, why in the world would I sit at their feet? Is God telling them each night what is happening around the world? Definitely there is a "knowing" in the spirit. All I "know in the spirit" is that Jesus is the Way and every other way is not the Way. However, when talking to someone who "KNOWS" all there is to know about man, I shift to a different topic to keep from going mad. I do not know how shellfish grow. I do not know how a caterpillar becomes a butterfly. I do not know why a hippo hates fires. There is so much I do not know, and maybe, just maybe, he will know about some of those things!

DAY 5
Addiction Defined

. . . for by what a man is overcome, by this he is enslaved.
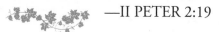 —II PETER 2:19

An addiction goes way beyond a habit in that it is really a coping mechanism with which we have built a relationship. Just as a controlling person keeps telling us we need him in our lives if we are going to succeed, so does Mr. Addiction. Just as the controlling person takes us down in order to bring himself up, so does Mr. Addiction. Just as our day can be going fine until all of a sudden the controller calls and turns our world upside down, so does Mr. Addiction. The controller hates us, uses us, fills us with self-hatred, and yet we refuse to say good-bye.

Many in our society are carrying on adulterous affairs with Mr. Addiction. Drugs—not only the kind sold by the corner drug dealer but also the corner drugstore—and myriad other vices control the lives of believers. Things that become addictions start out friendly enough, coming only when they are wanted. But once addicted, people come to them at their every bidding. While going about daily tasks, Mr. Addiction places a call to their minds. He asks, "Are you feeling depressed? Are things wrong at home?

Do you have stress at work? Is the teenager driving you crazy? Then stop by after work!" Something deep within the persons tells them to hang up, but throughout the day calls keep coming. Finally in a robot-like trance they subconsciously agree, leaving work with every intention of going home, but in the back of their minds knowing they have answered the phone in the affirmative. They find themselves unwilling participants with the old, controlling friend, Mr. Addiction. To make sure they never consider themselves to be above him, Mr. Addiction waits until the moment they have fallen into his suggestion before making an all-out verbal assault on their character. "You are a worthless, stupid failure," he says, for doing the very thing he had encouraged the people to do. Mr. Addiction knows if the ensnared ones focus on hating themselves, then instead of having to place several phone calls he can count on their answering on the first ring. In many ways we can thrive while still hating the world, but we cannot live well hating ourselves. Old buddy Mr. Addiction has one goal: sacrifice! That would be the sacrifice of people's lives—not to mention their sleep—at his feet.

DAY 6
Addiction Definitely Defeated

Wretched man that I am! Who will set me free from the body of this death? Thanks be to God through Jesus Christ our Lord! So then, on the one hand I myself with my mind am serving the law of God, but on the other, with my flesh the law of sin.

 —ROMANS 7:24, 25

Stop! You have punished yourself long enough. Though the way seems right at midday, life has already proven to you that by the next morning you will hate yourself and know for certain this is not the way. You need a divorce from your so-called friend, Mr. Addiction; let the thief that steals steal no longer. First, bring the matter before God, making it His responsibility. Let Him answer the phone. Let light meet darkness and see who gives way! Second, you must keep in mind that this is no friend at all; he is not concerned for your good. Say this to Mr. Addiction: "Satan, all that you hoped to destroy in me, I pronounce on you a thousandfold, in the name of Jesus." Say that for me even if you do not believe it; I have enough faith for both of us in this matter. Third, during times when the ringing sound seems to overwhelm you, live for the morning. Remember how you would feel the next morning if you did not say no and wait. One victory causes the same song in your voice as a sparrow's in the morning, and one victory encourages the next victory. The more you are victorious, the more you will desire victory. Your divorce with Mr. Addiction will definitely put a song in your heart and a lift in your spirit.

One last point: if there is an addiction to drugs of any kind, do not stop all at once. Rather, withdraw slowly. Set a goal of six weeks or months to be free. Decrease dosages and consult a physician. Take charge! All of life will support your decision.

DAY 7
Affairs!

*. . . having eyes full of adultery that never cease from sin,
enticing unstable souls, having a heart trained in greed,
accursed children; forsaking the right way,
they have gone astray . . .*

 —II PETER 2:14 & 15

Affairs are interesting in that only about 10% marry the person with whom they are having an adulterous affair, because generally speaking, a mate will fulfill 70% or more of a person's needs. An affair starts because of the search for the other 30% or less of unmet needs. These needs comprise a variety of things, including but not limited to the lack of conversation, sex, impulsiveness (not being on guard against temptation), stability, activities, or agreement. However, the hiccup is that though an affair is started because of seeking to meet the 30% unmet need, even if the 30% need is met, the other 70% of needs will not be met by this new person. Therefore, the affair does not last, and if the person has already divorced, he or she will ultimately find another person that meets the same old 70% of need met by the original spouse, in essence, marrying the same type of spouse he or she divorced.

The conclusion made would be to stay with (and true to) the current mate, realizing God does not intend any person to meet all of one's needs, and then, to the degree possible, work toward the meeting of the other 30% within the context of marriage. Those who are victims of divorce they never sought can remember they were meeting at least 70% of the wayward spouses' needs, so they need not listen to former mates' offensive blame and justification that they failed to meet the full 100%. Who could? God did not create us to be another's all in all; He is that to anyone honestly seeking Him.

"The LORD is near to all who call upon Him, to all who call upon Him in truth.

He will fulfill the desire of those who fear Him; He will also hear their cry and will save them." –Psalm 145:18, 19

DAY 8
Agreement With God

A double-minded man, unstable in all his ways.

—JAMES 1:8

God tells us we are free; we are created in such a way that we can choose. It is not the will of God that everyone chooses to obey every one of His commands. He would like for us to, but He does not will it. It is the will of God that we get to choose. Many times we want to do what we want to do, and yet we can see the wisdom in what He has asked us to do. When we continue to choose our way, the end result is double-mindedness and, ultimately, self-hatred leading to depression from the struggle of not agreeing with God. At this point many will see their freedom to choose as a curse and would like God to step in and make them robots programmed to do only His will. Such a mindset will keep us waiting for a long time, and the in-between time will become a mean time as we slowly return to the place we never left. Esau is interesting in that he regretted losing the birthright but showed not a hint of remorse about the soup. He still wanted the soup and the birthright. We want to continue in the self-gratifying ways of the past (good and bad) and still have a dynamic relationship with the Lord, and yet the two are incompatible. Hence, people get depressed and want to punish themselves for their misbehavior. This self-punishment is not repentance but something they deem sufficient to allow them to continue in THEIR ways while still pleading to God to make them be pleasing. Depression will continue to appear because of the knowledge that they are free but are choosing not to follow Christ. It is a conflict of doing the very things they do not want to do, and their way never builds them up but tears them down. This is where the world, flesh, and Satan are of benefit to believers, not a curse, by the way they make us aware of the principle of cost and benefit. The cost of self-hatred outweighs any possible perceived benefit of doing what we want. Christ has set us free, and when we get sick of being double-minded, we can use our freedom to follow Him and be at one with ourselves, discovering a peace that passes understanding. Remember, choosing our way as opposed to the WAY is like walking with a weak cane; one day it will break, we will fall on it, and it will pierce our very hearts. God's commands are for our good, not His.

DAY 9
All These Things Are Against Me

Through God we will do valiantly, and it is He who shall tread down our adversaries.

—PSALM 108:13

Let God arise, let His enemies be scattered.

—PSALM 68:1

I call upon the Lord, who is worthy to be praised, and I am saved from my enemies.

—PSALM 18:3

Are you finding that life is against you? Do you find the system to be causing you frustration? Do you believe if the devil were not against you, life would be easier and victory possible? As I traveled from place to place, country to country, and church to church, I found believers who were always fighting with the devil and professing that he is against them.

When Paul addressed the church at Colossae he highlighted the life, teaching, and resurrection of Jesus. To them it seemed Jesus was important, but not central; His prestige was considerable, but not preeminent; and so Paul writes to them in an attempt to restore Jesus, the Messiah, to the center of their lives. In this book, he emphasizes the work Christ has done and places everything as secondary to the person and work of Jesus, the Messiah, including the defeat on the cross of the devil and all that was contrary to true life.

How vital is our focus on, our belief in, and our understanding of what Jesus has done. It is vitally important to know that God and the devil are not at war; there is not an ongoing struggle between God and the devil. Jesus put the devil out of business at Calvary, and yet too often it seems Christians want to keep putting him back into business. There is no doubt that we live in an anti-God, truly unbelieving society, and much is seemingly against us. Like in Asaph's Psalm 73, we ask, "Does God really care? Does He know what is going on?" Someone has said that God is never late, but He misses some glorious opportunities to be early.

Make no mistake about it, the world's system and the devil are against the believer. We hear people say in a real defeated voice, "Oh, Brother, the devil is giving me a hard time," or, "The devil has been against me so much lately." At this I ask, "Did you think he would ever be for you?" Be assured he is not and never will be for you, for by his very nature he will always be against you. His mission is to steal, kill, and destroy. He does not have a nature to be for anyone, not even those who serve and fulfill his evil intentions. We see people who serve the devil and whose lives are being destroyed; his evil deception has brought them into bondage and even self-destruction. The devil is a liar. However, there is a higher revelation for the Christian, because the devil is secondary and being used by God for His purposes. As my English friend has said, "The devil is God's sheepdog to bring us to Christ." In the same way, the world squeezes us until we seek refuge in Christ and then squeezes us to reveal the Christ in us. How often have we moaned that all these things are against us, not recognizing the greater revelation in the truth that God is in all and to all, and because of Him all things exist.

In Psalm 56 David talks about all the enemies that surrounded and came against him, and then in verse 9 he said, "This I know, that God is for me." What a belief system that is, what a revelation that is, that when our enemies, modern-day type, come against us, this we know: God is for us!

In Romans, Chapter 8, verses 35-39, Paul speaks of all the things arrayed against us: tribulation, distress, persecution, famine, swords, nakedness, principalities, powers, and the list goes on. But he had already made clear the profound truth in verse 31: "What, then, shall we say in response to this? If God is for us, who can be against us?" [NIV] No matter the opposition, who can really be against us? Paul had already reminded us how mighty God is and how He is working in our lives to the extent that (verse 28) "we know that God causes all things to work together for good to those who love God, to those who are called according to His purpose."

Let me emphasize that we have a God, He is for us, and all of those things appearing to be against us are actually in His hand working together for good, as He correctly interprets it. We know our problems and negatives of life are working for us even though they started out against us from our perspective through the natural senses. In the midst of your enemies, declare like David, "This I know! This I know! God is for me." Believing this truth will change your lifestyle.

DAY 10
All Things TOGETHER

And we know that God causes all things to work together
for good to those who love God, to those who are called
according to His purpose.

—ROMANS 8:28

"Rather, let God be found true, though every man be found a liar," Romans 3:4. Carnal man is set on internal and external destruction, and he would take every man with him. Yet God is for us. Of the billions of people, to each one who turns to Him He gives the promise to cause all things to work together for good! What willpower, what a will of steel; nothing can bend it, nothing stops it, and it will be accomplished. All things will work together. It is important to remember the word together, for things standing by themselves cannot accomplish His goal. For example, many times an isolated event has worked to ruin people, like when an abuse, a hurt, a rejection, an accident, or a death is singled out to stand alone and is allowed to become the focus of life; no good will be found, only ruin. All things must work together. One bad event must wrap itself around a good event, and a good around a bad, and so on until all is one. In Him there is not good and bad. The cross and crown are not isolated but are one; to take me down to bring me up is not separated but one, and to put me out in order to bring me in both work together.

Look not at singular events in your life and then make the assessment that life is bad. Take the full spectrum of events and you will see they have all worked together for good. Do remember the concept of together and the will of steel that is working things together. It will change your outlook on life. What good are four wheels? You feel cheated if that is your graduation present. Or what good is a car with no wheels? Again there would be the feeling of disappointment. But if someone were to carry the wheels to the car, put them on, and give it to you, you would feel quite blessed. God is putting things together; when you see it, you will be quite blessed.

DAY 11
Am I Saved?

For God so loved the world, that He gave His only begotten Son, that whoever believes in Him should not perish, but have eternal life.

—JOHN 3:16

Scripture is clear on the point of salvation, or who is going to heaven. That gift exists for the one who believes in Jesus. I continue to find it amazing that many believe in the power of Satan to enter a life through a distant relative who had been involved in the occult, and yet Jesus just might not enter the lives of those who ask Him to. Let me assure you on this point! If you have ever verbally given your life to Christ or asked Christ to enter your life, He has! There are three ways to know without a doubt that you are saved. Any of the three are confirmation. First, if you ever wonder if you are saved, for only a saved person can be tempted with the thought that he is not saved. Second, if you have ever struggled with sinful behavior, for an unbeliever is often happy with his behavior. Third, finally, and most importantly, have you ever asked Christ into your life? This third point does not rest on feeling but on fact and faith. Your God is bigger than you! If you are held accountable for idle words, how much more, then, when with the words of your mouth Christ is acknowledged as Lord and Savior?

DAY 12
Anxious

And which of you by being anxious can add
a single cubit to his life's span?
—MATTHEW 6:27 [RSV]

Anxiety, worry, doubt, and fear! The worry list presented by most is nearly endless and usually includes relationships, personal responsibilities, children, finances, the future, job security, and health. These are indeed things for which you are responsible; it is your job to see them through. Now imagine that you can step out of your body, look back, and examine the worried, anxious you sitting in a chair. How would you describe yourself at your worst moments? Very likely you feel stupid, worthless, weak, angry, condemning, and like a failure and a liar. As you contemplate your weakness and all that you must do, how do you feel? If with all your responsibilities you are full of such weakness, how can you be filled with joyful expectation? You must perform, but you know your limitations and so you worry over the outcome.

Now imagine that sitting in the chair next to you is another person, Jesus. How would you describe Him? His eyes are filled with compassion. The warmth of His countenance, accompanied by His strength and confidence, is stirring. His empty hands are held open; of course there is nothing in them, for you have given nothing to Him! Your powerful Lord sits there inactive, resting, waiting, doing nothing.

The weak you seated in the chair is exhausted, because in all your frailty you had attempted to push uphill a wheelbarrow filled with all your cares. Within just a few short feet you had given up, angry that those you trust had not come to your aid.

The point is that the source of your anxiety and fear is trusting a weak self. Do you see why you need Jesus? You were not created to carry all the concerns of life; you were created to be dependent. You cannot fly, and neither can you carry anxiety. The only One Who can—Jesus—must carry the anxiety of every person. But how can He carry what He has not been given? Psalm 46:10 is clear: "Cease striving and know that I am God," or literally, get your hands off. Why do you keep your hands on? There is only one reason: unbelief. You cling to belief in your own ability to do a better job than He would. Psalm 46:10 goes on to say, "I will be exalted among the nations, I will be exalted in the earth."

"Do not be anxious then, saying, 'What will we eat?' or 'What will we drink?' or 'With what shall we clothe ourselves?' For all these things the Gentiles eagerly seek; for your heavenly Father knows that you need all these things," Matthew 6:31, 32.

Anxiety does not suit the disciple.

DAY 13
Appealing To The Flesh

For the kingdom of God does not consist in words but in power.

—I CORINTHIANS 4:20

Flesh-stirring sermons are the easiest in the world to preach simply by sitting back and thinking of a common problem humanity shares, particularly if it revolves around instinct: sex, self-protection, food, or unforgiveness. Such topics will pretty much hit everyone in the congregation. Then show Jesus as not having had any of these problems and talk about a few saints that supposedly never had these problems. At this point, you are ready for the final plunge of the knife: "How can you be a Christian with these problems? You must change." Then end the whole thing with a list of things they can do to change, a list you have never kept yourself. In the end, you will get nearly the desired 100% response.

However, there is another approach. Focus on and talk about Jesus, highlight the revelation that we cannot but He can, and remind the people that the commands of Christ are exactly His description of how He lived. Then move to a passage concerning the Christ who lives in us. End with a plea to rest in the knowledge that He understands our struggles, nothing we have done will make Him reject us, and He lived in a body and won the battle, a victory that will forever exist in His blood. Explain the Way and what is not the Way. See if the hearts cannot be stirred toward Jesus rather than guilt's being stirred, which makes people run from Jesus, when His presence offers the only possibility of such living. Remember that according to the parable of the sower and seed, three-fourths of your work is a complete waste of time. Relax and let God give growth to the seeds. Only a few may respond, but from those few you will see a 6,000 and 10,000% return, for they will not be acting like Jesus but allowing exactly Jesus to emanate from them.

DAY 14
Are They Saved?

That is, the word of faith which we are preaching, that if you confess with your mouth Jesus as Lord, and believe in your heart that God raised Him from the dead, you will be saved.

—ROMANS 10:8, 9

"Are they saved?"

"They are not true believers!"

"I don't think they are born again!"

"They couldn't be Christians and act that way."

The preceding are statements I have often heard and, to my dismay, have said. They are questions that are regularly asked. However, there is an inherent problem with asking such questions about others, namely that we embrace as our calling the ascertaining of who is saved by examining criteria and then judging another's salvation with our understanding. This heavy responsibility is obviously best left in the hands of God. Throughout church history the speculation over who is saved and who is not has led men to make incredible lists of qualifiers, including such things as dress, creeds, "spiritual" activities, hairstyles, attendance, language, and which day of the week to hold a worship service. Every believer must decide where to draw the line between who is saved and who is not. According to my own personal experience and perspective, I have decided where that line is. I ask the simple question, "Do you believe in Jesus Christ?" If the answer is affirmative I move ahead to acknowledge the person as a brother or sister in Christ, no matter what his or her apparent condition. I have had experience with believers who would not measure up to any qualifier on any list, but as I spoke to them as believers, they began to move as believers and soon were expressing Christ naturally. Often I will meet someone whose spouse has for years said that the person cannot be a believer because of certain behaviors. I have even had some say to me, "Well, I used to think I was a Christian, but my mate assures me I am not!" What a thing to say. How could anyone hope to satisfy when he has been told he is one big disappointment?

If you have accepted Christ into your life, He then became your life. You are saved, and we need merely look at the obstacles hindering the expression of that life.

DAY 15
Are We Teaching Passivity?

Show me your ways, O Lord, teach me your paths; guide me in your truth and teach me, for you are God my Savior, and my hope is in you all day long.

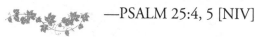

—PSALM 25:4, 5 [NIV]

I was sharing how some think we teach passivity. It is not so. In the morning we get up and commit the day to God, and then we move in all the natural areas of life, which are actually supernatural, for He holds them all together. When I meet a "situation," I yield and say amen, but that is not passivity. I will give an example. I get up and say, "Jesus, come and go with me" when I am headed to the airport to fly to another country. Upon arriving I discover that my bags are missing. I do not just say "Amen" and walk off; I work to get them. When it becomes obvious that I cannot get them, I recognize I have a situation. At that point I do say, "Amen," yield, and stop fighting it. In the moment I yield and see God in a situation, I no longer have a situation! However, the result of passivity did not bring me to this point but the very active choices of seeing God and yielding to His will.

DAY 16
Are You a Machine and Sin the Driver?

Knowing this, that our old self was crucified with Him,
in order that our body of sin might be done away with,
so that we would no longer be slaves to sin;
for he who has died is freed from sin.

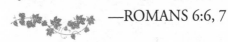

—ROMANS 6:6, 7

Many view slavery to sin as analogous to a machine and a driver. A machine has no will of its own, being completely dominated and controlled by the driver, who turns it on, moves the handles, expects response from the machine, and turns it back off. This is the "life" of a machine; its state of being without a will, without the ability to choose, shows a true example of passivity. Many unbelievers and believers alike have embraced the philosophy of the slavery of sin, viewing sin as the driver and the unbeliever or believer as nothing more than a machine. Sin has complete control over the unbeliever or the believer, who in turn must yield to its dictates. This view of life is soul killing in that it strips man of all hope. If one cannot choose, why even get out of bed in the morning? Why keep moving forward to a pre-determined judgment? When those in the world say their sexual orientation is predetermined, they have just confessed to being hopeless machine slaves. To convince a believer that he has an addiction is to persuade him that he has no choice. What, then, is there to do but allow sin to turn his switch to on, move him in its direction, and turn him off at its bidding? Oddly, we are told that the heterosexual can say no to sex, but somehow the homosexual cannot.

We are not machines, and sin is not the driver. Unlike the piece of machinery, we have free will. However, our Creator, the Master, has set the parameters of our choices. Though thus limited in our choices, we still have choice. As a slave, a person can work or not work, live or be killed, eat or not eat, sin or not sin, love or not love. There is a lot a slave can do and a lot a slave cannot do. Certainly he cannot leave. Spiritually, sin might be the master, but still the person can choose to do good (follow the Law) or choose to sin (disobey the Law). Now, sin does not sit controlling in the driver's seat on a believer or unbeliever; instead, sin manipulates by appealing to pride and the desires of the flesh. Sin cannot control; it is not allowed to do so. Sin gets its adrenaline rush from manipulating someone to choose against God, choose sin, but anyone can simply say no to sin. I have seen and met unbelievers who one day said no to this or that sin; they meant it and it stuck. How much more empowered is the believer? Sin is a big annoyance, it has the power to deceive, and it is relentless. When someone is the slave of sin, all choices are calculated by sin to serve sin. However, the capability is still there to choose, or how could an unbeliever choose Christ? Once Christ is chosen, a person is taken out of the dominion of sin and placed in the Kingdom of God. He is still a slave, but he serves a wonderful Master, the parameters are much grander, and the choices far more varied. A slave still must choose. We read in John 5:19, "the Son can do nothing of Himself, unless it is something He sees the Father doing; for whatever the Father does, these things the Son also does in like manner." Jesus did do something; He chose to do nothing on His own. That is not passivity.

I once finished a meeting and was verbally attacked by another. I did something: I prayed, I listened, I rested, and I heard nothing from Jesus, so I said nothing. It appeared to others that I did nothing, but I was actually doing a lot of choosing. As a slave of righteousness, I can do a lot of choosing. At other times I have actively done nothing by waiting and listening, and He spoke. In those instances I spoke what I heard, and it was redemptive, as Jesus always is. Again, it is soul killing if as a believer I think I am a machine without free will. I am a slave to Christ, but I do not just sit around waiting for Jesus to get in the driver's seat. I work within the parameters He has set for me, His slave, and I have so many choices and freedoms that He actually calls me His friend, His beloved, His brother, and His bride. This slave must put one foot in front of the other and walk by faith. This slave must deny his lying emotions. There are many things that my Master will not do for me, because it is His will that I do them for myself, and I am to obey my beautiful Master. What a wonderful kingdom is His; what a great day it is to be a slave! Now, the old slave died, so sin can no longer lay any claim whatsoever on me as a believer. If sin wants to grab back the old slave, it will just end up with a handful of spiritual dust.

DAY 17
Are You a Successful Christian?

*Do not love the world, nor the things in the world. If
anyone loves the world, the love of the Father is not in him.*

—I JOHN 2:15

There are many ways carnal believers judge the success
of their Christianity. Often I find them poking around
my marriage in an attempt to discount the ministry. My
children have laughed at the attempts made to get them
to reveal some hidden secret about our family. "Didn't you
resent your father's traveling? What is he like at home on
his bad days? Did your siblings rebel because of the time
your father spent in the ministry?" These are just a few
of the overt questions. There are many more covert ones.
My point is that in the United States, the "proof" of a
relationship with Christ is generally judged by the state of
finances, children, and marriage. Is that the proof?

Luke 12:51-53, "Do you suppose that I came to grant
peace on earth? I tell you, no, but rather division; for
from now on five {members} in one household will be
divided, three against two and two against three. They
will be divided, father against son and son against father;
mother against daughter and daughter against mother;
mother-in-law against daughter-in-law and daughter-
in-law against mother-in-law." Also, John 16:33, "These
things I have spoken to you, so that in Me you may have
peace. In the world you have tribulation, but take courage;

I have overcome the world." Then, I Corinthians 7:28, "But if you should marry, you have not sinned; and if a virgin should marry, she has not sinned. Yet such will have trouble in this life, and I am trying to spare you." The Old Testament is replete with stories of the great men of faith—such as Noah, Isaac, and David—and the failures of their children.

My point is threefold. First, I do not believe a person can say that a man's relationship with Christ is proven in a good marriage, perfect children, or financial success. There is, actually, more proof of a man's walk with Jesus in how he responds in a bad marriage with self-willed children and financial strain. Frankly, we do not know what a man is like when he remains untested. This is one of the lessons from Job. Second, I have only been a success as a husband and father as I judge myself by my own or another's standards of success. As I come under God's light I realize I have been far less successful. Once I admit it, no one has a leverage point in me, and when I discern that someone is looking for dirt to discredit my message, I respond, "I am a terrible husband, a worse father, and an idiot with money. Only when I have acknowledged these weaknesses and invited Him to be my strength, in that moment was I something different." That settles it. I am a weak man ministering to the weak. The third and final point is that I have met those who fulfill Paul's requirements of eldership, and I thank God for men like these. Paul's standard goes beyond the individual's manifesting the fruit of the Spirit to a commitment to those around him. Titus 1:5-9, "For this reason I left you in Crete, that you would set in order what remains, and appoint elders in every city as I directed you, namely, if any man be above reproach, the husband of one wife, having children who believe, not accused of dissipation or rebellion. For the overseer must be above reproach as God's steward, not self-willed, not quick-tempered, not addicted to wine, not pugnacious, not fond of sordid gain, but hospitable, loving what is good, sensible, just, devout, self-controlled, holding fast the faithful word which is in accordance with the teaching, so that he will be able both to exhort in sound doctrine and to refute those who contradict." The Prodigal Son's father would not have met the criteria. I can imagine the hints his friends dropped after hearing about the son's behavior. I am not above reproach. I have walked in the flesh. I have judged and slandered. I have gotten angry. I have competed with others. I have had children rebel, and most importantly, I have tried to steal what belongs to God: His glory! I am in good company, for nearly every Old Testament saint would flunk Paul's requirements. I am not making excuses, for I said that "I" was the one that made the mistakes. You might be like me, one who falls short and does not qualify, given such a list. What are we to do? Well, a lesser gives way to the greater. God is the greatest; my failures are the lesser. We will acknowledge that we abide in Him, focus on His successes, preach His successes, and relish the fact that nothing has separated us from His love. We will preach Jesus and nothing of ourselves. Should we be allowed to minister to the righteous? In no way; we are not worthy. Can we share with the hopeless? Yes, for we can share the fact that we, too, are hopeless every moment we are not focused on Him. In the end, we have no glory, but we glory in the glory of the One who has remained faithful when we have been faithless. Though you may not meet the list of qualifications for an Elder, it does not mean you cannot share Jesus. I have been told that if I did not meet everything in Paul's list, I should not be the head of a ministry. My response is, "I am the head of nothing. I have asked none to follow me or to imitate me; I am pointing to the One who is the head, who is to be followed, and who is to be imitated."

DAY 18
Are You Telling The Truth?

Jesus said to him, "I am the way, and the truth, and the life; no one comes to the Father but through Me."

—JOHN 14:6

In this day and age, truth is in short supply, so this question is all the more important. Do you tell the truth? No, I do not mean did you lie on your tax return, did you give the police officer correct information when questioned about your speed, or were you honest when asked why you did not make the meeting. There is only one Truth, and to tell the Truth is to tell of Jesus. In the Christian community I find more and more who do not tell the Truth. I am told what will bring healing, how to build a church, how to have a happy family, and how to obtain material blessings. However, I do not think in all those sermons I am being told the Truth, for after listening intently, I cannot hear the name of Jesus. In fact, walk around nearly any church institution, seminary, or organization and you will not hear the Truth. "If we say that we have fellowship with Him and yet walk in the darkness, we lie and do not practice the truth" (I John 1:6). I find that most who would confront and divide over a minute point of doctrine are never telling the Truth. Their little point is never the point. Jesus is to be the point. These people simply are not concerned for the Truth, for if they were, surely we would hear His name.

DAY 19
Aspen Trees

So then, just as you received Christ Jesus as Lord,
continue to live in Him, rooted and built up in Him,
strengthened in the faith as you were taught,
and overflowing with thankfulness.

 —COLOSSIANS 2:6, 7 [NIV]

The aspen is an interesting tree, growing to great stature and yet having no great root system. When it reaches gigantic proportions, the winds collapse it and it becomes reachable food for the deer in the winter, for the bark is high in protein.

So it is with many Christian leaders who reach great height, but because they neglected to remain rooted in Christ, the wind caused them to fall in times of winter.

Do not be discouraged! There is much to be learned from a fallen Christian. The warnings are food for us, and there is often much to be eaten.

DAY 20
At Whom Are You Really Angry?

So if the Son makes you free, you will be free indeed.

—JOHN 8:36

How much power does man have over you? Do you surrender your peace to men? Can someone really make you miserable? As a slave was being beaten by his Hindu master for preaching, the master said, "Now what can Jesus do for you?" The slave quickly replied, "He can help me love you!" The slave never surrendered his peace to a person. When you are mad because someone has upset you, and then you vent your frustration on that person, you are venting in the wrong direction. It is impossible that someone upset you. What really happened is that you allowed yourself to be upset. You should be mad at yourself; however, in pride, it is much more pleasant to say that it is another person's fault, though it simply is not.

Many men are angry because their wives will not follow. In reality they are mad at themselves for not taking a stand and leading. Living in such a way—"I am mad at myself, but I will say I am mad at you and blame you"—yields any solution for happiness into the hand of another and doubles the anger, but remember, you gave the person this power over you.

DAY 21
Avoiding Winter

As an example, brethren, of suffering and patience, take the prophets who spoke in the name of the Lord. We count those blessed who endured. You have heard of the endurance of Job and have seen the outcome of the Lord's dealings, that the Lord is full of compassion and is merciful.

—JAMES 5:10, 11

"Because the harbor was not suitable for wintering, the majority reached a decision to put out to sea from there, if somehow they could reach Phoenix, a harbor of Crete, facing southwest and northwest, and spend the winter there. And when a moderate south wind came up, supposing that they had gained their purpose, they weighed anchor and began sailing along Crete, close inshore. But before very long there rushed down from the land a violent wind, called Euraquilo," Acts 27:13, 14. There was a favorable wind, and mistakenly believing this was a sign to set sail, they departed, only to find a violent wind. We want so much to avoid winter that we look for every opportunity. We then make the mistake of examining the consequences rather than what caused the consequences.

Many believers would like to dodge winter in our relationships with the Lord and in our hearts, even though the mighty oak needs winter to strengthen. There is a way to avoid winter! The migratory birds take flight and escape winter. As they have discovered, the price of avoiding winter is never fully being able to rest, since birds on the move are always flapping and eating on the fly. I want to submit to winter as does the bear; spring, summer, and fall have prepared him for a relaxed time of hibernation. In contrast to the birds' avoidance of winter, the bear submits to it and rests!

As believers, we can simply submit to times of winter, resting in the Lord and waiting for the promised spring.

DAY 22
Ax the Root

And seeing at a distance a fig tree in leaf, he went to see if perhaps He would find anything on it; and when He came to it, He found nothing but leaves, for it was not the season for figs. He said to it, "May no one ever eat fruit from you again!"

And as they were passing by in the morning, they saw the fig tree withered from the roots up.

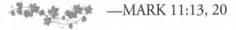 —MARK 11:13, 20

Jesus comes to us expecting fruit and finds nothing. We, of course, have myriad excuses for our condition of barrenness, such as our marriage, our condition of being single, the children, those at work, our less-than-perfect health, our past, or the future; each argument can be eloquently expressed and deftly defended, for much thought has gone into our exoneration. We simply are not to blame.

Yet Jesus, true to form, never listens to or accepts these excuses, these branches. Instead, He goes directly to the root. Notice that the fig tree withered from the roots up. If we remove all the leaves, lop off the branches, and even cut the trunk off at ground level, something will sprout up, because a tree must be destroyed from the root. In believers, the life of Christ is imparted to us once our root is dealt a deathblow and replaced with the new root of His very life. All who study His life have come to the same conclusion: A free, full, and satisfying life allowed Jesus effectively to live in a country with a belief system pitted against Him, in a family opposing Him, and with friends denying and rejecting Him.

I can assure you that those things considered by believers to be branches hindering them from the bearing of fruit are merely deceptions that keep them from the root issue. While teaching at a conference I made the statement that the purpose of marriage was to make us miserable. Immediately a woman in the back yelled, "Mine is a great success!" My point was that the root issue of misery in marriage is not the behavior of the mates but the self-centeredness revealed in us through their behavior. You see, we believers are without excuse! It gives me great comfort to remember each night that no matter what others have done, I have no excuse not to love. The root issue is my response, not the behavior of others.

Let Jesus use others to deal with the root in your life. Stop believing that the reason for misery and the lack of fruit is all the branches on which you cast blame. Having Him deal with the root will make you a happy believer!

DAY 23
Bad Memory Is Godliness

I, even I, am the one who wipes out your transgression for My own sake, and I will not remember your sins.

—ISAIAH 43:25

How wonderful that we are made in the image of God, who says, "I, even I, am the one who wipes out your transgressions for My own sake." When something is done to hurt you by those to whom you minister, those who minister to you, those you minister with, or those to whom you will never be able to minister, the thought of the transgression can haunt you for years. It only takes a name being brought up, an event of the past, or a painful experience to renew the transgression. If the hurtful person completely disappears from the scene, never to be heard of again, he can still take up residency in your head and heart. As I often note, the purpose of forgiveness in the Bible is restoration. However, there are those who do not want restoration; hence, they would see no need for forgiveness. There are relationships I have tried to restore in the past by asking for forgiveness, only to be told of more offenses and to stay away. For my own good, I need to forget. Oh, to able to forget, to wipe out a transgression, to remember the sins no longer, just for our own sakes.

When I got married, Betty quickly realized what was ahead of her, for each day I would ask, "Have you seen my keys? Have you seen my wallet?" Everything would shut down while we looked. Then a few years ago I got glasses, and we have added them to the list of things that are lost daily, along with a cell phone and the key to the mailbox. You get the picture. "Betty, have you seen my keys, wallet, glasses, phone, and key to the mailbox?" One day, justifiably, she said, "Can't you remember anything?" I jokingly said, "Forgetfulness is a sign of godliness. Only God could wipe out transgressions and remember no more, and we are in His image. I am glad that in His image, I can forget. I just do not want to remember everything from my past, and if not being able to remember where my keys are is part of not remembering, then it is a fair tradeoff." You can see why I can be difficult to live with! However, to forget is a great blessing. Research (if it can ever be trusted) says that the average person only loses about 10% of the ability to remember. The difference is that past age 60 it takes more physical effort to correct the forgetfulness. In the younger years, if we forgot the mail we thought nothing of running back to get it. In the older years the extra effort is a frustration. My grandfather used to complain about his memory loss, and I would remind him that I had worked with him most of my life and did not remember his ever having had a razor-sharp memory, only now it was annoying him. Start this day knowing that the Lord wipes out your transgressions for His own good. He does not want to think about your failures all day long, so why should you? Keep in mind that since He does not remember your sin, thoughts of it are utilized by the enemy, who likes to come from your past. Guilt is the undertaker's best friend.

DAY 24
Barking Dogs

For we wanted to come to you—certainly I, Paul, did,
again and again—but Satan stopped us.

—I THESSALONIANS 2:18 [NIV]

I know this: We are not strong men; we are protected men. I had a nice walk and was asking the Lord about a particular passage, 1st Thessalonians 2:18. As I walked down a side street in Borneo to the beach, a large sign came into view in front of a development site, although nothing had yet been built. Two old dogs were there; one barked, but the other just looked as I approached. I had no clue they were guard dogs. One disappeared through a hole in a fence and returned with an entire pack of well over ten dogs. The first dog to emerge after the leader had one eye; all had sores and were beaten-up, ugly mongrels moving toward me and fanning out. I began to back away slowly! Once I got out of their territory, they just stood and would not move out of it. I suppose with the right weapons I could have won the battle, but for what? There was not even a building there to look at; if I am going to fight dogs, I want it to result in some gain. The Lord said, "That is exactly how Satan hinders!" Well, I do not always need such a graphic illustration in response to my questioning! However, I got the point. The enemy and his "dogs" bunch up and take a stand. We are then hindered, chased off. We could stay longer and fight, but why? Later Paul did go to that place, and God gave it over.

Think of demons like dogs. There are various levels of demonic influence for unbelievers. Some people invite dogs in, some allow them to sleep on their porch, and some feed them out the window. Some dogs just come by to sniff around. Some are in the house, some just attached to the house, some fed occasionally. A dog looks cute, so it is invited in, but what can it really do for a person? It always wants something and has to be provided for. When Christ comes into a person, the house is swept clean of dogs, but the dogs still come back around in hopes of being fed. If you want a dog to leave, neglect it. Many give attention to the demonic, unaware that giving it attention will encourage it to stay around. Many of us have thoughts from dogs: thoughts from the past, thoughts of doing something we would never do now, thoughts of hatred, thoughts of self-glory! They are all dogs returning in the hope of being fed, and it is best to say no to the barking-dog thoughts.

DAY 25
Be Content

Not that I speak from want; for I have learned to be content in whatever circumstances I am.

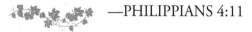 —PHILIPPIANS 4:11

We are to be content. He gives, in His love, the exact things that will make us contented persons. Can you be content, or does He owe you something that will make you content? Does He owe you a better marriage, children, or vocation? If LIFE has cheated you, then LIFE must owe you something that will make you content.

The Christian community has fed believers' lack of contentment insofar as we are actually taught not to be content. Many seminars are calculated to make us feel discontented. I have seen many men who love God in their jobs. However, a speaker comes and tells them they should be in ministry, and by saying this he is spreading discontent. I have seen women in difficult marriage situations; others feed discontent by telling them they would not put up with such behavior from a husband or with being in that kind of position.

I have discovered that being content in my situation is not as difficult as having others content with my situation. Beware of discouraging another person by fueling discontent with his situation. Encourage him to seek and praise Jesus.

DAY 26
Bears!

He turned around, looked at them and called down a curse on them in the name of the LORD. Then two bears came out of the woods and mauled forty-two of the youths.

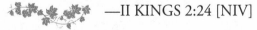 —II KINGS 2:24 [NIV]

An interesting thing about bear cubs is that they actually like humans. In fact, if you were to admire them, walk near, and give them a pat, they would actually follow you. They are so cute it would be easy to encourage them in this. The problem is that unseen somewhere around you is the mother, who will come with a vengeance to kill you once she spies you playing with them.

So it is with addiction. I was traveling with Betty in a foreign country. It goes without saying that I found a budget hotel. As we went walking outside, we noticed the addicts in the stairwells, rubber tubes wrapped around their legs and arms, shooting heroin and rocking back and forth. When playing with the cute cubs of the initial drug experimentation, did they ever imagine the viciousness of the mother? It is sad to see a wasted life, but I believe God can use this in their lives. They go to the very bottom, where the contrast to Jesus is so tremendous that one day all their heart might see is His great light beckoning.

DAY 27
Being Like God?

And God created man in His own image, in the image of God He created him; male and female He created them.

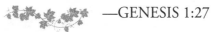 —GENESIS 1:27

Often I am asked how I can believe in a God who permits suffering. My response is, "How can you continue to believe in mankind that causes it?" Man seems to love playing God in science, social issues, in the world, and in relationships. One fellow told me that while watching a loved one die, he realized he could be God! Incredible!

However, man's playing God and imitating God seems to come to an abrupt halt when it comes to forgiveness. If man is to imitate God, why not imitate all of God, His forgiveness, love, mercy, kindness, and will? Why not love as He loves, forgive as He forgave, and be a leaven in the world as He was? In the end, we see that man does not really want to imitate God; He wants to be God on his own terms. Man, as God, would quickly prove himself to be self-serving, self-centered, void of forgiveness and compassion, violent, and indifferent. We end where we began. Why trust man who causes suffering? There is a Way and a "not the way." Jesus is the Way and every other way is not the Way.

DAY 28
Being Put On the Spot By the World

Do not give what is holy to dogs, and do not throw your pearls before swine, or they will trample them under their feet, and turn and tear you to pieces.

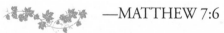 —MATTHEW 7:6

Unbelievers have a habit of asking questions to take the spotlight off of their ignorance and pride. However, I have a habit of answering only half of someone's questions. In fairness, they must then answer mine and defend their system. A question, by its very nature, does not reveal intelligence; the most ignorant person alive can ask a question. The person who knows does not ask. Somehow the world believes that its questioning reveals great minds at work. Amen, the world is always upside down. Correct answers from the mouths of the worldly do reveal a measure of intelligence. I can ask difficult questions, also, for example, "How does a chemical store a memory? In evolution, which calf developed the ability to nurse, and how did the calves that did not know how to nurse ever come into being? Where is the proof that there is not a Master planner to the universe? Can you prove that you can do whatever you want if it does not hurt another? You have a god, and it is self; how can you prove it is helping you?"

A Mormon came to my door wanting to put me on the defensive by asking if I were a Christian and then starting the normal accusations. I told him I did not respond to his knock on the door to answer his questions, and since he had come to my door it was his responsibility to answer my questions. "Why were they polygamists? Why were they bigots?" (Joseph Smith prohibited African Americans in the Mormon system and women are considered to have a lower status than men.) "Why did the Mormons slaughter the innocent in Utah? In Joseph Smith's own handwriting he says that his direct descendants are to rule the Latter Day Saints; why is he not listened to on that point? Why all the Masonic writing in their book and Masonic symbols in the temples?" I then said, "Read something from the book of Mormon that makes sense, something that would make me want to convert. Why is there so much immorality and divorce among the Mormons?" I must admit I enjoyed being the foolish one who only asks questions. He did not have answers. We do have answers, and we can give a defense of the faith, but I am not doing it for the disingenuous or for those who, when I answer their question, instead of acquiescing just resort to asking yet another question. We are not here to answer all of the questions people devise in their attempts to negate Christ. We witness to Him, always mindful that pearls are not cast before swine.

DAY 29
Belief Versus Faith

However, they did not all heed the glad tidings; for Isaiah says, "LORD, WHO HAS BELIEVED OUR REPORT?"
So faith comes from hearing,
and hearing by the word of Christ.

—ROMANS 10:16 & 17

We must say over and over again what every translator will repeat: "We stand and fall on our definitions." Certain words are nearly worn out among Christians and yet are rarely defined. Two such words are *belief* and *faith*, which generally are used interchangeably, and that merits clarification for Christians' daily living. Romans 12:3, "God has allotted to each a measure of faith." Faith is given from God and is something all men have and are born with; it is something received. Faith is the organ of the spirit that allows man to receive what God is doing. With "faith as a mustard seed" is an easy passage [Matthew 17:20] to understand when faith is defined as an organ of the spirit that receives. God gave a very small eye to the mouse and a very large eye to the whale, and yet both do the same thing, they receive. Likewise, faith receives what God is doing.

Galatians 2:20, ". . . the life I now live, I live by the faith OF the Son of God." A good case is thus made for the fact that I live by the faith given and proceeding from Jesus to me. Hebrews 12:2, "Jesus is the author and perfecter of faith." Man must have this received faith; without it he would not cross a street, get in a car, or fly in an airplane. "Faith is . . . the conviction of things not seen," Hebrews 11:1. We do not see what is coming ahead, and therefore, man must have a given faith, something within him that enables him to move on into an unknown future. Ephesians 2:8, "For by grace you have been saved through faith; and that not of yourselves, it is the gift of God."

While faith is God-given, belief is my response to that gift. No matter what level of faith God has given to me, it is my responsibility to respond in belief. Do I believe the word of Christ? Now, if I have the faith of a mustard seed (God-given), and this faith, proceeding from Him, is telling me to move a mountain, I must exercise my belief and act. However, if I decide to move a mountain and endeavor to generate my own faith for doing just that, it is another level of playing God as I next attempt to exercise my belief in my own faith and not in His. This error causes some silly statements, such as, "If you have faith, you will be healed." "If you have enough faith, you will get pregnant." "If only you have faith, you will keep your job." "If you have faith, you can move your 'personal mountain.'" All of these are silly because we should say this: "Did Jesus tell you that

He had given you the faith to be healed? If so, exercise your belief." "Did Jesus tell you that your mate would be raised from the dead?" Faith-in-faith teachers have caused much harm. Faith and belief are two different things; faith originates from God and belief proceeds from man.

Remember, faith is a fruit of the Spirit and therefore must come from God. Here is a fun exercise. Go through the book of Romans, and every time the word "faith" is used, replace it with, "The faith that proceeded from God and was given to me." In this context, what is a believer? Someone who has responded to the faith that proceeded from God; someone who has responded to Jesus.

DAY 30
Believing

But these have been written so that you may believe that Jesus is the Christ, the Son of God; and that believing you may have life in His name.

—JOHN 20:31

A man does not fall because he fails, but because his faith fails. In the course of ministry I have met many who have lost hope. They have lost hope in themselves, which is good and necessary; unfortunately, they also lose hope in Jesus, and this we must never do, for He promises life, gives life, is life, and provides the way for life. It is said that if He takes the credit (for life), then He must also do all the work.

A gifted evangelist and I were walking in his Eastern European country when a guard came to throw us off the beach. I noticed he was carrying a Jehovah's Witness booklet. We told him we were believers. He responded that he knew all believers were hypocrites. I asked, "Are you married; do you have kids?"

"Yes."

"Then let's assume all believers are hypocrites; what is that to you? How does that affect your marriage?"

At that he proclaimed, "Hindus have a trinity, and Christians have a trinity. The doctrine of the trinity is simply Hinduism."

I said, "Let's assume all believers are really Hindus at heart. How does that help your marriage?"

He retorted, "Christians believe that Jesus was God, when He is only a creation of God!"

I said, "OK, suppose Jesus is just a creation of God and not God. What does that do for your marriage?"

He finally shrugged, "None of it helps my marriage."

"Neither does a thing you read in the 'Watch Tower.' Nothing you are doing applies to life. Jesus does apply to life! He is not just words upon words, concepts upon concepts, and knowledge! He is life."

The evangelist then began to share the gospel, and in the end the fellow said he was going to go home and ask Christ into his life. Faith was being stirred in this fellow, and faith keeps the discouraged from falling!

DAY 31
Bible and Division

You search the Scriptures because you think that in them you have eternal life; it is these that testify about Me; and you are unwilling to come to Me so that you may have life.

—JOHN 5:39, 40

Of course, there is as much dynamite in this passage as in John 14:26, "But the Helper, the Holy Spirit, whom the Father will send in My name, He will teach you all things." Together they can blow apart most religious institutions. Having acknowledged how odd it is for the Bible to be the cause of so much division in the Church, one might say it is the cause for out-and-out hatred. I have imagined that each day, somewhere in the world, there is a church split over what the Bible says, and one thing appears to be at the root of this conflict. When the Bible is used to prove itself, there will be division. The flesh of man loves to systematize. Religious flesh will develop a theory concerning a system and then twist any passages that do not fit, until what started out to be a theory has become an absolute. It has been reported in medical journals that a majority of absolute medical discoveries will be shown as flawed within ten years. Science is used to prove science, and soon things are askew. When the Bible is used to witness to itself, things quickly go awry. Some very conservative "theologians" change the Scripture to fit their systems, not overtly but covertly, through the back door of their commentaries. I believe unity will be maintained among believers as long as the Bible does not witness to itself, but rather, as Jesus said, is allowed to testify to Him. We would then have a synthesis around Jesus rather than a dissecting by a system. Of course, in all of this, pride enters in, making "theologians" go deaf and blind.

DAY 32
Birth Of Simplicity

. . . you are worried and bothered about so many things; but only one thing is necessary . . .

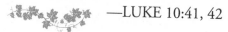—LUKE 10:41, 42

You may remember how once when I asked God to give me a deeper insight into the birth of His Son, a still, small voice whispered, "It is the birth of Simplicity."

The Pharisees lived a complicated life with a thousand rules, but with Jesus came the advent of simplicity, for those with eyes of faith. He reduced life to two rules: love God and love man. This helps show the genius of Jesus.

"So make up your minds not to prepare beforehand to defend yourselves" (Luke 21:14). Why? Self-defense makes life difficult and complicated, tying us up inside. Jesus allowed life and time to speak against His accusers. It has been said we must wait till the years and the centuries speak against the hours. Small men defend themselves; big men can afford to wait till time will defend them. I have observed that if any good exists in any culture, Christ will be found at the source, not Buddha, not the Romans, not a Pharisee, only Christ! His life has been defended.

God's greatest gift truly was Jesus, the gift of simplicity. How do we share in His simplicity? First, we recognize that to have simplicity without, we must have simplicity within. Inner conflict creates outer chaos. Many are divided within, wanting to be loving and forgiving but at the same time desiring to be served, never mistreated, and never told anything negative. Within they desire to live as sparrows, free from anxiety, and yet they view money as security. We must allow the *divided desires* within to come to light, but never fight the desires once they are revealed. Next, we must decide the direction we will go. Notice I said *decide*, not do. We do not uproot a tree by shaking a branch; this only wears us out. However, a tree will fall over naturally if the roots die. As we make the decision and then surrender to God everything that complicates us from within, He begins to kill the division at its root, for if a believer's actions are complicated, he will be complicated. The second step is equally easy. We now begin to focus on the simple motives of Christ resident within every believer. A simple motive (the motive to love, allow offense, serve an enemy) within will bring the outer life into order.

We can start each day with a simple statement, a simple goal, a simple united desire within. "I have no responsibility today except to live abiding in Him" (John 15). It is only unbelief that makes life difficult.

DAY 33
Bitterness

But I tell you that anyone who is angry with his brother
will be subject to judgment.
—MATTHEW 5:22 [NIV]

Obsessing on the hurt caused by others never brings relief even though it may promise satisfaction, self-justification, and the fantasy of punishing the offenders. In the end we punish ourselves, for we are frustrated, sentenced by God, cheated, destroyed, physically sick, and often suicidal. We learn that if we cannot live with others, we cannot live with ourselves. If we hate, we will be hated. If we are resentful, we are resented. Internalizing bitterness is similar to swallowing a grenade. Bitterness is a ticking time bomb; approach it from any angle and we will be hurt.

Bitterness does not suit us, and as believers we must decide on which level we are going to live: as a demon, dishing out evil for good; as a legalist, planning evil for evil; or in Christ, the Way that fits us, offering good for evil. This makes us rulers of the world.

Go ahead and allow others to think you are wrong. Let the years speak against the hours. You have no need for instant vindication. Allow others to use you; you will not be destroyed. Expose your bitterness to the One you have treated worse than anyone has ever treated you—Jesus. Then look within when you cannot stand the view of the world outside. There you will find Him and find love. Live in the way that suits you.

DAY 34
Bitterness In Relationships

Let all bitterness and wrath and anger and clamor and slander be put away from you, along with all malice. And be kind to one another, tenderhearted, forgiving each other, just as God in Christ also has forgiven you.

—EPHESIANS 4:31, 32

Finding the way out of bitterness requires the revelation that the person toward whom we are bitter has become, through our inappropriate attention of him, our god. Where there was one problem—the other person's despised behavior—now there are two, for self-hatred also arises when worshipping someone who caused offense. The third problem occurs when the actions of the one toward whom we are bitter begin to control our actions and even our personality, making us a distortion, no longer ourselves. The behavior of the one who "made us bitter" is blamed for all behavior.

"If only you knew what had happened to me, you would be acting even worse than I am right now."

"Of course I am not sleeping with you; do you not understand my pain?"

"Of course I am in a bad mood; under similar circumstances you would be in a bad mood, too."

The person who caused the bitterness is in control of every aspect of the "sufferer's" family and relationships.

However, Jesus tells us to love an enemy and pray for those who persecute; by so doing, the perceived enemy will remain the same, but we will walk away free.

I was told of a man who, upon hearing of terrible hurricane damage in New Orleans, immediately got in his truck to bring a family to his state and help them get started in a new life. He had trouble finding a black family that wanted to live with a strange white man from the north, let alone in his basement (they do not have basements in New Orleans). At last a pastor persuaded an old woman, with her daughter and granddaughter, to go with the man. They arrived to discover the white man lived in a mansion, and the basement had been completely remodeled for them; it was a walkout basement with a beautiful view. The family had never been in such surroundings. Six weeks later, the white man found the old woman weeping in the kitchen. He approached her, put his arm around her, and said, "I am sorry! Are you homesick? I know it had to be hard to leave everyone you knew! Is there something here we could change that is making you uncomfortable or unhappy?" The old woman looked up with tears flowing and said, "None of those things are bothering me. See, I was raised to hate white people, and all my life I have done a good job of it. Yet your kindness has proven me wrong, and I am so sad that I would have acted and talked that way." His love had broken the stronghold bitterness had on her. Now her family is settled on the east coast, and the two families take turns annually hosting one another for Thanksgiving dinner!

I must repeat myself over and over again: Anything which could be done without Christ cannot be Christian.

We cannot love an enemy but must ask Him to love the enemy; we receive the victory He gives simply by walking across the room and loving. Often I will be in a place where someone has developed hatred toward me. Inviting Jesus along, I go over and start talking to the person, asking his opinions, what work he does, what about his children, his take on the government, and more. At first his head appears to be spinning with a real look of confusion, for on the one hand, it was settled in his mind and emotions that I was some kind of deceiving monster. On the other hand, I cannot be completely hopeless, because we have found common ground. This is Christian life; the first person to lose is the first person to win. Take up your freedom and walk away from bitterness.

DAY 35
Blast! A Woman's Desire Will Be For Her Husband?

To the woman He said, "I will greatly multiply your pain in childbirth, in pain you will bring forth children; yet your desire will be for your husband, and he will rule over you."

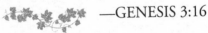 —GENESIS 3:16

Amen, what a thing to say. However, if we see the Lord and His love, we can appreciate the two wonderful types of faith into which only a woman can enter. "I will greatly multiply your pain in childbirth." In the giving of birth, a woman becomes completely other-centered, exactly the attitude that sent Jesus to save mankind; He was other-centered. Normally the most self-centered woman will become other-centered upon the birth of a child. This is an experience that no man will have. The second great move of faith comes from trusting a husband who has flaws. "Yet your desire will be for your husband, and he will rule over you" (Genesis 3:16). What a step of faith for a woman! God did not put woman under man because man is superior; on the contrary, He put the woman under the man so she might exercise her faith. Rather than seeing man in the relationship, she would see the God who gave the command and move up in faith to trust Him who asked her to put herself under a flawed man. It is not the command but the God of the command in which a woman must trust. The danger comes with the temptation to put the husband under a magnifying glass to amplify his shortcomings and use those as reason enough to refuse to come under the husband's headship. Remember, it is not the man but the God of the man under which the wife is to come. If the man were perfect, she would need no faith; a flawed man insures that his rule must be an act of faith in God for a wife. God is not out to get women; He is not an inherent chauvinist. He is all about our learning trust and faith, and a husband and children will make a woman learn just that.

DAY 36
Blessed Simplicity

But I am afraid, lest as the serpent deceived Eve by his craftiness, your minds should be led astray from the simplicity and purity of devotion to Christ.

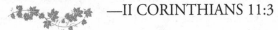

—II CORINTHIANS 11:3

Exhausted souls! We believe the grace of God will adequately provide us with heaven in the future, but we live as though His grace is not sufficient for daily burdens. Is it really as simple as, "Believe on the Lord Jesus?" I believe so! However, we must understand that simplicity requires faith; without faith one can never enter into simplicity. Simplicity reflects faith; complexity is unbelief. Unbelief will always subtract from God and add to man; therefore, complexity is self-righteousness, while simplicity is pure humility. We cannot come to Him having pride. An addition is impossible to faith, for every addition cancels faith. Additions are born of pride. If something of man is added to "believe on the Lord Jesus," complexity and unbelief also are added. Man will find cause to boast and cast Jesus aside. Complexity cancels the complete work of Jesus. Truth is not preached but demonstrated. We let the years speak against the minutes. Those who add to Jesus will be embarrassed! Faith people are doers. We do more than others, but our doing is never an addition to Jesus.

DAY 37
Boasting In the Lord

In God we make our boast all day long,
and we will praise Your name forever.

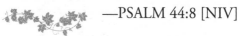

—PSALM 44:8 [NIV]

"Let him who boasts, boast in the Lord" [I Corinthians 1:31]. While trekking with a small group in the Amazon region, an older gentleman was telling anyone nearby about how cute, smart, and funny his grandchildren were. It is always delightful to see the love a grandparent has for grandchildren. It has been said jokingly that the reason grandparents and grandchildren get along so well is that they have a common enemy—the parents!

Nevertheless, I imagine some of you have received newsletters in past Christmas cards that read something like this:

Dear friends, Johnny has been tested, and it has been determined that he is, in fact, a genius. We knew he was because he was reading at a 6th-grade level when he was two. By the way, we have purchased a luxurious home with the proceeds from Tom's latest promotion. We traveled extensively in Europe this past year . . . blah, blah, blah, blah.

Perhaps you have also received a Christmas card with the following type of message:

Dear friends, It has been another year of miracles and God's goodness and faithfulness. As you know, our daughter with Down's Syndrome was never expected to read or write, but thanks to your prayers and many long hours of work, she is reading at a 2nd-grade level. Isn't God good? My husband has lost his job, yet we look forward to how God will provide. God has done so much, how could we not trust Him now? I was watching a sparrow sing after a storm, and God spoke to my heart, "So shall you sing after this storm passes."

Which family was blessed? Which family speaks of God and His goodness? Who has been drawn near to Him? I thought of two things as I read the cards. First, is a mental handicap or the loss of a job bad? What appears to be bad to us may be good to the Lord. Second, many are left feeling that they have been cursed because of the rebellious child, the loss, or the learning-disabled child because they allow comparisons. The events in life this past year, good or bad, were to bring us to the Father's feet, where alone we can receive blessing. The intelligent child is a gift of God, but how often does God get the glory? All boasting should be in Him. The handicapped child is a gift from God; again, we boast in God. I cannot emphasize enough that we Christians are not to allow others or our perceptions of others to define success. Allow the relationship that is built with our Lord through the good and the bad to define success, and then always boast in the Lord.

DAY 38
Boundaries: We All Want Them

Be pleased, O LORD, to deliver me; make haste,
O LORD, to help me.

—PSALM 40:13

Man was made for boundaries and the security they give. I have often noticed that children who are allowed to do whatever they like soon hate themselves and whatever they do. They grow increasingly dissatisfied with life and begin to make everyone around them as miserable as possible. The weak-willed parent just keeps pleading with the child, "You can't have that. You can't have that. You can't have that! OK, you can only have that one. Now, just take one. No, don't throw that!" You get the picture. The child is craving and crying out for a boundary even as he spirals into a deepening misery. As soon as the parent is firm about the boundary, says no once and enforces it, the child will cry initially but soon will be happy. The parent, through a boundary, has delivered the child from a self-centered spiral out of which the child cannot climb alone.

A boundary does for man what man cannot do for himself. Everyone desires an authority that can deliver him from self-centeredness when he cannot deliver himself. Often I have talked to someone who is caught up in an affair and knows it is wrong but cannot get free from it. I have, on occasion, picked up the phone, called the person with whom he or she was involved, and said, "It is over.

You are never to see him/her again." The one who felt trapped now senses freedom. I have also noticed that adults who were never disciplined nor given boundaries while being raised will, when married, try their mates with out-of-control behavior, secretly wishing that the mates will get frustrated enough to set a boundary. The self-centered one cannot deliver himself from his situation and is craving intervention. Instead, the weak-willed, good-hearted, or people-pleasing mate just keeps pleading, as did the parents of the past: "Oh, it will be all right. I know you will calm down. I am so sorry I said something to upset you. Let's both try harder." What the Selfer wants to hear is, "That's enough! Stop it! You are not talking like that! Go to the Lord! Grow up!" He would react to begin with and maybe shout a little louder, but later a sense of security would come over him. A boundary is set that he is really loath to cross over, having become sick of his own behavior, as well.

One of the proofs of the operation of the Holy Spirit in our lives is that we experience boundaries. We can only go so far in the flesh before He will pull us back. We want a strong God, as did David, one that will deliver us, set a boundary, and pull us back if we cross over it. Christianity is not a type of mushy living. It is built in the strength of a love that steps in to set a boundary and deliver. Pity the society that has no boundaries nor strong men that pull people back from error.

DAY 39
Boys, It's a Relationship

"Love the Lord your God with all your heart, with all your soul, with all your mind, and with all your strength. You shall love your neighbor as yourself." There is no other commandment greater than these.

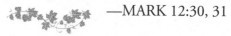

—MARK 12:30, 31

When my boys were young I explained just how important it is never to allow Christianity to become anything other than a relationship, for all our *"doing"* is to grow out of a relationship with the living Christ.

I am quite sure that if we included in a mother's job description the shuttling of every kid on the block to various activities, with the passing of time that mother might become resentful. However, that same mother thinks nothing of providing for her own children. As she does the laundry, picks up after them, cooks, runs them to various activities, cares for them when they are sick, and confronts when they are wrong, the thought of motherhood's being a burden does not enter her mind. Why? The mother has a relationship with her children.

Few working fathers are vexed by the thought of working to provide for their families. In fact, a job that is disliked is actually tolerable if one is providing for others.

In contrast, children can believe themselves put upon when required to act on behalf of the family. That is, they do not yet see the relationship as the foundation of the doing. As they mature and reach adulthood, they who rebelled at the smallest inconvenience will begin to take care of and provide for parents in times of need, not from duty but as a normal outgrowth of the relationship.

We must be careful to emphasize the relationship that we are to have with God. Within the context of this relationship, anything asked of us is a privilege, not a duty. We are not told to perform so that God will not get us, but from love. Obedience becomes vexing when presented as duty, as proof of love, or as a sign of commitment and spirituality. Obedience is an enjoyable blessing amid a loving relationship with our Lord.

DAY 40
Breakups

More than that, I count all things to be loss in view of the surpassing value of knowing Christ Jesus my Lord, for whom I have suffered the loss of all things, and count them but rubbish in order that I may gain Christ.

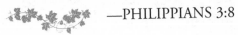 —PHILIPPIANS 3:8

It is interesting that in India, where arranged marriages are the rule, very few have ever had to experience the hurt of a breakup. Yet in the West it is a common, painful occurrence. A breakup can be likened to a pot with several issues in it. First is the pain, which is normal and natural, even though many make the mistake of thinking that the absence of pain would be the proof that their decision to break up was the right one. Where there is a breakup and no pain, there was nothing invested emotionally. Someone without pain proves he or she lacked the maturity necessary to be in a relationship. The majority of people will experience pain; it is an absolute for the mature and will be present whether the decision to break up is right or wrong.

If God has taken you out of a relationship and the other person had no pain from that, bear it and consider your being out as a blessing. Like any other grief over a loss, this pain will first stand on your head. With time, it will walk beside you. Finally, you will stand on the pain, though to some degree it will remain as a part of your growth. As you go through the pain it is important to move toward closure through understanding why the breakup occurred, what went wrong, what could have been done differently, and what the will of God was in the breakup.

The first thing to be determined is the peace of God, for the peace of God is to rule in our hearts. You may not know when the peace of God comes, but you will always know when it leaves. The absence of the peace of God must precede a breakup. You are praying, asking for the will of God, and His peace leaves. Your spirit becomes uneasy. You cannot see yourself living 365 days times fifty years with this person. Less and less do you experience communication, working things out, understanding, prayer, respect, love, and joy (all too frequently I see dating couples having more trouble than longtime married couples). The peace of God will lead you, and I must remind you that the peace of God settles it. I reiterate, the peace of God settles it. Do not tell someone that you are breaking up because you lack peace and then list off all that is wrong with him or her. If you do that, the peace of God is not really leading you; it is your flesh. It also reveals that your love is based in performance, and not in the will of God. If the positive performance of your potential mate is all that is keeping you, get out now. Relationship in marriage must be based in God's behavior toward you. He has been faithful when you were faithless. You love because He first loved you. You are to love your mate even when positive behavior is absent. If you cannot do that, again, you may not be mature enough to be dating.

Once you understand the peace of God, you will not only be dealing with pain, but you will also have to deal with your belief system. This is actually the hardest. The will of God is not the opposite of evil. The will of God is the mind and heart of God, how He determines to work. He can take you out to bring you in, take you down to bring you up, make you weak to give you strength, bring death so you can give life, and yes, put you in a relationship just to bring you out! Why? There are things you can only learn in the purifying fire. Can you receive it? It will depend on what you believe. Do you believe I Peter 3:14? Do you? "But even if you should suffer for the sake of righteousness, you are blessed. And do not fear their intimidation, and do not be troubled." One "Praise God" before you understand the purpose of a breakup is worth one thousand after the understanding. Whenever your breakup crosses your mind, the first thing you should say before chasing all the "what if" thoughts is, "Praise You, God! This is Your will; this is exactly what I need. Thank You!" You will be surprised to see the relief this brings.

Having settled that there is pain and it is normal, the peace of God is to rule, and your present situation is the will of God, you are ready to work through closure. Write a letter or make a phone call or an appointment with the person. Ask the questions you need to know. What did I do wrong? Why couldn't we communicate with one another? Where was Jesus in the relationship? Was it the peace of God? Are we reacting to rejection or responding to the fact that the peace of God is absent? What were our biggest misunderstandings? How are believers to act in a breakup?

In all of this, one issue will muddle many others: sex. When there is sex outside of marriage, a couple will have an unnatural bonding. I have counseled many women who, upon having the peace of God leave them and knowing they are in a wrong relationship, reveal that they have been having sex with the person. They feel they are married in the sight of God and therefore must go through with marriage. Well, the Bible does not consider sex as equal to marriage. Sex outside of marriage is fornication, no light matter since under the law it carried the death sentence. However, the believer is under grace and must confess it as sin, not enter into the condemnation that comes only to those outside of Christ. The act of sin needs to stop whether the relationship is continuing on or dissolving, for either way it is wrong. Though sex is not marriage it can produce a false loyalty, allowing the enemy to use false guilt to keep the believer in a place the peace of God is telling him or her to leave.

All of the discussion above does help in bringing closure, but here is a warning. Seldom after a breakup is the Lord leading people back to one another. If you do not let the peace of God rule, you will react to the rejection, get back together, and repeat the miserable process of breaking up all over again. If you get married, the enemy will constantly remind you of the time you broke up, did not listen to God, and returned to the person. There will be pain when you break up, but in time it will subside. Taking the shortcut by going back into a relationship with the person to soothe the feelings of rejection will only start the pain all over again the next time you break up.

Now some of you will break up with a manipulator, who is more often a man than a woman, just because a carnal man sees a woman as a possession. Think of a man who has a gun collection he never looks at, and one day the wife says, "Let's sell it!" Immediately he reacts and says, "No! They are my favorite guns!" Next he is fondling them and making over them, all stemming from the fear that he was going to lose them. Someone who would treat you as a possession acts the same way. He does not care about you until he feels he is going to lose you; then he does everything to change your opinion. However, once he gets you back, it is the same old treatment; you are just his possession. My advice is that you run! Many know this is happening but are just too weak to say no. To them I give the advice to stay away from the manipulator. There is nothing wrong with admitting weakness. Own where you are in order to leave where you are. Otherwise, because of all the false loyalty and pain, you will return to the one with whom God has given you no peace to stay. The best place to kill a snake is in the egg. Kill the thought of going back by avoiding the person's phone calls, calculated meetings, and advances.

Finally, do you believe God has been in this whole relationship thing? If you do not see Him, then instead you will choose to see chance, lost opportunities, and stupid mistakes, and you will live in regret. You must never, never, never live in regret, which will waylay you today and wreck your marriage in the future. God has been leading. This is the will of God. Praise God, who has used all that you would have fought.

DAY 41
Bring Faith To the Table

Therefore, holy brethren, partakers of a heavenly calling, consider Jesus, the Apostle and High Priest of our confession.

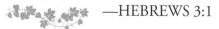

—HEBREWS 3:1

Too many go through life spreading unbelief to others. Unbelief can be presented in a variety of packages, such as wrapped in understanding due to the reasoning that if we understand, we will live. It may be bundled as methods and formulas to be followed, or sold as willpower. It can even present itself as another person to be followed. The flesh of man loves unbelief and will always rally to prop it up to make it appear to be something of importance, all the while avoiding faith. Many will even fight for their particular system of unbelief. As we come to the table to meet with others, do we bring unbelief or do we display faith, not trusting methods, lists, men, or systems, but trusting only God? When in that trust we bring Jesus to the table, with Him come His abilities, power, Spirit, work, faithfulness, mercy, liberty, and compassion; these things laid on the table stir not the mind of man but the spirit. I am constantly amazed at how when He can be brought into even the worst of situations, faith in Him turns the tables on what become the most blessed of experiences.

What is it in the Christian life that presents my biggest struggle? To me it is obvious: whether to focus on Jesus or myself. I suppose I often write about that weakness because it is the one thing capable of turning a day into joy unspeakable or the torment of hell. It is faith to see Him and unbelief not to. We can tell what is most important in the Christian life by how hard the enemy tries to keep us from it. The enemy has seemingly put minimal effort in keeping me from studying the Bible, church, ministry, and discussing Christianity, but I have felt the enemy's full force as I wanted to do one simple thing—consider Jesus . . . just lie on my back and look to Him. Why? Because His nearness overcomes all else! Plus, this is so simple that anyone can do it. The enemy must hide the simple issue of faith. If the "average" believer were to discover this simple truth, marriages would be restored, churches revitalized, addictions cast aside, holiness ushered in without effort, families renewed, and love released. The enemy fears this one thing, and our lives prove it.

DAY 42
Building Yourself a Cross

For I could wish that I myself were accursed, separated from Christ for the sake of my brethren, my kinsmen according to the flesh.

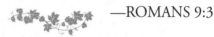

—ROMANS 9:3

Love will force you to intervene in the lives of those around you; Christ's love in you will not permit you to escape. At the very moment you love, you build for yourself a cross. Christ's love is much different from worldly love that takes; His love gives. He will give His life in need and also give yours. When you love with Christ's love, you will suffer more for the sin of the ones you love than they do. How many parents have experienced the truth of the cross and love? The children go on, often pleased with themselves in their sin; they take no thought of it; they have no fear; the misbehavior was nothing more than a passing pleasure. Yet the parents lie awake at night weeping, wondering, praying, and suffering. When you love, you build yourself a cross.

DAY 43
Burnout and Depression

Encourage the exhausted, and strengthen the feeble.

—ISAIAH 35:3

There is a movement afoot to diagnose people so easily as having exhaustion or, as the world calls it, burnout. So many are burnt out, especially within the pastoral "profession." What an interesting concept burnout is! I have learned how easy it is to get tired; in fact, all that is needed is the propensity toward being an idiot. In my foolhardiness I have ministered, worked, and traveled way too many hours, just as many people have done. It is not a sign of spirituality but rather a sign of stupidity. However, being burnt out is something much different; it comes from serving in the power of the flesh. It seems to be a common occurrence for many believers to require more out of their flesh than God does. They do not believe themselves to be acceptable to God simply because of the work of Christ, and therefore they continue to work in an attempt to gain acceptance. This misconception has led many into self-affirming deeds of the flesh, a malady unfortunately encouraged by many pastors as they guilt manipulate the congregation into self-validating work that, more importantly, also validates the pastors. "The mind set on the flesh," as the Scriptures tell us in Romans 8:7 & 8, "is hostile toward God . . . and those who are in the flesh cannot please God." An attempt to validate a relationship with God based on anything other than Christ is doomed to failure. However, what is vexing is that instead of seeing that such attempts are futile, the believers become depressed over their flesh's inability to do better! It is internal anger over an outward failure to live with conduct suitable to and in line with what we saw in the life of Jesus.

Yes, I know we are being told that 80% of people have a chemical imbalance; this comes from amazing "research statistics" pointing to the number of manic depressives, people with depression, people with ADHD, and sufferers of a variety of dysfunctions not listed. In one report the average American would have to have three mental maladies for the statistics to pan out. I have, of course, had contact with those with a true chemical imbalance, and that topic is addressed in a different article, "Can a Christian Take Antidepressants?" I am not knocking those who have physiological problems.

What I am addressing is the depression which comes from the realization that we cannot live the Christian life. Of course we cannot! Jesus alone can and did, and He can live it through us as we admit to Him our failure, release it to Him, and wait. Wait! It seems so many dislike the WAIT word, though WAITING goes hand in hand with faith, and we must remember we did not decide in the flesh to change our flesh, but rather it was the conviction of God, with whose light will come the might. First comes the conviction that something must change. Second, we will attempt to change it ourselves and get depressed because we cannot, and finally, we will rest and let Him do the operation to free us from the cancer consuming us. Yes, wait, and do not miss the rest of the Lord. In burnout we will learn something wonderful, and afterward the phrase, "I cannot," that previously prompted weeping, will make our hearts sing. "I cannot, but He can" is a glorious statement that will lift us to heaven.

DAY 44
Butchering Chickens

The thief comes only to steal and kill and destroy; I have come that they may have life and have it abundantly.

 —JOHN 10:10

One time I spent a day with my grandfather on the farm butchering chickens. As I walked to the chicken coop and grabbed a chicken by the legs, it began to fight and flap; I would grab the wings with the other hand. It took both hands to carry the chicken, which made it difficult to open and close the gate, not to mention getting the bird butchered! After repeating this procedure several times, I stepped around the corner of the barn to see how my grandfather was carrying his chickens. There he came with a chicken neatly tucked under one arm as it rested contentedly on his side. He had a free hand to do the butchering, and the bird did not appear to be one bit worried. I was rough with the chickens and they fought; he was gentle and they went quietly, even though they were experiencing a false peace.

What is the point? Certainly I am not trying to keep anyone from eating chicken! It is this: On occasion I have believers tell me that once they give in to a sinful practice such as homosexuality, they actually feel a peace, and so maybe God is telling them it is all right. I have spoken to others who have left their mates to find true happiness and do find themselves much happier once they are away from the conflict. This is the false peace the butcher gives as he maneuvers to suit his own purposes. It is not a peace that comes from God; it is dangerous, deceptive, and does not last. "The thief comes only to steal, kill, and destroy" (John 10:10).

DAY 45
Can a Christian Take Antidepressants?

We were afflicted on every side: conflicts without, fears within. But God, who comforts the depressed, comforted us by the coming of Titus.

—II CORINTHIANS 7:5, 6

"When sick, seek the Lord. If there is no sin, then visit the physician, for God has made him."—The Apocrypha

There are several issues to be considered concerning depression.

—Depression is often internal anger. There are things in our lives we cannot control. It can be something from our past, present, or future. If this is the case, we need an expanded vision of God, one that allows us to rest.

—Depression can come from obsessive thinking, finding one negative thing in our life or the life of another and making it our total focus, like pulling an ink pen so close to our eyes that we can see nothing else. This is the result of an undisciplined mind. If this is the case, we must learn "not to go there." When the thought comes, we refuse it, setting our minds on the things above.

—It has been said that depressed people are 60% more realistic about situations. Depression can come from seeing things as they are. However, we are to walk in faith, not seeing the situation but seeing God. Faith is the assurance of things hoped for! Depression can be a faith issue.

—Depression can come from believing that our "chooser" is broken and we cannot change our lives or our situations. We are deceived into thinking we are stuck, so we give up.

—Depression can be an addiction, the way we have learned to cope with life. Depression gives the excuse to be lazy and is actually very addictive. Many have a vested interest in being depressed, when the advantages far outweigh the disadvantages. Advantages can include not having to work, having an excuse, avoiding risk, self-absorption, and attention getting.

—Depression can come as oppression of the enemy. All things true are not the Truth. For example, it may be true that I am not getting along with my mate, but it does not mean the marriage is over; that is something true ending at hopelessness. Instead, it is true I am not getting along with my mate, but the truth is that Jesus has made us one. In this case, write on a piece of paper all you know to be Truth (Jesus is the Truth) and mediate on it.

—Depression can have its roots in diet. If you feel depressed after drinking coffee, tea, or after eating heaps of sugar, there can be a very good chance you have low blood sugar. Just by eating differently you can escape the depression cycle.

—Depression can be the result of sin. Carl Menninger, the famous psychiatrist, said he treated the symptoms of guilt his whole life, and toward the end of his life he realized that people felt guilt because they were guilty. He then published a book, scorned by his colleagues, *Whatever Became of Sin?* The depressed person must ask himself or herself, is there anything I am doing that God does not want me to do?

—Having said the above, you can see that the fight to be free from depression can be daily. I have fought it most of my life. Anymore, if I feel depressed, I simply say to myself, "Like the tide that rises and lowers, this tide will go out with time. I will feel myself again; therefore, I will continue working and not focus on the emotions."

—This brings us to the final point, which is considered after all others for a reason. Can a Christian take medication? Of course! Can there be a chemical imbalance? That has been proven. Any of the above can create a chemical imbalance. However, if the imbalance (consequence) is treated and the cause allowed to go untreated, the long-term use of anti-depressants causes more damage than good. In my opinion only about 2-3% of people on anti-depressants do not have a core issue causing the depression. I am not opposed to anti-depressants when accompanied with a detailed examination of the cause. However, I rarely find this to be the case. Many general practitioners are writing prescriptions with no expertise in the field. They would not march in and do heart surgery if unqualified, and yet they treat the fragile brain chemistry girded with only the pen and pamphlet given to them by a drug representative. Not only are they unqualified, but they spend at the most 10-20 minutes asking the patient a few questions. They then treat the symptoms (the same symptom can have more than one cause) rather than the person. I find this very unethical.

There is one more point. If the above-mentioned are the cause of depression, medication can help in the short term if there is a commitment to working on the cause. A true chemical imbalance will respond to medication, so the person taking it would begin to feel much better within a few weeks. If not, a return to the physician is in order. After I did a complete six to eight hours of counseling with a few people I have known, no cause was found. After they visited a qualified psychiatrist and began the medications, relief came quickly. Praise God. I personally am very grateful for the physician who diagnosed my migraine headaches as coming from food allergies and gave me the non-narcotic medications to treat them. Amen!

DAY 46
Captive To Something How?

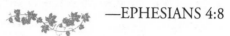

Therefore it says, When He ascended on High, He led captive a host of captives, and He gave gifts to men.
—EPHESIANS 4:8

So many of us at some time in our Christian lives believe ourselves to be enslaved to something, and whether it is a returning habit or a new one, the slavery seems very real. God, as our Shepherd, cannot lead us if we are sitting. We must move to be led, and that means we must move into a truth to discover the reality of the truth. He has taken captive everything that could have held the believer captive. We are free! Growth for Christians does not comprise a series of efforts to make us free, but rather a series of revelations to make known our freedom. We look at our Red Sea and wonder how WE will part it to obey and go forward. In reality, we step into it and discover HE is the one who parts it, but only so far as needed for us to place one foot at a time in it. That is the life of faith. It is a lie to say we are enslaved or captive to anything but Christ. However, the voices of sin, Satan, the world, and flesh are so loud that sometimes we sit in the chair and bemoan a condition we do not even have.

The glory of God is in choice, and there are none freer to make a choice than the believer. I have counseled people in a variety of situations, among which are several prisons, orphanages, alcohol and drug treatment centers, and with couples in troubled marriages. I have given them information and witnessed some miracles, but the information was never what set the people free; it was their choice to act on the information and to walk in the freedom Christ had already given them. The one dispensing information can never take the credit for a changed life; it was simply that the believer chose to walk in the purchased freedom given by Him.

I am happy that since I was obsessed with Betty long before she knew it, she chose me upon her discovery of my love. I chose her first, but she responded by choosing me. I am happy she was not forced to marry me but responded to my choice with her choice.

God has chosen you, He chose to set you free, and now you will thrill Him by choosing to walk in the freedom. It is a hard pill to swallow, but if you can choose not to go shopping naked, you can certainly as a believer choose not to walk in what you believe to be a behavior to which you are held captive. Admit where you are so you can leave where you are. Admit that you are choosing to stay in your state and let God work with your honesty.

DAY 47
Cause Or Consequence

Examine me, O LORD, and try me;
test my mind and my heart.

—PSALM 26:2

Often we find ourselves examining the spider webs rather than seeking out the spider, or as a friend says, "Cause leads to consequence! Do not examine the consequence, but the cause!" II Peter 1:3, "Seeing that His divine power has granted to us everything pertaining to life and godliness, through the true knowledge of Him who called us by His own glory and excellence." If God has indeed given us all we need, then the cause of failure must rest within us. I admit, from personal experience, it is more enjoyable to examine consequence, avoiding my responsibility in cause. However, cause is the issue. We fail others and ourselves for one reason: pride. Because of pride we turn from God's presence to something else and are left with our inherent weakness. When we discover the cause of our failure, we must once again purchase forgiveness with the currency of self at the counter manned by the offended person. We cannot purchase it through a third party. As children of God, our goal is to purchase so much truth with self that in the end we go to heaven flat broke!

DAY 48
Charley

Jesus said to him, "I am the way, and the truth, and the life; no one comes to the Father but through Me."
—JOHN 14:6

Whoever slaps you on your right cheek, turn the other to him also.

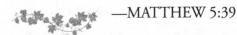

—MATTHEW 5:39

I woke up this morning thinking of an old friend, Charley, who was my friend from junior high on. His mother ran a bar and his father was absent, an alcoholic. One day Charley and I stole the car parked in his neighbor's yard, and when we got it up to 40 mph we discovered why it had been sitting so long; it did not have brakes. Another friend, Clark, had us drive close to the ditch, and he jumped out. Charley and I continued on until we realized we could simply turn off the engine. He was a good friend and taught me how to hop the train from the intersection near the school to my house a little over a mile away. One day in high school a boy from the local reform school told Charley I had said something about his girlfriend, though I had never said it. Charley confronted me and would not believe I did not say it. He insisted on a fight. That afternoon after school we fought until someone called the police. Here is what is vexing me: If only I knew then what I know now, I would have let Charley hit me and never struck him back. There is The Way and a not the way. Jesus is The Way and every other way is not The Way. Why did I think of that? Why do I wish Charley could have hit me unopposed? I suppose I am projecting current revelation on the past, and that is dangerous, for it can cause something demonic called regret. However, I really wish I would have stood still and let him hit me. Well, amen. Charley, like most all of my childhood friends, died young, in his case by the time he was 33 (one friend died with a brain tumor, one was hit by a train, and another was killed in a traffic accident). He had quit school to work as a laborer; out in the country one night, sitting in his car trying to persuade his wife not to leave him, he shot her and himself. I wonder if I had let him hit me, would it have made a difference in his life?

I am no David, but I am becoming like David in my attitude. When he was with his mighty army and a man came cursing him, David simply said, "Leave him alone; it may be God." He could see God in everything. I should have let Charley hit me. I have "hit" Christ many times, and yet He has never hit back. Well, amen! Only Jesus knows, but this morning I am thinking of Charley.

DAY 49
Children In Crisis

*For by grace you have been saved through faith; and
that not of yourselves, it is the gift of God; not as a result of
works, so that no one may boast.*

—EPHESIANS 2:8, 9

It seems that adolescence has as much to teach the
parent as it does the child. Many parents experience full-on
panic attacks as their children enter adolescence, and this
reality speaks volumes about the faith of the parent. First,
I do not believe parents are taught the normal progression
of God's work with man, which is that a person is given
independence, messes up his world, and chooses Jesus to
sort out the mess and himself. People are too often told that
if they follow certain formulas, they can bypass God's order.
God's order can never be undone. Every single person who
comes to Jesus will come in some form of brokenness.
Christianity is for those at the bottom rung of the ladder.
The servant God, who became a man, a carpenter, started
it. The "founders" were largely simple, uneducated men
from a variety of walks of life. Given the state of the
original founders, why is Christianity continually put forth
as something exclusive? Well, fleshly men want to make
it exclusive; they cannot stand the fact that it is for the
weakest. Wanting to be special, they always seem to have
a valuable formula which, if followed, will set apart and
make disciples more exclusive. Those in the exclusive club
do not believe we all are equal in Jesus. Parents fall victim

to these esteemed formulas because they want to believe that formulas, if followed, will eliminate problems with their children and increase their own comfort. The fault for being deceived lies with the parents. I am asked, "Well, what about all those kids that never have any problems?" My answer is the same, "What kids? All have sinned, have they not?" In counseling I hear things the parents never will; there are no "perfect" kids. A child must follow God's order! Before a child can believe, he must first have been unbelieving. In adolescence pride (unbelief) is active, which causes independent decisions that often result in failure and sin. The consequence is the revelation of the personal need for Jesus. Again, it is the order of things.

However, what I see happening in the parent is often more vexing than what I see in the child. In his unbelief and bad behavior the child pulls the parents into lack of faith. The preferred dynamic would be the parents' pulling the child up into their faith in a God big enough to care for all of them. But the opposite is true, and soon they are as unbelieving as the child. They cannot believe God will work, the order of things is wise, or the child—like the prodigal son—will return. This unbelief gives rise to a flood of activities and covert messages. The teenager is forced into the youth group, where, it is hoped, since God has dropped the ball and is not working, maybe the youth leader can do something. There is a search for a person or place that can "fix" the child. There can be a need and a place for faith-based intervention, but not when it is replacing the need for faith.

Now at this point, as I am talking to parents, the complaint comes, "Well, are we just to let our teens go do whatever they want, ignore the consequences, and give up?" That statement actually addresses three separate issues. First, stop thinking about what should be done as a parent and start thinking about what to do as a child of the Most High God. What should the parent be doing today? What is God telling him or her to do, not just with the kids but with the family, mate, job, and, most importantly, with God Himself? This is the advice Samson's parents received when they questioned the angel as to what they were to do for their boy. Live separated to Him, obey Him, and a person will be the believer he needs to be. Everything else will flow from that. Second, I am not saying a parent does nothing, but is faith in the doing or in God? I liked having family devotions at night because I believed God wanted me to have them. However, I never for a minute believed the devotions would make my children Christian; that is God's job. Yes, we do have standards, we do enforce them, we do what is good for the child, and we do fight for our stands. But unless God puts His fire in a person, none of the above will change him. We do protect our children, for one day we will hand their lives over to them, and we want to give something of value. Third, it reveals that the parent sees only two options: Either the child is formed into the image of God by the parent or an image of the world by the child's own choices. What about Jesus? What about the Holy Spirit? What about the promises of God? What about God? Here I end where I began, with parents who are hitting the panic button because they live as though they have no God, or have not activated their faith in Him!

Your parents did not put the fire of God in you; I cannot imagine you will put it in your child. However, you can trust God to do it as He follows His order. It is very easy to tell the difference between the child who has been touched by his parents' teaching and the one who has had a personal touch of God. Which do you want?

DAY 50
Choice Is Important

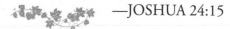

Choose for yourselves this day whom you will serve . . . but as for me and my household, we will serve the Lord.

—JOSHUA 24:15

Choice is very important when the subject comes to judging our thoughts and lying emotions, looking to God to be delivered before walking in the flesh, walking across the room by putting one foot in front of the other to kiss an enemy, acknowledging the fact of abiding, believing His work and not my own, and thousands more choices. But choice is not a factor in how and for what purpose God makes me. "Does not the potter have a right over the clay, to make from the same lump one vessel for honorable use, and another for common use?" (Romans 9:21) God does set some aside to express a particular living message; they did not set themselves aside, nor could they have passed all the tests required to be set aside, apart from His grace. It was not choice or effort that made them what God wanted them to be. Boasting is excluded, except in God. Therefore, all are to be content with where God has placed them, for the choice was His, not theirs. I Corinthians 7:24

exhorts, "Brethren, each one is to remain with God in that condition in which he was called."

I find it vexing when one Christian is measured against another and the one most obviously in a position of serving the Lord becomes the standard. I can remember several of us from the '70's Jesus Movement being told that since we loved God, the next step would be fulltime ministry. However, dedication to God is never equated with vocation. I was dedicated to God when I was a janitor, and then the Potter decided to do something different with this pot of clay, not by my choice but His doing. No matter in what vocation I am placed, abiding in Christ is my choice; putting me in the Vine and placing me where He wanted me in the Vine were His choices. Therefore, we are not to go about choosing to be like certain ones of those we see in the ministry, but choosing to be whom God in His high calling has chosen us to be.

DAY 51
Christ Is In You!

Now all these things are from God, who reconciled us to Himself through Christ and gave us the ministry of reconciliation, namely, that God was in Christ reconciling the world to Himself, not counting their trespasses against them, and He has committed to us the word of reconciliation. Therefore, we are ambassadors for Christ, as though God were making an appeal through us; we beg you on behalf of Christ, be reconciled to God.

—II CORINTHIANS 5:18-20

Jesus is there for us. In every situation He is there; there are no obstacles; He is in us. We can pray for that revelation. It was a beautiful experience to preach on this in a Chinese church as the Spirit began touching people. One by one in the Chinese language they began to shout, "Jesus, Jesus, You are so beautiful! Your presence is in us!" For over thirty minutes the sound of it got louder and louder but was never imposing; it was gentle, like I would imagine angels sound. It was very peaceful; Jesus' touch is so gentle. I was just happy to be there. When it stopped, the peace remained, and everyone carried it away with them, for Jesus had revealed His presence within. It was not a "sing me happy" service, but a simple revelation of Jesus within, a move of God.

I had a fellow tell me the Spirit always moves in his meetings, and people pray and repent. But I watched his meeting; the people had no choice! They were forced to the front, forced to sing, forced to confess, and forced to pray. Although it is within the allowable will of God, that kind of worship cannot be maintained. The quiet fellowship of the soul turned toward the Spirit is possible all day long, anywhere. Prayer in the flesh cannot be maintained; prayer in the Spirit can be ceaseless. This same fellow asked if I belong to a particular denomination. I confuse him because I let the Spirit move me, and the meeting as well, rather than trying to move the Spirit by scheduling Him to show up and express Himself in a certain way or do anything I might expect or want. The Spirit moves as the wind and engages Himself as He wills, and sometimes that means we witness, preach, write, or rest. In Acts they prayed and the Spirit filled them. Then they spoke the word of God in boldness.

DAY 52
Christ, the Giver Of Life

For am I now seeking the favor of men, or of God? Or am I striving to please men? If I were still trying to please men, I would not be a bond-servant of Christ.

—GALATIANS 1:10

Jesus said, "I am the way, and the truth, and the life . . ."

—JOHN 14:6

I was wondering if others have been seeing what I have, many successful businessmen, ages 50 - 60, telling me they have lost all motivation. They have low levels of depression and will say things like, "I should have set my sights higher; I should have had greater challenges," etc. Also, they have the feeling that if they just kept sending the check to the wife and kids, no one would miss them. I explain it this way to them: Life with a small "l" only gives X amount of satisfaction through vocation, marriage, and rearing children. For argument's sake, let us say that sex, marriage, the kids, or the vocation, on a scale of one to ten, can only give a ten. Marriage at its very best can give a ten in satisfaction. Many marriages are chugging along at a three when they could be a ten. However, there is no eleven, fifteen, or twenty on the life scale, there is only a ten. Many sex addicts, particularly in the gay community, want out of sex what sex cannot give. Generally speaking, mankind has unreal and ignorant—and therefore unmet—expectations. All of this is just to say that the men I am seeing have hit the ceiling concerning their vocation, marriage, and everything else that life with a small "l" has to offer. The end result is disillusionment, which I believe is exactly what God wanted to accomplish in life with a small "l." Now instead of sinking into feelings of a lack of fulfillment, this awareness is useful in driving man into Life with a capital "L," for Life with a capital "L"—our Life in Christ—has no ceiling and always has much more in a much more gospel. There is so much to know and experience in this LIFE.

DAY 53
Christian Buddhism

But I say, walk by the Spirit, and you will not carry out the desire of the flesh. For the flesh sets its desire against the Spirit, and the Spirit against the flesh; for these are in opposition to one another, so that you may not do the things that you please. But if you are led by the Spirit, you are not under the Law.

—GALATIANS 5:16-18

Christianity does not center on what man does, but what Jesus has done; our command is that we live out of His work. "Apart from Me you can do nothing" (John 15:5) and "I can do all things through Him who strengthens me" (Philippians 4:13). Christian Buddhism is very simple to describe; it emanates from the tree of the knowledge of good and evil as the religion of lists. Its directive is to do the good and not do the bad. It takes a variety of forms and is easily understood by the carnal mind, because, frankly, it is based in the carnal. Let me give an example. I can be a Cat Christian or a Dog Christian. Cat Christians are all about themselves, and Dog Christians are all about God. Well, amen! There is something true there. The problem I have is in the "how to" of moving from a cat to a dog. Not only can a cat never be a dog (I push the illustration too far), but also, the solution religion presents to becoming a dog lies at the believer's feet. So the teaching comes full circle. A Cat Christian is consumed with self, but in the power of self a Cat Christian is expected to transform into a dog! Self will never improve self. At first the believer is consumed with what self can take from God, and then he is encouraged to move to being consumed with what self can give to God. Again, any teaching that ultimately ends at man's feet is some kind of Christian Buddhism from the tree of the knowledge of good and evil. However, any teaching that ends at choice, and the choice is Jesus, comes from the tree of Life. There are no Cat or Dog Christians; to prefix the word *Christian* is to nullify the word *Christian*. Like an oak that is three inches tall or one that is a hundred feet tall, both are fully, in all ways, a complete oak. The little oak does think only of self. It cannot give shade or fruit and needs to receive constantly from God. As God tends the little oak, it will begin by thinking only of itself. The day we believed in Jesus, we only thought of ourselves. However, God is the glory, and He must be the ultimate goal. He will begin to put us in situations we cannot handle so we will turn to Him and discover how great a salvation we have.

Each day that we simply choose Jesus (as opposed to choosing to be like Jesus), we are brought out of ourselves toward a place where He is all that matters. Soon we will find ourselves naturally saying, "I count all things to be loss in view of the surpassing value of knowing Christ Jesus my Lord" (Philippians 3:8). We have not gone from being cats to dogs, but rather have grown in the revelation of what we have been from the first day we believed, the temple of God. We are not the focus; it is not about us. He is the glory. We do well to remember that the flesh, or humanity (our being under the influence of something other than Christ and our attempt to play God in that condition), will never depart. There is always the potential of walking in the flesh and looking just like an unbeliever, ALWAYS! It is God's stronghold that keeps us near to Him. Flesh and humanism simply present us with clothes we can no longer comfortably wear, but we give latitude for the reality that at times believers are not abiding. The residue of the old man (part of the flesh) never goes away.

If you live long enough, some day you could be lying in bed shouting, "Where is Eddie? He took my puppy. I hate Eddie!"

The younger relatives will be asking, "Who is Eddie?"

The old ones, though, will remember Eddie. "Oh, he lived next door to him on the farm." You might even be yelling something much worse, for in your senility you are not able to activate your choice to bring your mind in subjection to Christ. There is nothing wrong with this condition; it is the way of things. My point is that the residue of the flesh never goes, and subduing it requires the activation of the will, choosing Jesus. I like it all. I like the way it all works together. You will act like a cat, only thinking about yourself, when you have the door to His life closed. You will act like a dog, wanting Him, when the door is open.

DAY 54
Christian Counseling?

For the word of the cross is foolishness to those who are perishing, but to us who are being saved it is the power of God.

—I CORINTHIANS 1:18

Once I listened as a brother began to explain how spiritual maturity was to be judged. He used criteria for spirituality neither the other brothers nor I had ever before heard. In a matter of minutes issue was taken with his position as one of the brothers simply asked, "Where is your criteria found in the Scriptures?" At that the one who began the conversation became quiet; there were no Scriptures for this position. It was merely *his* position, *his* experience, and how *he* felt, but it was not a New Testament barometer of spirituality. If what we had heard taught were crucial to Christian life and maturity, why did Paul, John, or Peter not mention it? My point is simple: It is easy to be sidetracked.

I have noticed that Christian Counseling has actually become a denomination of sorts, with its own language the uninitiated will not understand, concept of man, knowledge, and explanations of behavior that generally have nothing to do with Scripture. In fact, one would be hard pressed to follow the theme of most Christian counseling in any portion of Scripture. This *is* meant to be critical, for my prayer for the body of Christ each day is that we not be led astray, our focus on Him will be maintained, and we never forget that His presence can cure us from every ill. He may not deliver out of every situation, but He will deliver in the midst of every one, and in this there is greater joy!

It is not enough for a counseling ministry to teach an experience; the call is to teach Christ, not lose Him in the midst of examining and understanding problems. Quite a movement is afoot to "feel the pain" of others, which is said to be accomplished by being honest and explaining that we have defeat, are angry, and are often left scratching our heads in bewilderment as we see babies die, crime increase, and myriad unanswered prayers. To say the above is not so, according to this movement, is denial, and denial is bad.

In fact, I am amazed at the large number of Christian teachers who admit to constant defeat, lack of understanding, bewilderment toward God, misery, and hope that lies only in the assurance that things will get better in heaven. Some of them have gone so far as to label anyone who teaches that things will get better in this present life as a false prophet. Once again, "Where is this taught in Scripture?" It may be these teachers' experience, but this type of lifelong experience is not Scriptural. Even more amazing is that this open approach can be considered intellectual and spiritual, when it is an obvious case of their inability to lead to where they have not ventured.

Yes, I have had times of defeat, personal and financial crises, and plenty of hiccups in the past. However, life has gotten progressively freer, easier, more enjoyable, quiet, peaceful, and happy. All trials first pass through the hand of God and are planned and needed, bringing with them a degree of maturing for the believer. I do not scratch my head in bewilderment at the Christian life; I cannot wait to see what tomorrow has to offer. When I was a child I could get mad at God, find excuses, and attempt to justify my defeat as the normal Christian experience, but it is not, and trying to make it so is immaturity. Scripture does tell of hard times (I Cor. 4; II Cor. 4), but it speaks much more of joy. Jesus makes it clear He came that we might have joy, peace, and victory and be more than conquerors, filled with His Spirit, with power over the forces of darkness. Paul, Peter, John, and Luke all echo the same. There is the downward path to the cross where we learn to give up on self (even self-examination), but there is also the upward path from the cross where we learn to trust Him intrinsically, where daily victory and joy become the course of the day in the midst of all circumstances.

When I listen to a teacher I want him to have been where I am going, not where I have already been! I do not want someone who "feels my pain"; I already feel it! I must know the way past it. How do I go beyond it? As I draw near and follow the One who passed through pain and came out the other side free in victory, His story will become mine. When Jesus appeared to the disciples after the crucifixion, the proof of His resurrection power was the marks of death. But death is not pointless; there is life that comes after death. Without death there is no life! "Unless a grain of wheat falls to the earth and dies it will remain by itself, but if it dies it bears much fruit" (John 12:24). Notice the "much fruit." To teach that the Christian life on this earth is a miserable existence is the *denial* of basic Christian teaching. Beyond that, it is Buddhism, plain and simple. To say we must understand all our hurt before we get on is Gnosticism and more *denial.* Too many look to the teaching of Christ, but when failing to experience His freedom, change the concepts to fit themselves.

The answer is so simple. Spend thirty minutes reading Psalm 139, be quiet, let the living God speak to you, and you will discover that you are an overcomer. Paul sang in prison. The term salvation in the New Testament refers to today, not the future. Yes, we want to get into heaven in the future, but salvation is for today. Let no one steal that. We "are being saved" (I Cor. 1:18) TODAY; it is Scriptural. Do not settle for a life of mediocrity when an abundant life is so easily received. If the solution to being free lies in how much you can understand, the last 25 years of Christian counseling have rendered its verdict: You cannot be free. But if God gives freedom for the asking in Jesus' name to the weak man, it can be yours. Never allow joy to become difficult or just for a chosen few; it is for you!

DAY 55
Christians Are Hypocrites!

Why do you look at the speck of sawdust in your brother's eye and pay no attention to the plank in your own eye?

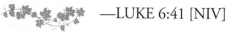

—LUKE 6:41 [NIV]

I once heard it said that the difference between a spiritual and a carnal man is that the spiritual man will stab you in the chest rather than in the back! A pastor recently described his congregation as whining, sniveling wimps; he was sick of them. I sit in my office while believers enumerate the many experiences of disappointment with others in the Church. It is easy to conclude that many believers are self-centered, self-absorbed, judgmental, critical, greedy, harsh, impatient, indifferent, insensitive, manipulative, materialistic, unreliable, slanderous, proud, and just plain rude. To prevent arguments, let us just say that 95% of all believers do fit into the above categories. Now what? Two possible responses to this assertion come to mind. First, pointing to others' carnal behavior to justify one's own carnality, leading to increased self-righteousness. Second, using the carnality of others to reveal one's own and making a conscious decision to walk with Christ. The behavior of others will either suck a believer into like conduct or move him or her into Him. However, know for certain that the decision concerning which way a believer goes is all his own; others cannot be blamed.

Frustration comes from spotting faults in and trying to change others; relief comes when we only have to deal with ourselves. For example, I had a large sum (large for me) of money taken. I related the offense to an elderly brother, who responded, "Mike, you were deceived." I respect this man and was happy he saw I had been victimized, but he continued, "Do you know, Mike, that deceivers are deceived?" I knew immediately what he meant. God had initially warned me about getting involved in a business deal with the deceiver, but for reasons which at the time had seemed fine to me, I did not listen; I deceived God, or so I thought. I told the brother I knew exactly what he was talking about; the carnality of another had merely revealed my own. He then said, "Go to your room and confess your stupidity. God shows grace and mercy. Consider the loss of money a cheap lesson." I did what he said and felt great! The carnality of another had at length succeeded in pushing me into spirituality, and I could thank God for the person.

DAY 56
Clinging To Jesus!

And behold, a woman who had been suffering from a hemorrhage for twelve years, came up behind Him and touched the fringe of His cloak.

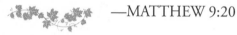

—MATTHEW 9:20

On a trip to Brazil and Argentina I stopped at Iguassu, the largest waterfall in the world. Beneath the largest of the falls I noticed a rock sticking out; the full power of the falls hits the rock but cannot move it. Protected under the rock was a small plant, which was close enough to the power of the falls to reap every benefit, yet it was shielded from destruction. What gave it life could easily destroy it if not for the rock. It was a good reminder of how Jesus is the Holy Transformer. None of us could handle the full power of God or His presence, but passing through Jesus it becomes safe for us. In Jesus the very power that could destroy us nourishes us. In Jesus we are quite safe and washed with God.

A woman had suffered for so long, and all it took to be healed was a touch. Later, there were those who were clinging to Him, something we can all do to be safe in Him.

DAY 57
Coming To a Place Of Deception

But each one is tempted when he is carried away and enticed by his own lust.

—JAMES 1:14

But I say, walk by the Spirit, and you will not carry out the desire of the flesh. For the flesh sets its desire against the Spirit, and the Spirit against the flesh; for these are in opposition to one another, so that you may not do the things that you please.

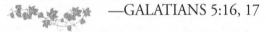 —GALATIANS 5:16, 17

I am starting to believe that people are deceived because there is something in them desiring the deception. First, if Satan has the ability to deceive all men, then all men would be deceived. Obviously he does not have that kind of power. So what is it he looks for in a man that would allow for a deception? Satan is looking for something in the heart of man where the deception can begin. It would be impossible for Christ to deceive any person, for in Christ is nothing the flesh desires. True Christianity cannot deceive, for again, nothing in the flesh wants anything at all to do with Christianity, since its one message for the flesh is, "Move over!" So what will make man's heart open to deception? I believe it is the desire of a heart to be independent from God, perhaps even going so far as to say, "I can be God." This is why the Mormon religion is so successful; it is cleverer than the early Catholics who embraced or simply gave different names to the local gods of the people, to the end that some countries are rife with blends of Catholicism and witchcraft. Haiti is an example. However, the Mormons offer something more: Man can actually become a god and can invite his wife to his celestial kingdom, where she can be eternally pregnant. This "deception" has incredible drawing power for those who have suffered under the hand of their unjust god, or who have served a god all of their lives. After all, who would not want to believe that he could become the one who hands out punishment and receives gifts from others? Such a person is deceived with a ludicrous teaching, but moving past the cobweb to the spider, we see at the root a heart that says, "I want to be God." Deceptions all offer the flesh something, and Christ is always taking something away from the flesh. When someone converts to Mormonism, or any of the other "-isms," I never have the sense that the Mormons won one while the Christians lost one. Instead, I believe that the person, in believing the deception of Mormonism, actually revealed a heart within that is anti-Christ. Again we see that nothing is working against us. God is permitting all the "-isms" for the revelation of hearts. The germ of every cult is this promise of keeping the flesh alive through some form of playing God. The amazing thing is that it holds any attraction, when it is so much easier to have a God than to play God.

DAY 58
Coming To Know Him

God is not a man, that he should lie, nor a son of man, that he should change his mind. Does he speak and then not act? Does he promise and not fulfill?

—NUMBERS 23:19 [NIV]

Witnessing, preaching, and teaching are all interesting in the way we start out talking about the One we do not know and yet who knows us perfectly. Since we do not know Him we inadvertently preach ourselves by telling what we believe God is like, actually making Him in our image. So many times a judgmental person will preach about how God is vengeful. The perfectionist will make God out to be all about the Law. The rejected will make God a rejecting God who is impossible to please and requires more and more work. Actually, preaching more often than not reveals more about the preacher than it ever does about God. Therefore, God must step in, for we are in His image and can reveal something of Him. Often this revealing will take the form of breaking down any false concept we have attributed to God. For example, if the legalist believes God is all about the Law, God will lift His hand and let the legalist break himself against his own rules. If one believes that God will refuse to forgive certain types of sin, he may find himself in that very sin. God only does what is redemptive and within the context of the fact that He is love. He merely would like us to understand and represent what and whom He really is when we are talking about Him to others.

Look at the Apostles. God turned out to be something at the end of their lives that confounded what they thought He was in the beginning of their lives. The Religion makes too much of the Apostles' and Saints' sacrifices, because whatever it was they had given—even when giving up their very lives—was not to be compared to what they had received.

DAY 59
Commentaries

I testify to everyone who hears the words of the prophecy of this book: if anyone adds to them, God shall add to him the plagues which are written in this book; and if anyone takes away from the words of the book of this prophecy, God shall take away his part from the tree of life and from the holy city, which are written in this book.

 —REVELATION 22:18, 19

Much is said about the inerrancy of Scripture, upholding the belief that every word is inspired. One would not have to go far to read an article detailing the debate. Within the context of the battle, the Catholics are often mocked for their position, which allows the Pope ex cathedra speech. In effect, the Pope can add to Scripture. The majority of Protestants see this as wholly unacceptable, taking the position that the Scriptures are not to be changed.

Fundamentalists have as a stated goal the protection of the Scriptures in its present state. Interestingly enough, though Fundamentalists would never go in the front door and change the Bible ex cathedra, they seem to have no hesitancy changing the Bible with commentaries, going in through the back door. Many conservative teachers are busy telling us what the Bible "really" means. For example, the explanations of what the term "baptism" means varies from the Charismatics to the Calvinists to the Armenians; all are conservatives, all fundamentalists, and all are protecting the inerrancy of the Bible. It is argued between groups that the "others" have changed what the Bible teaches through commentary. The point of this article is not to resolve who is right and wrong. Disagreement among scholars is proof enough that someone is changing something. In fact, I would like to move in a completely different direction, one in which we are not continually making commentary on Scripture but allowing the Scripture to make commentary on us. What, exactly, is the passage saying to us today? As we read, we listen for the divine "amen" of the Spirit within, God's speaking to us through the Scripture that is making commentary on us. This reading is in fellowship with Him, so that what we glean comes with power and life. In this regard, "All Scripture is inspired by God and profitable for teaching, for reproof, for correction, for training in righteousness" (II Timothy 3:16).

DAY 60
Compatibility

*For you were called to freedom, brethren; only do not turn
your freedom into an opportunity for the flesh, but through
love serve one another. For the whole Law is fulfilled in one
word, in the statement, "You shall love your neighbor as
yourself." But if you bite and devour one another, take care
lest you be consumed by one another.*

—GALATIANS 5:13-15

Is it true that many couples are just not compatible? I
often hear it said of a marriage that it got off on the wrong
foot because of incompatibility; therefore, I would like to
discuss the issue.

I have had a difficult time getting marriage counselors
who subscribe to the absolute necessity of compatibility
to define *compatibility*. I would like to know what it looks
like, but the more specifics I request, the more vague the
absolute becomes. For example, does compatibility mean
that people who like the same things get along better? If so,
then why do business partners who have identical passions
and goals split up? Does compatibility mean doing the
same things? If that is true, why do expeditions break
up? Is compatibility wearing the same kind of clothes?
Then why do soldiers in matching uniforms fight with
one another? Is compatibility enjoying the same ideals
about life? Why is there infighting among communist
party leaders? We discover that when compatibility is the

issue, we are actually chasing a non-issue. Marriages do not break down from incompatibility. On the contrary, incompatibility is the greatest grounds for oneness. The expedition is a success when the people do their varied jobs with excellence. Obtaining a business partner who does with passion what the other hates to do makes for rapid, harmonious success. A family wherein mother and father split the responsibilities makes for wholesome children.

In marriage, compatibility is not the issue; when it comes to getting along, the issue is the flesh. "But I say, walk by the Spirit, and you will not carry out the desire of the flesh," Galatians 5:16. Ultimately, marriage is not a personality or compatibility issue, but a flesh-versus-the-spirit issue. When flesh wars against spirit in the marriage, the things desired cannot be accomplished. What does the Christian couple desire? Without exception the desire is for peace, joy, love, patience, kindness, goodness, faithfulness, gentleness, and self-control. Personally I have never met a couple who set out from day one to ruin their marriage. After the wedding vows, no husband and wife immediately started to make lists on how they could mess up their mate's life. I see many couples each year in a marriage discipleship setting, and none enjoy being there. True, couples have done things to make their marriages miserable. My point is that they never intended for the marriage to get to the miserable shape it is in today; that happened not by plan, but through walking in the flesh. (Flesh = man under the controlling influence of anything other than Christ, i.e., selfishness, anger, others, habits, past, lying emotions, sin, etc.) A muscle gets bigger the more it is exercised. The more one exercises control, the more of a controller he becomes. Flesh begets flesh. If a couple decides to relate to one another through strife, enmities, anger, disputes, dissensions, and factions, the more miserable the marriage becomes. Walking in the flesh creates the exact opposite of what a Christian couple wants; it creates more flesh.

I have often said that the purpose of marriage is to make a person miserable! It is true, for we are only miserable to the degree we are in the flesh. If we desire to get out of the misery, we must walk in the Spirit. Love as portrayed by the media is most often a body love, which is falling in lust with another's appearance. Less frequently love is portrayed as soulish love: same thoughts about each other, similar emotions, and a common drive. However, the Christian marriage is true love that finds its center in the Spirit and receives oneness in Him. The spiritual marriage simply does not need to be perfect in body or soul; spirit begets spirit, and all outer dissimilarities are inconsequential. Since spirit is the issue, though, every couple must be warned of the enemy's attempts to take them out of the Spirit.

The most volatile situation in a marriage exists when one mate is in the Spirit and one is in the flesh. When both are in the flesh, the couple can coexist; when both are in the Spirit, it is a taste of heaven; but one in the Spirit and one in the flesh equals a living hell. However, it can be short-lived if approached properly. When in the flesh, the life of the flesh makes perfect sense, so we will react to any who attempt to move us from that place. Therefore, when the mate who is in the Spirit approaches, the first response is to pull him into the flesh. Why? Spirit contrasts with and heightens awareness of flesh. The flesh of man cannot stand contrast.

For example, I can remember being at parties as a young teenager. I was the only one who was not smoking. No one around me was comfortable with my not smoking. I did not care if they smoked; it was just that I had asthma. Yet they would continue to pressure me. Those in the flesh hate contrast.

It was contrast that got Jesus killed. If only He would have acted as did the other religious leaders, paid homage to those in the flesh, and used worldly methods to obtain a kingdom, He would have been left alone.

If the husband is in the flesh, an uncomfortable place for a believer, and he can push enough buttons to pull the wife into the flesh, then the pressure for him to change is gone. His flesh is now justified by the wife's reactions in kind. There is no greater love than to lay down one's life for another. The mate in the Spirit must lay down his life for the carnal mate. When the husband is rude, the wife must recognize the condition, walk across the room, and give him a kiss. Once this is done, a contrast is created. The husband will not immediately respond in the Spirit; on the contrary, he will try even harder to pull the wife down. Once again, she must die, refuse to react, and give another hug. As she does this, two things happen. First, she senses an incredible freedom from outside circumstances. This is Spirit control, the freedom enjoyed in the Spirit. The words and behavior of others are not controlling her words and behavior. Second, the husband must now come face to face with his own carnality. In his wife he sees the divine contrast, his carnality is in his lap, he has to (as the Africans say) carry his own monkey, he cannot blame anyone but himself, and he must return to life in the Spirit. Paul says,

"Death works in me, but life in you." Therefore, the greater truth that includes the lesser is this: Life in the Spirit makes for perfect compatibility, even during disagreements.

DAY 61
Complaining? Stop and Enjoy the Lord's Presence!

Because you did not serve the LORD your God with joy and a glad heart, for the abundance of all things; therefore you shall serve your enemies whom the LORD will send against you, in hunger, in thirst, in nakedness, and in the lack of all things; and He will put an iron yoke on your neck until He has destroyed you.

 —DEUTERONOMY 28:47, 48

If we are complaining, we are not enjoying the Lord's presence. This statement can take a lifetime to move from head to heart. However, as we dwell on it, it will make more and more sense. We did not become Christians to work for God or to please God; the work has already been done, and the Father is well pleased with Jesus. We became Christians for God, and God alone. As the understanding of our position in Him expands, we see that His presence is in us, just as it was in the Holy of Holies. Christ Himself dwells in us! We are temples of the living God (II Corinthians 6:16)! All of life's experiences have been moving us toward that revelation, and once we have it, everything changes. We can enjoy His presence in heavy traffic, in a hospital room, at a birth or a funeral, waiting for a taxi, sitting before the banker, walking or riding, or whatever we do. His presence is an absolute, and the peace of it is never to be surrendered to a situation. If we are looking without, we will find much to complain about. If we are looking behind the veil and seeing His presence with us in the midst of what we thought was a place of discomfort, we can have great joy. Once again we see that on this earth we make our own heaven or hell.

DAY 62
Consequences, Those Awful Consequences

For I will be merciful to their iniquities,
and I will remember their sins no more.

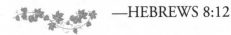

—HEBREWS 8:12

A large number of believers think sin from the past will continue to exercise power over them through consequences. It is true that sin and punishment are one and the same. If one gets drunk, has a wreck, and loses an arm, it is a consequence of the sin. But fear of consequences is too often emphasized in Christian teaching in order to motivate believers. Fear of hell, fear of punishment, and the fear of consequences have been used by the ecclesiastical machine to keep believers under its bondage for centuries. In this environment of control, there is a fairly strong overemphasis on hell for the believer and unbeliever alike, but this gives rise to an observation. When the groom woos the bride, he does not end the proposal with, "If you do not marry me, I will send you to hell." He may, however, end with, "If you do not marry me, any other life you choose will be hell. For I will love you and take care of you."

I do not minimize the horror of experiencing hell because of the rejection of Christ, but I know God is not so interested in consequences as in results. Parents do not want to punish a child forever; rather, parents are looking for results. The controller whispers, "Consequence, consequence, consequence!" in order to attain superiority and base others' inferiority on comparisons. Remember, the controller will always compare things only to those areas in which he has been successful. We will hear nothing of his failures. God whispers, "Results, results, results." What is the result? Have we believers learned that the blood of Jesus allows God to use our mistakes and not continually punish them? Have we learned our acceptance is in Christ because of His righteousness? Have we learned that in weakness we are safe, and in our strength we fail? Read in the book of Judges about the cycle of God's people as they forget God, are judged (consequence), return, and are blessed (results).

Immediately the legalist will shout, "A person sows what he reaps!" The Bible is full of this analogy, though we are also told that some sow and never reap, that others do not sow but reap, while still others neither sow nor reap. However, the one constant is that sowing and reaping generally last for a season.

I talked to a young Christian involved in an immoral situation. She had lost her glow, the lift in her countenance, and her peace. She had sown to the flesh and was reaping it.

We made the decision for her to move on, reject the activity, renounce it, and move back to Christ. She subsequently wrote me to say, "I am now consumed with the love of Jesus, and I cannot get enough of the Bible." There is the result! She was now sowing to the spirit and reaping its good fruit.

Coming from a farming community, I sat on a tractor more than once thinking how nice it would be not to do this chore every year! Every farmer knows the truth that he cannot sow once and then keep reaping for the next seventy years. Sowing and reaping last for one season. Therefore, if applied to consequences, they, too, are for a season. Sow to the flesh and reap to the flesh; sow to the spirit and reap to the spirit. These are short-term consequences. No one can sow to the spirit once and expect to reap the consequences of that act for the rest of his life. The same is true for sowing to the flesh; for that season the flesh will be reaped. The answer is to start sowing to the spirit in this season and the next. Each new season will be full of reaping something new, beautiful, fresh, and living. Instead, by sowing to the flesh, the reaping will be death.

It makes no sense that a Christian would commit a stupid act of the flesh and God would keep him under bondage, placing him for the rest of his life in a new category entitled "Second-class Believer"! Again, if it were possible to commit one sin that would cause suffering the rest of his life, then it would also be possible to commit one act of righteousness that would carry a person through his whole life. But abiding is for the moment, the season. God is not interested in punishing us for the rest of our lives. Often believers think everything that goes wrong is a consequence of a past mistake, such as marrying the "wrong" person, succumbing to temptation and sin, or betraying a loved one. Very likely it is not the past that is causing misery but today's walking in the flesh.

DAY 63
Contrast

They heard the sound of the LORD God walking in the garden in the cool of the day, and the man and his wife hid themselves from the presence of the LORD God among the trees of the garden. Then the LORD God called to the man and said to him, "Where are you?" He said, "I heard the sound of You in the garden, and I was afraid because I was naked; so I hid myself."

—GENESIS 3:8-10

Here is a secret: God does not fight our failures; He uses them! One aspect of the Glory of God is that He is never undone, wringing His hands in the hope that we will come through with a plan, for He always has one. He does what He wants, and He uses all things! "For My own sake, I will act . . . And My glory I will not give to another" (Isaiah 48:11). The Glory of God is a wonderful thing; who can comprehend it? Especially if it is hidden! God will not give His Glory to another; every one of us is "another" and, therefore, a threat to the Glory of God. But how are we a threat? Only one thing will mask the Glory of God: a man's own counterfeit glory, which is pride. Consequently, God does not work in the midst of the self-righteous, those who are up and out. Their own glory blinds them from seeing the true Glory of God. Adam walked with God and had his own glory. Adam was not perfect, for had he been he would not have fallen. His imitation glory hid the true Glory. Adam's glory allowed him to take lightly the Glory of God, so lightly that he would sell it for a piece of fruit. However, after the fall a contrast was created, and Adam could see the Glory of God, appreciate it, long for it, and seek it as something valuable. God used Adam's failure to allow him to lose his own glory and discover the Glory of God. "For this reason I say to you, her sins, which are many, have been forgiven, for she loved much; but he who is forgiven little, loves little" (Luke 7:47). The Prodigal Son is another example of deceitful glory. He had lived so long in the father's house that somehow he had come to believe he had made some significant contribution toward all he had experienced. In the pigpen he fell out of pride into reality.

Many leaders have lived so long on the borrowed gifting of God that in deceitful glory they start to think they are the source. Failure is their awakening! Oh, for the recognition of the Glory of God.

As I have failed throughout the Christian life I have often thought all was lost. Yet in my fallen state I have seen His Glory, a glory I had previously never imagined in my self-satisfied, self-exalted state . . . and I worship! Before, He had not been pleased with me, but He revealed Himself in my failure when I could appreciate it, and He was pleased to do it. "For all have sinned and fall short of the glory of God, being justified as a gift by His grace

through the redemption which is in Christ Jesus," Romans
3:23, 24. Oh, for the glory of God!

DAY 64
Crucified With Christ

And if Christ is in you, though the body is dead because
of sin, yet the spirit is alive because of righteousness.
But if the Spirit of Him who raised Jesus from the dead
dwells in you, He who raised Christ Jesus from the dead will
also give life to your mortal bodies through
His Spirit who indwells you.
—ROMANS 8:10, 11

The moment I believe in Jesus for life in heaven, He
binds me, so I must not be able to live the life on earth. I
am seeing it clearly. How can I be bound and then required
to do something? Do you remember the Head, the man
I saw in the Amazon region without any limbs? He is the
full image of Jesus. What can He do but rest? This is our
inner life. We cannot perform; we cannot do it. I am sick
and tired of beating myself up over requirements I have
made for myself; He did not make them for me, because
He bound me. No more waking up full of self-hatred,
regrets, and guilt; He never required those things out of
a dead man. His death was for sin, and my death was for
Life. The purpose of my crucifixion is so I will be forced to
live on the earth the same way He did, in full dependence
on the Father, doing nothing on His own.

DAY 65
Culture

In which there is no distinction between Greek and Jew,
circumcised and uncircumcised, barbarian, Scythian,
slave and freeman, but Christ is all, and in all.

—COLOSSIANS 3:11

I have nearly stopped working with missionaries simply because I am weary of being told what I cannot do. They have said I can never minister because I do not know the culture or the language, or because the message I present is too complex. Well, amen! Jesus did not have my culture, He did not speak my language, and He was not from the same race, and yet everything He does and says cuts deeply, past my flesh into my spirit. Sometimes the human culture, which is the foundation for every subculture, is common among man. Jesus spoke of things not of His culture but of mankind. It is our job also as missionaries to speak of things common to man. In so doing I have discovered that people on every continent, of every educational level, and of every race are ministered to. I really believe that culture is far overrated as an influence in or detriment to understanding the Gospel.

DAY 66
Daily Miracles

As soon as He was approaching, near the descent of the Mount of Olives, the whole crowd of the disciples began to praise God joyfully with a loud voice for all the miracles which they had seen.

—LUKE 19:37

We want to experience the supernatural, and yet we are experiencing it daily. If we awoke and were able to smell for the first time, hear for the first time, and touch for the first time, would we not say we had experienced a miracle? Had we never seen fire, what would we think the first time we saw it? If we had never walked, what would we think upon taking the first step? We are living the miraculous! This is why Jesus said it is a wicked generation that seeks for a sign, a wicked people who cannot see the miracle of life every day of their lives. If we cannot recognize God, we want something more to add to the miraculous. For those who do not recognize God, there will never be enough. It would be a miracle to see the lame walk, the blind see, a leper healed. Yet we walk, see, and are being healed every day, so why would people say we never experience miracles? I have walked on water . . . when it had become ice. Why am I not walking and leaping and praising God like the healed lame man? I have been healed, and yet like the carnal—blind and unseeing—I do not recognize God and His glory, considering it to be mundane.

DAY 67
David Versus Solomon

And He has said to me, "My grace is sufficient for you,
for power is perfected in weakness."

—II CORINTHIANS 12:9

David vs. Solomon? It is vexing to see the number of people who claim to abandon their mates for a relationship with a "soul mate." The infatuation with another leads them to forfeit all other relationships for this one that supposedly will bring ultimate satisfaction. In one way I think marriage conferences feed it, in that the speakers feed a fantasy of what marriage in Christ is really like. They present a portrayal of family in which children do not leave footprints on the floor and the home is nirvana. The goal of Christianity is no longer Christ but idyllic relationships with those around us. They do not seem to point out the reason why we have conflicts, disagreements, and frustrations with a person from whom we cannot escape. The Lord works it out beautifully as we are forced to grow in weakness and failure, allowing Christ to become our strength. We are obliged to let His love flow through us when we have run out of our own carnal love.

Why bring Solomon and David into this discussion? So I can ask a question. Ready? Which would you pick, the Song of Solomon or the Psalms? Both describe nearly perfect relationships; one describes the relationship with another, the other with God. Which would you prefer?

Personally, I would rather see husbands and wives fulfilled in their relationships with the Lord than in the relationship with one another. Why? The lesser must always give way to the greater. If the wife and husband first had a vibrant relationship with God, I believe their relationship with one another would be very, very, very fulfilling. We encourage one another in Christ. When we have Him as the priority, we are softer, more easily forgiving, harder to offend, and more selfless.

DAY 68
Decision-Making and
the Peace Of God

And the peace of God, which surpasses all comprehension, shall guard your hearts and your minds in Christ Jesus.

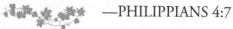 —PHILIPPIANS 4:7

The peace of God is God, for all that God is stands in agreement. The decisions God makes are in light of the context of His peace. There are no outside influences. I sometimes illustrate the peace of God as a circle within which lie all the attributes of God: His will, His judgments, His provision, His wisdom, His mercy, His love, and His word. Complete agreement and absolute peace exist among His attributes. Therefore, when He decides something, it is perfect. When He gives direction, it is infallible.

Contrast that with man. We are never at peace. All of our attributes (mind, will, emotions, and body) disagree. Add to the confusion inside us the confusion outside of us. To make a decision we must have everything right. We cannot get it right, though. We must take into account the actions of others, hoping we judged them properly. We must consider how our decision will affect others. Is it the right thing? Will it work out in the long run? There are so many variables in decision-making that most people approach it with fear and apprehension. Who could blame them? What is the solution for those of us who are fragmented? We turn to the only one that is One! "The Lord thy God is One God." There is no division in Him; there is peace.

Therefore, let the peace of God rule in your heart. You say, "I do not know the peace of God!" Not so! You do know the peace of God. You may not know when it comes, but you have always known when the peace of God has left you. Judging when it leaves is the secret. I decide to buy a car, and the peace of God leaves me. I decide to discipline my child in a particular way, and the peace of God leaves me. I decide that I will fix my relationships by withdrawing and no longer caring, and the peace of God leaves me. When the decision I have made is the wrong one, the peace of God leaves. Let every decision be rooted in this peace. Move with this peace, and you will be moving perfectly. It is easy!

DAY 69
Discipleship

So that the man of God may be thoroughly equipped for
every good work.
—II TIMOTHY 3:17 [NIV]

There are two forms of discipleship in the church today. The predominant program emphasizes what may one day be possessed through hard work and uses guilt to manipulate the disciple through constantly comparing him with successful others who have arrived. The approach less often utilized reveals what a believer already possesses, stressing things to be experienced through His work today, stirring action through understanding of the love and compassion of God. It is unfortunate that the former agenda reigns in Christendom today.

It is worthwhile to examine the differences between these approaches to discipleship. In the former, success is determined by grand accomplishments: numbers, individual decisions, buildings, giving, programs, attendance, passages memorized, rules kept, levels of separation, submission gained, and devotion to structure. Exaltation, superiority, and authority are the buzzwords, not equality. Discipleship takes the form of a mold that can make parrots of those deemed superior in discipline, while God's loving hand in the lives of the weak, defeated, and failing is never considered. Neither are these seen as cherished traits: the desire to wait on God while receiving nothing, the giving of a kind word when slandered or misunderstood, nor the ability to love the unlovable. A full notebook and head of knowledge are preferred to a heart full to overflowing. Knowledge of the Bible takes precedence over knowledge of the Author. Law of and for the earth is more valuable than grace originating in heaven. Disciples are equipped only to see the steps needed to secure God but remain ignorant of God's work to secure them. They are continually taught how to change, yet remain untutored regarding the secret of the expanding life, His life, which is already possessed. These disciples are in the bondage of comparison, never enjoying their youth in the Lord. Soul and spirit are not divided, leading them to believe that great talent, intellect, and ability will equal both great spiritual power and pleasure to God. Slow, steady, natural growth is abandoned for the promised one-time fix. The person in charge sets the standard for success in anyone's walk with God, using his own experiences and attainments as the standard rather than God's allowance for individualistic success. Many are the victims of legalistic discipleship.

DAY 70
Divine Omissions

You shall not add to the word which I am commanding you, nor take away from it, that you may keep the commandments of the LORD your God which I comand you.

—DEUTERONOMY 4:2

*Pray, then, in this way: Our Father who art in heaven,
Hallowed be Thy name. Thy kingdom come.
Thy will be done, on earth as it is in heaven.*

*Give us this day our daily bread. And forgive us our
debts, as we also have forgiven our debtors. And do not lead
us into temptation, but deliver us from evil. For Thine is the
kingdom, and the power, and the glory, forever. Amen.*

—MATTHEW 6:9-13

We love what is called the Lord's Prayer. It is so beautiful, so simple, so complete! It covers all the bases. It makes prayer simple and natural, and it brings such peace. Many have written about it, finding significance in every word. Who could disagree? However, few have written about what the prayer leaves out. Divine omissions are very important. Nearly nothing we are told we need or must do today, nor the sought-after experiences, are in this prayer. Again, we must get the first things right. I find the "moves of God" (all too often simply the stirrings of the flesh) quite boring. See the people behind the stage or look into the next week, and you will know what I mean. It all centers on man, what one man is offering, what another is giving, and what another one has. It does not center on Jesus and is not needed. If it were needed, it would happen in every place, without coaching. I am not saying that God does not cause all things to work together for good, and even this He will cause for good. My point is that no one should get too upset over lauded occurrences he has not experienced when they are divine omissions. Often I am asked what I think about a particular expression of what is called spiritual. I simply respond, "What Scripture are you talking about?" There never is one, just a vague reference to some Old Testament passage, "Eye has not seen, ear has not heard!" In the Lord's Prayer, Jesus is clearly telling us what we really need. His kingdom (it will not be weird), His will (not something scary), daily provision (not security), forgiveness (for our own good), and deliverance from temptation. Additions are often Divine Omissions!

DAY 71
Divine Umbilical Cord

Beloved . . . it has not appeared as yet what we will be.
We know that when He appears, we will be like Him,
because we will see Him just as He is.

—I JOHN 3:2

Picture an umbilical cord running from God to Jesus on earth. The Oneness flowed into the man named Jesus. The Word in God became a man. Jesus had the body and soul of a man but the very life of God. When Jesus spoke, the words were God's. This man, Jesus, who did everything, actually did nothing except what was done by the Father through Him. In the lifetime of Jesus, the body and soul of a man struggled with His Spirit; Jesus won, and the body, soul, and world became a place of victory for Him. His body was no longer bound to the world. This Spirit, this life that wins, comes out in the blood of Jesus, for as we are told in Genesis 9:4, "The life is in the blood."

On the cross, Jesus would have liked the cup to pass from Him. What was the cup? It could not have been physical suffering, for He acknowledged that flesh and blood do not enter the Kingdom. The cup was the intimate connection with the Father that He had always experienced, even before time. The umbilical cord was cut by the Father, and instantly Jesus' spirit was isolated. Sin immediately took its opportunity, encasing His spirit as though weighted in concrete. He who knew no sin became sin. His spirit began to sink; just as David prophesied, He was descending. Then death encased what was already encased in sin, and further into the abyss He sank. In hell, captivity added one more layer. Though sin, Satan, and the world could not defeat Him in the body, into the dark place they had now taken Him, encased in sin, death, and captivity. Their celebration, though, was premature, for light is greater than darkness. All three encasements broke open and Jesus emerged. He took captivity captive, broke the power of sin and death, and plundered hell itself. He was reconnected to the Father, Who moved Him back to His body, raising Him from the dead.

Our spirit can go only where the body, its earth suit, takes it. But when the Spirit of Jesus returned to His body, the Spirit was now so much greater that it actually transformed His body, which then would go where the Spirit wished. Since the Spirit could move through doors, so, too, could the body. Once He ascended to heaven, He took with Him the spoils. He is the Son of man in heaven, having overcome the body, sin, Satan, the world, the law of sin, the law of death, and captivity. He is united in perfect peace with the Father. Every bit of the victory gained by the Word is now brought into the Divine oneness as a part of the Father. As Jesus moves through the Holy Spirit into new sons, the umbilical cord that comes from God, carrying with it all that God is, attaches to the new life of believers, who then share in the life that is the Living Word.

DAY 72
Divorce

I press on toward the goal for the prize of the upward call of God in Christ Jesus.

—PHILIPPIANS 3:14

There is much I could say about divorce without getting into the debate as to whether or not a Christian can get a divorce. I am not taking a position on that topic; that is not the purpose of this article. I have worked diligently for decades to see every marriage stay together. Unfortunately, that effort was not always rewarded. Root issues are at play in every divorce, heightening the issue of self-centeredness and often leading to the destruction of families. The fact is that marriage does not create as many problems as it reveals. Much could be said, but, as is my custom, I want to move to a greater truth. Can you believe that God causes all things to work for good? Can you believe that His primary goal is not a good marriage? Can you believe that His goal is the revelation of Christ in you, the loss of your glory to obtain His, the destruction of pride that you might have His strength, and the dissolving of your kingdom so you might enter into building His? I am vexed when any particular deed of the flesh is exalted above another, such as when self-righteousness will put a person in leadership and unrighteousness will take him out. We have all walked in the flesh, all been stupid, and some of us have gotten divorces. Laying aside the issue of the right or wrong of divorce (my efforts speak for themselves), I want to raise a different question: Do you believe that once divorced, a brother or sister is doomed to a life of being a second-class Christian, never to rise above mediocrity, with the work of Jesus having ceased in his or her life? Do you believe God is limited by divorce? I do not! His goal is Jesus. I have actually met people who came to Christ because they had a divorce! They tried restoration and the other was not interested; in fact, the mate had thought them quite mad. It vexes me when any believer, because of any failure, believes he has now been put in the hopeless bin. My goal is Jesus. If some really come to know Jesus in a good marriage, a bad marriage, or no marriage, I rejoice in Jesus. Guilt and condemnation are of the devil and will only make a person stall out. We must first and foremost press on to, and in, Jesus.

DAY 73
Doctrine Of Failure?

For I know that nothing good dwells in me, that is, in my
flesh; for the willing is present in me,
but the doing of the good is not.

—ROMANS 7:18

Because of how religion infiltrates the Church, so few have a doctrine of failure. The one very big problem with this is that we all will fail! Most are emphasizing a one-time fix, meaning that better understanding or some conference will free a person from all future conflict. It is not so with us. Our system not only allows for failure but plans for it. Do any believe that the early Church did not have failures? The Epistles were written because Christians were failing, not getting it, and, most importantly, had moved away from their focus on Jesus. Without their failures we would not have those books. We have all learned through their failures, but also, if they learned through theirs, is it not true that we will learn from ours? Paul used the occurrence of believers' going to temple prostitutes to explain the principle of oneness. He did not tell them they were hopeless; he told them to stop and explained why they should not be doing it. Peter was a tremendous failure after being taught by Jesus for three-and-a-half years. From his example, what do we learn about soul strength in our attempts to serve God? What did he learn? If we are prepared for failure, when it comes (and it will), we will not have to enter into condemnation or unbelief and become a Galatian.

The flesh does not change, which really is a beautiful thing, because if we do not want to walk with Jesus, we will be the same mess we were before . . . well, actually worse, because with Adam's life within us, wearing sin was natural, but with Christ's life within, wearing sin is very abnormal and miserable. The hardest thing to get across is that we are not improving, but only abiding longer. I knew a man in a mental institution who came to see Christ as his life, and as Christ flowed from him, people could see Jesus. However, he believed in a one-time fix, so when he was not abiding he still acted very psychotic, only it was more of an "acceptable" Christian psychosis. Well, amen.

An elephant can live 65 to 100 years, and if it achieves natural death, it dies of starvation. It has six sets of teeth; as one wears out, the next set comes in, and so on until it has no teeth, can no longer eat, and dies. Like the elephant, so to speak, we have many sets of spiritual teeth for eating at different stages of our life: teeth for the milk of the early things and teeth for the later things. Until the day we leave this body there will always be something on which to chew, and if we chew long enough we need a new set of teeth. We have chewed long enough on heaven vs. hell. It is time to chew on the fact that Christ is in us. As by choice we invite Him to live through us, He will today, but for today only. This is not to say He is coming and going, but that we must choose to relate to Him in a certain way. If we do not invite Him today to live His life through us, we will discover the hard way that we have not changed, and God will use the ensuing failure to bring the point home.

DAY 74
Does An Affair Break Or Ruin a Marriage?

Do you not know that he who unites himself with a prostitute is one with her in body? For it is said, "The two will become one flesh."

—I CORINTHIANS 6:16 [NIV]

There are, of course, several ways to experience oneness. The sexual relationship is one of them. The question I am posing is, does an affair ruin a marriage? When Paul was addressing the Corinthians' habit of visiting temple prostitutes (male and female), he admonished them to stop, arguing that it is not right to be one in flesh with someone other than a mate. He says the ritual is to stop; he does not say marriages are over for all the believers who participated. Does the sex act ruin or break spiritual oneness? I do not see how, in light of Scripture. It is an act that is to cease, for it is sin, but it is not the end of the marriage. I have seen more than one marriage weather an affair. I want to go lightly on this topic, especially in an age where the sex act has become something less than special, and if sex is not held as sacred or special before marriage, it is easy to understand why it is not sacred or special to so many after marriage. However, I must speak my convictions on the matter and give hope to those who have so suffered. An affair of the flesh cannot break spiritual oneness! After all, if it could, then so could a rape, and that would not even make sense to doubly punish a victim.

DAY 75
Does the Flesh Continue To Grow?

What is my strength, that I should wait?
And what is my end, that I should endure?
Is my strength the strength of stones, or is my flesh bronze?

—JOB 6:11, 12

The Bible makes the point that once we have believed in Jesus, the old man is crucified, we receive a new life, and what was true of us is no longer true, what we did we never did, what happened to us never happened to us, for "if any man be in Christ, he is a new creation" [II Cor. 5:17, NIV]. The old man is gone but the flesh—the condition of being under the influence of something other than Jesus—has not changed and will never change; we just abide longer with it under His influence, so it may appear that it has changed. The flesh is not improving, nor does God intend for it to, for it is His stronghold to drive us back to Him. In fact, once we have Christ within us, the flesh will make us more miserable than it did when we had Adam's life in us, for now it does not fit what we are.

This brings me to an important point: The flesh can continue to develop after we believe in Jesus. All we have to do is walk after the flesh, and the flesh will find new idols, new ways of coping. It will continue to grow. In Fiji I got a fungus, a very tricky thing that started out very small, but when it would itch, it felt so good to scratch it, and though the pain in the center was intense, it always felt good to scratch around it. Through the scratching it spread; soon it covered both feet. The flesh is the same: Scratch that itch and it will grow.

A perfect example of the flesh's continuing to expand is its increase in those (men and women) who struggle with internet pornography. This was something unheard of not so many years ago, but now there are few families not affected. It actually is worse among believers than unbelievers, for if unbelievers want sex, they will generally just go for it. But the believer draws an invisible line in the sand and tells the flesh, "You can go this far and no further." To them, porn is not the same as adultery and is therefore allowable. There are many in ministry struggling with this new development in fleshly expression.

We stand in our why. Are we saying that we can stop doing something because our flesh got stronger, or are we saying we can stop doing something because we have moved up a gear in faith and believe what He says He has done for us? We can do all things through Christ who strengthens us. Action is to be based on His previous action. We are to walk sinless because His action makes such a walk possible. We live a very high life based on a work He has done. We need to take up our mats. The man in the Bible had to take up his mat, but his action was based on something Jesus had already spoken. Some can only say they will not look at porn if the why is based on the fact that Jesus has set them free. And if Jesus has set them free from one thing, then how many things are included after the one? One will lead to many. We should never vow that we will not do something if it is because we think we are strong enough to keep the vow, but if we have had the revelation of Him keeping the vow in us, then that is the proper order.

This awareness of the weakness of the flesh and its propensity to grow should not discourage us, but rather encourage us to remain near to Him, for we know the moment the Lord is not our focus, we will move into the flesh, which has not improved. God has orchestrated the whole of the Christian life to center on abiding in Him.

DAY 76
Do I Encourage Sin?

For if while we were enemies, we were reconciled to God through the death of His Son, much more, having been reconciled, we shall be saved by His life. And not only this, but we also exult in God through our Lord Jesus Christ, through whom we have now received the reconciliation.

 —ROMANS 5:10, 11

Many times I have said that no one is set free from the thing on which he focuses. I wish the problem with humanity were as simple as telling people no concerning their behavior and then watching them quit it; however, this does not work out in real life. For instance, do you know of sin in your life and in the lives of other believers that has not stopped? No one is set free from the thing on which he focuses. If the homosexual were focused on staying away from it or focused on doing it, his focus would not be on Christ, the only Source of his deliverance. My goal, unlike that of many, is not to see people set free from their sin. If I know someone out of fellowship with

Christ and practicing homosexuality or someone out of fellowship with Christ but not practicing homosexuality, what difference is that to the man's soul or to the desire of God to fellowship with the man? He must first enter into fellowship with God and then allow the Gardener to do the pruning as Jesus said He would. I am not advocating sin of any kind; I am advocating fellowship with Christ. God does work in an order, and I believe that fellowship with Christ comes first in that order. We do not clean ourselves up to go to God; we go to God and let Him clean us up. Should sin be an excuse for not going to God? Never! When Christianity is viewed as a religion, it is like all other religions in that success rests at the feet of man, but Christianity is no mere religion. There is only one faith, the Christian faith, where our success rests at the feet of Jesus! I trust those who have questions will completely read my books and understand this teaching.

DAY 77
Do Not Despise the Carnal

And as for you, you meant evil against me, but God meant it for good in order to bring about this present result, to preserve many people alive.

—GENESIS 50:20

I really dread reflections on my time in Bible college, those days when we sat around discussing how ignorant congregations were, how they did not do what they knew was right, and how they could be so stupid. I cannot stand those memories primarily because all my judgments befell me. It is so easy to stand on the work of others, carnal or spiritual, and make judgments. For years I actually believed that my thinking was my own, that I owed no one. I would read the Ante-Nicene fathers and think, "How could they believe that?" It was easy to look back through history and assess what was right or wrong with those believers. With a bit more maturity I have come to see that I stand on their shoulders, that what many have done, in the light they had, has brought me into a greater light. I am not independent of them. I am not smarter. I was born in this age, with this education, all for a time to come. It is too easy to look at some doctrine believed by a Luther or Calvin and judge it. However, I stand in my reality and judge them in theirs. My point is twofold. First, everything, whether good or bad, the believers before me have done contributed toward making me what I am. I am indebted to them and not as independent as I would like to think. Second, I should never despise the work of God accomplished through the good or the bad in a saint.

For instance, perhaps you are angry over the bondage you underwent while in legalism, despising those who taught it to you and then manipulated and controlled you through it. This is not necessary, for it was not their teaching that brought you into bondage; it only revealed that you held a righteousness of your own. Only a self-righteous person would attempt such a journey with that type of teacher. It is your own fault you were in bondage. You went along with it, and God permitted it because He knew you needed it! Being in bondage was what made you long for liberty and what today makes you acknowledge freedom as so precious. Therefore, bless those who used and abused you, bringing you under bondage. God used them to make you long for the contrast.

DAY 78
Double Yellow Line

To whom God willed to make known what is the riches of the glory of this mystery among the Gentiles, which is Christ in you, the hope of glory.

—COLOSSIANS 1:27

But encourage one another day after day, as long as it is still called "Today," so that none of you will be hardened by the deceitfulness of sin.

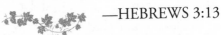

—HEBREWS 3:13

Once while traveling outback in Australia with my father, he asked if he could take the wheel, for he wanted to be able to say he had experienced driving on the "wrong" side of the road. What I witnessed next could only be duplicated by another farmer! He steered with his knees, holding a cup of coffee in one hand and a beautiful dessert in the other. As we approached the top of a hill, he unconsciously began to move into the right lane. I yelled out, "You are crossing a double yellow line! You are moving into the wrong lane on a hill!" He just kept sipping his coffee! Suddenly, I got my first glimpse of the roofline of an oncoming truck. I grabbed the steering wheel and pulled us into the left lane, but instinctively, he grabbed the wheel back to whip the car back into the right lane. Once again I grabbed the wheel and pulled us into the left lane just as the truck headed in and out of the ditch. We noticed in the rearview mirror that the driver had regained control and therefore did not see any reason to turn around, explain we were from America, and check his spiritual condition! As for the destiny of the coffee and dessert, that is another story.

We have a saying at ALMI: "I know what I am saying, but I am not always sure what is being heard." On occasion, I will receive a letter questioning some of the things I teach on audio, in print, or through seminar messages. One friend in Ukraine told me that much of what I am saying could easily be misinterpreted. Another in the States remarked that after examining Scripture in light of what ALMI taught, he really liked it; he had not thought it could possibly be in the Bible. The problem, he said, was that these emphases are not often made by others, making the teaching sound foreign. I have been accused by legalists of leading some astray. I always ask that the "some" be identified and organized, so I can get together with them and clarify any misconceptions having arisen. To date, the accusers cannot come up with a list of the "some," for in truth it is painful only to them; I am stepping on the toes of their pet predispositions. I would not defend all that I say to press any point apart from Christ as Life or defend a teaching outside the hub of the wheel, which is Christ, because I want to continue to make the focus "the simplicity and purity of devotion to Christ" (II Cor. 11:3).

There is a story of two giants sitting next to one another. An unseen elf in the tree kept throwing pebbles at one or the other giant when he was not looking. The giants each blamed the other and in the end became so angry they beat one another to death. The enemy loves to throw pebbles to separate believers, so we must all be aware of them. However, it does not mean we do not welcome honest, heartfelt observations. We receive them in the Lord and are grateful for all such inspection. Brothers and sisters in Christ can keep us from crossing the double yellow lines and having a head-on collision. Therefore, when I receive a question, an attempt is made to clarify my position. I really liked it when Eric Maddison from England visited me and asked, "Are you continuing to preach Christ as life?" He was an elder brother checking up on me. Different ministries have different passions; we thank God for them. ALMI's passion is the revelation of Christ in you, the hope of glory, praying always that nothing sidetracks us. "Now I urge you, brethren, by our Lord Jesus Christ and by the love of the Spirit, to strive together with me in your prayers to God for me" (Romans 15:30).

DAY 79
Dreams

In the last days, God says, I will pour out my Spirit on all people. Your sons and daughters will prophesy, your young men will see visions, your old men will dream dreams.

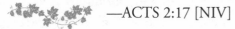

—ACTS 2:17 [NIV]

When we have a daydream our minds are wandering, but an outside stimulus such as noise or movement can break the concentration and bring us back to reality. However, in a dream there is no outside stimulus to interrupt the flow; the thought is able to run its course without direction from the conscious mind. Often several items in the subconscious are blended together to make for some strange happenings.

Another aspect of dreams occurs when salvation (freedom), after working in the conscious mind, begins to work in the subconscious. People will begin to dream about past events, some hurtful, but there is no need to panic. Pray, for God is cleaning out the garbage. Dreams can also put us in touch with the spiritual world. Why? When awake, the mind is most often consumed with running the body. However, during sleep the mind can turn to the spirit and its realm. At this time, Satan can attack. Just as we stand in our body and people walk past, we have a spirit, and spirits walk past and talk. Again, there is no need for concern; just pray, learning to do it even in dreams. In many dreams I have had to rebuke the enemy. He has no glory. Also, of course, God can speak in dreams. In our state of physical inactivity God often can most easily speak. Notice in the Bible how often God speaks when a man or woman is inactive, either in prison, in a pit, asleep, or on a lonely mountaintop. Satan's interruptions into our sleep have his thumbprint, fear. The dreams inspired by God are crystal clear. Subconscious-inspired dreams are often nonsensical; the mind is initiating. "I need Thee every hour, in joy or pain. I need Thee; oh I need Thee, every hour I need Thee."

DAY 80
Ecology

*For the anxious longing of the creation waits eagerly
for the revealing of the sons of God. For the creation was
subjected to futility, not willingly, but because of Him who
subjected it, in hope that the creation itself also will be set
free from its slavery to corruption into the freedom of the
glory of the children of God. For we know that
the whole creation groans and suffers the pains
of childbirth together until now.*

—ROMANS 8:19-22

*Then God said to Jonah, "Do you have good reason to be
angry about the plant?" And he said, "I have good reason to
be angry, even to death." Then the LORD said, "You had
compassion on the plant for which you did not work and
which you did not cause to grow, which came up overnight
and perished overnight. Should I not have compassion
on Nineveh, the great city in which there are more than
120,000 persons who do not know the difference between
their right and left hand, as well as many animals?"*

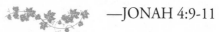

—JONAH 4:9-11

In Scripture we see that creation has suffered by the hand
of man and that redeemed man treats creation differently.
However, the lesser will always give way to the greater, and
man is the greater. It is amazing to watch as people show
more compassion to plants and animals than to people,
to live in a society where it is more important to protect a

bird egg than the heart, mind, and innocence of a child or the life of a human fetus. Often the reason why people are that way is because they have been hurt by others, which makes loving a pet or a tree safer than giving themselves to others. I can only imagine the rejection and suffering Jonah had experienced at the hands of others, so much so that when he was commanded to go to people, he fled. How often do we flee when God tells us to give ourselves to those who have hurt us? One amazing thing about Jesus is that where we fail, He succeeded. Though everyone rejected Him in the end, we see Him going forward to a cross to give Himself for all those who had hurt Him. We must admit where we are. After so much hurt, many of us have decided never again to give ourselves to others. However, if we invite Christ to be our love, we will find that what is impossible for us is easily possible for Him.

DAY 81
Endurance

For this reason I endure all things for the sake of those who are chosen, so that they also may obtain the salvation which is in Christ Jesus and with it eternal glory.

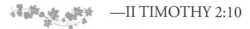 —II TIMOTHY 2:10

Endurance is a relevant topic today, when there has been so much loss to endure over the years: loss of personal freedom, loss of family, loss of property, loss of integrity, loss of steadfastness, loss of relationships, loss of friendships, loss of dreams, loss of vision, loss of loves. It cannot be regained; it is gone forever. Have you ever asked yourself the question, "How do I settle things that cannot be settled?" or "How do I live with loss?" You can, of course, live in regret, the world of "if only," blame, and giving up. That, however, does not lead to optimal living. You must go to the Lord and ask Him for yourself how to live through what must be endured to the end. A lifetime of endurance is actually not very long in view of the big picture. In Him it is actually possible to endure loss with joy and find perfect peace. Do you believe it? What are your options? Do you know that by His grace He has allowed you to endure until this present time? He will keep you, because He is love. Do you know that? Do you believe it? Do you believe that God loves you? It is an important, serious question to which an answer in the affirmative is crucial. If you believe He loves you, then believe that everything coming into your life, even the things not settled, are rooted in His love and are what you needed. One of my Chinese friends, upon telling me everything that had gone wrong in his life, reflected, "Can you believe God loves me that much? You would not let those things into your son's life unless it was for his good. Such great pain reveals a great love." He was settled. God's love settles everything.

DAY 82
Eternal Man

For since the creation of the world His invisible attributes, His eternal power and divine nature, have been clearly seen, being understood through what has been made, so that they are without excuse.

—ROMANS 1:20

When gazing at an ocean all the way to the horizon, some believe they know the limit of the ocean, while others understand that the horizon is merely the extent of their vision. In light of the new understanding concerning the complexities of the makeup of man (DNA, genetics, microbiology, brain chemistry, etc.), evolutionists must rethink the age of man. The time needed to bring about these minute but complex changes must be expanded. Man is not a trillion years old, but trillions of trillions of years old. More accurately, man's age is eternal. It would take eternity to create man. How can man be eternal? Man has always been in the mind of God, who is eternal. Therefore, man is eternal. Eternity closes the loop on the beginning and the end of time. Eternity is as a circle. If we stand in the center of the circle and look out to eternity, the place where we presently look is the only thing of which we can be aware. The age of the thing we look at is proportionate to how long we have been looking at that spot. Man is in eternity, for he dwells in the mind of the eternal One. At the point in eternity where we notice man, the age of man from our perspective begins. Therefore, the eternal man has been noticed for 6,000 years of recorded history and, hence, only recognized as existing for the amount of time he has been noticed. Man's existence is then, in a sense, limited by man, who can only discern his existence from the moment he became aware of it. Man then limits the understanding of man. The only true way to know the eternal man would be to move into the One who is eternal. At this point we come to know man not from our awareness but through awareness outside of us. The conclusion is that man can never know man. Knowledge based on a point in time can only perceive that point in time, like a penlight shining on a great piece of artwork and we only see where the light hits. We must stand in a greater light to see the whole picture. The lesser must give way to the greater, and as we stand in The Light, we can discern much more. Attempting to judge the age of something by looking at the visible, when its actual age must be based in the invisible, is absurd.

DAY 83
Everything!

Knowing that from the Lord you will receive the reward of the inheritance. It is the Lord Christ whom you serve.

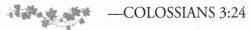 —COLOSSIANS 3:24

I have written elsewhere about the fellow who returned home to take care of his dying father. After the death the son became very depressed, unable to live with the truth that he had returned not for the sake of caring for the one who loved him, but to secure the inheritance. God has given us everything from the very beginning, including everything pertaining to life and godliness. Why? So we can enter into the relationship of Jesus, who seeks the Father for the sake of the Father alone. If we keep thinking there is something to get out of God, we will be tempted to seek Him for something other than Himself. Everything, if you are interested in things, has been given to you. He gives us everything from the beginning. We go to God today not to get something, but simply because we want to be with Him, to enjoy the fellowship of a relationship renewed daily with no strings attached. There cannot be, as He has given everything pertaining to life.

DAY 84
Exchanging Negatives for Positives?

Have you not made distinctions among yourselves, and become judges with evil motives? Listen, my beloved brethren: did not God choose the poor of this world to be rich in faith and heirs of the kingdom which He promised to those who love Him?

—JAMES 2:4, 5

We believe that if we have a negative in our lives, others can feed us enough positives to make it go away, so we are always trying to make a positive out of others or hoping they will admit the negative they have put in our lives. In reality we need another negative to feed the original negative in order to enlarge it so much that we will, by revelation, see the stupidity of trying to get undone the negatives in life. This will make us stop trying to change it and put it on the shelf called flesh.

I see many dissatisfied believers, and often they are motivated not by need but want. They see their lack of goods as a negative and want to get a positive. Some cheat to do so. After their accomplishment of milking a positive out of someone, they remain a negative. By all appearances, an African friend appears to have many negatives in his lack of this world's goods. He asks for nothing, is not materialistic but Christ-minded, and is very positive, for he does not see his situation as a negative; he sees Jesus. One time I gave him a computer, and later I was erroneously thinking I had sent two. I wrote and asked him to give one away to another brother. He immediately wrote that he would. Then I discovered my mistake and explained it, told him to keep the computer, and said I would purchase one for the other brother. "But," I asked, "how could you so easily give back the computer you need so much?" His response was, "When your mother cooks a large meal and asks for some of it, would you not give it to her?" He is a full and free man, not trying to change the negatives.

In fact, at the highest revelation of Christ in us, there are no negatives, for He is working all things together for the good of those who love Him and are called according to His purposes.

DAY 85
Faith Believes God

What then shall we say that Abraham, our forefather
according to the flesh, has found? For if Abraham was
justified by works, he has something to boast about, but not
before God. For what does the Scripture say? "ABRAHAM
BELIEVED GOD, AND IT WAS RECKONED TO HIM
AS RIGHTEOUSNESS." Now to the one who works, his
wage is not credited as a favor, but as what is due. But to
the one who does not work, but believes in Him who justifies
the ungodly, his faith is credited as righteousness, just as
David also speaks of the blessing upon the man to whom
God credits righteousness apart from works: "BLESSED
ARE THOSE WHOSE LAWLESS DEEDS HAVE
BEEN FORGIVEN, AND WHOSE SINS HAVE BEEN
COVERED. BLESSED IS THE MAN WHOSE SIN THE
LORD WILL NOT TAKE INTO ACCOUNT."

—ROMANS 4:1-8

Man can never obligate God; the Sovereign can never
oblige Himself to the thing He has created (save out of
love). He cannot do that and remain true to His character.
Paul makes it clear that what makes the Law appalling is
the attitude that can accompany it. As always, it is not
what a person does but why he does it. When the Law
is kept with an attitude that the Creator is now indebted
and obligated to the Law-keeper, that Law-keeper has now
become the enemy of God. I have watched this attitude

covertly manifest itself over the years, usually revealed in a hint of frustration.

First, do you believe that if your sin, behavior, or flaw were to leave you, God would then do something for you? Rather, do you believe that God would actually owe you something?

Why do Christians say things like this?

—"I did everything the Scriptures said and my unwed daughter got pregnant."

—"I went through premarital counseling and prayed, yet my marriage fell apart."

—"I have served God my whole life, and yet my mate died and I am left alone."

—"I followed the advice in all the books on financial responsibility, and still I lost my house!"

"I have done all this myself" goes the assertion, and a close listen reveals there is a hint of the "God owes me" attitude, the attitude of keeping the Law, obligating God, and becoming an enemy of Christ. There are many religious programs that feed this attitude: prayer programs, child-rearing programs, and relationship and church-growth programs. Do this or do that, pray all night every night, and God will owe you a blessing. As we have mentioned, there is a big difference between religion and faith. Religion is man-based, gives man activities, and then asserts that this earns for man the "right" to ask (require) something from God. Faith recognizes and values the activity of God, whose action toward us is what is important, and it is not based on our behavior. Faith is based in our response to His activity. Many wonder why keeping the religious law (whatever flavor that takes today) leaves them depleted, feeling hopeless, and somehow unacceptable. The explanation is simple; the attitude of doing in order to get is anti-Christ. God will never become anyone's debtor. "God so loved the world that He gave." God is the initiator; He loves and He gives. There was no arm-twisting by man to get the Father to give His Son, and to think that a created being could do that kind of arm-twisting is error. Remember, if man could twist His arm at one point by keeping the Law, he could twist it at another. Hence, Abraham was accepted by faith; he was not receiving what was worked for. Abraham's life played out for us that which is in line with the character of God.

Well, I have never been known for rededication services, for asking people to bow their heads and raise their hands. I am not known to motivate people to surrender to entering the ministry or the mission field. I do not ask that people choose tonight never to have another fight in their marriage, never to take another drink, or never to look at porn. Why? Those activities do not work. However, there is something I would ask the reader to do.

There is a wonderful story of Jacob's encounter with God in Genesis 28. To paraphrase, God met Jacob in a dream, and Jacob realized he was dealing with the one true God. Acting on that revelation, Jacob in effect said, "I want to make a deal with You. I see that You are God. I am going on a journey, and if You keep me safe, give me food, clothe me, and make me wealthy, I will do two things for You. I will let You be my God and give you back a fraction of what You give to me." Wow, what an offer! I can just see God talking to an angel in heaven and saying, "My, how do I pass up that offer?" Jacob was offering nothing for everything! God's response was, "OK!" Jacob was living in faith, not by the Law. He was not offering something as a bargaining chip and then obligating God. He simply recognized God and let God give freely to him. I wonder if what went through Jacob's head in the following days went something like this: "My God will not accept anything from a man and yet gives everything. My God does not want anything from me except my recognition. He is a God who loves and gives. This God is not like a man; He is the one true God." Jacob was justified by his faith. Before he departed, he put a stone in that place and called it, "God is in this place." He had an encounter with the true and living God, who is so outside the box of all the false gods that are claimed to demand activity before they are even reputed to listen. Remember that all false gods have a type of contract relationship with man, waiting for man to perform before they do. The one, true, living God establishes a covenant relationship with man. He does, period.

Back to what I would ask you to do today, I would like you to make an exchange with God, make the deal that I made with Him. One day I said to Him, "I will give You nothing if You will give me everything." He said, "OK," and since that day I have received, received, and received the revelation of Christ in me, the hope of glory. Can you offer Him your nothing? Is there anyone too weak to have a "nothing" to trade? Do it and you will move into faith and an experience of God so precious that all other things will be counted as rubbish. Do it and you, too, will say, "God is in this place." But first you might say, "There you go again, talking about all that God does and leaving us with nothing to do!" Well, I must give you something to do: rest and receive. You will receive not because you kept the program but because God loves and gives. Until the above happens all attempts to keep the Law will end in disaster. He did not give to you because you obligated Him through the keeping of the Law, but because you gave Him your nothing, so what is left in which to boast? "Let him who boasts, boast in the Lord" (I Corinthians 1:31).

DAY 86
Faith Without Works

Ask and it will be given to you; seek and you will find; knock and the door will be opened to you.

 —MATTHEW 7:7 [NIV]

God became man and walked among the multitudes in order that He might be touched by them and thus they be made free. Have you learned that He still walks within the heart of the believer, waiting to be touched? Turn to Him and touch Him with your fear, sin, failure, and hurt. You will find healing.

Faith is made up of two opposing elements becoming one: self-reliance and other-reliance melded together. "Faith without works is dead." I must reach out and touch Him, I must ask, I must walk toward Him, I must look within to find Him, I must confess, I must seek, and I must work! But it is He who is found, who does the healing, who draws me near, who lives within, who does the forgiving, and who makes my work a delight. He and I blended together equal faith.

DAY 87
Falling Out With Others

The LORD God commanded the man, saying, "From any tree of the garden you may eat freely; but from the tree of the knowledge of good and evil you shall not eat, for in the day that you eat from it you shall surely die."

—GENESIS 2:16, 17

It is the opinion of many that bad relationships come from misunderstandings, selfishness, varying relational definitions, bondage to the past, financial struggle, likes and dislikes, the inability to give or receive love, and more. Often the struggles appear to be endless and overwhelming; it seems like just too much effort to attempt to fix a bad relationship. Therefore, we want something concrete that we could begin with today, something a weak person could accomplish that would reap immediate results.

However, I would like to look not at the struggles in relationships, but rather at the one reason for good relationships, which work because of a simple understanding. Adam and Eve fell out with God before they ever fell out with one another. We all fall out with God before we ever fall out with others. Falling out with God has a domino effect. All struggles find their source at this one point. Man does not have the resources to sort out struggles; he is incomplete, deficient, in need of a new engine, a new life, a life that is not just near to God but in God Himself. Therefore, when in the midst of relational struggle, the first thing that must be done is to fall back in with God.

Often someone tells me he has had enough, that life and others have finally beat him down. I always request that he spend time alone with Jesus in order to gain the strength needed to continue. To date no one who spent time with Jesus failed to move ahead. Once we have fallen out with God, the enemy's voice makes sense. When we fall back to Jesus, life does not beat us down, the enemy's voice is discerned, and LIFE holds us up. We fall out with others when we have fallen out with Him.

DAY 88
Fatalism

I again saw under the sun that the race is not to the swift and the battle is not to the warriors, and neither is bread to the wise nor wealth to the discerning nor favor to men of ability; for time and chance overtake them all.

 —ECCLESIASTES 9:11

A prominent philosophy expounded is fatalism, which simply put depicts life as meaningless, since whatever happens is bound or decreed to happen; everyone ceases to exist, and man is powerless to change that. Therefore, if someone is of a mind to, he could take everything possible that looks good, or he could even just suicide out of the mess. Man travels toward nonexistence, so what is chosen—good or bad—cannot be an issue. Solomon examined this approach in detail.

We ask ourselves the question, "Are there absolutes in life?" and conclude there are two. Faith is an absolute. Every single person lives in faith, for he cannot communicate without making a statement showing belief in something that cannot be seen. Second, fact is an absolute not derived from any individual's subjective perception. Where facts are concerned, independently of one another mankind will observe the same thing. All men with functioning eyes have seen the sun. Therefore, the sun is not perception but fact. Consequently, there are two absolutes on the earth, faith and fact. Where faith and fact meet we will find truth.

A philosophical system utilizing only faith is as erroneous as one with only fact. It is not right for someone to ask us to believe without facts or to walk in the facts without faith. Simply to say, "I believe," is error. Simply to say, "I have the facts," is error. Truth can only exist where there are both. Hence, what one believes must be proven by the facts. Fatalism is erroneous in its belief that man ceases to exist without the facts to prove it. There is only one system wherein faith and fact meet perfectly, though actually it is not a system, but a person: Jesus! In Him we see faith and fact flowing perfectly together to form The Truth. What we are asked to believe is proven in the facts of daily life. When Jesus appeared to the five hundred (I Cor. 15:6), there was a perfect blending of faith, in that they were awaiting Him, and fact, for He had been raised from the grave. In Christ these two absolutes merge, and we have the confidence that Love is interceding for us and there is something beyond the grave.

DAY 89
Fathers Who Lead

*It is for discipline that you endure; God deals with you
as with sons; for what son is there whom
his father does not discipline?*

—HEBREWS 12:7

Today children are waiting for direction, wanting to be stopped if going the wrong way. The world is a confusing place, especially if one does not yet possess a compass. But what do many fathers do? They ask a small child what the child would like to do. They spare the rod. In fact, they give no direction. The children do not respect the father, and if the leader cannot be respected, the followers will lose self-respect. The father who avoids the certain conflict which comes from leading is opting for a much greater conflict later. Many fathers are frustrated with the lack of submission in the family. The solution is not to browbeat the family into a position of submission. No, the solution is to begin to lead. When the father leads, no one has a choice but to follow. Where he leads the family is to Christ.

Hundreds of books are written on how to raise children but only a couple of passages in the Bible give such direction. Does that strike you as odd? If we attempt to have an answer for each possible situation, then perhaps like Abraham and Sarah we will really not be prepared for parenthood until we are nearly a hundred years old. Fortunately, this is not the case. The Christian life is far too simple for that.

DAY 90
Fathers Who Lead, Part II

Furthermore, we had earthly fathers to discipline us, and we respected them; shall we not much rather be subject to the Father of spirits, and live?

—HEBREWS 12:9

The father need only address the Father in heaven when wisdom is needed for relating to the child. Yes, we address the Father, for He is a Father also, and it is one father's heart appealing for the wisdom of another Father. Therefore, the most important aspect of being a father is staying near the Father in heaven, who possesses all the answers we will ever need. I marvel as fathers from around the world share with me the wisdom God gave them in differing situations with their children, many involving the explanation of concepts that have been studied and researched for years untold. Its genius produced results, for it came from the Father with power.

It is possible never to discipline a small child from anger but to say, "No," once and spank if the deed is repeated. Soon the child knows what "No" means, saying no once is all that is needed, and the father is not pushed to a point of anger. Discipline is the most valuable tool a father has. It should be used sparingly but applied at the proper time and place to reap great results. I have witnessed the unhealthy fear many children have for fathers who have allowed the behavior of their children to elevate their frustration to the point of explosion. This is inexcusable and avoidable. To this day, I possess a healthy fear of my grandfather and my father. I do not tremble, but I have a sincere respect for these men who not only demanded respect but also earned it. I submit gladly.

DAY 91
Fathers Who Lead, Part III

If any of you lacks wisdom, he should ask God, who gives
generously to all without finding fault,
and it will be given to him.

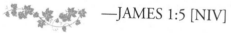

—JAMES 1:5 [NIV]

When a father must dialogue with the adolescent, it is helpful to remember that usually no decision has to be made that day. He can wait until tomorrow or the end of the week to confront the issue. This gives him time to pray and ask for guidance. The Father in heaven will hear and give the needed answer. The issue can be approached with compassion, love, and caring. The answer may be harsh treatment, grounding, restitution, or simply talking about it and forgetting it. Each such session should be ended with prayer.

It is also to be kept in mind that in every area of the Christian life we do not allow others to define what is normal for us; we allow the definition to rest in God's hand. A father who leads must do so as God has revealed to him in his individual way. For example, a "good" father is not necessarily one who is athletic, likes to box, hunt, and can fix almost anything that breaks. A "good" father may not possess any of the above. He may instead set an example in the way he loves the unlovable, is devoted to prayer, is confident in witnessing, or pursues doing all things as unto the Lord. Never allow anyone but God to define leadership. Men simply need to lead. The style is allowed to be different, the goal the same, for every father.

DAY 92
Feeling Heavy

Humble yourselves, therefore, under the mighty hand of God, that He may exalt you at the proper time, casting all your anxiety upon Him, because He cares for you.

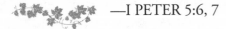 —I PETER 5:6, 7

Once when Alex Mathew spoke at ALMI men's and women's retreats, he made an interesting observation. The body is made in such a way that the mouth takes in things good and bad. During processing, the nutrients are absorbed and the waste is expelled, just like an engine, which with intake must have exhaust. However, mind and emotions are constantly taking in with no way to expel what is not useful. The result is a constipated mind. Chemically, the brain actually becomes loaded and causes the heaviness many feel. The obvious question is, "How do I get things moving out of my mind and emotions?" We know that God designed our tears to carry certain toxins and hormones from the body, but more importantly are the simple commands, such as I Peter 5:7's "casting all your anxiety on Him, because He cares for you" and I Thessalonians 5:17's "pray without ceasing." Through our fellowship with God we are able to release what has us mentally constipated. In Him we will find everything we have looked for elsewhere in vain.

DAY 93
Feeling Sorry For Others?

Arise, O God, judge the earth! For it is Thou who dost
possess all the nations.

—PSALM 82:8

It is not a fairy tale. God throughout history has judged the nations. He is judging nations today. It is therefore possible for human knowledge and compassion to get in the way of God's judgment. It takes the peace of God to guide a believer in giving where God wants him to give. We all know from personal experience that had provision come before faith, we would have been cheated. Suffering is permitted, not caused by God. Man causes the suffering and God out of His love and wisdom uses the suffering for His goal. It is pride that causes men to be blind and deaf to the things of God. Suffering opens the eyes and ears of the nations to God. We are to feel sorry for people, but sometimes we should feel sorry that they cannot hear God, see God, turn, and repent. This is the spider, and anything else can be a mere sweeping of the cobwebs. We are conditioned to be consequence-minded and not cause-minded. Often the suffering is a consequence. Worldly humanism attempts to fix the consequence and never looks at the cause. After all, humanism often is the cause, so it is like putting the fox in charge of the chicken coop. If we are cause-minded, we can look at a situation and go to the root. Could it be that some sickness, starvation, and death has its cause in sin? If so, we must go to the cause, making secondary the fixing of the consequence. If suffering does not have its root in a discernible cause, then let the peace of God rule in Christian compassion. It is Jesus we are seeing in prison, hungry, naked, and lonely.

DAY 94
Finding My Buttons Pushed . . . Please Change YOUR Behavior

Set your mind on the things above, not on the things that are on earth. For you have died and your life is hidden with Christ in God. When Christ, who is our life, is revealed, then you also will be revealed with Him in glory.
—COLOSSIANS 3:2-4

We have said before that to see God in a situation brings a move in Him; to see only ourselves yields a move in self. This is not to endorse an offensive or ignorant person's behavior. However, if someone pushes our buttons, there are issues each of us can address, in order.

1) What button is the behavior pushing and why am I allowing it to be pushed?

2) Why am I choosing to become a distortion in my response? "I really want to be a joyful person around you, but I am changing to a punishing, withdrawing, obsessive person."

3) If I must manipulate the crowd through people-pleasing or cut them off by isolating myself to make sure they do nothing that would push my button, at this point I am a slave to others and not free in Christ.

4) After having addressed the above, I can legitimately address others' behavior.

5) As persons learning to find our life as Christ alone, we must be dysfunctional to become functional in Him. While yet looking for fleshly equilibrium, we swing from self-justification to self-hatred. Spiritual equilibrium comes from seeing that in our weakness, there is strength from Christ.

6) Likewise, we must have inferiority and worthlessness to invite Him to be our worth. Once we find our worth, security, freedom, love, and all other needs met in Christ, we can set others free to be themselves and not demand that they never push our buttons. Because our fleshly response need not automatically come from button-pushing when the eyes and heart are set on the Kingdom of God and not our kingdom of the flesh.

DAY 95
Flesh Against Flesh

*For the love of Christ controls us, having concluded this,
that one died for all, therefore all died; and He died for all,
that they who live should no longer live for themselves, but
for Him who died and rose again on their behalf. Therefore
from now on we recognize no one according to the flesh.*

—II CORINTHIANS 5:14-16

At certain meetings I have the people rub their hands together until they are hot, explaining that likewise, flesh against flesh creates friction. There is always agreement, since we all have experienced it. The simple point is: If we walk in the flesh and our mate walks in the flesh, there will be aggravation. As long as we see people only in the flesh, we in turn will be moved into the flesh, and the resulting friction will cause irritation and anger. Paul had the secret, which is to see no man according to the flesh. If we see our mates according to the flesh and not according the heart, there will be heat. However, seeing others according to the spirit will make us minister to their spirit and move them and ourselves out of the flesh.

DAY 96
Flesh Is Hostile,
Even a Child's Flesh

That which is born of the flesh is flesh, and that which is born of the Spirit is spirit.

 —JOHN 3:6

I really was not what you would call a good kid! I was an even worse teenager. My early college days are not worth mentioning, with so many mistakes and so many things I would like to think I would do differently. I will leave my past at that. There is no value in elaborating. Flesh is flesh.

I do not know what I was thinking, but for some reason, in the back of mind, I believed that I could keep my children from doing or becoming anything like me. I think somewhere along the line of Christian teaching, I was covertly told that my kids did not (or should not?) have flesh. Therefore, I set out to correct in them everything I was never able to correct in myself. Imagine the blow when I discovered them doing some of the same things. Well, amen. God has been faithful. I have wonderful kids, and they all have flesh. On any given day they either walk with Him or they do not. Either way is obvious. However, to this day I would still like to correct their flesh. What amazing thinking, since I have never in decades of being a believer improved my flesh. When not acknowledging that I abide, I find myself in the same flesh patterns, yet I seem to believe this not to be true in my kids when I continue

to emphasize, covertly and overtly, that certain behaviors and attitudes can be changed in their own strength. I teach one thing and tell them another. Many tend to fall into this same trap with those closest to them. In these many years as a believer I did not need to learn how to change the flesh; I needed to learn that I could not change it and therefore needed Him every moment of every day. My children will learn the same thing, the same way. As a parent the question is this: "Is my God big enough? Does He need my help? Will He be faithful to work the revelation of change in them?" I think so. I rest. I do not enter into condemnation or worry, for my God is big enough.

DAY 97
For the Birds

For the creation was subjected to frustration, not by its own choice, but by the will of the one who subjected it, in hope that the creation itself will be liberated from its bondage to decay and brought into the glorious freedom of the children of God. We know that the whole creation has been groaning as in the pains of childbirth right up to the present time.

—ROMANS 8:20-22 [NIV]

In the Amazon, among the brightly colored macaws in their cages, I notice the less colorful, smaller birds darting in and out of the cages at will and eating the larger birds' food. To me this is such a good illustration of wealth and beauty versus simplicity and poverty. The size and beauty of the large bird make it a trophy, while the smaller bird is not noticed at all. The one adulated and important to the world is actually in bondage. For the smaller bird there is no cage and complete freedom. Wealth really is bondage. So many people have proven the luxury of poverty. I know of a home in the mountains that cost twenty-two million dollars and takes five hundred thousand dollars a year to maintain. The owners are rarely there; they must stay busy making enough money to maintain it. Do riches bring freedom? There is so much to be said for being plain, for possessing little, for being unnoticed, and for being free. I will not say I have not questioned these thoughts when I have to pass through the first-class section of the plane on my way to coach. I comfort myself with thinking the people in the tail are most likely to survive in case of an accident!

DAY 98
Forever Victory

For whatever is born of God overcomes the world; and this is the victory that has overcome the world—our faith.

 —I JOHN 5:4

From believers around the world I often hear the same thing: "There was a time when I felt I had victory over my anger, my unforgiveness, my sin; but then it seemed to return, and there does not appear to be anything I can do about it." We believers would like to have victory forever through a one-time fix, something that would rid us of those cursed behaviors that make life and others around us miserable, things that bring condemnation. Many seminars and books promise just such a fix, though it does not exist. The only way to have a forever fix is to daily abide in the One who is FOREVER. FOREVER is not an event, an explosive experience, or a dynamic teaching; FOREVER is a Person. "Today, if you hear His voice . . ." (Hebrews 4:7) Today is the word. Today as you abide, the forever victory of the FOREVER ONE becomes yours in this moment.

"Well and good," you say, "but now my problem is not finding the fix but abiding, and I do not know how to do either." Satan will always have the believer working for something instead of *from* what the believer already is.

Exactly what is abiding, or rather, keeping our focus on Jesus? I use the example of taking water in our hands. If we squeeze our hands we will lose the water; work makes us lose it. Abiding comes not as a result of work but from His work. Abiding and focusing acknowledges His work. This is how to abide, and no one is too weak for such a life. Actually, weakness is an asset.

I do not say, "I choose to abide; I want to focus on You; I want to experience Your crucifixion; I desire to be obedient." That is working; it is unbelief. Faith acknowledges, "I am abiding; I have an obedient life; I have been crucified with Christ," and then the experience comes. Often I go to sleep simply recounting what Jesus has done for me and what I believe. I go to sleep in faith. I go to sleep abiding. I go to sleep in the FOREVER ONE.

DAY 99
Foundations

Husbands, love your wives.
—COLOSSIANS 3:19
Wives, be subject to your husbands.
—EPHESIANS 5:22

When the foundation of a house is bad, cracks begin to appear in the walls. For cosmetic repairs the cracks can be covered with plaster, but they will only return unless the foundation is fixed.

In the Christian life, a bad foundation must never be neglected. Let me illustrate. Thousands of books have been written on marriage. With only a few foundational scriptures, myriad books present ideas on how to fix the plaster in marriage, but the foundation must be addressed first. "Husbands, love your wives." "Wives, be subject to your husbands." These two verses will foundationally fix ninety percent of marriages, but the number of objections to them is really quite astounding. The first things from the mouths of the husbands and wives are a series of reasons why they are correct for not obeying. The husband cannot possibly love someone who will not listen, is not affectionate, or questions his every move. Surely a wife cannot be expected to respect a man who is such a spiritual drip, lacks basic wisdom, and just sits in front of the television! These lists attempt to justify rebellion against the simple commands of God and absolve responsibility until such time as the other person changes enough to MERIT this love or submission.

There are problems with such thinking. In trying to justify our rebellion we are in danger of having Jesus tell us a story of the man who owed one million dollars he could not pay, and the man who lent him the money forgave him. Unbelievably, the defaulter went straight out, found someone who owed him just a few dollars, and beat him. The previously forgiven man was thrown into prison. We never justify ourselves by pointing out the failures of others.

The Christ who created us and holds us together has written His way in us. The commandment to love a wife is not for the wives' benefit but for the husbands' sake! If husbands decide not to love, thereby inviting in another way not written into their texture, they have invited in chaos and misery. The same is true for the wives who decide not to respect their husbands; they punish themselves! It is impossible for a husband to continue to love himself if he does not love his wife. It is impossible for a wife to refuse to respect her husband and still maintain respect for the person in the mirror. They are punishing themselves!

DAY 100
Freedom In the Loss Of Image

So Jesus was saying to those Jews who had believed Him, "If you continue in My word, then you are truly disciples of Mine; and you will know the truth, and the truth will make you free."

—JOHN 8:31, 32

Isn't image interesting? If we could be free from image, we would be free indeed. But to be free from image, we must see God, not ourselves. In some Third World countries I am given great respect only because of skin color, dress, and money. People give way on the street and few would argue with me. However, if I were, say, a "common" tea picker, people would chase me away with a switch if I crossed their path. I would be dressed differently, my skin would be a little darker, and I would have no money. Image dictates a lot considering that all of us came naked out of the womb, and naked we will leave in the end. There is no difference in men; there are only images. Image makes us treat the poor man with contempt or compassion and the rich man with respect or a hatred mixed with the jealous desire to be like him. The fear of the loss of image can keep us from taking a risk, making a phone call, looking for a new job, going to a restaurant considered out of our league, or disagreeing with the pastor. Some image groups cannot stand it when other image groups consider themselves better, so they use slander or riches to try to bring the others down and build themselves up. Do you see why Jesus dealt so little with the world's system? It is a circle; it is the same, and it goes nowhere. "All things are wearisome, more than one can say. The eye never has enough of seeing, nor the ear its fill of hearing. What has been, will be again, what has been done will be done again; there is nothing new under the sun. Is there anything of which one can say, 'Look! This is something new'? It was here already, long ago; it was here before our time" [Eccles. 1:8-10, NIV]. Once we are free from image, we will free everyone else from image. We will neither pander to the rich nor show compassion to the poor. We will minister to the individual! We will see beyond image to the exact need Jesus saw in man. Our teaching will change; our emphasis will change. How to be free? We must admit where we are to leave where we are.

Admit that you are a slave to image and ask Him to free you. He will do it in a way you had not imagined. Many believe the way to the loss of image is to be humiliated through a sinful defeat. This does not destroy image; it just draws attention to it and gives a person a different image. God's way is different. You will see. Just ask.

DAY 101
Freely He Gives

We have not received the spirit of the world but the Spirit who is from God, that we may understand what God has freely given us.

 —I CORINTHIANS 2:12 [NIV]

I was talking to a group of the brothers and asked them to do a simple exercise: "Take a sheet of paper and draw a line down the middle. On the left-hand side write down everything you thought you would receive in life, and on the right-hand side list what you have actually received." In the end, everyone agreed that the list on the right was much bigger; all had received far more than they had ever imagined. That being the case, I asked if their objectives in life had been as good as the Lord's plan. We have ideas of what we want that are often based outside of the love of

God. That is, we do not fully trust that what He gives will be better than what we can obtain in the power of the flesh.

I remember a friend saying to me with conviction, "I do not want my own will! I have had it, and it is not as good as God's." Well, amen. We have a history with God that proves to us His is a better way. I am getting through with plans and simply saying each and every day, "Thy will, not mine." Why not relax? He has done a great job up to this point.

"Do not worry then, saying, 'What will we eat?' or 'What will we drink?' or 'What will we wear for clothing?' For the Gentiles eagerly seek all these things; for your heavenly Father knows that you need all these things. But seek first His kingdom and His righteousness, and all these things will be added to you. So do not worry about tomorrow; for tomorrow will care for itself. Each day has enough trouble of its own." [Matthew 6:31-34]

DAY 102
Generosity Is Getting What You Need

Abram believed the LORD, and he credited it to him as righteousness.

—GENESIS 15:6 [NIV]

In Matthew 20 Jesus tells a story now known by one and all. A man hires workers at different hours of the day; some work a long day and others a short one. In the end, every man gets paid the same. However, those that worked from the beginning were expecting more than the late men got. "Is it not lawful for me to do what I wish with what is my own?" They were rebuked, for the master was free to pay what he wanted, and what was it to them if he wanted to be generous? Every man, from the one arriving early to the one who arrived late, got exactly what he needed! The master was much fairer, compassionate, and generous than anyone imagined; he knew the need was the same for every man, so he met the need accordingly. The master was generous with his initial offering to the men who worked the longer day, but since the first men were in need of a job, I believe they would have worked even if the master had squeezed them and given them less than their need. All of the men were looking for a job; some found it in the morning and some in the afternoon. Which would you rather be? I would want to be one who found it in the morning and knew my need would be met. Think of the stomach churning the men hired last had gone through, wondering if the day would end, their need would go unmet, and they would have to go home to hungry children. They had to learn to trust in God and lean on Him all morning, while the others worked in the fleshly confidence that through their own labors their need would be met. God rewarded the greater faith of the men who worked only a few hours by meeting their need, also.

The story is built around men who had to wait with faith in God. As you wait in faith, He will meet your need.

DAY 103
Get Real!

*For I am afraid that perhaps when I come I may find
you to be not what I wish and may be found by you to be
not what you wish; that perhaps there may be
strife, jealousy, angry tempers, disputes, slanders,
gossip, arrogance, disturbances . . .*

—II CORINTHIANS 12:20

The Koreans are a noble people who, I have often thought, might be the most polite people on the planet. Therefore, it was a shock for them to encounter the American Press during the 1988 Olympics. The Koreans had gone to great efforts to make the Olympics a wonderful experience for everyone involved, having cleaned the city, built apartments and new roads, and completely revitalized the river. Yet predominantly reported in the American news were a fight and a couple of old men under a bridge, and both news items were embellished. The Koreans were speechless (as I said, they are polite). I joked with them, "Do you know how to tell when a reporter is lying? His lips are moving." Press coverage simply is not real.

I remember an elderly believer once telling me, "Christians tell it like it isn't." Paul was real as he dealt with real problems, and yet he was always a positive, for he knew if a believer's behavior was beneath his expectations, that person was merely falling short of his own heritage. Rarely have I had to confront someone over his sin; he would have already condemned himself. Among believers there can be strife, jealousy, angry tempers, disputes, slander, gossip, arrogance, and disturbances. Believers do fall short because we are all growing. As this occurs we must be honest, as was Paul. Of the many areas in which believers need to be real, I only want to venture into a couple.

I was staying with what I consider to be a very spiritual family, one I admire greatly. The husband and wife have a policy never to go to bed angry. I believe that throughout the course of their marriage, they have held to that approach; however, I also believe there have been nights when they did not get to bed before 6:00 AM. One morning before church they had a disagreement, which was no secret, since both are quite animated and vocal regarding whatever is causing their unhappiness. The argument was not resolved by the time the church service started, but the fellow preached one of the best messages I have ever heard. When we arrived back at his home, another guest questioned him: "How can you furiously argue with your wife and then get up and preach such a dynamic message?" The response fascinated me, "The two are not related!" He explained how it is not real to think spiritual husbands and wives never disagree. Relationships are always expanding and, therefore, being worked on. He is committed to his wife and has no intentions of leaving; being vocal is how they work out their relationship. They could choose to withdraw, pout, run away, write letters, or call up friends, but they choose to voice their complaints, clearly express what needs to be worked through, and pray about it. This works for them. They are real people, and real people do disagree. He added, "My relationship with my wife does not have to be completely worked out before a church service, but my relationship with God does. It was, and I preached."

To me that man was real, not hiding or putting on a false front, and he revealed how we as believers must work through disagreements. Today I have the feeling that the Church's concept of a spiritual couple involves two people who are always unruffled and would not talk louder than Michael Jackson. It vexes me to have dinner with a spiritual couple embarrassed about their teenagers. I have had three teenagers; what will their teenagers do to surprise me? I liked my teenagers, and I will like theirs, too. Often life has to mature the teenagers before teaching them of their need for Christ. I do not expect teenagers to sit next to me and ask if we can please read the Bible together. Real life can involve their telling about their car, some fights at school, or why dating is so miserable, all while they make a mess they do not intend to clean up. That is real. I listen to them because someday, when the Holy Spirit has prepared them, I want to be able to share with them.

Another area in which being real is important can be illustrated by how often I have sat in a meeting and been told to bow my head and ask the Lord to tell me what needs to change in my life, how I can serve Him better, and secret areas of sin. In years of participating in such things, I have rarely heard God say anything. Being a speaker, I realize how little thought can be put into some of the things I say. I pop off, so to speak, and someone else takes it to heart. Do the majority of speakers really believe that all we have to do is ask and God will speak audibly to us? That is not real! Central to Christianity is faith. All that happens to me is to build faith. If every time I made a noise, God made one, would there be faith? We ask and do not always hear, but we believe. This is the normal course, pleasing to God. I believe that He hears, watches, directs, keeps, and provides, most often in silence.

I want to be real, and the beauty is that I have a God who works in the midst of the average daily life I experience and through those things makes me supernatural.

DAY 104
Give To No Man;
Give To Every Man

But Jesus, on His part, was not entrusting Himself to them, for He knew all men, and because He did not need anyone to bear witness concerning man, for He Himself knew what was in man.

—JOHN 2:24, 25

If anyone wants to be first, he shall be last of all and servant of all.

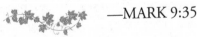

—MARK 9:35

I find it interesting that Christ leads us not to live to man, and yet we are commanded to go out and give ourselves to every man. How can this be? First, we have become too accustomed to milking out of others what we think we need and believe they can give us. We have looked to others in the attempt to have needs met that only God can meet. Unsatisfied, we continued our search in new areas of worldly living. God must cure us of this! Because He is love, He allows everything apart from Himself to fail us, thus driving us back to Him. Once we find the Christ within and all the riches we need, we no longer look to others or the world for satisfaction. Now we can go as commanded back into the world, giving ourselves to others for their redemption, seeking nothing for ourselves, and free from being tyrannized by their rejection. We go back differently! Once we were beggars, now we give from the rivers of living water within. However, we must remember that giving ourselves to others came only after giving ourselves to no one until we knew that the Lord meets our needs. Herein lies a problem. Many are persuaded that within the confines of the church we can give to others without first experiencing our giving to no one. The end result is a group without the foundation of finding their all in Christ attempting to give themselves and receive from others. Quite simply, this is flesh attempting to minister to flesh. Impossible! Before we can operate effectively as the body of Christ, we must first recognize that we, individually, are a part of His body, that apart from Him we can do nothing, that what is true of Him is true of us, and that the old man, old nature, old life is now crucified. Only when we realize we have lost all of the old self and gained all of the new life in Christ do we have anything of value to give in our oneness, and only then do we realize that we can receive the offenses of others with love within the Body. This is the foundation on which oneness in Christ is built.

DAY 105
Given Over to the Flesh

For this reason God gave them over to degrading passions; for their women exchanged the natural function for that which is unnatural, and in the same way also the men abandoned the natural function of the woman and burned in their desire toward one another, men with men committing indecent acts and receiving in their own persons the due penalty of their error. And just as they did not see fit to acknowledge God any longer, God gave them over to a depraved mind, to do those things which are not proper.

—ROMANS 1:26-28

Over the years God has been gracious to give me some very real and loyal friends. I have a few very close friends who struggle with homosexuality. If you were to meet them, chances are you would never guess that was the area of flesh with which they struggled. Why? Because they have never given themselves completely to the deeds of the flesh, for deep within they know they have given themselves to Him. Though they stumble, they do not have to bear it in their own bodies. The misery in these believers is proof of their love for Christ. They rule over their passion, the passion does not rule over them. I remember one brother in frustration saying, "I give up! I will not fight the desires any longer; I am moving in with another man." I stopped him, "Brother, so far God has not abandoned you to your passions, and you have never had to bear your failures in your body. I am begging you, do not abandon yourself to your passions, for He will give you the desire of your heart."

In these end times I am meeting more and more people who have given themselves over to their passions, and now the passions rule over them. They barely possess anything of the image of God. A young woman passed out in the shower from overdosing on ecstasy. The parents could cope with the burns but not with the brain scan that showed three cigar-sized spots of brain-dead tissue. The girl had abandoned herself to her lust and now will bear it in the body. It is not God doing these things but mankind doing them to themselves. It sickens me because all are forms of self-mutilation, proof again that if a person can do whatever he wants, he will hate himself and what he does. Come quickly, Lord Jesus!

DAY 106
Giving To Bless and Giving To Curse

But if your eye is bad, your whole body will be full of darkness. If therefore the light that is in you is darkness, how great is the darkness!

—MATTHEW 6:23

I have a dilemma common to many in missions: I get deceived! I give money to what appears to be the most sincere person and find out later I was lied to. I know of a business school in another country that, when the director of a particular denomination shows up, replaces the sign hanging out front with one proclaiming that it is a Bible college. The director is none the wiser because he cannot read the language. One fellow asks that prayer requests be accompanied with a donation. He was caught on camera rifling through the mail for money, not even noticing the name of the person or the prayer request. I could go on, but why? My point is that I have given money I thought was going for one thing and then discovered a greedy pastor behind it all. Why did God not make me aware of it beforehand? Should I stop giving altogether?

I believe not only do we give to bless, but we also give to curse. In the short span of a human's life, God must either perfect us, if we are saints, or bring us into complete judgment if we are unbelieving. Sometimes money is used to perfect the saints. We learn the lessons of trusting Him for our daily bread to the point that we can be responsible with earthly riches. On the other hand, there are those who are unbelieving, cheating, stealing, and deceiving for their own gain. We give to them for their judgment. One day they will stand before God and have to give account for the fact that they called out to Him for a need, He sent someone, and they stole the money. Ananias and Sapphira could have given and been blessed, but their giving cursed them because of deceit. God will actually lead us to give to places where the money will be abused. It is all in His hands. We are not to worry. The important thing is that we listened to Him and obeyed in our giving. He had a reason for it.

DAY 107
Go Sell All You Have

Looking at him, Jesus felt a love for him and said to him,
"One thing you lack: go and sell all you possess and give to
the poor, and you will have treasure in heaven;
and come, follow Me."

—MARK 10:21

I have received from one man a measure of indoctrination concerning saving and financial responsibility. Well, amen, many have been stupid with their credit cards. Some have, in reality, stolen money through poor management; there is no question they need to rein in their spending habits. However, reining in probably is not the root issue. More often than not I find those with high debt attempting to meet spiritual needs through the material world. Some feel empowered with what they can purchase. Others get a false sense of control. Still others have been so hurt by relationships that they find security in having more things. Then there are those just meeting an obsession or compulsion.

Having said that, when does the teaching of financial responsibility merely become a mask for carnal living? When does it cross the line and cause an obsession with security in money and even feed unbelief rather than faith? As I look at the books written on this topic, I generally find authors more obsessed with money than with Jesus; their security actually appears to be in money. I wonder what these authors would do if Jesus approached them and said, "One thing you lack; go and sell all you possess and give to the poor, and you will have treasure in heaven; and come, follow Me." The man I mentioned above who was talking to me had taken financial responsibility too far. It was time that the Master reined him in. At any point He may, in a like manner, rein us in.

DAY 108
Goal Of Marriage

I press on toward the goal for the prize of the upward call of God in Christ Jesus.

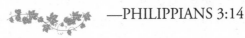

—PHILIPPIANS 3:14

I attended the wedding of a good friend's daughter. At the beginning the groom spoke of how they had, throughout their lives, the wonderful opportunity to follow Jesus. However, from this day forward they had the wonderful opportunity of following Jesus together. I like it. It was all Jesus: Jesus when single and Jesus when married. The focus was not primarily on the couple; it was on Jesus. Is not Jesus the goal of our marriages?

What is the goal of your marriage? I have often discovered believers putting my marriage under a magnifying glass for the purpose of finding something with which they can disqualify my teaching. They seek something wrong to be able to say, "Ah! Your teaching does not work." They also do it with my relationship with my kids. Sometimes the kids have said it was nearly comical as they were asked, "What is your father really like at home? Does it affect you negatively to have him travel so much?" Some of you have experienced the same type of thing. Well, I have a good marriage and a good relationship with my kids, but that is not proof of a walk with Jesus. It is proof that I am walking with them in harmony. "If possible, so far as it depends on you, be at peace with all men," Romans 12:18. On the other hand, if I were not getting along with my wife or my kids, that would not necessarily mean that I was not walking with Jesus. The carnal believe and preach that good family relationships are proof of walking with Jesus, being pleasing to Jesus, and lacking hypocrisy. Family relationships often mean everything to the carnal, but does this reflect what Jesus taught? Is harmony in the home proof of spirituality? What did He say? "Do not think that I came to bring peace on the earth; I did not come to bring peace, but a sword. For I came to set a man against his father, and a daughter against her mother, and a daughter-in-law against her mother-in-law; and a man's enemies will be the members of his household. He who loves father or mother more than Me is not worthy of Me; and he who loves son or daughter more than Me is not worthy of Me," Matthew 10:34-37.

Have you heard this teaching? "You can tell how well you are doing in the Lord by the look in your wife's eyes!" In a pig's eye! Proof of a walk with Jesus is loving when offended. If you are never offended in your marriage or family, how will we know if you walk with Jesus? The real proof of a walk with Jesus is how you act when all hell breaks loose, your mate leaves, the kids rebel, or no one listens to you. Then we will know.

Note this: Some who have a good marriage are only keeping the peace by living in submission or superficiality and getting what they really want, for their goal is comfort.

DAY 109
God Does It All,
Not By Man's Efforts

They said therefore to Him, "What shall we do, that we may work the works of God?" Jesus answered and said to them, "This is the work of God, that you believe in Him whom He has sent."

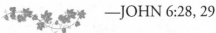

—JOHN 6:28, 29

First, we know that a lesser must give way to a greater. If a message is not effective because the music was not moving enough, the service was not seeker friendly, the big-screen projector was not working, or the skit director was missing, then all of those things just mentioned are greater than the message. If it takes something to support a message to make it effective, then the thing that supports it is greater. Isn't it great that the message of "Christ in you" does not need any external support? It is a message not needing support by man but is merely witnessed to. Paul said he did not come with clever speech; he just came! There are those who will argue, but in the end it will be discovered that they really do not want the message; they want those things used to "support" the message. They are there for the flesh and not for the things of the Spirit.

Second, David loved God, and I believe that was a constant. "I have found David the son of Jesse, a man after My heart, who will do all My will" (Acts 13:22). That assessment never changed. God always felt that way about David, before, during, and after the affair. What was missing in David was not a deep love for God; what was missing in David was the recognition of God's deep love for him! That revelation could only come through failure. David needed to fail to have the circle complete, to see the love of God. How else do we learn the love, the mercy, the forgiveness, and the greatness of God? Am I saying God sanctions affairs? May it never be! Am I saying that God's plan for man is conditional? Not in any way. He knows exactly what He is doing, why He made the earth, why He put us in flesh, why He permits the devil, and what is to be the outcome of His permission.

Third, I had an interesting experience. In the busyness of getting prepared to leave on a long trip, I generally let my relationship with Jesus suffer. It is stupidity, but I do it. I was surprised the other day that when I did return through the Door that is Christ to recognizing the Father's presence, I found myself before Him in the same state of confidence I would have had if focused on Him every moment of every one of those days. It was as though when I moved through the doorway of Jesus I was stripped. Stripped of everything. Stripped of my righteousness, my unrighteousness, and my self-righteousness. I stood there in Jesus, in perfection, with no hindrance between God and myself. It so surprised me to see how my neglect of God had not created any kind of barrier between Him and myself. He knew what I was thinking and He spoke to me,

"When you come through Jesus, this is how you always come!" Amazing! Jesus is much better than the blood of bulls and goats! At any instant we can come to Him, and the past does not matter. Jesus makes the moment perfect. "Today if you hear His voice" (Hebrews 3:15).

Fourth, there is a very important question to ask every believer. Be honest when you answer it for you must own where you are to leave where you are. The question is: Do you believe God shows partiality? 99% of believers do. It is a crucial question. Deuteronomy 10:17 states, "For the Lord your God is the God of gods and the Lord of lords, the great, the mighty, and the awesome God who does not show partiality, nor take a bribe." It was said of Jesus, "You are not partial to any" (Luke 20:21). "For there is no partiality with God" (Romans 2:11). Well, what difference does it make? If you believe that He shows partiality, how does it affect your life? It affects your life in every way, for those who believe there is partiality never rest! They believe that other believers have greater ministries, wealth, health, happiness, and blessings because they are doing something to garner the favor of God! They do not believe that God, in His love, has given them exactly what they need. In fact, those who believe in partiality are showing partiality. Those who believe in partiality are unbelieving in Jesus. Those who believe in partiality are fighting against the circumstances in which they find themselves. Job said, "He will rebuke you if you secretly show partiality" (Job 13:10). When God deals with your belief in partiality, He is dealing with your deepest areas of unbelief. Do you believe that God has given someone a better mate than you have? Partiality! Do you believe that God has given another a greater church and ministry? Partiality! Do you believe that God has given another greater intelligence, talent, and ability? You are despising the perfect and exact work of the love of God in your life. I am telling you, the belief in partiality is a curse to you and others.

Fifth, stop and think for just a moment. Do you believe that the Bible is simple and for all people to read? Do you believe Jesus is simple and for all people to receive? Do you believe that Christianity is a profession? Do you believe there are different levels of acceptability into which Christians are arranged? I do not! Therefore, can you see how utterly absurd it is to study the Bible, which was made for the masses, as a profession? Man in his flesh just cannot stand equality, and therefore he must make a pyramid he can climb in hopes that others cannot make the ascent. Sometimes I find it comical to hear a teacher explain the Greek word, exactly what it means, and then watch him give someone the "California wave" when someone pulls in front of his car on the highway. As a profession Christianity does not work. As a degree program it does not work. As a body of knowledge to be known, it does not work. Christianity is Jesus, and Jesus is for the very weakest. It is as though the "elite" (in their minds anyway) just cannot stand the fact that something as important as Christianity is actually suited most for the weak and uneducated. They have to make it exclusive by making it difficult. They must build a pyramid to climb. Jesus never asks us to climb a pyramid. He meets us at the bottom, not the top. Also, never mind the fact that the "professionals" only make it difficult for the weak; they never can arrive at the standard they set as Jesus-plus people themselves.

DAY 110
God For God

For am I now seeking the favor of men, or of God? Or am I striving to please men? If I were still trying to please men, I would not be a bondservant of Christ.

—GALATIANS 1:10

Something that at first may be very difficult is seeking God for God, but try it! It is much tougher than it sounds. Try to go one day in fellowship and prayer without asking anything for yourself. If the kids are a problem, do not mention them. If the marriage is falling apart, pray and do not mention it. If the finances are wrecked, talk to Him just about His wonder. It is harder than you think. I have prayed before meetings and never mentioned the meeting, though amazingly those are the best meetings. Again, Jesus is the issue. Try one day of mentioning nothing but Jesus!

DAY 111
God Is In the Negatives

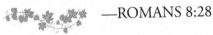

And we know that God causes all things to work together for good to those who love God, to those who are called according to His purpose.

—ROMANS 8:28

While I was a young believer at university, our campus fellowship had a yearly potluck celebration before Thanksgiving break. All of the young women brought the food, and the young men would bring their appetites! The celebration during my senior year turned out to be the most memorable experience. After the main course, several of us fellows had discovered a wonderful pecan pie. As we stood off by ourselves eating, someone asked, "Who made the pie?" The cook was mentioned and a dialogue ensued with comments such as, "She really is sweet," "A very gentle spirit," "Really loves the Lord," and so on. The more I listened, the more I was forgetting the pie and thinking about the cook. I slipped away from the conversation and looked up the cook. I wanted to appear spiritual, so I asked if she would mind getting together for prayer! Of course, my motives were not entirely spiritual. After just a few months of "prayer and fellowship," I asked the cook to marry me!

I was very excited for our wedding. We had invited all our brothers and sisters in Christ. The night before, my friends came to a Christian stag party to pray for me. A good friend was performing the marriage, another read poetry and brought a salvation message, and still another led the music. My oldest friend, Gregg, took some photos. I had borrowed a suit from a roommate, and I must admit I looked pretty good. I still remember how beautiful my bride looked to me the day she walked down the aisle. The ceremony fulfilled every expectation, and afterward we headed off for a two-week honeymoon.

As soon as I returned home, I went to Gregg's small basement apartment just off campus to get my photos.

Gregg handed me an envelope, but it was full of negatives! I could not even recognize the couple in the pictures. My bride was not beautiful, her dress looked all black, her face blotchy, and I, why, I was unrecognizable! I said, "What is this?"

Brother Gregg responded, "These are the negatives!"

"But I don't want the negatives, I want the positives!" He told me not to get rattled, for hidden in the negatives were the positives I wanted, the images for which I was longing.

Now let me ask you, what did you think the Christian life would be like? What did you think marriage would be like? What did you think your job would be like? What did you think having a family would be like? Have you been handed the negative? Do you want to throw away the negative because in it you cannot find any of the images for which you had hoped? Do not, for in the negative you will find the positive for which you long.

Next Gregg invited me into his darkroom. I do not like dark rooms, but he assured me that there I would find what I was looking for. We must all enter the darkroom of faith, wherein we cannot see, feel, experience, or understand what is promised. Seeing nothing around us, we believe ourselves to be alone. But in this room faith is developed. We give God something no angel in heaven can give Him, for we believe His promises without seeing Him. Like Joseph, we first believe the promise has ended in a pit, where rescue leads to a prison. But in the end, His promise does come forth.

In that darkroom I looked as an image began to appear, a beautiful bride and groom just as I had imagined. I wanted to grab it and run. Gregg told me if I did, it would soon fade; I first needed to fix it in acid. That did not sound too good to me. But the destruction of self-centeredness always takes place in a vat of acid. The cross works as the acid, and at the cross I lose self. The true test of a believer is not walking on water but walking across the room to love an enemy, which does feel like a swim in a vat of acid. In the end I left the darkroom and walked into the light to gaze at something I loved so much. In the negative I had found the positive.

Do you believe that God is in the midst of your negative? He is! Your faith is the size of a quarter, the situation is the size of a plate, and you are in crisis. Do not attempt to shrink the situation; yield to it. Say amen (so be it), let faith grow, enter the darkroom, and let God reveal the positive.

DAY 112
God Takes Charge Of the Cleanup

I do not condemn you, either. Go.
From now on sin no more.

 —JOHN 8:11

God is definitely the God of the cleanup! We charge and charge again on our credit cards, not thinking about the end of the month when we must pay. We charge against our sin account, and in the end He must pay. Isn't it amazing that He is the God of the cleanup? When there is a teen pregnancy, turn to Him, and He cleans it all up. When a man or woman has had an affair, turn to Him, and He cleans it all up. When someone has fallen into homosexuality, turn to Him, and He is in charge of the cleanup. Who has a God like ours, a God who will take charge of the cleanup? He causes all things to work together for good.

DAY 113
Good and Evil, the Enemies Of Christ

The woman said to the serpent, "From the fruit of the trees of the garden we may eat; but from the fruit of the tree which is in the middle of the garden, God has said, You shall not eat from it or touch it, or you will die."'

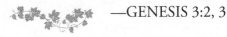 —GENESIS 3:2, 3

The unholy trinity—sin, Satan, and the world—attempt to keep the believer's eyes on good and evil. However, it must be remembered that both are the enemy of Christ. Man is either in rebellion and acting out of evil or in self-righteousness, acting out of good. Both keep the flesh alive and keep man from the Father. Good is the enemy of the best. Therefore, if Satan cannot keep our eyes on evil, he will make sure our eyes are on good. This point is especially important to make during an election year. Governments are very important to the enemy. I listened to a talk-show host for ten years. He would constantly hit the panic button over the bad that is happening and become elated over the good that could happen. He eloquently described all the bad one political party has been able to accomplish and the supposed good of the other party. He sure made my flesh feel good! Yet after years of supposed bad, and the people being enlightened to the good, nothing changed. Nothing! Both parties agreed to loot Social Security with pork-barrel projects. Do you believe that if the President is exchanged for another from the same system the government will be more holy? Of course not! What that mainly tells us is that we have a priority; an earthly kingdom will not advance the kingdom of God. It never has. It cannot, for the world's kingdom is opposed to the kingdom of God. Has any candidate proclaimed that Jesus is the Way and every other way is not the Way? Maybe to a certain voting bloc for the sake of winning those votes, but not openly and consistently. Governments are inherently kingdoms of the world and therefore opposed to His kingdom. We accept that. We are not trying to change the nature of the beast. We have a different goal, to see Christ manifested through those who have Him and to introduce Him to those who do not have Him. It is vexing to see ministries devote themselves to worldly kingdoms. Jesus, when offered the kingdoms of the world, refused them. I believe that if the Founding Fathers were to come back from the grave, the first thing they would shout is not, "Get back to the constitution!" No, they would shout, "Get back to God!"

DAY 114
Governments Are Counting On Your Pride

*Pride goes before destruction, and a haughty
spirit before stumbling.*

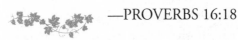

—PROVERBS 16:18

One day I was watching a boxing interview when one of the boxers inadvertently threw to the ground the flag of the country of the opposing boxer. It was an accident. However, he had to flee in the midst of bodyguards. The people were in a rage. I remember doing a radio interview in Ukraine and being asked by the interviewer what I thought of Ukrainians. I said, "Oh, I grew up hating them. They were the frontline troops for the Russians. We hated the Ukrainians and the Russians. We wanted them all dead!" She looked quite surprised. I continued, "But then I came to Ukraine. The people gave me their food and went without. They gave me their bed and slept on the floor. They heated water for me and went without. They loved without even knowing me! I am broken, and never again will I allow a government to tell me who my enemy is." We are to love our enemies, that is true. It is also true that we are often told about enemies that do not exist. In traveling in over 100 countries and staying in the homes, I have discovered the commonality among families all over the world in how our concerns are about the same things.

Governments count on our pride to take attention off their actions and put it onto others. We are angered at the Chinese who stole our military secrets. Would that have been possible without our government's allowing it? We are mad at the Japanese for the trade deficit. Is it possible without our government's allowing it? We do not like illegal immigration. Is it possible without our government's tacit approval? Our foreign aid is being wasted. Is that possible without our governmental policies? Often I am in a country where the people are so frustrated with the damage the U.S. has done to their country that a discussion about it cannot be avoided. Every time I feel a defensiveness swelling up in me. First, our government is not to blame, for their own government allows the abuse but encourages the attention to be on the U.S. Second, and most importantly, I must check my insidious pride. Every believer belongs to the Kingdom of God and has a holy leader. Everything in His kingdom is righteous. We must lay aside the pride we might have invested in earthly kingdoms and unite in His. I refuse to defend the wicked, and wicked rule the world. I must love my brother and let no one or any bit of pride make another my enemy. As believers we have no enemies because we have no enemies. The wicked are nearly genius in getting us to hate one another to avoid our thinking about their behaviors.

DAY 115
Grief, from India

Blessed are those who mourn, for they shall be comforted.
—MATTHEW 5:4

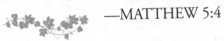

I remember talking to a woman in India who had lost her young daughter to a gruesome auto-rickshaw accident. The woman asked, "Why did God allow my daughter to die?"

I said, "I have a great answer to your question. [I really did.] I have an answer that makes sense, I have an answer that is biblical, and in three years if you write me I will tell you the answer!"

She asked, "Why three years?"

I said, "Because the best answer in the world will not take away any of the pain."

It is interesting that answers will not take away pain, but Godly mourning will. Mourning takes three years. The first year we walk with pain standing on top of us, the second year we walk side by side with pain, and the third year we stand on top of pain. The pain never leaves, the memories of the person never leave, time does not heal all wounds, but the experience of the pain of loss is absorbed into our being permanently, and the person for whom we grieve is a permanent part of what we are from that day forward. Mourning is truly of the Lord.

DAY 116
Guilt

The way of a guilty man is crooked, but as for the pure,
his conduct is upright.

—PROVERBS 21:8

Being restored to our former state is not the purpose of repentance. In repentance we will always lose something, most often our pride. The Lord must increase and we must decrease. To retain the sense of guilt after forgiveness is simply to mourn over what was lost.

You can imagine the strange feeling a person would get when crossing a desert, hearing an unusual noise coming from the car's engine, and knowing something is out of sync. To feel guilty is to feel strange. We all know that feeling of sensing something is wrong and in need of fixing. We are created by Christ, held together by Him, and He is written throughout our being. To invite something anti-Christ into our being will make us feel strange, since His life is repelled by it. Sin is simply anything that is anti-Jesus and contrary to what is laid out in Matthew 5, 6, and 7. This "strange" feeling will not leave us until we invite the sin out through repentance. In the Old Testament the sin was taken out of people and placed upon a ritual animal, thus providing a sacrifice for sin. There is a tendency to focus only on the sacrifice of Jesus for sin, but the freedom from guilt is equally important and comes at the point where the sin (the thing that was anti-Christ and had been invited in) is taken out of the person; the Christ who holds man together stops fighting against the sin, and the former sinner has peace. To have all our sins placed on Jesus, to have the struggle of our being cease, and for Christ Himself to flow unhindered in us brings a peace that the world does not know. Any time we are sick of feeling "strange," we can confess the sin, invite it out and on to Jesus, it will leave, the struggle will stop, and we will have peace.

Simple? Well, what about the person who goes on feeling guilty long after he has confessed the sin, invited the anti-Jesus thing out of his being, and, according to the authority of Scripture, has been forgiven? Why does the feeling of guilt hang around in some people? This lingering feeling of being "strange" has led many believers to the conclusion that they were not forgiven at all, that they are, in fact, castaways, that they have fallen from grace, and that they have crucified anew the Son of God. They begin to consider themselves analogous to Esau. Hebrews 12:14-17, "Pursue peace with all men, and the sanctification without which no one will see the Lord. See to it that no one comes short of the grace of God; that no root of bitterness springing up causes trouble, and by it many be defiled; that there be no immoral or godless person like Esau, who sold his own birthright for a single meal. For you know that even afterwards, when he desired to inherit the blessing, he was rejected, for he found no place for repentance, though he sought for it with tears." This is an interesting passage in light of many others, such as I John 1:9 & 10, "If we confess our sins, He is faithful and righteous to forgive us our sins and to cleanse us from all unrighteousness. If we say that we have not sinned, we make Him a liar and His word is not in us." The mention of Esau is used to reinforce the difference between law and grace. However, many use Esau as an example of a man who had gone too far, so God was in no way going to receive him back. How can that be? Well, we stand or fall not in what we do but why we do it. Esau was not repenting because he felt "strange," felt guilt; Esau was repenting because he had lost something other than the peace of God and wanted back what he had lost. His repentance was faulty. Repentance based on losing something other than the peace and fellowship of God is based in the lust of the flesh, the lust of the eyes, and the boastful pride of life. Look at Judas, the betrayer, for example. Judas and Peter both denied Jesus and sold Him out, one for silver and one for the comfort of his own flesh. Peter found repentance, for he had invited in something anti-Jesus, he felt very strange, could not stand to feel that way, invited it out, and received the forgiveness of Christ in his soul. However, Judas' repentance was based in pride; he was so upset and obsessed with his poor performance as a man that he killed himself. Often guilty people commit suicide, and the root of that is always pride! They just cannot come to grips with their failures. If Judas could have gone back in time to undo his failure, he could have stayed in pride; his bad flesh could have remained hidden and his good flesh put on display. But Judas would still be Judas, not as interested in Jesus as in his own desires! When Judas saw he was not ending up looking too good, he wanted to die. If he were fundamentally interested in Jesus, he could have failed and still had Jesus, just as Peter did. Judas could not come to terms with his failure. Pride! Esau wanted to go back in time, but what did he want when he got there?

In reading the Bible I cannot find a reference wherein God says anything positive about man (with the exception of The Man). Do we think He is surprised by our failings? No, He is not, and therefore He has made a provision for them. When we have felt "strange" long enough, we can truly repent, the sin lifts, and His peace comes. However, it is no good seeking forgiveness so we can have something returned to us other than the full flow of Christ. Many look for repentance to have their image restored, to feel good about their flesh again, to undo a mistake that cost them financially, to be able to stand again in a place of self-righteousness, to avoid embarrassment or shame, or even to have emotional experiences, and all of this is done with tears. This simply is not the appropriate purpose of repentance. Did Esau want God and the joy of moving forward, or did he want the ability to go backward for the birthright? In Hebrews it is quite clear what Esau was up to; he wanted the inheritance, period. The purpose of repentance is not to go back and undo a mistake. The purpose of repentance and forgiveness is to go forward with a greater revelation of the love and peace of God. HAD ESAU REPENTED BECAUSE HE WAS FEELING "STRANGE," HE WOULD HAVE FOUND RESTORATION. That does not mean he would have gotten his birthright back, but if the peace of God were the goal, he would not have cared. Esau's heart was revealed. We are in this life for Jesus, not for any material or self-righteous attainment. If I lose all my self-righteousness, my possessions, and my image but retain the peace of God, then amen!

Any time we have a sense of feeling unforgiven even though we have confessed, we can ask ourselves a simple question: "Did I repent for the return of His peace, or did I repent to regain my lost ground?" Then we need to say, "I do not care about the attachments of the flesh or about the past; I invite out everything that is anti-Jesus. I recognize even my desire to regain what I lost as anti-Jesus, and now I want You, Jesus, to fill the vacuum left when my sin was placed on you." Everything we seek we will find once we are looking for the right reason. We can tell if we are repenting in order to have something other than the peace of God return to us. It will be revealed if when the enemy reminds us of stupid things we have done in the past, our response is an ensuing sense of dread or fear. If God has forgiven us, why do we have the sense of fear and dread? Both of those have their roots deep in the fear of man or our own pride. We cannot stand to remember how we failed and are no better than others (pride), or we fear the loss of image. If we do not like the fruit, the solution is to lay an axe to the root. Invite out the fear of man, the embarrassment of failure, and the disappointment over a loss of standing. Let Christ come. Repent of both the initial sin and the pride wanting Jesus plus something else. Actually, it is pride to think about how if we went back in time, we would do better!

DAY 117
Guilt-based Motivation

*Whether, then, you eat or drink or whatever you do,
do all to the glory of God.*

 —I CORINTHIANS 10:31

The easy way to motivate someone is through guilt. Having inherited a life that rejected God, man is born fallen and guilty. Much has been accomplished in America through the use of guilt-based knowledge. When a picture of a starving child is shown, a statement follows: "For the cost of an average pair of shoes, you can provide for this child for one year." The message behind the message is, "Would you please feel guilty buying a pair of shoes and not helping this child?" History is being rewritten with the permission of guilty people. Frankly, I have not abused anyone because of race or religion. However, I know people who believe they must confess the sins of their race for all injustice done in the past. The thinking is that if one hundred to a thousand years ago someone of a like race abused another race, the people now living must make amends. This is illogical but made plausible because of the context: We feel guilty. A friend from Eastern Europe sat scratching his head one day questioning Americans' obsession with race. He concluded, "I do not feel guilty about race, so I get tired of the discussion. I am about as interested in your color as I am your gray hair. Can we please get on to Christ?"

Guilt is used to manipulate those within the Church. A video of teenagers is shown, followed by the statement, "Without a new youth complex, where will these children be? With the money you spend on hamburgers each year, we could build it." I cannot even enjoy my hamburger now. I feel guilty. Teenagers are going to hell because I want a hamburger. Husbands are motivated to love, and wives to respect, because otherwise they are destroying their children. Believers are motivated to change behavior, read the Scriptures, witness, and pray, all by guilt. We even begin to feel guilty watching television when it is realized we have not bought our children a good pair of Nike tennis shoes. How will they ever "just do it?" Many in the psychological, educational, health, ministerial, and political professions would not know how to talk to people without employing guilt.

It is an issue of obedience to Christ as He speaks to us concerning the poor. I asked an African friend, "Do you give money to all the beggars who ask?" "Only to the ones the Lord tells me to," was his response. But again, we allow others to motivate us because we feel guilty. If we were to be delivered from our guilt, we would not be "others-motivated," but we could become Christ-motivated. The issue is not what others think we should do, but what He thinks we should do.

DAY 118
Happiness and Divorce

Yet I wish that all men were even as I myself am. However, each man has his own gift from God, one in this manner, and another in that.

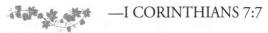
—I CORINTHIANS 7:7

It is said that marriage is a fortress; those inside want out, and those outside want in. I have heard single people boast about how they have gone the distance without a mate and married people boast in having completed the race. Some of the married take delight in the statement, "For in the resurrection they neither marry nor are given in marriage, but are like angels in heaven" [Matthew 22:30]. I only want to make one point. If happiness is the goal of marriage, then absolutely every married person on the planet has had cause for divorce at one time or another, period. We all have flesh. Do we think our flesh is better than our mate's flesh? Do we believe it is always fun living with us? To make a list of how unhappy someone makes us is quite telling. People do at times have aspects of their behavior that is likely in need of immediate improvement, but in reality we are the ones who surrendered our happiness to another.

Wouldn't it be wonderful if in this life I made the discovery of just how free, truly free, He has made me from another's behavior? I start with one "perceived" problem. Next, I surrender my peace to the person's behavior. Then I obsess on the misery, after which I begin to hate myself for letting the whole situation get to me, and finally, I am carrying the behavior rather than letting the other person wear it. One problem has turned into five, and I am left thinking the other person is making me miserable. This is the fruit and not the root. Surrendering my peace and looking to another to make me happy is the root. As long as the root is unchanged, cutting off the fruit leads only to more fruit to come.

One last thing: There are people married to very annoying spouses. If you are married to such a person, you must never defend him or her or feel embarrassed by his/her behavior. Let the mate throw a fit and let everyone see it. Stop wearing the other's behavior; no one is holding you responsible for your spouse. If people love you, they will love your mate and separate the spouse's behavior from yours. Do not run around attempting to make everything "right." Just let it rest.

DAY 119
Hating the War Between the Flesh and the Spirit?

But I say, walk by the Spirit, and you will not carry out the desire of the flesh. For the flesh sets its desire against the Spirit, and the Spirit against the flesh; for these are in opposition to one another, so that you may not do the things that you please.

—GALATIANS 5:16, 17

Often I hear the complaint, "I hate the war against the Spirit. If only I could stay in the Spirit." These complaints lead to a common teaching in the Church, one attempting to encourage us to "fight the good fight" and to "look forward to heaven, where this battle no longer takes place" . . . a heaven, I presume, where there is no choice. (It sounds as though we will all mindlessly be singing praises to the Lamb, and not because we choose to. Of course, choice seems to be a curse in the minds of many, and they would relish the thought of ridding themselves of that troublesome capacity.) Well, I would like to go on record as saying I do not hate the battle between the flesh and the Spirit.

Certain topics definitely need to be settled. Is God attempting to oversee chaos, or is God the God of order? If

He is overseeing chaos, then there is a great battle between good and evil, and Satan (in the minds of many) has power equal to God's, we are caught in the middle, and we must somehow muster up the spiritual, emotional, and physical strength to side with God and win this great battle. Wow! Honestly, this thinking, which is not hard to find, is one of the enemy's greatest coups. It can be subtle, but we hear it in e-mails pleading for believers all over the world to pray for protection, healing, and blessing and to pray against the advance of the enemy, disease, and poverty.

Actually, if you are a believer and no one prays for your cancer, do you believe that your chances of being heard personally by God or enlisting His activity in your life are lessened? Do you believe that if no one prays for your unbelieving mate, and yet you in your belief pray, God does not hear you? Do you believe that when you pray in your loneliness and isolation for your daughter, who is living with someone who definitely does not appear to be good for her in any way, that God does not hear you? There is one mediator between man and God, and it is the man Jesus. We need a paradigm shift. God is in charge! Satan is not! Disease is not! Man is not! Financial markets are not! Doctors are not! Ship captains are not! Your pastor is not! Your employer is not! Your children are not! God is in charge, period.

Prayer is a participation in what God is doing, and we must get over the notion of an arm-twisting fight against a defeated foe. Honestly, from Genesis to Revelation, God is in charge. Yet, with the wrong glasses, which seem to be handed out in many Christian religious circles like 3-D glasses at the movies, it looks like God is attempting to win, Satan is gaining, and we are the determining factor. Our flesh is not in charge! Our flesh is not the problem! The flesh is permitted by God as the means of pushing, even driving us into the life of the Spirit.

It might sound odd, but I like my flesh; I like what it does for me. If I do not like the expression of my flesh, then I must simply allow it to accomplish the goal God intended of driving me to the Spirit. Sometime today I will get angry, so what will be my response? "Oh, my rotten flesh! If only the flesh did not make me angry!" Or this: "Oh, my flesh always acts the same way, and now it is reminding me that I began this day somehow believing it could live just fine without an active submission to the Lord. Who do I think I am? Jesus was God among man and yet said of Himself He could do nothing. Jesus, You are welcome here; come and be my joy and peace today. Thank You, Jesus, for giving me a body of flesh which reminds me that life can be Life on this earth." It depends on what glasses I am wearing, or better yet, what eye surgery I have been given.

Heaven held some hellishness when angels, who are not even created in the image of God, decided they were gods in and of themselves. What kind of world would this become if no one had flesh? More specifically, what kind of person would you be without flesh? You would be a monster living in the midst of monsters. My flesh has been an ugly mirror that has made me take my assessments, my treatment of others, and my disdain down a notch, or rather, three, four, five, and one hundred notches. A man was bemoaning what his former alcoholism had done to his family. I looked him straight in the face and delivered this word, "You are an ass! If you had not become an alcoholic, the flesh—your pride, arrogance, drive, and self-righteousness—would have done a thousand times more damage to your family than the alcohol." There was no argument in his eyes; the flesh had humbled him. We all need humbling, and the flesh is sent by God to do it. The world idolizes men who are a 1% success at playing God, but then the facts of their flesh become known: they were thieves, drug addicts, perverts, adulterers, self-centered, and there were attempts to hide all of this through threats, courts, and disclaimers. The fact is that the flesh is bringing them down to the level of admitting their need for Jesus in order to live just one day, something humanists do not want to acknowledge. One famous man's picture appears in nearly every Christian home on a particular continent, though he is an atheist and has participated in murder; in short, he has flesh, and yet any mention of that fact is avoided and met with shock. The "positive" side of his flesh is attested to as something to be idolized and worthy of attainment.

Those who hate the flesh will look for the good in the flesh. The most unrighteous will become the most self-righteous. Those who despise the negative will attempt to obtain the positive. However, when someone sees God, he gets off the rollercoaster and understands that the flesh is not there to be hated or loved; it is there to drive man to Life. In hating or loving it, a person will become a monster, nothing short of a distortion. I saw a woman obsessed with the "Barbie doll" and had all the plastic surgery to become an exact replica; she had become a monster. I saw another man obsessed on the art of Salvador Dali; in the end, he became a monster. It is all relative, but flesh, good or bad, will make anyone a distortion, a monster. I have seen men who were monsters standing on and speaking from the platform at Christian conventions. The flesh will distort us if not seen as something driving us to Him to allow Him to be for us what the flesh can never be. I do not hate my flesh, and neither do I love my flesh; I see it as a marvelous tool in the hand of God, who is in total control and has my very best interests nestled in the deepest part of His heart.

DAY 120
Hating Your Sin Is a Revelation

But put on the Lord Jesus Christ, and make no provision for the flesh in regard to its lusts.
—ROMANS 13:14

If you hate your job, it is because you have emotionally quit it. It appears obvious that once you hate something, it will soon follow that you want nothing to do with it. Let's apply this simple principle in a different way. If you hate your sin, it is because you've emotionally divorced yourself from it and want nothing to do with it. The next step is to acknowledge the fact of it and embrace your freedom.

Many people would rather do what they think they want to do and beat themselves up in self-hatred later than do what the Lord is asking them to do and be happy. Why? Why do they spend a lifetime doing this, when they could recognize that the sinful desires no longer reflect who they are in Christ and could develop a hatred for the sin?

DAY 121
Have You Felt Separated From God?

But your iniquities have made a separation between you and your God, and your sins have hidden His face from you so that He does not hear.

—ISAIAH 59:2

I hate the fact of separation. I invite in sin, so the glue (Jesus) that is holding me together begins to retreat from my mind, my will, and my emotions. I sense that I am losing something. I am out of sync. It is terrible. He does not leave me but only retreats to give me what I thought I wanted: freedom from His will. The break between Him and my mind, will, and emotions is really a state of neurosis, for my life that is bound up in His had attempted to break away. It is sickening, but it does work for Him, because eventually I cannot stand my will and cry out, "Thy will, not my will," and invite the sin out. I invited it in; I can invite it out. Next He returns and I am complete once again. Well, all of that is of my own doing. Jesus has experienced the very same thing, but by our doing, not His own. The sins of the whole world were cast on Him to the degree that it drove His life out of Him. I am so happy He has identified with me, He knows this sick feeling that comes from separation, He works and moves me back to Him, and He always floods back through my whole being the moment I repent. He knows the joy of reconnecting with the Father, and He wants for me the same joy. He will never leave nor forsake me, and He understands everything about me. Though Jesus' experience of being separated from God did not come by way of inviting in sin, it did come through the cross, and therefore He knows the feeling of separation. He has entered into our humanity completely.

DAY 122
He Bore My Sin

For you have been called for this purpose, since Christ also suffered for you, leaving you an example for you to follow in His steps, Who committed no sin, nor was any deceit found in His mouth; and while being reviled, He did not revile in return; while suffering, He uttered no threats, but kept entrusting Himself to Him who judges righteously; and He Himself bore our sins in His body on the cross, that we might die to sin and live to righteousness; for by His wounds you were healed.

 —I PETER 2:21-24

When I have the opportunity to walk and pray, I like to ask questions of the Lord. I enjoy His voice, the voice that every believer hears. "My sheep hear My voice." It is not something one believer has and another does not. Listening to God begins with hearing the first whispers of "yes" and "no" and grows from there. One morning I asked, "How exactly did Jesus bear our sin and separation? Why do You make people pay for their sin? Why did Jesus bear our sin?" This is, of course, standard doctrine: Jesus died for our sins. I was always told that someone had to pay, and that someone was Jesus, but why, I wondered.

I want to use some examples, but my intention is not to pick on a particular class of sinners. All have sinned; I only use these cases to clarify the point. Please bear with me to the end of the article!

Sin is not created but is a result. When a created being, held together by the Creator, does something unnatural, there is a result. Creation has suffered because of results (the natural doing the unnatural). "The creation waits in eager expectation for the sons of God to be revealed. For the creation was subjected to frustration, not by its own choice, but by the will of the one who subjected it, in hope that the creation itself will be liberated from its bondage to decay and brought into the glorious freedom of the children of God. We know that the whole creation has been groaning as in the pains of childbirth right up to the present time. Not only so, but we ourselves . . ." (Romans 8:19-23, NIV).

Example 1

The homosexual has the result of AIDS.

Created beings have a reaction, which is judgment, to any result. The purpose of a judgment is to hinder the further production of results. This is creation's attempt to love and protect the rest of creation. Hence, the judgment on the homosexual is death! The world, in ignorance, mocks any who label this a judgment. But if the first person with AIDS had been destroyed, millions would have had their lives spared. Judgments arise from laws. Laws are weak; they cannot kill a result once it comes into being. Law can only hinder results by attempting to stem the domino effect and cover up the mistake so creation can get on naturally.

Example 2

Created beings Adam and Eve did something unnatural: They chose to disobey God. The result: independence from the Creator, a recipe for disaster.

The Creator now reacts to the result; a judgment comes. God is not perched in heaven waiting with bated breath to make a judgment; He has no great joy in making it. Judgments are reactions to results. The unfortunate thing is that there ever was an act by creation that yielded a result! If there were no results, there would be no reactions, and God, Who is love, would be very happy with that.

Law comes. The judgment is made. The couple must leave the garden to dwell with pain and suffering. The judgment, law, is the very best that can happen in this situation. It cannot undo the result, but it can slow the ripple effect by making man aware of his need for his God. The judgment/law tries to cover over the mistake, but it cannot make things perfect again. Was Adam punished? He thought so, but the judgment was the best that could be done to address the result. If judgments are punishments, then they are unrighteous. Why? The punishment never fits the crime. The death sentence for a murderer is not fair when it is the exchange of a bad man's life for a good one's. The death sentence is a judgment that accomplishes many different things.

How much wisdom must be in the judgments, or laws of God? Only He Who knows all could make them to infuse the best into a bad situation. The Old Testament saints saw the wisdom of the judgments of God and gloried in them, knowing they were good. Does it surprise us, then, that we are commanded not to judge? We see a result in a person's life and make a judgment on what he ought to do. Our IQ is not high enough to do that. In fact, if our judgments were followed, things would get much worse. Thus another judgment issues forth from God, "Judge not!"

Finally, why did Jesus bear all the results? Let me give a weak example. So far the AIDS virus cannot be killed. A man in South India has volunteered to be infected with the virus; he says that his system can overcome it. If so, there would be a premium on his blood that had the ability to conquer a result, a non-created thing.

Jesus did just that. The law could never kill results, but only contain them. "The former regulation is set aside because it was weak and useless, (for the law made nothing perfect), and a better hope is introduced, by which we draw near to God" (Hebrews 7:18-19, NIV). All the results and reactions entered Jesus: sin, separation, guilt, law, sorrow, suffering, pain, sickness, and death. He became sin Who knew no sin, judgment Who deserved no judgment, separation Who knew no separation, and every other result and reaction of creation to the result. They chose to fight where they thought they had the best chance—in the human body and soul—and He fought them on the ground they had chosen. They were given every advantage, yet He did the unimaginable, what the laws and judgments of God could never do! He put them to death one by one in His own body! Now there is a blood possessing a life that is more than a conqueror.

DAY 123
He Is Not a Tame Lion

And I began to weep greatly, because no one was found worthy to open the book, or to look into it; and one of the elders said to me, "Stop weeping; behold, the Lion that is from the tribe of Judah, the Root of David, has overcome so as to open the book and its seven seals."

—REVELATION 5:4, 5

In C.S. Lewis' book, The Chronicles of Narnia, Jesus is portrayed as a Lion. As the plot unfolds, the comment is made, "He is not a Tame Lion!" Those who approach Him maintain this attitude, for though He is welcoming, there is a healthy fear. Children who have been disciplined properly have a healthy fear of their father. A boy once told me of his respect and admiration for his father and told of a time when he (the son) was verbally bashing his mother. His father never got angry, he just stared at his son and said, "You will never do that again." The boy in his healthy fear knew that he was never to do that again, and he never did. I am making this point because when it comes to dealing with Jesus concerning our growth, our prayer life, our requests, our experiences, and our desires, it must be remembered that "He is not a tame Lion" and approach him with a healthy fear.

In my own experience I have watched Him turn this way or that way; I cannot, nor have I ever been able to, plot His course. I am reminded of an afternoon in Perth,

Australia, when I had the afternoon off, was feeling a bit blue or out of sync, and wanted to talk to Him about me. I left the hotel, and as I was walking I said, "Jesus, what will we talk about today?" I asked it knowing full well my predetermined topic. Instantly His voice spoke, "Not about you!" In my healthy fear I never brought up the topic of myself to Him that day. I am glad I did not, as what I learned about Him that day made my heart sing. This one revelation kills all calculated church programs. With a tame lion a person cracks the whip and gets the response desired. Why is Jesus called the Lion? No one will tame Him; there will always be a wild element. Read the Book of Acts to remember the wild rides the apostles and early Christians were on as they followed Him! Read descriptions of Him in The Revelation. I have seen a lion in the wild, and I know a person can shout, scream, plead, and more, but the lion is king and will not give way to the requests.

How does that affect us? A program calculated to deliver a given response is useless, for the things of God cannot be orchestrated by man; He is not tame and does not jump at the crack of a whip. Man is not the initiator in the relationship, because the Lion acts according to His unlimited knowledge, foresight, and purpose. He knows what He is up to and does not consult man for advice on a "better" way of doing things. He is King of Kings and Lord of Lords forever. "For the Son of Man is going to come in the glory of His Father with His angels; and will then recompense every man according to his deeds" (Matthew 16:27).

DAY 124
He Is the Light!

Then Jesus again spoke to them, saying, "I am the Light of the world; he who follows Me will not walk in the darkness, but will have the Light of life."

—JOHN 8:12

When lost in the dark, shining a light is the best thing to do to be found most easily. Conversely, when in a war, you must never shine a light unless you want to be seen and do battle. Jesus was the light that shined out of the darkness. He wanted to be found by those seeking the light, though He was accessible both to those who hated darkness and those who loved it. All who sought found Him. "Whosoever believes" in John 3:16 really means whosoever! He did not hide from those who would do battle with Him; He made His presence known. Death came to the light, Satan came, captivity came, sin came, and hell itself. They were a bit like the dog chasing the car, for when they found Him, they wished they had not. He defeated them all. All! He saved every friend and defeated every enemy. He is still the light. In our dark days we must run to Him. It is not difficult to go to Him. Do not be deceived. You abide in Him. When the enemy thinks he is coming for you, he will again find Him. There will not be a battle but rather a simple reminder of the accomplishment of his defeat.

DAY 125
He Learned Obedience Through the Things He Suffered!

Therefore, since Christ has suffered in the flesh, arm yourselves also with the same purpose, because he who has suffered in the flesh has ceased from sin, so as to live the rest of the time in the flesh no longer for the lusts of men, but for the will of God.

—I PETER 4:1, 2

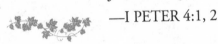

"Although He was a Son, He learned obedience from the things which He suffered," Hebrews 5:8. We immediately tend to equate suffering with punishment for disobedience, so when we read the passage with our emotions, it seems to say, "He learned obedience through His disobedience." It confuses us, for we know that He was never disobedient. However, it is clear He learned obedience through what He suffered. I have a question: Is there a suffering which does not come from disobedience? Does all suffering have at its roots disobedience? How can we suffer when we are obedient?

We can suffer without a hint of disobedience. Let me give an example. We are commanded to love. Obedience to this command has caused more suffering than any other, for the day we choose to love, we build a cross on which one day we will hang and suffer. As we love our children, one day we will find ourselves on a cross. Rarely does a child suffer for his sins as much as a parent does. Often, in pride, children see nothing wrong with their sin, yet the parent lies in bed unable to sleep, vexed and weeping. However, in the end love is triumphant. This makes obedience all the easier. It is actually a circle. Obedience begets suffering, and suffering begets more obedience.

DAY 126
He Will Blot Out Your Name

The LORD shall never be willing to forgive him, but rather the anger of the LORD and His jealousy will burn against that man, and every curse which is written in this book will rest on him, and the LORD will blot out his name from under heaven.

—DEUTERONOMY 29:20

He who overcomes will thus be clothed in white garments; and I will not erase his name from the book of life, and I will confess his name before My Father and before His angels. He who has an ear, let him hear what the Spirit says to the churches.

—REVELATION 3:5, 6

And if anyone's name was not found written in the book of life, he was thrown into the lake of fire.

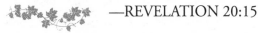 —REVELATION 20:15

From the foundation of the world it was God's desire that none should perish. God even sent His own Son to that end. Therefore, from the foundations of the world everyone has his name written into the Lamb's book of life. It does not seem to be a matter of choosing Jesus one day and then rejecting Him the next, thus having one's name blotted out of the book of life. However, there is a choice to stop believing in Jesus. It is interesting that children want to believe in Jesus. In fact, they have to be taught not to believe in Jesus. It is not so much our making a choice that gets our name *in* His book; rather, we make a choice that gets our name *out* of His book. I often hear from people, "One day I just stopped believing." Unbelievers like to lay all blame at the feet of God and yet maintain their freedom to choose what they want. If someone has his name blotted out of the book of life, it is because he specifically wanted it erased. It is getting the desire of his heart. God will not go against the heart; if the heart wants out, it can get out.

DAY 127
Hearing the Voice Of God!

Truly, truly, I say to you, he who does not enter by the door into the fold of the sheep, but climbs up some other way, he is a thief and a robber. But he who enters by the door is a shepherd of the sheep. To him the doorkeeper opens, and the sheep hear his voice, and he calls his own sheep by name and leads them out. When he puts forth all his own, he goes ahead of them, and the sheep follow him because they know his voice. A stranger they simply will not follow, but will flee from him, because they do not know the voice of strangers.

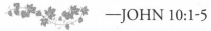

—JOHN 10:1-5

Often, as you know, we stand or fall on definitions. The voice of God is distinct to each individual; you cannot judge what His voice is to you by what it is to another. For example, a mother drops off her sleeping baby in the church nursery and tiptoes out. When she returns and quietly starts talking to the attendant, her baby begins to cry upon hearing her voice; none of the other babies cry, because they do not know that voice. The baby knows the voice that does not stir the other babies.

In a like manner, everyone hears God's voice in a unique way, and you can discover how you hear Him. Let me give you a couple of exercises. Begin to read the Psalms; something will jump out to you that does not jump out to others. That will be the voice of God as you hear His unique voice for you. Stop and really examine why that segment spoke to you and what the awareness of needing to pause and ponder feels and sounds like. It is His voice. The second exercise is this: The next time you start to do something wrong and you sense a dip in your spirit, a conviction, a loss of peace, and a little voice that says, "No," stop and meditate on what it sounds like. I can promise you are hearing the Lord, but you may have been unaware of it because of using others' definitions of what God's voice sounds like. How else could you write things that are revelation? When the revelation comes, what does it sound like? What is it like when the thought comes into your mind? Take time out to begin to examine these things.

Another point on hearing God is that there may be a problem of hearing too many voices, but you can be certain that His is one of the voices you hear. It is important for you to discern the voice of the Lord, for His brings love, joy, peace, longsuffering, gentleness, goodness, meekness, self-control, and faith, when the voices of the flesh, the world, and the enemy bring everything else. You may have a flood of doubt. "How can God be talking like this to me? Why is everything He says to me so positive? I am only talking to myself and telling myself the things I want to hear." You may even think you are crazy. But His voice is always just that positive, and what He tells you about yourself and the Son can be witnessed to in the Scriptures.

DAY 128
"Here Are Two Swords"

He said to them, "But now if you have a purse, take it, and also a bag; and if you don't have a sword, sell your cloak and buy one. It is written: 'And he was numbered with the transgressors'; and I tell you that this must be fulfilled in me. Yes, what is written about me is reaching its fulfillment." The disciples said, "See, Lord, here are two swords." "That is enough," he replied.

—LUKE 22:36-38 [NIV]

What in the world were the disciples doing with two swords? Why did they have them? Did they think they were hidden from Jesus? How long had they been packing the swords waiting to use them? Had they returned to something they never really left, the trust in the sword? So quickly came the revelation that they had two swords and had finally heard the words they longed to hear, "Buy a sword." They were going to be able to use the sword.

I meet people every day who carry easy, carnal fixes for their problems. They may know they should be praying about their problem, but give them a minute, lean a little toward the flesh, and you will see the sword come out. Yes, they will love their neighbor, but if he goes too far, out comes the sword. They have yet to make a break with the past. We need to see that our battle is not against flesh and blood, God is in all things, and this world is a place where we are perfected.

Peter finally, after three years, was able to take his sword with him. He went for the man's head to protect Jesus, and all he got was an ear. Then he discovered that just as Jesus loved him, so did Jesus love the man and healed the ear. The man who would capture Jesus gets a healing, and Peter gets a rebuke. Resolving things in the power of the flesh and not seeing God in all things will always end in a rebuke. Plus, it is not effective. We will only get the ear in the issue; we will never get the head.

DAY 129
His All, My Nothing

The God who made the world and all things in it, since He is Lord of heaven and earth, does not dwell in temples made with hands; neither is He served by human hands, as though He needed anything, since He Himself gives to all life and breath and all things.

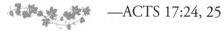 —ACTS 17:24, 25

The history of God and man is divided in two. There were those who wanted to offer God something and by so doing cut a deal of some sort. There were those who could offer God nothing except the acknowledgement that He was, in fact, God. We see the recorded history of men caught in this battle, not the history of good against evil but man's glory against God's. The disciples wanted so much to offer something and earn a special place seated beside Christ in His Kingdom or be the greatest among them. They felt they had given Jesus everything: time, allegiance, and more. Yet when push came to shove, they all scattered and left Him alone. We see, though, that there are those who offered nothing along the way but were heard and found what they needed: the centurion with a sick child, the blind man who had nothing, the widow, the woman who touched His garment, the woman in adultery, and more. In their nothingness, they received His all.

The history of the Christian religion is a history of man wanting something to give God. In this struggle, like the disciples that forsook Him, man has nothing to give and must be filled by the Giver, the Lord.

Closely associated with this is the battle with God over what is "mine." If He is the creator, then everything is His. "Or who has first given to Him that it might be paid back to him again? For from Him and through Him and to Him are all things. To Him be the glory forever. Amen" (Romans 11:35, 36). Man playing god in this battle of "mine" is constantly thinking that something is his. The "mine" mentality runs from people to jobs, possessions, positions, countries, and more; it is an entitlement mentality. However, man did not make it, so how can it be his? The deception is that he was allowed to make it, but allowance does not equal possession.

Your wife is not your own; she is not a "mine." But the attitude that she is leads to the belief that if she is mine, then she must exist for me and my happiness, for what is "mine" is primarily for my good. Your wife, however, is first and foremost the Lord's.

DAY 130
History and Choices

Humble yourselves, therefore, under the mighty hand of God, that He may exalt you at the proper time, casting all your anxiety upon Him, because He cares for you.

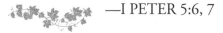

—I PETER 5:6, 7

We are commanded to take up the cross and deny self. Beautiful. I have seen for many years that the only thing to satisfy self is the denial of it . . . amazing but true. I spend hours with believers so they might understand how they act and why they act that way. For example, if someone were adopted, once he reaches his twenties, especially after marriage and having a child, he will gaze at the child and the enemy will whisper, "Why would anyone give up such a beautiful thing as a child? You are obviously worthless, unlovable, and more." These "feelings" can lead to a plethora of behaviors that can be summed up as looking for enough outward confirmations to undo the inward condemnation of himself as not worthy to be on the planet earth. He is looking for validation and constantly trying to yank it out of others, and when validation is not perceived, he moves into a variety of carnal behaviors. In short, he will do nearly anything to get a small measure of acceptance. Amen, we can understand it and work with it. However, problem number two often appears when in his frustration, the rejected person escapes into the ugly deeds of the flesh, perhaps moving to drugs, alcohol, or sex, or into the good deeds of the flesh: performance, accomplishments, and titles. I have discovered that if I confront such a one on his behavior, he uses the past as an excuse. I do not buy that.

I was in one African country in the midst of a war. The rebels were raping, cutting the hands off of children, and actually cannibalizing (sorry to be so graphic; I am using this extreme example to make my point). The "excuse" was that it all was permissible in the context of war: they needed to win and they were hungry. No, no, and no! That answer does not sell with me. In the West we are told of the "blood diamonds" which led to the dismemberment of African people simply so women in the West could have diamond engagement rings. No! There are enough diamonds in the world for every person to have an eight-ounce cupful. Faulting a woman in Kansas for wanting a nice diamond by saying it causes the hands of children to be cut off simply does not compute for me, period (although humanists like to go to people whose hearts have Christ as the foundation and play the blame game to elicit funds). A man is a man, and every man must be accountable to God. The man made a freewill choice to cut off the hands of a child, and it has nothing to do with an engagement ring; the man who did such a thing will stand before God to give an account, and attempting to offload the blame for his behavior onto a woman in Kansas will not help.

Some people have been abused, rejected, conflicted, taught dysfunction, and more. Understanding the past and the hurts of the past will help them see the self that must be denied. However, to use the past as an excuse to be immoral, greedy, rejecting, self-centered, and even annoying is unacceptable. More and more I see people who have a vested interest in finding the "one" thing in their past to justify their behavior and allow them to be labeled "victims," and yet they can choose to clothe themselves in the morning; their choosers are not damaged. When their past hurts are used as a pretext for dabbling in the flesh, they hang themselves, on the one hand saying that what went before is bad and on the other hand using it as the excuse to dive into the deeds of the flesh. They will become divided and unstable in all their ways. Paul said this, "Forgetting what lies behind and reaching forward to what lies ahead, I press on toward the goal for the prize of the upward call of God in Christ Jesus" [Philippians 3:13, 14]. When the "victims" refuse to do this, they have a vested interest in maintaining the appearance and identity of being victims, because it justifies the feeding of their flesh. At that point we can ask them to invite Jesus into the middle of the situation and leave. Jesus can do what we cannot. We let Jesus handle the situation, because we would go mad trying to deal with the dual messages presented by a divided person. It takes the discernment of the Lord to know if and when someone has used a horrific event in his past as an excuse to offload his behavior and remain a victim.

DAY 131
Holy Spirit

*But the Helper, the Holy Spirit, whom the Father will
send in My name, He will teach you all things, and bring to
your remembrance all that I said to you.*

—JOHN 14:26

A question often heard is, "When I feel happy or sad, is it the Holy Spirit or just emotion?" This, of course, is an excellent question. The basic problem is our definition of how the Holy Spirit manifests Himself. When that definition can be given to various other objects and experiences, then the believer is left with the overwhelming task of discerning the source of the emotion. For example, feelings of elation, laughter, sadness, depression, and happiness can be rooted in several sources. If the Holy Spirit is considered one of these sources but not the exclusive source, confusion arises when attempting to ascertain from where exactly the feelings might come. This is our first indicator that our definitions of the work of the Holy Spirit are wrong. "For God is not a God of confusion but of peace, as in all the churches of the saints," I Cor. 14:33. The work of the Holy Spirit is unique.

How can we keep from being confused? Simply, the work of the Holy Spirit is the work of Christ. The Holy Spirit is the Spirit of Christ. The Holy Spirit will manifest himself as Christ was manifested on the earth. The experience of the Sermon on the Mount (Matt. 5-7) is without question the legitimate work of the Spirit. The experience of all the fruit of the Spirit (Galatians 5) is His unique expression. We need simply look to Christ to judge our definition of being full of the Spirit. Did Jesus attempt to drive Peter to suicide after his denial? No! Did He condemn the woman at the well? No! He only told her the truth. Did Jesus keep secret His disappointment with the carnal behavior of the disciples, leaving them looking under every rock to find clues indicating whether Jesus was unhappy with them? No! Was Jesus filled with sadness or laughter to the point of being uncontrolled? No (self-control being one aspect of the fruit of the Spirit)! Did Jesus dangle the happiness apple in front of others, requesting that they figure out the puzzle before they could eat from it? No! Once there was repentance, did Jesus continue to remind the one that failed? No!

The whole Bible gives to the Holy Spirit a definition of behavior so unique that it cannot be confused with the myriads of human experience. Unfortunately, the Church is filled with those who stand at the top of the spiritual pyramid defining the fullness of the Holy Spirit in terms of what they have naturally experienced. The proof their definitions are wrong is when they could apply them to so many sources other than the Holy Spirit. I want to be full of the Holy Spirit, and two signs of His work in my life will be loving an enemy and freedom from guilt. Definitions of this type will not be confused with any other source.

DAY 132
Hope For a Hardened Heart

*Then He got into the boat with them, and the wind
stopped; and they were utterly astonished, for they had not
gained any insight from the incident of the loaves,
but their heart was hardened.*

—MARK 6:51, 52

We often assume that when Jesus picked the twelve
disciples, He was picking the best, men above the rest,
men who were holy and especially talented for the task
ahead. Yet here we read that these men all had hearts that
were hardened. They had just participated with Jesus as He
fed the five thousand and calmed a storm, and yet they still
had a hard heart. They were witnesses of a miracle and yet
Jesus received nothing from them by way of recognition or
trust. This is additional proof that Jesus does not expect us
to meet Him at the top rung of the ladder, but He comes
to the bottom rung to get us.

There are times when we know our hearts are hard;
whenever we choose the flesh, we have a hardened heart.
What sticks out to me is that Jesus kept working with the
men until they had soft hearts. More had been given and
more was required. If Jesus did not give up on men who
had seen miracles and remained hard, how could it be
possible for Him to give up on those of us who have seen
no such overt miracles and yet possess hard hearts?

The bottom line is this: If He did not give up on them,
He surely has not given up on you!

DAY 133
Hormones

You have heard that it was said, "YOU SHALL NOT COMMIT ADULTERY"; but I say to you that everyone who looks at a woman with lust for her has already committed adultery with her in his heart.

—MATTHEW 5:27, 28

If the message you get from what I am about to say is that I am somehow justifying immorality, please reread the article. Immorality is sin. However, I would like to make one small point concerning the passage quoted: It is written to those who are married. A single person can commit fornication but not adultery. Fornication is prohibited for the single just as adultery is for the married. Why make a distinction? It is simply in order to recognize the fact of the hormones of youth. God has created men and women with a sex drive for attracting the opposite sex, for procreation. When the hormones are raging in a young man, it is impossible, in the power of self, not to look on a girl with lust, so the Lord can use the sex drive to reveal the weakness in a young person's flesh. I have seen so many young men under condemnation because they had sexual thoughts about a young woman and applied the verse above to themselves. That is unrealistic and leads to condemnation. Is there any dating or engaged person who has not thought about the day when as a married couple they could be in bed together? Is this adultery? Are these thoughts fornication? I do not believe so. Can such thoughts go too far and be sinful? Yes! How to tell the difference? Simply let the peace of God rule in your heart. He will tell you when you have moved out of the natural into the unnatural. However, remember, condemnation will not help you.

DAY 134
How Believers Fall Into Sin and Defeat

Now the deeds of the flesh are evident, which are: immorality, impurity, sensuality, idolatry, sorcery, enmities, strife, jealousy, outbursts of anger, disputes, dissensions, factions, envying, drunkenness, carousing, and things like these, of which I forewarn you, just as I have forewarned you, that those who practice such things will not inherit the kingdom of God.

—GALATIANS 5:19-21

Paul communicates what is one of the most vexing of all life's experiences, "I am doing the very thing I do not wish" (Romans 7:20). For many years I have had the privilege of ministering to believers who struggle with such things as, "How can I say I love the Lord yet fall into sin and defeat, even hurting those around me I love?" When I say "privilege," I do mean it, for distress over sin and defeat reveals a heart for God. Therefore, I have had association with what I consider some of the greatest hearts for God existing on the planet! These great hearts wonder how they can love Christ so much yet act in a way so unloving to someone they love. The "up and out" legalist has a simple answer for them: "You do not love the Lord." This I will not accept. Believers who love God do fail both in behavior and attitudes, and they are vexed. If believers who fail are excluded as being false, then to what purpose does so much of Scripture call back failing believers? I have a simple formula I follow in my office: "Hate your sin and I love you; love your sin and I hate you." If you have ever failed and are vexed by that, Abiding Life Ministries Int'l stands behind you, and the Lord Himself holds you up. "Brethren, even if a man is caught in any trespass, you who are spiritual, restore such a one in a spirit of gentleness; each one looking to yourself, lest you too be tempted" (Galatians 6:1).

Now on to the why: When discussing unwanted defeat, the participation of Christ must be addressed, for if Christ is not brought into the equation, the topic will quickly center around an individual's *will*. Is it the *will* that makes all the difference? This is the approach of the Buddhist, Hindu, Mormon, and New Ager. A basic problem with making the *will* of man the issue when it comes to failure is pride. The foundation of life is Christ and our relationship with Him, not the strength of our *will*. We are not successful because we *will* it.

We Americans are unique in that so often professionals have done everything from cleaning toilets or flipping hamburgers to construction before they settled into their careers. Through hard work and, yes, willpower, they moved from low-paying work in their early years to higher paying professions in their later years. But in a country with a caste system, what part does *will* play in a hopeless man's condition? When an American observes a person in India making cow-patty heating fuel with his hands, it is natural to think, "If he works hard, someday he will have his own business." But that is not possible for an East Indian, who could *will* all he wanted, but in reality will continue in the occupation his father was in. I take great pleasure in the fact that if he knows the Lord, Christ will meet him there and make the production of cow-patty fuel a fulfilling vocation, but it becomes obvious that there are obstacles to man greater than his *will.*

Scripture clearly states that God causes no one to sin.

"Let no one say when he is tempted, 'I am being tempted by God,' for God cannot be tempted by evil, and He Himself does not tempt anyone" (James 1:13).

Scripture is also clear that if we do good, it is actually His doing in us. If we are kept from sin, it is His keeping, and if we overcome, it is His overcoming power.

"For since He Himself was tempted in that which He has suffered, He is able to come to the aid of those who are tempted" (Hebrews 2:18).

". . . for it is God who is at work in you, both to will and to work for His good pleasure" (Philippians 2:13).

"But in all these things we overwhelmingly conquer through Him who loved us" (Romans 8:37).

"For who regards you as superior? What do you have that you did not receive? And if you did receive it, why do you boast as if you had not received it?" (I Corinthians 4:7)

Victory is a gift, just as is salvation. However, too often when listening to victorious believers, we hear that a successful life is the result of intelligence, ability, right choices, personal power, theological correctness, Biblical knowledge, spiritual formulas, and the very favor of God. Contrary to this, I have found that spiritual men and women prefer to give the credit and glory for a successful spiritual life to God, and God alone. "ASCRIBE to the LORD, O sons of the mighty, ascribe to the LORD glory and strength" (Psalm 29:1).

The point is that the ability to walk away from failure rests in the grace and glory of Christ. Failure is our responsibility, choice, and fault. Please read that again lest I be misquoted as saying God causes our sin. He does not! However, He does passively allow it instead of stopping it. For example, if I stand with you on a curb and see but do not stop you from stepping out in front of a moving bus, do I not passively allow your action? When a believer is kept, it is God's keeping; when the Christian sins, it is his doing with God's passive allowance.

Man has an animal outer body, a soul comprising mind, will, and emotions, and also a spirit. The soul determines our choice to look for life in the body or in the spirit. It is important to note that satisfaction in either is only temporary. "Fire never says, 'Enough'" (Proverbs 30:16). Fulfilling the lust of the eyes, the lust of the flesh, or the boastful pride of life is completely and utterly temporary. If one has fed the desire of the flesh a thousand times, it will still long for the 1,001st. The same is true of the spirit. The one who draws near to Christ 1,000 times will still desire the 1,001st.

I give Christ the complete credit when I have chosen to live in the Spirit; I refuse to take the glory. I also refuse to give God any responsibility for the times I have chosen the flesh; however, I recognize His passive allowance of it.

Here is a glorious secret! "And we know that God causes all things to work together for good to those who love God, to those who are called according to His purpose" (Romans 8:28). If God Who is love passively allows me to choose the flesh and also causes all things to work together for good according to His purposes, I must ask what is His purpose and what must be learned from those times of my choosing the flesh.

On a scale of 1-10, the failing believer immediately assumes that his particular deed of the flesh (slander, sex, food, anger, depression, etc.) is a 10 and is the real issue. After all, had he not chosen that thing, he would be free from suffering and more acceptable to God. However, I have found that God's real 10, real issue, and real purpose is not the obvious failing, but rather what that failing reveals.

For example, a believer stumbles into sexual sin. Believing the sexual sin to be the real problem, his thoughts turn completely to avoiding it; sex becomes the focus. Focus is an interesting thing. I noticed hundreds of pregnant women back when Betty was pregnant. However, since that time I have seen very few pregnant women. Is it true that in my city of two million only a handful of women are pregnant? Of course not, but then I am no longer thinking about pregnant women. If *any* sin is *the* focus, the believer will never be free from that sin; if a believer hates what he has done, a sure way to continue in what he hates is to focus on it. Satan knows this better than we do, tempting us to focus on doing sin or on avoiding next time the sin already done; either way, the focus is not Christ.

God's guilt produces a focus on Christ; Satan's version of guilt produces a focus on the sin. "If we confess our sins, He is faithful and righteous to forgive us our sins and to cleanse us from all unrighteousness" (I John 1:9). Do you see a complete change in focus? "There is therefore now no condemnation for those who are in Christ Jesus" (Romans 8:1). The first thing I say to a believer who is vexed over failure is, "There is therefore now no condemnation"! The response is often, "You do not understand! I have hurt others, I have been so stupid, all around me is chaos, etc., etc., etc." I know believers feel that way, and in many ways their turmoil speaks well of their hearts. But to be true to God, we must believe it: "There is therefore now no condemnation." We may not feel it, but we can believe it and refuse to participate with the enemy. The doing of the sin is bad enough without the regurgitation of the doing. Both have roots in unbelief.

When we believe our sin to be a 10 on the 1-10 scale and, after all, we may have struggled with it all these years to no avail, we also might fear we would be rejected were we to confess it openly, and the constant accusing voice of the enemy has not gone unnoticed: "You are hopeless, a hypocrite, worthy of death, a failure, stupid, unfaithful, and an embarrassment to the cause of Christ." Yes, the behavior is sin, it is error, and it has been our choice. However, it has been passively allowed to reveal the true purpose of God, which must be understood or the failure is a waste. I have witnessed the true purpose in thousands of failures and am excited about how God works. There is no one like Him. Never undone by our failure, never surprised, never manipulated by the enemy, never lacking in love, abounding in kindness, with the softest of hearts, and focused while we sin. Sin is not the issue; Christ died for the sins of all, so the sin issue has been dealt with. Therefore, the issue is what sin reveals: all that is a hindrance both to our relationship with Him and to the expression of His life in us. If sin and failure force us to climb dependently into the lap of a loving Father, then failure is not the devastating enemy we perceive it to be. "Now if their transgression be riches for the world and **their failure be riches for the Gentiles**, how much more will their fulfillment be!" (Romans 11:12, emphasis mine). God can take our failures and make them riches for others. Riches! "[God] comforts us in all our affliction so that we may be able to comfort those who are in any affliction with the comfort with which we ourselves are comforted by God" (II Corinthians 1:4). Failure is affliction! I have had migraines, I have had ulcers, and I prefer both over failure in my relationship with God. But my God comforts in affliction and causes my failure to be riches to others!

DAY 135
How Believers List Lessons Learned From Failures

He will not always strive with us; nor will He keep His anger forever. He has not dealt with us according to our sins, nor rewarded us according to our iniquities. For high as the heavens are above the earth, so great is His lovingkindness toward those who fear Him. As far as the east is from the west, so far has He removed our transgressions from us.

—PSALM 103:9-12

Therefore, as discussed in the previous article, on a scale of 1-10 your failure, your sin, is not a 10 to God, and if you continue to focus on what you believe is primarily important, you run the risk of missing God's priority, His 10 revealed through your failure. What is life teaching you? Could you have learned these things any other way than through failure? After asking many discouraged believers these same questions, I have quite a list of responses.

1. For the Christian, sin and punishment are one and the same. One need not concern himself with the punishment of a sinner; made in God's image, the believer who has allowed sin in his life has suffered a state akin to drinking poison.

2. Unbelieving-believers suffering condemnation after confessed sin actually set Christ aside, as though right behavior is more important than the blood of Jesus. To say it another way, they are full of pride. Their confidence before God rests in their own righteous behavior; this is proven in their withdrawal from Him when they sin.

3. The worst punishment one can impose on himself is self-hatred; nothing is worse than looking in the mirror and hating the person who has chosen the emptiness of the flesh over the love and fellowship of God.

4. The flesh and the spirit are only satisfied for a moment; hence, we were created for ongoing relationship, which satisfies moment by moment. We either have a relationship with the flesh or the spirit.

5. Humans naturally gravitate toward the whole of a relationship. Many believe they can be married and yet still have "deep" friendships with the opposite sex, including communication, private meetings, the

sharing of hurts and troubles, and physical flirting, yet never have sex. Each element listed is one of the total called relationship. Accept one part and we will ultimately accept the whole. We are weak, but pride has made us believe we have strength. Many actually believe the animal side of man is easily overcome, when only one man, Christ, ever overcame the body.

6. Sin complicates life. Sin never allows life to smooth out.

7. We become depressed when we have "lost everything"! Why? We have been too proud to see that all we ever possessed was Christ. "I am my beloved's and my beloved is mine" (Song of Solomon 6:3).

8. I can breathe on land and not in the ocean. Why? I am a human. I cannot breathe half of the time in the ocean and half on land. I do not have two natures. I prove my nature by diving into the water and then very soon, craving air in my lungs, returning to the land. I prove my true nature—that being a child of God—through experience. I dive into the flesh and nearly drown. I now know who I am and where my life cannot be found. The knowledge has moved eighteen inches from my head to my heart through experience. Now that I know, it is so much easier not to dive off. The fact that I am vexed by failure is proof of my being a new, holy creation with the old nature crucified and demonstrates I am not suited for a relationship in the flesh. I must stop punishing myself! God isn't! My true child-of-God nature has been revealed. Everything done in the flesh I regret, while nothing done in the spirit has ever made me sorry.

9. It does not show spiritual weakness to avoid those things so attractive to the animal body. Avoidance is wisdom!

If we desire to stop eating sweets, we stop buying them. It is possible to fill our homes with sweets and pray our way through each and every minute of the day, never tasting, but why put ourselves through the turmoil? "Avoid it, do not pass by it; turn away from it and pass on" (Proverbs 4:15).

"The fear of the LORD is a fountain of life, that one may avoid the snares of death" (Proverbs 14:27).

The above list helps reveal some of God's 10's; when they are the focus, those fleshly failings we consider to be most significant naturally lose their appeal and drop off. What we learn through failure does not come on a written page but from life; it need not be memorized only to be forgotten later, for life cuts it deeply into our inner being, leaving scars as reminders of what was experienced, not heard or read.

David, the writer of Psalms, blesses me. Can you imagine my being blessed by a man who had an affair? Most fellowships would never allow him to speak after such infamy, but he is a blessing in that through his wrong behavior, he found his heart was suited only for God, and through witnessing his failure I am helped in finding my own heart. He loved God and he failed; however, the failure gave him something success never could. "I LOVE the LORD, because He hears My voice and my supplications" (Psalm 116:1).

Like David, we learn to love the Lord through failure. We do not let failures be a waste; through them we learn to love the Lord. "I love the Lord"! "Return faithless people; I will cure you of backsliding" (Jeremiah 3:22, NIV). Focus on Him and all else will fall into place.

DAY 136
How Long Have You Camped There?

But one thing I do: forgetting what lies behind and reaching forward to what lies ahead, I press on toward the goal for the prize of the upward call of God in Christ Jesus.

—PHILIPPIANS 3:13, 14

I have been camping in one place or another in this country and outside it for many years, and sometimes, out of nowhere, I remember camping at a place. I cannot remember at all many of the places where I camped, yet others left an impression I have never forgotten. I was wondering why, and then the simple explanation came to me. The places I remembered the most were the places I stayed in the longest.

Camping in the flesh is the same way. Often we take a diversion into the flesh for an hour, a day, or even longer. When we come to our senses, we repent and press on. I have had people come up to me and tell me something I said in my early Christian life that I cannot remember saying; the conversation was just not long enough for me to remember it. However, if we spend years at one point of the flesh, one day come to our senses, repent, and decide to move on, that memory and place of the flesh can randomly pop up in our heads for years to come. The solution is simple: "Forgetting what lies behind and pressing on to the high call." This is particularly important to understand for those who camped at their abuse, their loss, their addiction, their molestation, or their personal pain. Of course, it is much better to take up the cross and deny self than to camp at it, but amen, we do camp at it. When we decide to move on, it is important for us to let the old campsite, when it comes as a memory, be something that comes and quickly passes. It is true that the best place to kill a snake is in the egg. Anyway, I have returned to old campsites, and they were never the same. I have moved on!

DAY 137
How To Begin the Journey Of Denying Self

. . . fixing our eyes on Jesus, the author and perfecter of faith, who for the joy set before Him endured the cross, despising the shame; and has sat down at the right hand of the throne of God.

—HEBREWS 12:2

Actually, it is quite simple. Life becomes complicated as we look at ourselves with a view to fixing the problems we find. Upon further examination, we soon realize the impossibility of our situation, for flesh will not improve flesh. However, life is simple when the focus is on the Lord. In Jesus' teaching, He does not cover myriad topics but generally sticks to one theme, "I and the Father are One." To see Jesus is to see God. Therefore, in this journey of denying self, our focus must be on Jesus; this is where we begin.

Pick one area of life that you obsess on continually. It can be your weight, how you look, your failures and regrets, your worthlessness, your lack of accomplishments, your embarrassments, your financial condition, your lusts, or your pride. Determine for one day not to think about the one main topic, the one thing that has been consuming you. Here is what you will discover: Not thinking about that one area of Self has a domino effect. The obsession with self is all or nothing. There is no such thing as a "little" obsession, because your mind, like a light-switch, is on self or off self, period. If you do not spend the day in self-loathing, you will not spend the night in fear. If you do not spend the day in pride (pride which can manifest as negative things, such as self-hatred, embarrassment, depression, and more), you will not spend the evening in lust. Just practice the domino effect. Now to add some spice to the equation: Try obsessing on just one of the characteristics of Jesus/God. Has He shown you mercy, do you love His humanity, or do you like the fact that He really, truly lives? All of this will help you to begin the journey. Always remember that you and your flesh are boring both to you and to Him. To date, you have never fixed a single thing in your life.

The State of New York did a survey on a fish market in California where the men had terrible jobs; all their workday held in store for them was a very early beginning to their morning and a return trip home reeking of fish. Yet something changed in the men and they began to have heaps of fun; now people come from all over to buy their fish and just watch the men work. Here is what was learned from the men:

Play: It's about having fun, enjoying yourselves, and being spontaneous and creative. Life is too short to spend it frowning, and FISH bring a smile to your face.

Make their day: It's about doing something special for your customers and co-workers. When you make people's day, you have given them a special gift they will not soon forget. It feels good to give it.

Be there: It's about being totally focused on the moment and on the person or task in which we are involved. When we are fully engaged with our customer, we listen deeply, and important opportunities do not escape us.

Choose your attitude: It's about accepting full responsibility for all our choices, even our attitude at work. A positive attitude is a decision we make moment by moment.

Charles R. Swindoll, Insight for Living Ministries, wrote the wonderful and now well-known piece on attitude and its importance to daily life. He wrote, "The longer I live, the more I realize the impact of attitude on life. Attitude, to me, is more important than facts. It is more important than the past, than education, than money, than circumstances, than failures, than successes, than what other people think or say or do. It is more important than appearance, giftedness or skill. It will make or break a company, a church, a home. The remarkable thing is we have a choice every day regarding the attitude we will embrace for that day. We cannot change our past, we cannot change the fact that people will act in a certain way. We cannot change the inevitable. The only thing we can do is play on the one string we have, and that is our attitude. I am convinced that life is 10% what happens to me and 90% how I react to it. And so it is with you; we are in charge of our attitudes."

"Have this attitude in you that was in Christ Jesus" [Philippians 2:5]. We must, in order to be happy, give ourselves to something greater than ourselves, and for that reason we must begin with that one thing: to obsess no longer on self.

DAY 138
How Would You Like Being Hated?

The night is almost gone, and the day is at hand. Let us therefore lay aside the deeds of darkness and put on the armor of light. Let us behave properly as in the day, not in carousing and drunkenness, not in sexual promiscuity and sensuality, not in strife and jealousy. But put on the Lord Jesus Christ, and make no provision for the flesh in regard to its lusts.

—ROMANS 13:12-14

The mind set on the flesh is hostile toward God; for it does not subject itself to the law of God, for it is not even able to do so.

 —ROMANS 8:7

Often two or three topics get blended together, which gives the enemy opportunity to bring about confusion. It is wise to separate the topics. The following is just such a blended topic.

Homosexuality is abnormal behavior and is sin, period. The world is attempting to build an argument one foot above the ground in hopes we will all forget there is no foundation. Even evolutionists would, given the framework of their scheme, have to admit that such activity is abnormal and not how man was meant to live. The Bible is not even needed to make the point, because the resultant diseases scream that something is wrong. Sin and punishment happen at the same time. I often ask those who advocate homosexuality as an alternate lifestyle how they felt the first time they participated in the act. They say they nearly came apart. Having a "gay pride day" is just as absurd as having something like an adulterer's pride day, a contentious one's pride day, or a drunk's pride day! I expect sinners to sin and I expect men of God to fail, since things are learned in failure that cannot be learned in success, as we know from our own experience with the flesh (flesh being the mind, will, and emotions under the rule of something other than Christ). Therefore, homosexuals do what homosexuals do. However, I am opposed, vexed, and burdened by their constant, wicked recruitment. Enough said.

We all walk in the flesh. If you do not know what your particular expression of the flesh is, just ask God or someone around you to show you. It is a shorter list when man does it, for once you fall under the gaze of God's light, you will be completely undone and never be the same. When you see your flesh as He sees it, there is nothing to do but cry out: "Then I said, woe is me, for I am ruined! Because I am a man of unclean lips, and I live among a people of unclean lips; for my eyes have seen the King, the LORD of hosts" (Isaiah 6:5). Flesh is flesh. Is homosexual flesh worse than jealous flesh? Is homosexual flesh worse than prideful flesh? Is it worse than any other flesh?

DAY 139
Hungry Flesh

And He has said to me, "My grace is sufficient for you, for power is perfected in weakness." Most gladly, therefore, I will rather boast about my weaknesses, that the power of Christ may dwell in me.

 —II CORINTHIANS 12:9

It seems the flesh needs only a crumb to stay alive and active—a pinch of praise or a bit of condemnation. Thoughts of self-hatred and self-adulation are alike to it, just so it gets attention. If it can stay alive, it knows that a time will come when it can gorge itself. As hard as it is to accept, the fact is that our flesh will never change or improve, but we can abide longer and more consistently. If we do not understand abiding—recognizing our fellowship with Christ—we will come to the place where since it is simply too difficult to attempt to ride the flesh beast, we will decide to feed it. Jesus lived in a body and has overcome it all, but apart from Him, we can do nothing. When we weep over our condition due to the discovery of how weak the flesh is; we discover what He always knew, and it depresses us, though it did not Him. He knew that God would be to, in, and for Him everything He was not, and therefore, He gladly acknowledged what He could not do. When we are sick we say, "I can't." When we are old we say, "I can't." But the very Son of God in His prime said, "I can't." There must be something in that for us.

DAY 140
Hypnotism Of the Masses

Leave them; they are blind guides. If a blind man leads a blind man, both will fall into a pit.

 —MATTHEW 15:14 [NIV]

As one dictionary put it, insidious is something awaiting a chance to entrap, treacherous, harmful but enticing, having a gradual and cumulative effect.

Insidious! That is what it is, insidious. The unholy trinity, consisting of sin, Satan, and the world, is insidious. Some are often lauded for taking a long-term approach to management and growth. In their management schemes immediate results are not sought, but rather a successful day is recognized as a part of the gradual work toward a determined end. Sin, Satan, and the world are much more patient than we are comfortable acknowledging, and it would appear as if that patience is close to being rewarded, perhaps not in the immediate future, but close. There are millions of publications, millions of hours of television, radio, and websites, millions of billboards and advertisements, thousands of political views and carping, and then all the uncountable medical cures. Oh, and let us not forget all the preaching we hear that is program-centered and not Christ-centered. Additionally, the list above does not come close to mentioning all the things truly going on, all dedicated to a slow but steady mind-numbing and brainwashing to bring about the widespread belief of, "There is no God! Life is to be found in the world! If you do not have life it is because something is wrong in your world!" Eventually the message from the unholy trinity sinks into the deepest recesses of man, even the believer, and then we wear our world glasses and believe (yes, it is a complete belief system) if only, if only, if only something could change in my world—my mate, my children, my finances, my community, or myself—then, and only then, could I be happy. Insidious!

I have fallen prey to this scheme of the devil so many times. I look at finances, friends, family, and myself and am overwhelmed. I find myself thinking, "What can be done?" just as if there is no God whatsoever. I am saying and preaching that we have a God, but all of a sudden I unwittingly and mechanically put Him on the shelf and flow seamlessly into what some would call my subconscious, where the world has deeply buried its messages. Like a person under hypnotism with buried triggers placed in the recesses of the mind, when I see or hear what pulls those triggers, I immediately revert to a preprogrammed behavior. I see a certain situation and all those millions of hours of being brainwashed kick in, with the awareness of God essentially out of the picture. "What must I do? What is going to happen to me?" Of course, this is not verbalized because over the years it has been planted in the subconscious, although it obviously is taking place, for the symptoms are clear: worry, doubt, fear, anxiety, and depression. In times of absolute quiet and meditation, stopping to recognize and praise the One who holds all things together, there is not a care or a worry; but then I step out the door, turn on the radio, look at the billboards, receive a phone call, or pick up the newspaper, and it is just as though He never made anything, does not exist, and is completely passive in the affairs of my life. I am being reprogrammed. Fortunately, the Word who became flesh is much stronger than the words of man. Either there is a God or there is not a God. Either He has numbered every hair of my head or He has not. Either the events in the world and in my life are permitted by Him or they are not. Either He is intensely concerned for my family or He is not. So much around me is taking my attention from the facts. So often it feels like it cannot be true that we have an involved God in our lives. He is silent, nothing is happening, and all is bleak.

I remember years ago challenging myself to go one full day without thinking about myself. It took seven years. To go one full day knowing that He is God and to rest is a far greater challenge. Isaiah said, "In repentance and rest you shall be saved, in quietness and trust is your strength" [Is. 30:15]. What a promise! We need to let the challenges of life reprogram us rather than letting them set off the triggers of unbelief systematically and insidiously planted in the brain for years by sin, Satan, and the world. We must remind ourselves, "I have a God, and often He has chosen to work in what appears to be silence and inactivity on His part. However, He is holding all things together, and He is active in the very middle of my crisis. I must rest."

If we do something twice a day for thirty days, it becomes a habit. Make the awareness of God a habit.

DAY 141
I AM

Jesus said to them, "Truly, truly, I say to you, before Abraham was born, I am."

—JOHN 8:58

Whatever you are looking for, His word to you is, "I AM." If God wants to reveal a lot of His Son in you, then there must be very little of you in you. Come to grips with it. If you have nothing to offer, you are blessed by God and have caught His eye for filling and the revelation of His Son. Stop complaining about what you do not have and rejoice. No one can put water in a full cup.

DAY 142
I Feel So Lost!

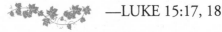

But when he came to his senses, he said, "How many of my father's hired men have more than enough bread, but I am dying here with hunger! I will get up and go to my father, and will say to him, 'Father, I have sinned against heaven, and in your sight.'"

—LUKE 15:17, 18

I often hear believers say they are feeling lost. An interesting thing about feeling lost is that a person cannot feel lost unless he has a home. When Satan was questioned about where he had been, he responded, "Going back and forth across the earth." He had no home and was not lost. Truly lost people do not know they are lost; they are blind and deaf. Therefore, one can only have a feeling of being lost if he is away from home. I have had the sinking feeling of being lost when I was many miles from home, and with each passing minute the awareness intensified. My point is, one who feels lost does so because he does have a home, a place he has left.

Years ago my Indian teacher was talking about our place, that all of human history was a struggle over finding a place. Our place as believers, he maintained, was in the vine with Jesus. If you are feeling lost, it is only because you have moved away from Him. Move back, acknowledge that you abide in Him, and the feeling will leave.

DAY 143
I Hate Divorce, Part I

"For I hate divorce," says the Lord, the God of Israel, "and him who covers his garment with wrong," says the Lord of hosts. "So take heed to your spirit, that you do not deal treacherously."

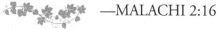 —MALACHI 2:16

I remember quite a journey, a mountain I climbed. Walking through a stream, I twisted my ankle. A 100-foot-tall rock wall had to be scaled in sleet; I slipped and slid all the way up. I do not think I have ever fallen so much in my life. Bruises and scratches abounded, and having a twig poke me in the eye was the final straw. I reached the top and proclaimed, "I hate mountains!" You can see why I said it. Those two words, "I hate," had definition for me because of what had preceded the statement. I did not just walk to the base of the mountain and for no reason say, "I hate mountains!" Had there been no hindrances to my ascent, I would never have made the comment about hating mountains.

When God says He hates divorce, He is not merely saying He hates the act of getting a divorce, the signature on the dotted line. Many things led up to His declaration, and had those obstacles been resolved, He would not have made the statement. Many Christians have a very narrow view of His statement. I have observed Christians who have struggled in their marriage for years with problems that have included alcohol, drugs, adulteries, control, lies, deceit, nagging, lack of respect, backbiting, dissension, strife, abuse of every kind, and basically all of the deeds of the flesh listed in Galatians 5. The children, too, were dragged into all of the conflict. Of the couples I have talked to encumbered with the aforementioned behaviors, 99% were never directly confronted about the bad behavior by anyone from their church. However, once the couples said they were divorcing, they were brought before the church for discipline and warned that if they were to get a divorce, they would be excommunicated! Immediately every Biblical passage concerning divorce was presented to cause guilt and fear in the couple so they would come back together. The signing of the divorce papers was presented as tantamount to the unpardonable sin. Because of this, many simply separate, never to return to one another, but at least they have not committed the "unpardonable sin" of divorce. I find this approach mind-boggling. I also find it unconscionable when a person has lived years displaying every one of the Galatians-listed deeds of the flesh, and when his or her abused mate decides he/she cannot go on, the Selfer becomes all consumed with the innocent one's need to keep the command not to divorce and constantly questions the innocent's commitment to Christ. Now, it is easy to discount my point by assuming I am for divorce and therefore against the Scriptures, but that type of detractor would be wrong on both counts. However, I am making a point that God did not hate the signing of the divorce papers. Rather, what He really hated was all of the sinful activity that led up to the signing; when He says that He hates divorce, it is erroneous not to include the "garment with wrong," not taking "heed to your spirit," and dealing "treacherously."

When discussing life choices with a struggling couple, many pastors or counselors say the easy thing: "Get divorced." Or they may say something even easier, which is, "Divorce is wrong, and you must stay together." Both camps have chosen the lazy way and are not really interested in the life of the couple. After many years of investing my life in believers' marriages, I can say that working through the root (behaviors, attitudes, ignorance in communication, and normal flesh issues) that brings about the fruit (divorce) is very difficult and will often give me more sleepless nights than it does the couple. When God says He hates divorce, He is saying He hates those root problems that brought the marriage to the looming point of demise. Jesus moved to the root of divorce when He said Moses allowed it because of the hardness of heart, for a hard heart makes room for every deed of the flesh. If there had been no hard heart, there would have been no divorce. I see couples where one has not walked in the flesh and the other has and intends on continuing. The Selfer wants the divorce or legalistically wants to prevent the divorce, but in reality the couple has already accomplished everything at a root level that in a practical way makes for divorce. To press the innocent to live in sin, tolerate and covertly condone sin, and make more sin possible under the guilt/fear of God's hating him or her, again, is mind-boggling. Paul makes the same point: If the unbeliever does not want to live with the believer, the believer is not bound. An unbeliever is someone who does not recognize Jesus; many we call *unbelieving believers* are in that category. My heart's desire is for no one to divorce, but that word divorce has definition for me. With that as my heart, I work with people on the root issues that brought them to the place of desiring divorce, and I witness to God's being at work amid the root issues. Often I have said to a young fellow, "What you are doing now will be soul killing to your wife later," in hopes that the root will be dealt with before the fruit of divorce develops.

Three things that make for a good marriage are communication, intimacy, and common goals. Too many relationships have none of the three, and addressing and adjusting this root issue will allow for the avoidance of divorce. However, this takes time, enlightenment, and the ability to see God in the struggles of daily life.

DAY 144
I Hate Divorce, Part II

For I hate divorce, says the Lord God of Israel.
—MALACHI 2:16

Let God be true and every man the liar: God does hate divorce. However, He does not say that he hates those people who get a divorce. I am still baffled and incredulous concerning the interpretation of Scripture by some who spread the notion of no divorce at any cost. I do not understand that, when there can be child abuse of every kind, addictions that deform the whole family composition, children overdosing on drugs, and Christians holding a handgun to their heads and pulling the trigger, all because of a bad marriage. Come and live in my shoes, hearing what I have heard over the decades of marriage counseling, and see if somehow perspective changes. It will never change the fact that God said, "I hate divorce," but it might make us wonder if He does not more greatly hate the things that lead to divorce, the "hardness of heart." If the lesser gives way to the greater, then is not the end result of the divorce the lesser in view of the more terrible sins that led up to the divorce? I so often wish other believers could plug a jack into my head and hear the screams from the children who lived with parents who decided to stay married to be obedient. Mind you, the parents' behavior was not dutiful to any other directives indicated in the Gospel, but somehow not divorcing became to them the supreme act of obedience and a feat in which they could boast. I see this same conviction being widely promulgated by believers.

If you have had a divorce and were a stupid person in your behavior, we at ALMI stand with you. If you have had a divorce after staying in the marriage even beyond when the peace of God left you, we at ALMI stand with you. If you are struggling today, ALMI stands with you. Jesus came that you might have life and have it abundantly. Our desire, like His, is for you to find abundant life. Remember, we have all failed Him according to Scriptural directives, but He has never left us nor forsaken us. We can honestly tell Him the facts of our humanity and be open to what He will work into our lives.

I remember a couple in the situation where everything was going wrong. The husband held two jobs, the wife was sick and yet kept going to work, the teens were rebelling, and their house was in foreclosure. I just said, "I have nothing to give that will relieve your situation. Will you do one thing? Invite Jesus into the pit in which you have found yourselves. Every situation into which you invite Him is one for which He will take responsibility. Only Jesus can lift your spirit." The next week they arrived with a big smile. I mistakenly assumed something wonderful had taken place—perhaps a new job, kids turning around, or the dynamics of the marriage changing—and I asked what had happened. The husband said, "Well, I lost one of my jobs!" That did not explain the smile until he continued on to say, "We invited Jesus into the pit! Nothing changed but our attitude, and now we have hope."

Invite Him in. Relationship is the hardest and messiest thing you will ever experience. Marriage can be a tough pit; ask Him to enter in. Either we have a God or we do not have a God! Brothers and Sisters in Christ, we have a God. Remember, God does NOT hate you. Do not be a pessimist about marriage; there is no waste in God, and past bad experiences bring new life into today.

DAY 145
"I Hate Your Sacrifices"

After saying above, "Sacrifices and offerings and whole burnt offerings and sacrifices for sin Thou hast not desired, nor hast Thou taken pleasure in them" (which are offered according to the Law), then He said, "Behold, I have come to do Thy will." He takes away the first in order to establish the second. By this will we have been sanctified through the offering of the body of Jesus Christ once for all.

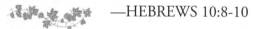

—HEBREWS 10:8-10

Prefixing or suffixing Christianity in word or deed nullifies Christianity. All relics, icons, and idols scream, "Jesus is not enough!" Every candle lit, every act of self-punishment, every knee bowed to an idol, and every prayer uttered to an icon rises to heaven with a mighty shout, "Jesus is not enough!" Every doctrine fought over, every denominational sign, every "new" wave that goes through the church, insinuates that, "Jesus is not enough." Go ahead and admit your failure and accept the label of being a Baptist, a Pentecostal, a Methodist; let the title proclaim that Jesus is not enough. Give yourself a title and an image and be known as the millionaire, the doctor, or the intellectual; let the admiring throngs go ahead to announce you and then proclaim the truth of the matter, that Jesus is not enough. With every bit of religious garb, every cross hastily fingered across your chest, and every cross bowed to, you are shouting to God, "Jesus is not enough!"

What will happen when He has had enough? When the Son of Man comes, will He find faith on the earth, or will He find religious people? Do not question the what but the why. All right, if you are praying to the saint of protection, then why? Jesus said to ask in His Name and the Father would give. Bowing with your body is to show that you are bowing in your heart, but to show whom? Surely not the One who knows your heart! Where in the Bible do we see mention of the candles, incense, and all the other trappings? They are the additions of men, and men desire us to cast our bodies upon the things they have attached to Jesus; we are to keep them warm with our affection and attention. Well, curl up around a stone Madonna and see what happens. Will the stone ever become warm? No, it will chill you to your bones. When I die I would like to hear this from the Father, "Michael, you ultimately always thought that Jesus was enough."

DAY 146
I Make My God Too Little

. . . to whom God willed to make known what is the riches of the glory of this mystery among the Gentiles, which is Christ in you, the hope of glory.

—COLOSSIANS 1:27

My unbelief astounds me! The fact that it astounds me reveals how I still think in my flesh dwells some good thing. You see, I knew Christ could live in the flesh of a man and conquer all things, but I never believed He could live in my flesh and conquer all things. What was I thinking, that somehow when Jesus moved into my flesh, His power was stripped away? What unbelief! Actually, when I had my last birthday, I just stopped and pondered. I never thought I would make it to that age. I did not think that He who had begun a good work in me would complete it. I did not think He would prove to me that He was love. It was all proof of my unbelief. Well, I want to testify that He can live in your flesh. He has lived in millions of people's flesh, and He is more than able. Not only that, but I will tell you one more secret: He enjoys living in you!

DAY 147
I Need To Know More
Than Grandma?

Whoever exalts himself shall be humbled; and whoever humbles himself shall be exalted.

—MATTHEW 23:12

Again, it is amazing that a religion (though I do not like calling Christianity that, for it is so much more than religion) started by a carpenter and intended to become inclusive of "whosoever will" is made out to be exclusive by the educated ones within it. Often I sat in class in Bible college or graduate school as the merits of education were touted. Those educated in theology like to answer a question beginning with, "We believe," or "We do not know," or "We know." In other words, "we" are the elite, the educated, those who have something most others do not have; "we" live on a higher plane. Yet, those same "scholars" (how odd to have scholars in a religion that centers on *being*), when asked to apply the same exclusivity rules (rules such as to have a working vocabulary in Greek and Hebrew, an active knowledge of archeological finds, etc.) to their wives, mothers, or grandmothers, refuse to do so. All of a sudden the wife, mother, or grandmother is a great saint even though not knowledgeable in all the things purported to be essential for the rest of us in order to know—really know—Jesus! My question is, "If Grandma did not have to know all these things to be a great saint, why do I?"

The disciples were uneducated men. If we want to learn anything about religion, we must turn to those who are specialists in this area, to those who have tested in their own experience what religion really means. We do not expect a dentist to understand auto mechanics. What do theologians and philosophers know about Christ? The specialists—the mystics, the prophets, and the men of prayer—are the ones we should talk to.

As I have discussed elsewhere, the ugliest religion in the world is Christianity, since every other religion is created to be a religion, centered in laws, places, rites, and ceremonies. Christianity centers on a relationship with the Founder, who is not a teacher of new rules but One raised from the dead, One who actually lives in and through the follower. Since no one can imitate Jesus, the religious have to come up with any number of laws, behaviors, and bodies of learning they can imitate and exalt themselves over others.

DAY 148
I Am Sorry

If we confess our sins, He is faithful and just and will forgive us our sins and purify us from all unrighteousness.

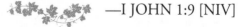 —I JOHN 1:9 [NIV]

One "I am sorry" before your sin is discovered by others is worth a thousand times of saying "I am sorry" after discovery. One word of repentance before discovery is worth 1,000 after discovery. It strikes all of us as hollow when someone is caught in the act and then repents. This is true from the behavior of your child to the behavior of the President. "If you had not been caught, would you be repenting? Is your repentance a bit self-centered, self-serving, and disingenuous?" What is my point? Well, God knows what you have been up to. Do not wait for discovery; repent today. Acknowledge where you are so you can leave where you are. God will take you onward. Confess to Jesus, the one mediator between God and man. It is worth so much on this side of discovery. Amen.

DAY 149
If Only I Knew Then What I Know Now

For I know that nothing good dwells in me, that is, in my flesh, for the wishing is present in me, but the doing of the good is not. For the good that I wish, I do not do, but I practice the very evil that I do not wish. But if I am doing the very thing I do not wish, I am no longer the one doing it, but sin which dwells in me.

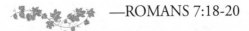

—ROMANS 7:18-20

Revelation does not come through effort; it will come through life and can take years to arrive. Revelation can never be forced; it is an outgrowth of our lives in a fallen body and in a fallen world. Revelation comes in the fullness of time; therefore, time is essential, and the longer one lives, the more revelation he will receive. Many exit at an early age, having been given the revelation needed for a move from this reality to THE reality. Life with a small "l" is constantly teaching us of Life with a capital "L." That is why revelation waits in the future for life to prepare us for what Life would teach us. In the fullness of time, we will receive what we would not have received at an earlier time. There is no need to be frustrated and make silly comments like, "I wish I would have known that sooner." At a sooner time we could not have received it and would not have "known" it.

This planet and our lives are not made up of random experiences. This world is the womb in which the things of God are made known to us, and just as a baby is methodically formed in the womb of the mother, the child of God is methodically formed in the womb of the world. God is the God of order, not of chaos; therefore everything comes in order. To say, "If only I had known this sooner" is assuming that "knowing" is what has made the change in us. Rather, it was revelation. Knowledge can come at any time, and yet revelation must come at the fullness of time as our duration on earth prepares the way. "If only I could go back and make different decisions!" Well, if we could go back, we would be the same persons we were back then, and we would make the same decisions. However, such a statement does reveal that we have grown, and the new persons we are today would never have made such decisions.

We have mentioned before that there are journey people and destination people. As believers we need to accept that we are all on a journey and enjoy the journey. Along the way and in the fullness of time, God is teaching us. We cannot hurry up that process (Bible schools and seminaries are the proof of that). If the process cannot be hurried, then we must accept the way of things on the earth and rest in Him. The Holy Spirit will bring the revelation—His teaching that moves from head to heart—in the fullness of time.

DAY 150
If The Counsel You Receive Can Be Followed Without Jesus, Is It Christian?

For there is one God, and one mediator also between God and men, the man Christ Jesus, who gave Himself as a ransom for all, the testimony given at the proper time.

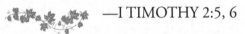 —I TIMOTHY 2:5, 6

Many are confused by the counsel/discipleship they receive; I can understand why. The approach is delivered, and as we listen, there seems to be something amiss in our spirits, something missing in the approach. That thing most often missing is Jesus. In fact, much of "Christian" counseling and discipleship is not Christian at all. Many counselors are only baptizing the world's methods they learned at a university and adding a vague passage here and there in an attempt to make it sound Christian. Take the topic of denial; given its definition, Jesus would appear to be one of the worst people in the world for being in denial. In the same way, many discipleship methods are nothing more than Buddhism baptized, with one list after another that could be achieved and followed by anybody. I could go on, but it would not help answer the confusion many have when hearing the latest advice on being set free. A simple way to judge the counseling and discipleship is to determine if the method includes Jesus, not in a peripheral way, but centrally, in its core. Can the advice given be accomplished without Jesus? If it depends on me, if it falls at my feet, if it falls at the feet of others, then it is not Christian. So much of what I hear can be done by anyone. Not so in abiding. Apart from Him we can do nothing. There is no need to talk about things done apart from Him, for we cannot do them. We cannot love, we cannot change, we cannot control our emotions, but we can choose Him and invite Him to be our love, our new life, and our peace. When Jesus is included in the method, that method has relevance for yesterday, today, and tomorrow; it is eternal. When He is left out, the methods are always changing, and what was needed for understanding twenty years ago is not needed today. Something is always being presented as new, when the old thing—Jesus and understanding His work—has not been understood.

DAY 151
Illegitimate Children?

The earth is the Lord's, and everything in it, the world, and all who live in it.

 —PSALM 24:1 [NIV]

Something every parent must come to grips with—and without it the task of parenting can be overwhelming—is the revelation that our child is not primarily our child; first and foremost the child belongs to the Lord. Having made an absolute point, "The earth and all that is within it belong to the Lord," the next statement will be equally absolute: The fatherless child is also the Lord's. Our foundation is not the parent but God. The issue is not the parent but the child who belongs to the Lord. As I presented seminars in churches around the world I met people who do not know their fathers and mothers or who are raising fatherless children. This is an increasing trend in the world. This type of child is left feeling uncertain where, or if, he belongs. When the mother describes the origins of the child, the explanation will often confirm just what the world and the child's emotions have been indicating. Whether the child was planned or not, this absolute fact does not change: The child belongs to God.

If you look in the mirror and see this child staring at you, or you look across the room and see this child sitting across from you, you must both cherish this same thought. The child belongs to God. Have you recognized it? As the child or the parent, have you acknowledged it?

DAY 152
Indecision

For in it the righteousness of God is revealed from faith to faith; as it is written, "But the righteous man shall live by faith."

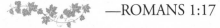 —ROMANS 1:17

Every person must live by some measure of faith. We have faith in the yellow line that separates our car from the oncoming traffic, faith in the restaurant owner not to poison us, faith in the city to provide basic amenities; yes, everyone lives by faith. All of life teaches that we must live by faith. Making a decision is the aspect of faith I want to examine, because the turmoil that comes from decision-making is actually a faith issue. Often when it comes to decision-making, understanding is picked up and faith laid aside. We want to know the outcome before we act, we fear the discomfort a wrong decision might bring, and we prolong the agony of choosing, when a quick decision is just as likely to be as good as a prolonged one without bringing all the discomfort of endless analyzing. Life teaches faith; therefore, life will never answer all the unknowns before action. We might analyze a decision for one week, one month, or one year, but at the end understanding and emotion will still fail, and God must be trusted as we choose. If there are 100 questions we feel must be answered before making a right decision, God might allow all but one to be answered, leaving us once again at a point of faith. "Why?" you might ask. It is too easy to trust something other than Him when we have to decide, so God structures our lives in such a way that we must enter the equation through faith.

Coming out of the garden, man wanted to be all-knowing. Decisions bring us back to reality and to a place of dependence, where we acknowledge that God is the Creator and we the creatures. To make the faith of decision-making simple, James, understanding that God has a plan for our lives (not a place), says that we need only make a decision and then follow it with this statement: "If the Lord wills, we shall live and also do this or that" (James 4:15). Paul echoes the same principle: "But I will come to you soon, if the Lord wills" (I Cor. 4:19). Make decisions based on the fact that you have a God who watches over you. Faith is not a cloud where nothing is clear; it is crystal clear. Indecision is what is murky. Simply say, "Father, this is my decision; I want Your will not mine." Then act.

DAY 153
Insanity Addictions

And you will seek Me and find Me when you search for
Me with all your heart.
—JEREMIAH 29:13

Come to Me, all who are weary and heavy-laden,
and I will give you rest.

—MATTHEW 11:28

Instances of what the secular world calls schizophrenia are on the increase throughout the Western world as families collapse. In a dysfunctional family a child often receives several negative messages about his worth and begins to feel worthless, unacceptable, and unwanted. Soon his behavior proves what he feels about himself. Next might come a series of attempts to improve (in his own strength) as he endeavors to be the opposite of what he feels. Therefore, at first appearance he is loving and caring, but soon with the mounting pressure of a relationship he falls back into the old feelings and behaviors. Anyone living with someone manifesting these actions has the feeling of living with two different people. The symptoms are compounded if the person is a "thinker" or "melancholy" by nature, for this type of person has excessive mental energy, high standards for himself and others close to him, and, often, obsessions about his ugly past. His mind is like a file cabinet; from youth everything hurtful from his past (either his own or others' actions) is put in the file and the drawer is closed, locked, and avoided. However, with the mounting pressures of life it becomes increasingly difficult to focus all of his energy on keeping the file locked.

Usually sometime between the ages of 35 and 45, the file begins to open, allowing a confrontation with the past. As a means of avoidance he then uses his mental energy to focus on something else, maybe a disease, the lines in paper, combing his hair, or anything else that keeps him from dwelling on his past and the failures.

There are two things to remember about insanity. First, it is calculated behavior. In a great majority of all cases, insanity is an addiction. It cannot be viewed as any different from alcoholism. With one exception there are many more advantages to insanity, and it is much more addictive than cocaine. Schizophrenia is ten times higher in the West than in poor countries. Why? It is a luxury of a wealthy culture. Insanity allows individuals to shed all responsibility, gives them an excuse for all behavior, and even demands that others feel sorry for them. With conventional drug treatment, most become worse, for drugs cause inactivity of the physical body, so more energy is diverted to the mind that is causing the problem.

Second, the addicted person is a complete controller. Through his behavior, others are forced to make him the center of their lives. If he cannot become the center of attention through nice behavior, he tries negative behavior; if that does not work, he will often tell others he is dying, anything to control and remain the center of attention. He goes completely out of control but remains in control of others around him. If a person is truly crazy, why does he still know when to eat and which food and drink he likes, and why does he often exhibit unrestrained sexual freedom? He knows what he is doing, but insanity is the easy way out: no responsibility, no self-sacrifice, no effort, and plenty of excuses.

There is no question the enemy is busy in the midst of all the self-deception and self-centeredness, whispering in a first-person singular voice that sounds like the afflicted person's own such assertions as he must be fixed, others do not understand, and he is hopeless. The spiral tightens. The greatest stronghold will be in the *feelings*, such as the *feeling* that he cannot get any better and life is hopeless.

Imagine you and I alone in a room when a wild bear breaks down the door. I would expect you to have an anxiety attack. As the bear attacked you, I would expect to see you depressed, and as I jumped through the window to save myself, I would expect you to be angry with me. All of that makes perfect sense. However, to have an anxiety attack, become depressed and angry, and then to drive all over town looking for a bear to justify the feelings is crazy.

Many have listened to the enemy's voice and the stirring of their emotions. They feel weak, stupid, hopeless, like failures, like something is wrong with them, and each morning they arise looking for the reason for their feelings. Life for them is turned upside down. At this point they are totally subjective and feel their way through life with false feelings.

That pretty much defines the problem, but what are we to do about it? How do we help the afflicted? What is our legitimate responsibility and what is theirs?

I will attempt to outline my approach and at the same time emphasize God's part in the human predicament. For whatever problem we create or others create for us, God is able to turn the darkness into light and immediately cause a reversal in our condition. Therefore, the beginning place is prayer for the afflicted, for his recognition of the addiction, his taking responsibility for something that has become his problem, and his personal turning to Christ for the strength needed. Then there is prayer for a change of focus for the defeated. Being consumed with self, past and present hurts, and the fear of one's future makes the mental hospital a place to remain *comfortable in one's misery*. As I have mentioned, there are several advantages to remaining miserable, for in such a state one does not have to put one foot in front of the other and walk toward Christ. Often someone who has had emotional problems will call me and say, "What you told me to do worked for about six months, and then it quit." My response is that if what a person was told worked five minutes, it could work five hours, it could work five months, and it could work for five years. If it worked at all it could work forever! The problem is not that *it* stopped working, but rather that the person stopped working! Challenge the person in the hospital to spend one hour not thinking about himself, only thinking about Christ, reading Psalm 139, and see what a difference there is. We need not prove Christ, for He will always prove Himself.

When others, or we ourselves, have a loved one so addicted, we must remember we have a God who is the person's Shepherd, Protector, Guide, Light, Life, and Hope, all those things we are not. One sheep simply cannot adequately take care of the other sheep, for there are things only the Shepherd can provide. We are not anyone's god, nor the one in whom he should trust or upon whom he should heap the responsibility of his wellbeing . . . only God is. We actually can get in the way of God when attempting to do what only He can do. Can we open the eyes of the self-centered, stir hope in the deepest recesses of a man's heart, move understanding from the head to the heart, or give the supernatural strength that allows one to say, "In Him all things are possible" as he gets out of bed and moves forward? God alone must work to accomplish that. If I work, He rests; if I rest, He works. It may sound cruel, but seeing the emotionally unstable become whole is not our responsibility, for the seat of dysfunction is untouchable by man. This is where man's wisdom reveals true ignorance, for in myriad mental wards those confined remain immaculately unchanged. For all the talk of what works and what is needed, all that has been discovered is what does not work. Therefore, the desire to help must be laid at the cross. This is true help and not pandering to a condition. Only the man empowered by the Holy Spirit can one day take the greatest step one can take, to say *no* to lying emotions, to walk against all they say, to listen to what God says, and to become a true man of faith.

There are far fewer cases of mental illness in less wealthy countries because time simply is not allotted for such a respite from life; all must go to work. I would suggest that those with mental dysfunctions be made to work, which disperses some mental energy into physical energy and thus decreases the symptoms. Hard work, not coddling, should be the course of the day.

Those addicted to insanity have predetermined what their healing will be like: a complete change in feeling and circumstance, all will be forgotten, and all fantasy will be realized. Is this God's definition of healing? If they seek for a definition that is not God's, then they seek for a false definition, and God will never confirm a lie. Healing is not feeling better about oneself, thinking better of oneself, or doing more for oneself, with *self* as the object. Healing is not feeling better about God, thinking more about God, or doing more for God. Whenever something must be accomplished before one can reach God, that one has false theology. Feeling, thinking, and doing do not come before God, period. Healing is God—no! God is healing—yes! The addicted must simply turn to Him. Each morning they must say, "Father, today I want You as my focus. Show me Your glory! You are my Creator and God! God is hope, God is love, God is help, God is health, God is all. Even if I spend my whole life without my emotions reaching God, God is greater." Every evening the afflicted put their heads on the pillow and say, "Without You, Father, I cannot exist. God is sleep, God is rest, God is peace, God is strength for tomorrow. Thank You, God!"

I will tell you something of my own life. For the last 40+ years my emotions have not confirmed that I am acceptable, loved, precious, forgiven, or good enough. But I no longer look for their confirmation; I have become a man of faith, and my life is much fuller than those who seek to whip up emotion, thoughts, and activity for God. I listen to Him, not to what a fallen body would tell me. To walk in faith is true theology.

How do we help the emotionally hurting? First, we put our trust in God alone, for we cannot lead where we have not been. We do not take responsibility that is not ours. Second, we wait on God, communicating gently to the hurting at every opportunity, "You have a God." The value of this truth is not hindered by mental collapse or medication, for man's spirit was made for just such truth; it can sink into his spirit no matter what his condition.

A question often surfaces about whether some, without doubt, could be helped by medication. The argument is between whether depression causes a chemical imbalance or whether the imbalance causes depression. I believe the former. However, one can be depressed for extended periods to the point that he cannot move past the focus of depression. In this condition, there is nothing "unspiritual" about taking medication, as long it is kept in mind that if the chemical imbalance is the true source, there should be some immediate results. If not, I would question continuing the medication. Doctors are from the Lord to minister to the body, but it is of no value for anyone to become a human guinea pig for them in their quest to understand what does not work!

DAY 154
Intimacy

For the crooked man is an abomination to the Lord, but
He is intimate with the upright.

—PROVERBS 3:32

To me, intimacy is one of the most misunderstood terms used as it relates to God and others. So many want intimacy with another. As I have said many times, we stand and fall on our definitions, and for most, intimacy has some element of the sexual attached to their definition. I have known believers caught up in an affair, and more often than not they will describe their "wonderful" experience as an intimacy they had never known before. For them intimacy is a connection in mind, will, and emotions that culminates in some sort of physical act.

However, intimacy properly defined exists in its purest form with God. God knows you intimately, and you are safe with Him. You can tell Him anything without fear of rejection. Safety with God is something to be valued, for how many people do you know that you can tell absolutely anything to, even your most absurd thoughts, and still be safe? Who do you know that upon clearly seeing your foibles will not utter a single judgment? Who do you know that does not secretly delight when your failure proves correct their opinion of you? "God is not a man," "God is love," and you are completely safe with Him. In Him is intimacy not found between humans. Intimacy requires safety, and there is no safer place than in the lap of perfect love. Your challenge is for the intimacy to run both ways. God was intimate with Job and Job with God. Once you are intimate with God, you cannot perceive that anything, no matter how it appears, can come to you in the form of harm.

Job simply said this, "The Lord gave and the Lord has taken away. Blessed be the name of the Lord" (Job 1:21). He could not conceive of God's doing something bad to him; intimacy does not allow for that. I have often acknowledged that I have no enemies because I have no enemies. I would have to perceive an enemy in my heart to actually have one. Two must agree on being enemies. I would have to perceive God as doing something bad to me before I could call something bad, and our intimacy does not allow me to do that. I am safe with Him, and therefore whatever comes from His heart to my life through intimacy is good. A man in Borneo related many terrible things that had happened to him and concluded by saying, "See how much God loves me? He would only allow such things if they were there to help me." In this man's heart of intimacy we see that nothing can be perceived as harmful. All of my actions, thoughts, failures, and stupidity are safe with God. I, despite of all these things, am safe. God is safe with me. Whatever His thoughts, His actions, pain or pleasure, He is safe with me. Intimacy does not question; it simply rests in a deep love that is safe.

DAY 155
Invisible Strings

And all in the synagogue were filled with rage as they heard these things.

 —LUKE 4:28

Jesus was giving a few illustrations from the Old Testament, and without warning the synagogue filled with rage. Have you ever had just such an experience? You are simply relating a few events from your life, when the one to whom you are speaking fills with anger! It was never your intent to enrage, and yet for some reason what you said on a scale of one to ten is a one for you but a ten to the other person. Why? Often the heart of man is trapped in an invisible web with hundreds of threads running to past events, ideas, hurts, and perceptions. We can inadvertently make a statement that pulls an invisible string attached to something other than what we think we are talking about.

Imagine a cup sitting on the table before you that is attached to your clothing by a string only you can see, and if the cup is moved at all, your clothing will drop off. When a person reaches for the cup, you will begin to scream at him for fear of what will happen. Of course, this totally unexpected reaction will be received with amazement by the unsuspecting person.

Many words, when mentioned, might pull at invisible strings to the heart, such as: married, single, suffering, death, children, material blessing, or doctrines. When conversing we should ask, "Why?" if there is a reaction—rather than a response—to what we said. Husbands and wives can attach motives to the words of their mates that often do not exist. Sometimes rage is inescapable, but if we do not counter a reaction with our own reaction, but rather respond in the love of Christ, we can usually discover why the other person is reacting and hopefully move past any misunderstanding.

One fellow often says, "I know what I am saying; I just do not know what you are hearing." I have found it valuable to begin an observation with a precursory statement: "Before I say anything, I first want to explain what I am not saying. I am not saying you are worthless, a failure, a no-hoper, a terrible mate, stupid, or that you have not grown in the Lord before you talked to me." It is important to use our time dialoguing about the real, not perceived, issues. As we listen, there can be actual discussion rather than debate.

DAY 156
Is It a Miracle, Magic, Or Flesh?

Do you not believe that I am in the Father, and the Father is in me? The words that I say to you I do not speak on My own initiative, but the Father abiding in Me does His works. Believe Me that I am in the Father, and the Father is in Me; otherwise believe on account of the works themselves. Truly, truly, I say to you, he who believes in Me, the works that I do shall he do also; and greater works than these shall he do; because I go to the Father.

—JOHN 14:10-12

A friend has a video of himself hypnotized and clucking on a stage like a chicken. I watched a magician as he hypnotized a whole group picked at random off the street. He told them they had just seen a flying saucer land and he was going to interview them. It was quite funny listening to the interviews. Charles Finney, being questioned over his dramatic techniques used to get people involved in meetings, responded that if someone could find a better way than his to get people coming, he would use it.

Just flick around the odd television stations and there you will see a variety of Christian expressions. In one night you might see screaming, strutting, people making animal sounds, uncontrolled laughter, and a variety of manifestations proclaimed to be of God. I know if I make a judgment and say those believers are deceived, I am in trouble. First, I am in trouble for judging if I am wrong. Second, I am in trouble if I am right, for God may turn to me and say, "Why is it you are not deceived? Who has kept you from being deceived?" Those who have an experience generally think less of those who have not, and those who have not think less of those who have. The debate over what is legitimate and what is deception has caused and continues to cause division in the family of God.

There is confusion over experience and its manifestations. Is it God, magic, or the flesh? I do not want to address the question; rather, I want to address the confusion. Not that I am judge. I understand that ultimately what I think does not matter. Not only does it not matter, but also God is listening to all my idle words. I know and respect many believers who have had some very interesting experiences. How can I keep from being confused? It is one thing to question another's experience, but quite another to have to question one's own. That causes real conflict.

If I do not want to be confused over a miracle—if I do not want to be left wondering if my experience is of God, magic, or the flesh—I should not seek the miracles and experiences that Satan, the flesh, or magic could imitate. The magicians duplicated the miracles Moses had performed. If we seek the same miracles the world seeks and then we have the experience, we will naturally be left questioning. I see so many things on TV I have also seen in various parts of the pagan world, the exact same manifestations. I am not saying the source is the same; I am saying the expression is the same. A Christian carpenter, it is said, drives a nail the same way an unbelieving carpenter does: same action, different sources. I see why people have doubts when they have similar experiences to occurrences in the unbelieving pagan world. Personally, I do not want that kind of confusion, so I have decided to pursue those experiences and miracles which Satan, the flesh, and magic want nothing to do with, miracles the enemy and flesh will avoid at all costs, miracles that will not confuse me; I will know it is God at work.

Let me give a few examples. I am sitting in my office pouting over a perceived offense. I seek God for a miracle. "Father, I am small, I cannot love; I invite You to come be my love." I get up, go in the other room, and love. Not I, but Christ in me. Another time I am invited to speak but am informed as I get up to speak I have only three minutes in which to say something. "Father, I need a miracle. My spirit is so bad that I just want to leave. I am angry with that man for not letting me share with this group as planned." Next God comes, and what comes out is the best three-minute sermon I could ever have imagined giving. The pastor and I become friends. Another time my family member is sick, and I know it will last for a while. "Father, come to me, give me Your strength, encourage me!" He does. Then there are the countless experiences of finding out a sin which once plagued me has just dropped off. Not one of these miracles have a hint of confusion in them. They are far greater miracles than those the world can duplicate, and they are miracles with which Satan and the flesh want nothing to do.

Jesus fed the masses and was soon being followed because of it. Food made people confuse Him with a political leader. They were interested in Him for worldly reasons. He began to feed the people with a greater miracle, the living Word. Food doling could be duplicated, but the feeding of the living Word, which burned in their hearts, could not. If we seek and receive miracles that cannot be duplicated, nor would they want to be duplicated by the enemy, we will have peace, not confusion.

DAY 157
Is Jesus All I Need?

Jesus answered, "I am the way, and the truth, and the life."
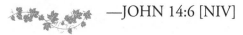
—JOHN 14:6 [NIV]

Consistently, each day since I accepted Jesus, I have been told that Jesus is not all I need. I was told all the way through Bible College and Seminary that Jesus was not enough; we needed to know Greek, Hebrew, the context of the gospels, history, archeology, and more. Jesus was not enough. Christian counseling often allows Freud to say more than Jesus; with just Jesus—so the contention goes—we would not be able to see emotions, marriages, or struggles healed. Nearly every day in my office or on the phone I am told of how the presenting problem is bigger than Jesus. It was not any different in the Campus ministry groups. One man came who was an "intellectual" believer. He could prove Jesus. Jesus was not enough; we needed the facts.

Do you believe that Jesus is all you need? It could well be that today, when the emphasis in the Church has so long been on what we need outside of Jesus, you may not know what Jesus did, who Jesus is, what He accomplished, or how the Jesus you read about actually lives in you. He wants to live through you as the Father lived through Him, and Jesus is really all you need.

It is the spirit of religion we are fighting, the additions that get hung onto Jesus until who He is actually gets forgotten. Today there is more understanding of what He is not than what He is. Some groups of believers I have been around for nearly thirty years know no more about Jesus than the day they accepted Him. Instead, as new waves of experiences or special knowledge come in, they have consistently embraced each new addition to Jesus. They are experts in the additions, but they could not explain the basics. How did Jesus conquer sin, death, hell, and captivity? How did He overcome the world in His flesh? What is His body and blood? How could He live in me? How is He released through me? What does it mean to hear He is Prophet, Priest, King, Leader, Guide,

Life, Lord, Mediator, and Peace? I am convinced and will not budge from the fact that Jesus is all I need! Jesus is all I need, He is all you need, and we will not rest until we know the One who called us.

DAY 158
Is Your Child Living In Sin With a "Partner"?

I wrote you in my letter not to associate with immoral people; I did not at all mean with the immoral people of this world, or with the covetous and swindlers, or with idolaters; for then you would have to go out of the world. But actually, I wrote to you not to associate with any so-called brother if he should be an immoral person, or covetous, or an idolater, or a reviler, or a drunkard, or a swindler—not even to eat with such a one. For what have I to do with judging outsiders? Do you not judge those who are within the church?

 —I CORINTHIANS 5:9-12

Paul basically said this: "We are to stay away from believers who sin but not away from sinners who sin." The topic in this article would have been unthinkable just forty years ago, and now it would appear to be the norm, although taking into consideration the media's proclivity toward pressing the concept of a norm that in fact exists only rarely. First, the Christian parents must establish that the situation is not all about them. Too many Christian couples have their identity tied up in the behavior of the children. When a child reaches the age of accountability, his choices do not absolutely reflect on the parents. Historically the Jews had a practice of beating a father if a child under age thirteen committed a wrongful act, but after age thirteen, the child received the punishment. Many parents do deserve beatings, in that their behavior has created monsters. I remember a counseling session wherein the parents told me they put cookies on the steps to their child's bedroom to get him to go to bed at night. Once the child entered his room, still eating the trail of cookies, the door was shut, thereby forcing the child to sleep. Imagine a young child so out of control. Amen.

The child who is grown up is making his own decisions. There is a Way and a "not the Way," and sometimes out of the freedom of choice God has given him, he has decided to choose what is not the Way and move in with a "partner." This has nothing to do with the parents who have never expressed any type of assent for such behavior, so why all the embarrassment? Could it be that the parents have a bit of image tied up in the child, and all of their boasting about him in the past is coming back to haunt them? Virtually all parents have done the same thing, wanting to put the most positive twist on their children's behavior. Again, it is not about the parents but God's working in the child's life.

I was speaking in South Africa about homosexuality in a manner that, in my opinion, was a balanced view. A pastor came up after the teaching and said, "I gave nearly the exact sermon one year ago to my church of 2,000, and today I am unemployed."

I responded, "Yes, and let me tell you who ran you out of the church: the mothers of all the gays."

He looked shocked and said, "Yes! But why?"

"Their identity is foremost in their children, not in Christ. They choose their mothering instinct over God. You were sunk when you said anything negative to mothers who have their identity tied up in their children. Criticizing the child seemed tantamount to condemning the mother, and hence the forceful reaction."

Remember, there are no second-generation believers. God must bring the situations forcing a child to choose. You have very little to do with that. In short, get over your pride and glory, move out of the way, and let God work!

Having said all that, what are we to do when we see a child living in sin? As in every area of life when we do not know where to go or where to hide, we must hide in the truth, for there we will find Christ, the Truth. Tell the truth to your child about how living with the opposite sex (outside of marriage) or the same sex is sin, period. It is not your judgment but the judgment of God. Too many parents make sin comfortable for their children, but any time the easy way is chosen today, a harder choice will be waiting ahead for later. Choose the easy way and one day the child will stand before God with no mother or father interceding, and when God speaks, no one speaks back. If I hear the following statement one more time, I think I will go mad. "Well, our daughter is living with a man, and we have decided just to LOVE them." Let us put that statement in perspective. What one really is saying is, "I am attached to my child more than I am attached to God. I could not stand to lose the child, so I am playing the 'love' card to keep him near and to keep the Bible from judging my passive participation in his sin, which will condemn him." A very worldly progression of reasoning goes something like this: "God is love. Love is unconditional. Love is acceptance. Acceptance is unconditional. If you do not accept the behavior, you do not love and are a person of hate." No! God is love, period, not "unconditional" love, which puts an addition to love. No, God is love. Love is why the world is not destroyed. I have a hard time wrapping my head around this, but God does love a pedophile, for the center of love is not a behavior but our God. Wow! However, God's acceptance is separate from love. He does not accept all behavior, and one behavior that is anti-God is living with someone other than a spouse. There are too many "ifs" in the Bible. God is love, period. He will be Love to every sinner until the end of that one's days. He is not unconditional acceptance. People do go to hell.

So what is there to do if a child is living with another? We tell him it is sin on several levels. Males and females are experiencing something meant to be reserved for marriage. Paul even says that one would offend his brother by having sex with someone he is not going to marry. Gays are experiencing something stupid. Yes, yes, I know all the causes, and I work on that level with Christians who struggle in order to support them. As I said to a Christian leader who struggled with homosexuality, "I would rather struggle with the temptation of homosexuality and be driven to Christ in humility and brokenness than never to struggle." Those persons are much different from the ones actively engaging in those acts and believing them to be the way. We are never to judge, for only the judgments of the Lord are true, and He has made His judgment that fornication and homosexuality are sin. We stand with Him and confront our loved ones with the Truth. Next, we must treat them as we would any other couple living in sin. We would treat them like our neighbors who are living in sin. We love, we share, we are available, and we do not reject them. Remember, though, we must always tell the truth as mentioned above. Truth can make others cut themselves off from us; we do not cut ourselves off from sinners. I say this to help prepare for the day we might be cut off because of telling our children the truth.

Again, Love is not unconditional. Love is love; do not add a term to it. Acceptance is conditional. Many refuse the sword brought by the Lord by saying what sounds so very spiritual, "We are just going to love our gay son." Yes, we must love all or the love of God is not in us. However, we should never allow love to be used as an excuse to accept a wicked behavior. Tell the truth and let truth land where it will. Many well-meaning and hurting parents have accepted their children, but they cannot act in love while accepting behaviors that kill a person. It will not work. Love the person and do not accept the sin. Love and acceptance are two words that have been blended for the sake of compromise. I have been amazed at the demands made by children that their behavior and decisions be accepted. No! They must bend and accept our convictions in Christ. When coming to your home, they are not to sleep together, the "gay" (my, what a fabrication that term is) couple is not invited to Christmas to gaze at each other in lust, hold hands, and make the rest of the family miserable as they press their deceptive point of having found happiness. Kill the snake in the egg. If they want to come to your house, they will sleep in separate bedrooms, and overt sin is not tolerated. After all, it is your home. In all this, the love of God comes. It is good for a child to know that when he is sinning, the parents disapprove. It takes a good bit out of the "passing pleasure" of sin. Remember, God gave the fulfillment of the law when He gave His Son. In a like manner, we can clarify the law through offering the Son. Do not be undone, for God is at work.

DAY 159
Is Your Conversion Normal?

If you confess with your mouth Jesus as Lord,
and believe in your heart that God raised
Him from the dead, you shall be saved.

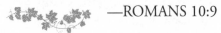

—ROMANS 10:9

I was reading an old devotional book; in it the author maintained he had found exactly what I have found, that there are two ways of entering into Christ. One is through an explosion with lots of fireworks that was preceded by depression, anxiety, and/or a severe breaking. The other involves coming into Christ slowly, methodically, through understanding that made the journey from head to heart over a period of time. It was noted that those who come to Christ slowly can rarely tell the exact day and hour they gave up on themselves and accepted Christ; however, their lives prove just such a thing has occurred.

Of these two methods of coming into Christ, the explosion is most often considered normal and desirable, so those who gradually grew into faith are left wondering if they really do know Christ as well as others. The most interesting note in the devotion was that in a survey, 60% of believers came to Christ the slower way while 40% came by way of the explosion. There is nothing wrong with either entrance, the important point being that a person did enter into life in Christ. Those who have never had the explosion need not waste time waiting for one, when they are in the majority and can simply press on in Him!

DAY 160
It Is a Miserable Life

He had his dwelling among the tombs. And no one was able to bind him anymore, even with a chain; because he had often been bound with shackles and chains, and the chains had been torn apart by him and the shackles broken in pieces, and no one was strong enough to subdue him. Constantly, night and day, he was screaming among the tombs and in the mountains, and gashing himself with stones.

 —MARK 5:3-5

Have you ever wondered what the day-by-day life of a demon is like? We often read the story of the demoniac in Mark 5 and relate it to the demons' recognition of Jesus, the miraculous deliverance, or the hardhearted people who would rather have illegal pigs than Jesus. However, something else can be gleaned from the story: insight into the life of a demon. They were many and therefore "strong," yet they were confined to living in tombs among the dead.

They did not have a dwelling place among the living. Also, we learn that day and night they cry and gash themselves. Obviously, they are in constant pain. Somewhat like a fish out of water, they were made for heaven but chose a pit; they hate the pit and yet now it is all they are suited for. Therefore, they surface into an environment (earth) held together by Jesus, which makes the whole world hostile to them. How can earth be comfortable for a demon? This is why we find them among the rocks, where there is less of creation, less of Jesus, to witness to them. Why would they choose to be here? Suffering on earth, with their sworn enemy, Jesus, is better than being with their leader in hell.

DAY 161
It Is All Dirt!

Brethren, I do not regard myself as having laid hold of it yet; but one thing I do: forgetting what lies behind and reaching forward to what lies ahead, I press on toward the goal for the prize of the upward call of God in Christ Jesus.

 —PHILIPPIANS 3:13, 14

One friend, a bit of a cowboy, has a way with words and will often paint a verbal picture that leaves me thinking for days. One day we were discussing our pasts. He made an interesting observation. "One day I started to dig into my past. I dug fifty feet and hit dirt. At one hundred feet I also hit dirt. At two hundred, dirt again, until finally I reached a depth of seven hundred feet, still dirt. I quit, figuring no matter how deep I went it would just be dirt." Well, amen!

Is that not really what examining the past is like? We never hit anything but dirt! The past has died and decomposed. It is the enemy who would have us believe there is something in our past, when uncovered, that would produce great release today, when in fact it is an elaborate scheme to steal the present. That is the enemy's job, to steal the present, for the present holds the key to the future. Steal the present and the future is his, too.

Many times I have sat and listened to believers as they talked about what it is like to be out of God's presence and fellowship, how they miss it, why they miss it, and what happened to precipitate their losing it. The whole discussion is a waste of time, for every moment the problem is being analyzed, it is allowed to continue. Analyzing the problem is actually feeding the problem. Stop analyzing the past and seize the present. He is as close as the words in our mouth. Call out to Him and stop wasting time; He is there. Jesus took care of it all; everything else is just dirt.

DAY 162
I Want To Sin and I Want To Be Forgiven!

Jesus answered them, "Truly, truly, I say to you, everyone who commits sin is the slave of sin. And the slave does not remain in the house forever; the son does remain forever. If therefore the Son shall make you free, you shall be free indeed."

—JOHN 8:34-36

What a place this is to live and what a state to be in when a person is pleading for forgiveness and yet knowing he will give himself willingly to the very same sin that evening, in the afternoon, in the morning, or the very next second. This is the man who is divided and unstable in all his ways ("But let him ask in faith without any doubting for the one who doubts is like the surf of the sea driven and tossed by the wind. For let not that man expect that he will receive anything from the Lord, being a double-minded man, unstable in all his ways," James 1:6-8). Many are waiting for people like this to be judged, which may come, but what could those waiting do to them that is worse than what they do to themselves? Paul described the struggle as doing the very thing he did not want to do; however, he was obviously doing it. Many could exercise their freedom from something, but it does not take much discernment to see they really do not want to walk away from the advantages they think they have where they are at and in what they are doing. It is just easier to beat themselves up, promise they will do better, and keep going.

They are already free because Christ is their life. We believers are always in the struggle of agreement. He has set us free from everything, even overeating, yet we refuse to accept the freedom and choose instead to work for it. Sometimes I think we prefer the work and the defeat because it allows us to continue in the way we are. The doctor said to me, "You are twenty pounds overweight, technically obese." I was so hurt and upset as I ate my ice cream that night! I said to the doctor, "Yes, I am twenty pounds overweight and here is why." He leaned forward to hear my answer, which was, "Because I want to be!" Could there be any other reason? Well, maybe the cause for this could be a thyroid or something gone wild in the body or a vile medication. But generally speaking, we are what we are because we choose it. We also choose to beat ourselves up over it, because there is no compulsion and not enough compunction to change.

I was happy to hear the report from a friend who was free from porn. He said to me, "Twenty years ago I told you my problem. All you said is that I was free and I would quit when I wanted to. You were right! One day I woke up and quit. I threw it all out of the house, and I feel wonderful." Amen. He was always free but did not really want it until the perfect time. Paul said that the one who would deliver him would be Jesus.

You are delivered but not ready to experience it. The best plan is to admit it to God. Period. Honestly, He sees you, and what motive of the heart can you hide from Him? "If we confess our sins, He is faithful and righteous to forgive us our sins and to cleanse us from all unrighteousness" –I John 1:9.

DAY 163
Joy Of Giving

"Bring the whole tithe into the storehouse, that there may be food in my house. Test me in this," says the Lord Almighty, "and see if I will not throw open the floodgates of heaven and pour out so much blessing that you will not have room enough for it."

 —MALACHI 3:10 [NIV]

Many are disciplined to pray and read but have not developed the discipline of giving. In short, they act stingy, not giving as it has been given unto them. As believers, our new inner nature includes the desire to share and give, and this desire is further developed in our fellowship with God, where His gifts are recognized and we cannot help but give in response.

Too many believers privately keep records of how many lunches they have bought, how much free time they have given, how many miles they have driven, and how many phone calls they have made without compensation. They keep track of how much money they are out. This is bondage! Freely we receive, so we can freely give! Our life does not hinge on a lunch or a gallon of gasoline! The lack of freedom and joy in giving nullifies the witness of prayer and reading.

DAY 164
Judgment and Poverty

First of all, then, I urge that entreaties and prayers, petitions and thanksgivings, be made on behalf of all men, for kings and all who are in authority, in order that we may lead a tranquil and quiet life in all godliness and dignity.

—I TIMOTHY 2:1, 2

In the Old Testament, poverty is seen as the judgment of God and a tool of God. Where there is poverty the people are to seek Him. He does not cause it; men walking in their way, despising The Way, are the cause. However, repentance and turning to Him is the answer. I am in many poor countries and always find corruption at the top that trickles down to poverty at the bottom. The moralist can try to give something at the bottom and yet will discover that neither they nor any they know have enough money to fix the bottom. Something needs to happen at the top. Who can effect change at the top? Only God can do in an instant what reform, riots, demonstrations, and international pressure try to do in a lifetime. If corrupt man sees God, he will change. Every leader of a poor country has exactly the country he wants. It is wicked and only the Almighty can touch such leaders. "Pray for those in authority."

DAY 165
Just An Old Dog?

"For My hand made all these things, thus all these things came into being," declares the Lord. "But to this one I will look, to him who is humble and contrite of spirit, and who trembles at My word."

 —ISAIAH 66:2

An old dog of mine has been around a long time. I remember what he was like when he was young. As soon as the garage door or gate was left open, he disappeared. On more than one occasion he even went home with strangers. I have spent a lot of time looking for that dog. I always had to walk him with a leash, for he loved to fight. His frequent barking in the middle of the night could drive any sane man over the edge. Much changed in the last couple of years as old age finally caught up with him. He can barely hear, is constantly down in the back, and his kidneys are gone. However, the instant I get close enough for him to make out it is me, his whole body begins to move, his ears perk up, and he wants to go with me. Our walks together are only about one-third the distance they used to be, but I no longer need a leash; he no longer pays attention to dogs or strangers, and he never leaves my side. Often he lags behind, and I have to wait for him; however, if I simply reach over and touch him, his energy resurges and he walks close to me. I can see that life has taught him a few lessons I was never able to. I think it would have been nice had he always stayed by my side, not listening to strangers or running off, but I probably appreciate him more now. I feel important knowing that in his broken condition and pain he chooses to walk beside me.

Once in India while gazing at a cow that appeared to be running wild, I asked my Indian brothers, "Who owns the cow; how does it get home?" The reply came with a slight laugh, "Michael, man is the only creature that does not know its master." Life will teach us all who the Master is, and though He must wait until our condition is broken, He enjoys our fellowship.

DAY 166
Keep Your Eyes On Jesus

I discipline my body and make it my slave, so that, after I
have preached to others, I myself will not be disqualified.

—I CORINTHIANS 9:27

The woman said to Him, "Sir, give me this water, so I will
not be thirsty nor come all the way here to draw."

He said to her, "Go, call your husband and come here."

The woman answered and said, "I have no husband."

Jesus said to her, "You have correctly said, 'I have no
husband'; for you have had five husbands, and the one whom
you now have is not your husband; this you have said truly."

—JOHN 4:15-18

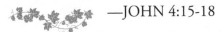

One can imagine that the hot topic of the day would
have been all the husbands this woman had. However,
Jesus brings it up, lets her know that He knows, kills the
topic, and moves to the real topic. In short, to the Master
her topic was boring.

May I be so bold as to say something true? Your life of
sin is boring, really, really boring. The Lord is actually tired
of the topic, and can you blame Him? If I had to think of
you all day, I would be bored, too.

A man was telling me of his truly horrific childhood, and
really, those who participated in his pain deserve death.
However, at the end I asked this question, "Have you told
this story to many counselors?"

His answer, "Oh, there have been very many, since I am trying to get in touch with my pain!"

At that, I responded, "Boring, all boring!" I really meant it. If rolling in the past helped, he would have been helped years ago. In reality, the past was keeping him from a glorious NOW! I see clearly what Paul meant when he said he "disciplines his body." It is not discipline as the legalists view it, for holiness is something given, not worked for. Instead, it is a discipline of not letting the center of one's life shift from Jesus to something else.

The flesh is amazing in its attempt to have control. It will use even the TV. All I have to do is watch a report I do not agree with, next I am thinking I know better, and the end result is a self-centered Mike, not a Christ-centered Mike. All I have to do is think about how stupid it is to be searched at the airport and what I would like to tell those workers, and what happens next is I am in the flesh and not Christ-centered. I am getting bored with Mike, really, really bored. I can be reflecting on praise I heard or mulling over condemnation, comparing what was said to what could have been said, avoiding sin or actively finding it, or I can be judging the carnality of others or participating in my own. The flesh does not care, just so it is the focus and can remain active. See? I am boring. I am bored with myself. I want to keep my eyes on Jesus; He is never boring.

Whether we think about how special we are or how ordinary, how intelligent or how stupid, or how spiritual or how carnal, either way the flesh reigns and our eyes are off the Beloved. It is a fight, a discipline, to keep the mind on Jesus, to know more and more of Him.

DAY 167
Keeping Your Wits About Sin and Forgiveness

If we confess our sins, He is faithful and righteous to forgive us our sins and to cleanse us from all unrighteousness. If we say that we have not sinned, we make Him a liar and His word is not in us.

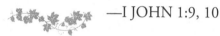

—I JOHN 1:9, 10

We understand the world's constant desire to maintain a trend toward redefining sin, but among believers it is disturbing to watch. Some parents regard homosexuality as sin until they discover they have a child engaged in it. That their special child is practicing it somehow legitimizes it. Baffling! Divorce is sin until a relative or friend gets one; arguments are then made for the "practicalities" of life. Sex outside of marriage has nearly become a foregone conclusion. Then there are the "minor" sins constantly being redefined. "It was just a white lie." Exactly what is the difference between a white lie and a "black" lie? Believers who redefine sin to fit their situation are most often labeled as hypocritical by people whose lives have not yet been touched by such "realities" of this life. Consequently, those who have yet to encounter a divorce in their families are the most vocal against it, and they will even saddle the innocuous former spouse with the responsibility to stay single until the adulterous and remarried mate returns. The legalist is so vocal about sin and yet so quiet when it comes to the topic of forgiveness. Well, as someone who has sinned, I have discovered I do not have to redefine, avoid, or wallow in my failures. "We all stumble in many ways," and that is a fact. Jesus sweat blood conquering the fleshly body; do we really think He believes we can conquer it? Only Christ living through us conquers the body of flesh, and none of us abide perfectly. We have all experienced defeat. Prioritizing the deeds of the flesh into categories of being worse or better is merely boasting in the flesh. We are called not to redefine sin, avoid it, or wallow in it, but to confess it. After all, there is no forgiveness for proudly living an alternative lifestyle, but there is for sin. If there were no forgiveness for sin, I could understand the desire to redefine it. However, since there is forgiveness for sin, there is no need to call it anything but what it is. The world redefines sin because the natural man wants not forgiveness but full participation in sin. In that case, those redefining sin do not have Christ and have a worse problem than their sin; they should move to the greater (Christ), laying aside the lesser (sin). It will do no good to convince them of their sin if they do not have forgiveness. The Bible is clear about there being forgiveness in Christ for every sin. If we had all done things differently, we would not have sinned. We did not, we did, and He forgives us. We are commanded to "press on toward the goal for the prize of the upward call of God in Christ Jesus" (Philippians 3:14).

Listen, if you have had an affair, practiced lying, been involved in homosexuality, had a divorce, or whatever, do not let others make you focus on it, and do not fall into the trap of justification. Just confess it and get on! Forgiveness settles the whole issue in an instant. Anyway, what is worse, the continual focus on a failure or the neglected focus on Him?

The Bible acknowledges the weaknesses of man's flesh. But all hope is in Him. Many times we hear brothers and sisters talk of the one sin that plagues them and always returns. Actually, there is one sin, only one sin that is manifested in a thousand variations. That one sin is allowing ourselves to give inner resources and attention to something other than Christ.

DAY 168
Kingdoms

Look at the birds of the air, that they do not sow, neither do they reap, nor gather into barns, and yet your heavenly Father feeds them.

But seek first His kingdom and His righteousness, and all these things will be added to you.

 —MATTHEW 6:26 & 33

I remember some years ago being visited by a man I greatly respect in international ministry. After spending the morning together, we said goodbye and Sam Jones left the office. Shortly afterward he returned, opened my door, and said, "One last thing, never build a kingdom." There has often been a little voice to whisper that admonition to me, "Never build a kingdom."

On one occasion when I visited a medieval castle I was struck by the thought of a castle's beginnings. One farmer enjoys farming, enjoyment leads to success, success brings more income, and extra income enables the building of a larger and larger home until it becomes the envy of enemies. To protect the home larger walls must be built, and even friends might be held suspect as they desire to warm their hands at a fire they did not build. The more indefensible the castle appears, the more others outside the walls want it, while those inside the walls have to be convinced to protect it. In the end all time is spent protecting the castle instead of doing the one thing most loved, farming. The ethics of a hardworking, nature-loving farmer give way to the rules and politics of a castle. Instead of enjoying the world God made all around, the man-made world becomes the focus and causes various forms of neuroses that are passed down to the children's children until all is in ruin. Sam's words returned, "Never build a kingdom!"

We believers must be careful not to give our hearts to what others have built, placed on a high hill, and then exalted above our lowly state, lest we, like the peasants, move inside the walls and give our all to protect it. What we have outside the walls in the field is something far greater than a kingdom! We have a King who has set up a kingdom in our hearts and reigns there. In His kingdom we are given some very significant commands. "Casting all your anxiety upon Him, because He cares for you" (I Peter 5:7). "Consider the lilies, how they grow; they neither toil nor spin; but I tell you, even Solomon in all his glory did not clothe himself like one of these" (Luke 12:27).

I do not want a kingdom; I only want Him. I do not want the life inside the walls; I want the life outside where everything proclaims Him.

DAY 169
Knowing The Difference

*But you must not eat from the tree of the knowledge of
good and evil, for when you eat of it you will surely die.*

—GENESIS 2:17

"Mike, how can you say that we do not know the difference between good and evil when God has told us what is good and what is evil?" Well, I said we do not know the difference; I did not say God did not know the difference. God alone does know the difference. When He tells me something is evil, then it is evil, or if good, then it is good; I must yield and obey. But on my own I do not know what is good and what is evil. When I see something God has not said is either good or evil, I am not to make the judgment. If I do, I will miss it.

For example, I have a flat tire. Does God say a flat is good or evil? No, He is silent. Therefore, if I make a judgment, I will get it wrong. I must just see God, say amen, and rest in Him. This is faith. What if I have the flat to keep me from getting to a place in the road where I will be killed? What if I had it to reveal to me the true condition of my flesh, and I angrily begin to yell? What if I had it because He has someone He would like to help me? You see, I do not know good from evil.

DAY 170
Knowing What Does Not Work

*Therefore what benefit were you then deriving from the
things of which you are now ashamed?
For the outcome of those things is death.*

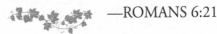

—ROMANS 6:21

In essence, Paul asks a great, pertinent question, "What did you gain from it all?" At the end of the day, what did we gain from our behavior? We are beginning to learn what does not work, such as the rollercoaster of self-loathing, producing only a self we hate. What have we gained from obsessing on hurts caused by those we love and the constant replaying of this or that offense? What have we won from recounting a disagreement or the slander of another, even if for argument's sake we are right? Remember three things.

1) We are to hold a crown above those we perceive to be beneath us so that they might even rise above us.

2) We cannot judge another slave of the Master.

3) We have not changed one hair white or black on our own head, so what do we think we will do for others?

It is time to move beyond the obsession with self or others and begin to consider the One, Jesus, who will bring a lift to our spirit.

"Set your mind on the things above, not on the things that are on earth," Colossians 3:2.

"Finally, brethren, whatever is true, whatever is honorable, whatever is right, whatever is pure, whatever is lovely, whatever is of good repute, if there is any excellence and if anything worthy of praise, let your mind dwell on these things," Philippians 4:8.

We do not ever get boring to Him, but we should realize that our little worlds and the drivel do get boring!

DAY 171
Knowing Your Call

Of this church I was made a minister according to the stewardship from God bestowed on me for your benefit, that I might fully carry out the preaching of the word of God.

—COLOSSIANS 1:25

The Apostle was very clear on what the call of God was for him. Yet many believers are unsure as to what they are to be doing. The confusion over their "call" is compounded by the onslaught of writings that purport to help believers discover their call. Just as an employer does not hire people when he has no idea what job he has for them, I would assume that God is not hiding from His children the call He has on their lives. I have discovered through my interaction with believers that before they can understand a "call," they must have a clear understanding of the purpose of the Christian life. If I were to take one digit out of someone's phone number and place it at the end of the number, the whole thing would be so out of order that I could never use the number to call the person. In God's order we must first know the purpose of our lives.

His goal is the revelation of Christ in us, and once our goal in life also becomes the revelation of Christ within, we will see that these two purposes meet perfectly in our unique sets of circumstances. From working in the yard to working in the corporate world, our life's goal and His goal remain consistent, the revelation of Christ.

We have all had friends for whom nothing seemed to work out; they always have a broken car and are in financial straits, and though amply qualified, they never get the good job. In the past I was vexed over that, but no longer! Once I could see the purpose of life, I could see how God had permitted them to be placed in situations that would best aid their advance into the great revelation of Christ. Therefore, we first define the goal of life, which will be expressed uniquely through every individual. I believe this is what many people define as a "call." On the Vine we are branches witnessing to other branches to the very same Life that flows in all of us.

I have said several times, "There are no great speakers; there are only great audiences able to respond to the message." Perhaps God has not spoken ahead of time into the hearts of the other branches; in that case, a speaker's attempts to witness to a message that is not in the listeners will not bear fruit. I was visiting a church in Asia where many of the men had taken mistresses. The pastor had chosen the topic on which I was to speak: prayer. It is a beautiful topic, but it was not where the Vine was speaking to the other branches. If I had the "call" of God to teach prayer, this was not the time, and we must be sensitive to our call.

It is very simple for a believer to determine what his call is. It is that which, when witnessed to by the leading of the Vine, creates a divine explosion in others. The secret is that since the life flows through the Vine, when there is an explosion in the receiver branches, there is an equal explosion in the witness branch! I am always telling people things they already know, for God has placed it in them. Yet when I see a spark in the eyes concerning the indwelling Christ, the love of God, the sufficiency of Jesus, and the hope we have in Him, I never know who gets more excited! For the explosion, by way of the Vine, is taking place in me, also. In short, the "call" is the work of God that is witnessed to and is exciting to a believer as he shares it. "Calls" are different. Paul makes this point to the Corinthians. We are all different members of one body, one Vine. In our "calls" we do not compete with the other branches but complete the work God has for all of us to do.

DAY 172
Laws, Laws, and More Laws

Saul was in hearty agreement with putting him to death. And on that day a great persecution arose against the church in Jerusalem; and they were all scattered throughout the regions of Judea and Samaria, except the apostles.

 —ACTS 8:1

It is said that every year in the U.S. over 50,000 new laws are passed, including local, state, and federal, but not including all the covenants that are passed. Why so many laws? First, the government would like a law to replace the conscience of man. The government believes in abortion.

How can there be abortion without a hardening of the heart? (That being said, I have met many who found that the intellectual argument for an abortion they underwent could not override their heart. For those, there has been repentance, forgiveness, restoration, and a moving on in Christ.) If conscience is dulled in one area, it is likely to decline in another, which will require more legislation than was necessary when the conscience of the society was healthier. The second reason for the multiplication of laws will be revealed in the future. Persecution for the Christian is coming to America. That would have seemed impossible until recent decades, since Christianity is the foundation for the constitution and laws, which guarantee freedom of religion. Christians will not be put in jail for their Christianity; that would be too overt. Christians will be put in jail for some other vague law that will have been broken. It was a joke in the former Soviet Union, "We will put you in prison and find the law you broke later." However, when it happens, it is never a joke.

DAY 173
Legalism and Grace

I do not set aside the grace of God, for if righteousness could be gained through the law, Christ died for nothing!

 —GALATIANS 2:21 [NIV]

Legalists exercise no knowledge of grace. For example, a legalist can be in the middle of an affair or other overt sin and still preach the next Sunday on purity. Why? How? It is simple: Legalism feeds the flesh. Sin and legalism are one and the same. In a person's being there is no pressure of a contrast between legalism and sin, because unrighteousness and self-righteousness both satisfy the flesh. However, a grace man cannot go on sinning, for the grace of God will rip him in two. When preaching grace, God will always come for a man's words. In really understanding grace, he just does not have an excuse. Enter the cross! I have been crucified, I am dead to sin, and how then can I continue to sin? If I do, with this understanding, I will come apart. The standard is so much higher in grace. It is the legalist who can actually practice sin without conviction. Embrace the message of grace, practice sin, and you will be ripped in two!

DAY 174
Let God Be True!

May it never be! Rather, let God be found true, though every man be found a liar, as it is written, THAT YOU MAY BE JUSTIFIED IN YOUR WORDS, AND PREVAIL WHEN YOU ARE JUDGED.

—ROMANS 3:4

Once I was talking to a fellow who had been on the mission field for several years but had by then quit. I questioned why he had "retired" from missions, to which he explained that God had left him, no longer listened to him, did not answer him, and had even reportedly told the woman to whom he was engaged that she was not to marry him because he had been cut off! He then explained that he had done everything possible to win God back: witnessing, praying, Bible reading, and more, but alas, God was silent. I turned to the fellow, put my finger in his face, looked him straight in the eyes, and said, "You are a liar!"

"What? he exclaimed.

Once again I told him, "You are a liar!" He appeared to be quite startled. I then explained how tired I was of those who lie about God. "Let God be found true, though every man a liar." Everything he had said about God was a lie! God does not forsake, leave, refuse to listen to, or finally reject us. Romans 8:39, "nor height, nor depth, nor any other created thing, shall be able to separate us from the love of God, which is in Christ Jesus our Lord." When we judge our feelings and experiences against the truth of who God is, the truth must win. The longer we listen to a lie, the more entrenched the lie becomes.

This fellow had tried everything to get back into the presence and favor of God except for one thing; he never tried faith. Faith is what God desires of man; there is nothing we can give Him of value aside from faith. It is a precious jewel in the sight of God. Faith is the assurance of things hoped for and the conviction of things not yet seen. We give God this precious gift when, though not feeling or sensing His presence, we thank Him for His nearness. We must all stop lying. Yes, I know that everything God was "supposed to" do for others or for us He has not done. I know the experience of the defeated. But I know something true and better: He never leaves or forsakes me. If I believe this, in spite of circumstances, then I give Him what He desires, faith.

DAY 175
Let's All Just Suicide Out!

But if we walk in the Light as He Himself is in the Light,
we have fellowship with one another, and the blood of Jesus
His Son cleanses us from all sin.

—I JOHN 1:7

Legalism leads to some very odd but logical conclusions. Legalism, as a means of control, teaches that Jesus gave us a standing with God, but it is our job to keep it. In other words, the gift was free, but it is up to us to hold on to it through performance, and that must be more toilsome than in any other religion, because the standard, Jesus, is much higher. If we mess up, we are slowly distancing ourselves from God; soon we may find ourselves so far away from God that return is impossible. A legalistic attitude also leads to very sick behavior. For some it is okay to lust and look at porn just as long as they never have sex with another. Since the former, goes the argument, is not as capable of taking one away from God as the latter, it continues. Weird.

Now, if we are given the gift, and yet from that day forward our lives are filled with mistakes that push us away from the gift, would it not be better to commit suicide a week after we accept Jesus? Is the damage done in suicide (which is not the unforgivable sin) worse than years of sin? Wouldn't the many sins of a lifetime be worse than the one sin of suicide? This is the type of reasoning possible when we do not have a clear doctrine of problems and failure, which in reality are not there to steal the gift from us, but for us to secure and understand the depth of the gift. Conviction of the Spirit is not to tell us God is through with us, but to reveal that what we are doing will ultimately make us unhappy.

Let me use an example. A man is undone over his "addiction" to porn. Is porn really the problem, or is it revealing deeper problems that if not dealt with will make the man miserable? Does he really believe that God comes and goes on the basis of what he looks at? Isn't God love? As a rock is a rock regardless of outside forces, is not God Love independently from outside activity? I question this man's understanding of God's love and of Jesus and the blood. I question his understanding of being free in Christ when he uses words such as addiction. I question what he is really getting out of porn. Is it the fantasy of acceptance? I can ask the same things of anyone's problem. Now if these foundational things revealed through the problem are not dealt with, how will the man come to see the gift that has secured him? Once the root is dealt with, the fruit drops away. When the real issues are dealt with, the man will be able to say, "All things are lawful (God will not cut me off), but not all things are profitable." For now God is meeting the real need, and it simply is not profitable to continue in sin. See, there must be a purpose in problems and suffering; however, once they have completed their purpose, why continue in them?

I will tell you of an experience I had, one I never want to happen to you. I was going along thinking everything was perfect. For reasons unknown to me, God shined His light into the corners of my being. Little things were revealed, seemingly insignificant things that in comparison to Him became huge. Attitudes, behaviors, anger, bitterness, judgments, and more were exposed. I was undone; I wanted to give up and die. I thought, *Who, then, can be saved?* Many positive things came from that encounter, and in particular it taught me this one thing. On any given day, we believe we are righteous and have done nothing wrong, only because we are judging ourselves by ourselves. Let the Lord judge and we will see that every day we are still sinning. Our concept of His love, steadfastness, and faithfulness will explode. We will see that He is not fighting sin but using it.

There is no need to suicide out. This earth and this body make up the womb in which the child of God is birthed.

DAY 176
Life Abundant

The thief comes only to steal and kill and destroy; I came that they might have life, and have it abundantly.

 —JOHN 10:10

If there is a large boulder you want to move and all you have is a steel bar, it is nearly impossible. There is a secret, though. Place a small rock under the bar, creating a leverage point, and you can move it. It seems impossible that a little rock could make such a difference, but that is what a leverage point does, allowing a smaller object to move a greater object with very little effort.

Your pride is the leverage point, the rock, which a weaker, carnal person will use to move you. Lose your pride and no one can move you. If no one can move you, you will only be moved by Him. If you are only moved by Him, you will have life that is abundant. Life is not abundant when a lesser can move you. Therefore, own and admit to everything. Do not defend a thing. When accused, if you did not do it, say so, and then tell the person something worse about yourself. I can promise he will not know how to handle you, for he was counting on your pride as the leverage point.

I was accused of not being holy. My response was, "My holiness comes from Jesus. I only have His; I never had holiness. But I believe your point is to find something in me with which to discredit me. Last night I was lying in bed with murder in my heart. I wanted to beat to death the men who stole my luggage. I fought to bring the thought captive to Christ. Finally I did. There, you have what you came for." The man just stared at me, not knowing what to say.

When accused of being stupid, admit it. If you did not do what the accuser is saying, tell of something you did do that was stupid. Soon you will find life abundant. It is another way of taking up the cross and denying self.

DAY 177
Life On Earth, Part I

And I heard a loud voice from the throne, saying, "Behold
the tabernacle of God is among men, and He shall dwell
among them, and they shall be His people, and God Himself
shall be among them, and He shall wipe away every tear
from their eyes; and there shall no longer be any death; there
shall no longer be any mourning, or crying, or pain;
the first things have passed away."

—REVELATION 21:3, 4

This passage is often used to keep the believer hanging on
through all of life's struggles. "One day this will all be over,"
it is asserted. "You will be in heaven for eternity." However, I
see it a different way. Humans get to experience mourning,
crying, and pain; those "negatives" are especially for us, and
they are essential to revealing our need and driving us to
the Lord. In mourning, crying, and pain we discover the
"God of all Comfort." David said it was good that he was
distressed, for it brought him to a deeper revelation of God
the Father (Psalm 59:16, 17; Psalm 118:4-9). This life is
our only opportunity to discover God's care, compassion,
grace, mercy, and love within the context of our being
in need. We are only human one time, and there is no
reincarnation. "And inasmuch as it is appointed for men to
die once, and after this comes judgment" (Hebrews 9:27).
For me, to say that there will be no more mourning or pain
encourages me more fully to appreciate encountering them
in my experiences on earth.

DAY 178
Life On Earth, Part II

Behold, the tabernacle of God is among men, and He will dwell among them, and they shall be His people, and God Himself will be among them, and He will wipe away every tear from their eyes; and there will no longer be any death; there will no longer be any mourning or crying, or pain; the first things have passed away.

—REVELATION 21:3, 4

Two things in this passage strike me. First, it is a deathblow to prosperity preaching, which raises its ugly head from time to time. The passage acknowledges that in this life, in a Spirit-filled believer, there will be pain. I read an article stating that the denomination with the healthiest, longest living members are the Seventh Day Adventists, not, apparently, those in denominations with constant harping on the need for exercising "faith" for health. I have discovered this: The clamoring for physical healing can be equal to a person's lack of inner evidence of the indwelling Christ. In the past I was baffled when I saw all of the longing for physical healing, but then I realized it was slanted more toward being validated by God than physical comfort. I did not say that, He did! "This generation is a wicked generation; it seeks for a sign, and yet no sign will be given to it but the sign of Jonah" (Luke 11:29). Does this mean we are not to pray for healing? Never! God does heal, but He does not do it to affirm His acceptance of us, to make a show of it, or to prove

Himself. We are commanded to pray, and we must. I like what Andrew Murray and Watchman Nee taught: Death is our enemy. We do not yield to our enemy until the day God tells us to. We pray for healing until the day we know God is calling us out of this body. Often I have had it in my spirit to pray for the healing of someone. I actually witnessed the raising of a child from the dead, and to my surprise it was not spectacular. It occurred in the normal course of ministry as Jesus was being Jesus, and no one stopped to get caught up in gawking at the miracle but simply continued on with Jesus. Also, I have told believers it was time for their departure when I knew that to be true in my spirit. I asked them to write letters to their families, sort out all of their finances (not to leave a mess for the kids to handle), and make sure all relationships were right. I am all for healing; however, I am also for God's using our sickness. I was very ill in Nepal and prayed through the night, "Lord, You must heal me, for I am not returning home. I have much work to do here." The answer came early in the morning, "I will not heal you, but I will carry you through this sickness. You will not miss a meeting, and afterward I will take you back home." It was remarkable to be carried in the arms of love from meeting to meeting. It took me a few days to enter into the faith of what was happening and to believe that He would take me back home again. But He did! Since that day, no matter how sick I am, I remember the experience of how "He carried me." That occurrence of having been carried is one I would not exchange for all the health in the world, for it has given me a wonderful confidence to move on, no matter how I feel, into the proclamations of "Christ in you, the hope of glory" (Colossians 1:27).

DAY 179
Life on Earth, Part III

Behold, the tabernacle of God is among men, and He will dwell among them, and they shall be His people, and God Himself will be among them, and He will wipe away every tear from their eyes; and there will no longer be any death; there will no longer be any mourning, or crying, or pain; the first things have passed away.

—REVELATION 21:3, 4

The caterpillar will become a butterfly without choice. A sapling oak will become a great oak without choice. "Choose" and "choice" are used one hundred forty-two times in the Bible. Man does appear to have a choice. I was surprised to discover that for lots of people one of the biggest appeals in exiting the earth and heading toward heaven is their silent belief in the absence of choice in heaven. The reasoning is pretty straightforward: Since sin is a choice and there will be no sin in heaven, that must mean mankind will finally be free from choice. Heaven will certainly be an interesting place if there is no choice. Once in the new heaven, new earth, new body, and Bride of Christ, it may be that the right choice is the only choice that makes any sense.

As for the passage quoted above with its implications for being in heaven, I am thinking of it differently. Instead of having a great sense of relief about a time in the future when there is no longer any mourning, or crying, or pain,

I am applying that passage to the present with a different view. God put me in a fallen world and a fallen body, He permits what He could prevent, and this is my only opportunity to experience mourning, crying, and pain, for those things will be absent in heaven. It is important for me to learn from those things while I have the occasion. How will I learn that He is the God of all comfort if I have never mourned? How will I know the mercy, love, and goodness of God if I cannot, like David, wash my face and move forward? The lame man went walking and leaping and praising God because he was in pain and God removed it. I have never seen a perfectly healthy person walking and leaping and praising God. We must stop seeing our lives in these bodies, in this world with its sin and its governments, as a curse. By so doing, I believe we are missing out on the human experience with its divine revelations of the One we love because He first loved us. To whom would the love of God mean the most, the one who has only experienced love his whole life or the one who has been a rejected untouchable? "We would see Jesus" is our cry in everything. He has much more for all of us. We have just a few years to enjoy the experience of being human. We will never again experience the wind on our faces, cups of cold water on a hot day, the release of emotions provided by weeping, intimacy with the one we love, a full moon, the heavens above, and more. We are privileged to be on this journey.

DAY 180
Life Out Of Death

Indeed, we had the sentence of death within ourselves so that we would not trust in ourselves, but in God who raises the dead.

—II CORINTHIANS 1:9

During a trip to Brazil my wife discovered a new favorite: palm heart soup. It is the best. However, the bad news is that the particular palm tree from which the soup is made must grow for ten years; then at the very top of the tree is the new growth where the heart for the soup is harvested. This new growth, when cut off, causes the entire tree to lose its life.

There is a message in that tree. We must always feed others with the new growth. The old growth is woody and cannot be digested. By abiding in Christ we are continuously fresh, being taught something new, sharing in invigorating truths, and always flavorful. Giving of our new growth will bring us death. Paul said in II Corinthians 1:9 that the death sentence was on himself. I often listen to believers who in depression say, "Nothing is working out for me." How could anything work out for a person who has the death sentence on self? In never being able to trust in self, we are never old and dry. We must go to Him each day to receive new growth.

I was told of a new variety of palm, one in which the new growth could be cut without causing the tree's death;

however, it reportedly does not taste as good. No, it would not. Paul also said, "Death works in me but life in you." We must give new growth to the body of Christ, and to do that, we must experience death to self.

DAY 181
Life Witnesses To Jesus

You shall not commit adultery.
—EXODUS 20:14

Once while talking to a Christian young woman living in an adulterous relationship, I asked her what the Bible had to say about her behavior. She responded, "I suppose that it says it is sin."

Correct answer, I told her, and then questioned her further: "What do you think of the Bible's command concerning your sinful behavior?" Her response was one I often hear from young people raised in the church today: "The Bible applied to a different generation. In light of the divorce rate, living together is a better option, so what I am doing really is not all that bad." In her mind, the commands were laws imposed outwardly upon persons, were unnatural, and, therefore, did not make sense.

What I said next surprised her, for she was expecting a sound Bible-thumping. I explained how if truth needs the Bible to prove it, then it really is not truth at all. The Bible is a truth witnessing to *the* truth, which is Jesus. Truth stands alone, not outside, but built within the very fiber of a person. Therefore, truth is not something imposed from without, but something written within that cannot be avoided. I next told her that her life also witnessed to the truth, and so I wanted to know not what the Bible said about her behavior, but what her life experiences had taught her about her behavior. She said that being in and out of relationships had resulted in an illegitimate child, sexually-transmitted disease, rejection, self-hatred, and the fear of lifelong loneliness. I said, "Your life and the Bible prove a truth." She did not argue but said she wanted a change. Jesus is truth, and life witnesses to this truth! Life is the loudest voice in support of Jesus!

DAY 182
Like God

For God knows that in the day you eat from it your eyes will be opened, and you will be like God, knowing good and evil.

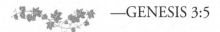

—GENESIS 3:5

Knowledge is a wonderful thing! "A wise man is strong, and a man of knowledge increases power" (Proverbs 24:5). Knowledge can allow man to *know* God. However, the hiccup comes when knowledge allows man to be *like* God. Many persons long for the knowledge that will make them like God. We want to know the future, to understand how to change a loved one, to be better prepared for life's obstacles, to discern the mind and motives of others, and to know how to change ourselves. Once those things were known, we would find it to be dead knowledge, for knowledge that makes man like God, since man is not God, always leads to frustration. Why? We may know the things of God, just like God knows them, and yet man does not have the power of God to act on what has been learned. Man knows, but cannot do. We may sit with others examining the behavior of a politician, a friend, or a relative and conclude that he is quite mad. But what is done with the conclusion, who does it help, and what can we do? Nothing. Therefore, Jesus gives a simple command, "Do not judge." Knowledge demands that it be followed and acted upon, but without the ability to follow, man will begin to condemn himself. Knowledge sets a standard that must be kept. If understanding is not obeyed, it will then judge. Therefore, the Law (the knowledge of God) will always condemn and judge those who come in contact with it. Man assumes knowledge will bring relief, something to boast in, and hope; rather, it brings bondage. Once the "at risk" person understands the folly of his way and yet continues in that way, the ensuing damage will be intensified by a whispering voice, "I told you so!" I personally have never met someone who did not know when he was doing something stupid, yet he did it, and who is to blame? Knowledge will never show compassion. Man is not like God, for what God knows, God has the power to do and does. His knowing and doing are one.

The believer is not interested in being like God, for he has the true and living God and does not need another. The believer wants to know God. The believer is happy to leave the future, his life, and others' lives in the hands of God. The believer is not consumed with knowledge that exalts, but a knowledge that brings confidence in God's ability to cause all things to work together for good.

DAY 183
Listening

And Eli said to Samuel, "Go lie down, and it shall be if He calls you, that you shall say, 'Speak, LORD, for Your servant is listening.'" So Samuel went and lay down in his place.

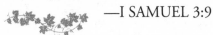

—I SAMUEL 3:9

I was shocked one day when asking an elderly saint how much time he spent in prayer to have him retort, "I have been delivered from prayer!"

That response stirred my curiosity, and without a thought I reacted, "What do you mean?"

He explained, "Mike, I have made enough requests to last the rest of my lifetime! I have found it much more profitable at this stage of my life to listen." He then told me he spent several hours each day just listening to his Father in heaven.

If it is true that communication is a lost art, how much more is the art of listening? "Like an earring of gold and an ornament of fine gold is a wise reprover to a listening ear," Proverbs 25:12.

"I can't hear God" is the response most often given when the topic of listening is broached. But we can, we have, and we continue to do so. His voice is the little lift we experience in our spirits when reading, talking to another about Him, walking, or listening to a teaching.

Refine your focus on that little lift and you, too, can spend hours a day listening.

DAY 184
Little Old Ladies and Their Flowers

*Now to Him who is able to do exceeding abundantly
beyond all that we ask or think, according to the power that
works within us, to Him be the glory in the church and in
Christ Jesus to all generations forever and ever. Amen.*

—EPHESIANS 3:20, 21

I cannot really say the railway stations in Europe are pleasant places. Packed with busy, expressionless travelers, often they are dirty, and foul smells from the lack of self-contained septic systems on the trains assault the nostrils. The stations are most often centrally located in an urban area, which makes for a convenient but uninviting entry to the city. One morning as the train I was on departed from a town and I rode, unimpressed with the whole procedure, I looked out the window and noticed an elderly lady coming from a very plain shack close to the tracks. She hobbled between the tracks and train traffic with what appeared to be a watering device. I then noticed what she was doing. She had planted beautiful poppies in the refuse along the track and was watering them with a smile on her face! It was simply beautiful—not just the flowers, but she was, too. Amid the smell, the noise, and the rush she had made her world more beautiful. In making her world beautiful, I got a respite from my world, and for the instant it took the train to pass, my world, too, became beautiful.

Didn't Jesus make the world beautiful for us? He pointed out all that is wonderful, for all the world is wonderful in Him. He revealed His life to us in the simple illustration of the vine. He told us stories about real people in real situations that lifted our spirits in the midst of the worst of conditions. He waded into the refuse of the world and planted a flower—the Church—that would reveal His heart and glory. I do not think I will ever look at flowers in the same way! Now they remind me of Him and His glory in the midst of a clanging and noisy world.

DAY 185
Living On the Fringe

Yet I hold this against you: You have forsaken your first love.

—REVELATION 2:4 [NIV]

We begin our Christian life finding Jesus, not a doctrine, emphasis, or activity, but a Person. In the beginning He, and He alone, was all important to us. We found Him and He gave us rest. We can liken our life in Him to being the hub of a wheel, with every spoke—every aspect of life—needing His support. The hub will turn by itself; however, spokes without a hub simply collapse. Therefore, lesser truth (the spokes) always gives way to the greater truth (the hub). Unfortunately, within a short time, the spokes (the lesser truths supported by Him) became our emphases and hence, avenues away from Him. We were led to believe the hub is not the primary focus in life, that we needed other experiences to make us whole and to support life in Him: intellectual pursuits, Scripture memory, evangelism, attendance at meetings, and mandated prayer and study times. All such things are good when they enhance the center, but weak when they become the focus and lead us away. As we move out of the hub, we become fringe believers, scrambling to succeed in competition with others who exalt life on the fringe. We no longer live out of the center, and every attempt to return is opposed by another new emphasis. Life on the fringe is shallow. How do we move back to the center?

The path back to the center is different in tone and severity for every person, but might include something like the loss of a loved one, dealing with a rebellious child, exhaustion from raising small children, illness, job insecurities, or any of myriad other circumstances that make us realize we need God alone in His rightful place back in the hub. There we find our rest in Him and acknowledge that no temptation, emphasis, doctrine, or experience is worthy of our trust or will produce abundant life. When others beckon us out with a new Jesus-plus emphasis, we are free to think, *Enjoy your detour; I am not leaving the center.*

DAY 186
Living To Your Mate . . .
An Absolute?

But one who is married is concerned about the things of the world, how he may please his wife, and his interests are divided. The woman who is unmarried, and the virgin, is concerned about the things of the Lord, that she may be holy both in body and spirit; but one who is married is concerned about the things of the world, how she may please her husband.

—I CORINTHIANS 7:33, 34

Of course, Paul prefaced this passage by writing it is "I," not the "Lord," speaking. My experience indicates there are just as many "divided" single Christians as married ones. Nevertheless, his observation is interesting and, for him, a near absolute born out of his experience. In thousands of hours of marriage counseling I have seen the same thing, but not from the same root. First, it has appeared to me that conflict comes not so much from trying to please one's mate as from trying to please oneself. Second, I have noticed that in mature couples this principle expounded by Paul does not play out. Every couple, as they move forward in the expansion of the Christ within, will become less and less as He becomes more and more. I just do not see it as an absolute, for I know married couples who are more concerned about pleasing the Lord than pleasing one another. I know couples who are one and do not have divided interests. People in marriage for the revelation of Jesus, and not fleshly happiness, are not divided. On the path to this discovery there is division, but I believe one process God uses in marriage is freeing both individuals from each other and then giving them back to one another as different people. We need to be freed from the self-life of the other just as we need to be freed from our own self-life. In this freeing process, He will make us sick of trying to feed our flesh and/or the flesh of our mate until in the end the only place to go is Jesus, where the spirit can be fed. Once the spirit's nourishing is the goal, there will be oneness of interests, all of which are rooted in undivided attention to the things of God. Seeing that there is no marriage in heaven [Mark 12:25], we can assume that marriage on earth is to have something more than a temporal impact on us. What is it teaching us that will have eternal value? There is so much to learn. We love but cannot live for another. We cannot get spiritual needs met from any human. We are selfish. Our peace is so easily surrendered to another, and it uncovers attributes of self hidden deep within. What wonderful things to be able to learn right alongside someone with whom we are one!

DAY 187
Losing Faith Or Religion?

However, when the Son of Man comes,
will He find faith on the earth?

—LUKE 18:8

So often believers tell me they have lost faith after surmising that God is not going to change their church, family, circumstances, relationships, or their own lives. They have given up, weary of the attempt to pull themselves up by their bootstraps time after time in the hope of starting over on a positive note, only to be disillusioned. If I attempt to refute the feelings of hopelessness, they give myriad illustrations to prove that God has done nothing and is going to do nothing.

The interesting thing is that these believers have not lost faith; they still believe Christ died for their sins, forgiveness comes through Him alone, and He is the Son of God. However, obviously they have lost something, which is actually their inaccurate system of belief—their false religion, if you will—that they (or someone else) can accomplish their own plans for such things as changing the rebellious child, the unspiritual mate, and the carnal pastor. Any such plan is a religion in the sense that it demonstrates a powerful hold on a way of trusting, thinking, and behaving. Of course, when their attempts to change others fail, they become depressed, discouraged, frustrated, and full of worry, but this is the failure of religion, not the failure of Christ.

Everyone needs to come to the end of religion and come to a complete trust in God. The process of accomplishing this involves the failure of everything in which trust is placed apart from Him. Deuteronomy 31:8, "And the LORD is the one who goes ahead of you; He will be with you. He will not fail you or forsake you. Do not fear, or be dismayed." Yes, religion fails, but the Lord never does. Lose your religion and cling to Him in trusting dependence.

DAY 188
Loss, Loss, and More Loss

Enter by the narrow gate; for the gate is wide and the way is broad that leads to destruction, and many are those who enter by it. For the gate is small and the way is narrow that leads to life, and few are those who find it."

—MATTHEW 7:13, 14

Once when preparing to retire for the evening at an old man's house, I asked a parting question, "What do you think is the purpose of life?" He never hesitated, just kept walking, and mumbled, "Death, death, and more death. Loss, loss, and more loss." With that, the door to his bedroom closed. I laid in bed for several hours just meditating on what he said. Then I heard Jesus speak through the Scriptures, "Enter through the narrow gate, the gate is wide and the way is broad that leads to destruction." I was then reminded of a recent trip to Vietnam, where I went crawling through the old war tunnels that sprawled underneath the ground. The guide said there was only one way in, and we had to leave behind all valuables, backpacks, cameras, and hats, because the way was just too small. Oh, how I wished I had not started that journey. At first I entered standing, and then the tunnel narrowed until in pitch-black darkness I was scooting along on my stomach, my shoulders and head were hitting the wall above me, and there was barely any air to breathe . . . nor was there any turning back. After several minutes we dropped into a rather large room (10x10x6), a storage area for everything needed to survive: rations, water, medical supplies, plus safety. What a trip to get there, though. This was the first of many such tunnels, with each one opening into a larger room containing something the soldiers during the war would have needed. Some rooms had been very dangerous, because bombs not detonated had been cut into pieces and drug through the tunnels in order for the explosives to be removed, the steel smelted, and hand grenades made.

We have a few years on this planet, where our goal is not gain but loss. Today many "Christian Clubs" promote the idea that we are to accumulate as much as possible until, in the end, it would take a wide path and train of elephants to carry everything sought after and found. It would never be possible to carry pride, wealth, success, intelligence, superiority, victories over enemies, or titles on the narrow path; that path is not made to accommodate such things. One day we will all reach the narrow path, and some will get on their hands and knees (a place they have often been) and pass through easily with their accumulated knowledge and revelation of Christ. Others will stand there dumbfounded, wondering what they are to do with their great line of amassed possessions. Again, the wrong thing can be said so many times that the right thing sounds wrong. Remember the Jews when they were so mad at Jesus for the pigs that ran over the cliff? My question would have been, "Why are you upset at losing the very thing you were never supposed to have had?" Many believers get depressed because they lose the very thing they should not have had. Some are so undone that the enemy whispers, "Suicide"; that shows a lot of pride.

It is no fun to lose and lose and lose, but it is the path you have chosen, and though He is the only comfort on the narrow path, is He not more than sufficient? It is no fun to lose family, friends, kids, security, or a marriage. Keep on that narrow path, for it will open into a secure place that has all you need.

DAY 189
Love and Affection In Marriage

Let us not become boastful, challenging one another,
envying one another.

—GALATIANS 5:26

At Abiding Life Ministries we often speak of a person's "unique self," or the uniqueness with which a person is born. We divide that uniqueness into three categories—thinker, feeler, and doer—with each person having a blend of the traits of each. In certain predominate ways, Jesus is the Way for the doer, the Truth for the thinker, and the Life for the feeler, although Jesus appeals to all three and to every blend. Jesus functioned as a thinker when He debated, a doer cleansing the temple, and a feeler found weeping at the tomb of Lazarus. Studying unique self is a study in the obvious, for every mother knows that each and every child has his or her own unique differences and traits.

Often physical affection in marriage is described in terms of male and female characteristics, as when it is said that for women the sexual relationship is emotional and for men it is merely physical. Experience, though, has taught that sex is far more emotional for men than women. When a man is denied, the wife need merely observe the pouting and rejecting behavior that ensues. Sex for the majority of men is equal to acceptance and significance. To respect a husband is to affirm he is wanted and significant, which sex does.

However, the purpose of this article is to look at the different outlooks on sex held by husbands and wives from the perspective of "Unique Self." In so doing, we will examine several blends of unique self and the difference those might make in what goes on during the physical side of relationships.

Generally speaking, in every relationship there is one who initiates affection and one who is the receiver. This aspect of initiation and receiving relates directly to being a thinker, feeler, or doer. The Feeler-Thinker (wherein the primary personality trait is feeler and the secondary is thinker) is one who allows affection to be initiated toward him; he is not the initiator. The thinker aspect causes two interesting manifestations where affection is concerned. This person does not want to take a risk; he fears the unknown and will wait for the other to initiate. Also, because a thinker keeps lists, he would like all turmoil of the past to be resolved before someone kisses him. His thoughts go something like this, "Do not kiss me until we talk about why you were so rude to me this morning." Husbands with this pattern leave their wives feeling as though something must be wrong with them; they must be unattractive or sexually undesirable. The wife also feels something is wrong if she is the one that must initiate. However, if the wife will notice, when the Feeler-Thinker husband does initiate affection, it is rather "clunky" or unnatural. The higher a person is in the thinker area, the less spontaneous he is. However, because the feeler is higher, attempts to touch him will not be rejected, provided there are not a lot of outstanding issues. If two people with this same personality pattern are married, very little affection is initiated. Both have a tendency to stand in the hallway wondering what the other is thinking.

Sex for the Thinker-Feeler in affection (thinker higher than feeler) is on a take-it-or-leave-it basis. He does not mind being involved and does not mind if he is not. He likes sitting next to his mate on Friday night watching a movie and holding hands, and he does not mind sitting by himself on Saturday night, across the room from his mate, doing his own thing. None of this behavior is intended to be rejecting toward the spouse.

Doer-Feeler (highest in doer) will initiate affection on demand. The thinker is lowest, so he does not have a list of requirements that must first be met; a very nice thing about the doer in affection is that he has forgotten all the offenses from the morning. What matters to the Doer is the goal, not the journey, so it would be helpful for this person to slow down, spend time talking, and have more of a "dating" mindset in the relationship.

Thinker-Doer (highest in Thinker) has high standards he has imposed upon himself and has the tendency to impose those standards on others. Consequently, the list for sexual acceptance becomes so long that neither he nor anyone else can ever meet it. The high Thinker plans so much to do that sex can be seen as an interruption to an otherwise productive day; during affection he can give a misread message of rejection as his mind begins to wander. For the Thinker, romance is not spontaneous but planned. If married to a Thinker, plan a romantic evening with plenty of advance warning. If you are the Thinker, go to bed without baggage; lay aside the list and unfulfilled expectations, which are valid but are separate issues from the romantic aspect of your life. There is absolutely nothing wrong with being a Thinker in affection.

The Feeler in relationship will have a tendency, when not under the power of the Spirit, to try to milk acceptance from the physical. By creation he is given to the senses, and sex can easily become a way of coping. The Feeler excels in the spontaneity of affection, delighting in coming up from behind and giving a hug. However, more often than not a Feeler marries a Thinker, to whom the surprise overt affection is seen as an interruption; the Feeler will assume this is rejection and reject in return. The Feeler will do well to show love in the "little" things of life that mean so much to the Thinker. Ask what is on the Thinker's list, help complete the tasks, and the Thinker will feel much more relaxed as more time is freed up for affection. If married to a Feeler, periodically surprise him with a show of affection. (I say periodically, because though the feeler thinks that he craves affection, he is really happier and more suited to showing it. He says he wants the other one to initiate, but he actually enjoys it the most.) A Thinker can learn to allow the Feeler to show his affection.

As in every area of life, we have a tendency to judge another's behavior from our own shoes and assume everyone thinks, acts, and feels like we do. Therefore, it is easy to attach a motive to a behavior that is more often than not wrongly judged. It is very helpful to understand the unique self of our mate. Always remember that sex is not an end in itself, but God did create it, and as with all of His creation, it is most enjoyed when He is the primary focus in our lives.

DAY 190
Lower Your Odds

But God has chosen the foolish things of the world to shame the wise, and God has chosen the weak things of the world to shame the things which are strong, and the base things of the world and the despised God has chosen, the things that are not, so that He may nullify the things that are.

—I CORINTHIANS 1:27, 28

It is easier for the camel to go through the eye of a needle than for the rich man to enter the Kingdom of God. We have this warning, and yet so many are attempting to get rich through clever investing, winning the lottery, or falling heir to an inheritance. Amazingly, they are hoping and working toward lowering their odds of entering the Kingdom of God. In the same way, God chose the weak and base things to shame the wise, yet the weak and base ones who are called into ministry are too often working, studying, and sacrificing in seminary to become the strong and sophisticated, decreasing the odds that they will be used of God; they are actually taking themselves out of the race. They may build their kingdoms, but they will be left out of the building of His. God's ways are amazing!

DAY 191
Making a Career Move

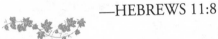

*By faith, Abraham, when he was called, obeyed by going
out to a place which he was to receive for an inheritance;
and he went out, not knowing where he was going.*

—HEBREWS 11:8

What are we to expect when we make a career change
or when we move from one place to another? What is the
way of things when we accept a different call? Here are a
few things we must know. First, before we can determine
to leave a place, we must understand that most of us
will slowly become unsettled with the place in which we
presently work or reside. God often makes us dissatisfied
with a place before He shows us the way, for if He showed
the way before we were dissatisfied, we might hesitate to
take it. Dissatisfaction with surroundings will make the
move of faith much easier. Second, like homing pigeons
released, we must circle, feeling lost, until something clicks
in our innermost being and we know the direction in
which we are to go. Third, we are being grafted into a new
place on the vine, and the dung must be packed around
the insertion to keep us in place and free from disease and
bugs. Fourth, there must be reversals before a fulfillment
of that to which we believe we have been called. Fifth, we
are like the caterpillar in that by our own choosing we have
built ourselves a tomb in which we cannot move and are in
the dark. Yet, in this dark place faith is being wrought, and
we will emerge from the cocoon looking much different
than when we entered into it.

In all of this, we must see that the whole process of shifting locations had faith as its goal. Faith is the assurance of things hoped for and the conviction of things not yet seen (Hebrews 11:1). Just as ships leaving the harbor must keep fixed on two points ahead to exit into the open sea, so we must stay fixed on this goal of faith in Jesus. When we have little needs, we will have the perception of a little God; big needs develop a little better sense of how big a God we serve. Shifting location will force us to recognize a bigger God. Beautiful.

DAY 192
Making Life Make Sense

*He is before all things, and in
Him all things hold together.*

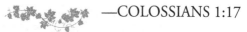—COLOSSIANS 1:17

Jesus makes life make sense. When we take hold of Him, we have the meaning to the universe and life itself. When anyone exposes all he is to the Lord, he changes! Life is full and has meaning. I can prove it! So can you! Take fifteen minutes with Him (Him, that most wonderful and personal word, Him) and you will not be the same.

Jesus must be included in life, for if the end result of life is me, myself, and I, then in the end I will fall apart. I must hold on to Jesus, the God/Man, the one I relate to. If I refuse the open invitation to fellowship, I pay the price of starvation at the point of my deepest need, for my new, born-again spirit is only fed by His Holy Spirit. When

He is neglected, I am neglecting my deepest need. Soon I will become cynical and lack depth in my life. If, however, my spirit is fed in fellowship, then I will find the drive to witness, to lose, and to forgive, and out of my innermost being will flow rivers of living water. To seek Him is to seek life, to find Him is to find life, to live in Him is to live life. I will give thanks for everything that drives me to Him! Even death will be the vehicle for the release of His life.

DAY 193
Male Validation

Therefore do not go on passing judgment before the time, but wait until the Lord comes who will both bring to light the things hidden in the darkness and disclose the motives of men's hearts; and then each man's praise will come to him from God.

—I CORINTHIANS 4:5

Peter's statement that "a woman will be saved in childbirth" is confusing until the word *saved* is properly defined. As used in the Bible, a majority of the time the term refers to deliverance in the present. Nothing hinders daily victory and joy as much as selfishness. Experiencing childbirth, a woman's self-life is given a severe blow as she devotes her own wellbeing to the good of another, her newborn child. This very loss of self-centeredness allows her to be more susceptible to daily victory in Christ. Peter's statement is not meant to be a dig to women who have not given birth to children any more so than to men, who also have never experienced childbirth. He is pointing to a greater truth, which is that selfishness needs a deathblow in order for mankind to find life. Childbirth seems to validate a woman's existence (not all women, but many) in the sense that once a woman is a mother, the course of her life is believed to be set, and she therefore has validation and purpose. Men do not have any such equal occurrence, and I find many who are still looking for purpose and validation. However, all of us seek for things that can only be found in the Lord.

I have collected several suicide notes from men over the years (more men successfully commit suicide than women). The notes are predictable and often carry the same theme: "I am sorry I did not amount to more"; "I should have done more with my life"; "I am a disappointment." In short, they never found validation, a fulfilled purpose in living. Within the context of discipleship I often play a suicide game. I pretend I am the person sitting before me wanting to commit suicide, and the person must take the name of Suicide. I say, "Suicide, why do you want to kill me?"

The answer comes in various forms, but always with the same general thrust: "Because you are worthless, you have not accomplished anything with your life, and you have not lived up to your potential."

I then respond, "Exactly what is my potential? How will I know if I have accomplished enough or lived well enough to fulfill my potential? Will it be when I have made a medical discovery, become popular, obtained my own television show, gained the praise of my family, or memorized the whole Bible? The problem is that I know of men who fall into all those categories of accomplishment and who have committed suicide, therefore proving your definition of validation faulty." Something very depressing to many is when they have "made it" in the world's sense and wake up in the morning being their same old selves. Validation from oneself, the world, or others is like taking a dry dishrag and wringing it for a full, thirst-satisfying glass of water. When man cannot find validation, he will live to the world, others, and self in an attempt to justify his existence on earth. I have not mentioned the things we do that actually, in our minds, do the opposite of validating us, such as the outbursts, the deeds of the flesh, the old habits that return, the failed marriages, and more. Men—even more than women—need to stop looking for validation in any place other than the Lord.

Naked you entered the world and naked you will leave. Frank Sinatra died and Las Vegas dimmed its lights for a short time. Wow! What a tribute. They then turned them back on full blaze and went on gambling. If the Lord validates you, you no longer must live to the world, yourself, or others. You will be free, free indeed.

He validates every man with a simple statement, "I will never leave you nor forsake you." That is enough. With that statement echoing in my heart, I am as happy sitting on a tractor turning up the grubs and watching the seagulls eat them as I am preaching before five thousand. I am as expectant in defeat as in victory. I am not watching myself obsessively, nor does the affirmation or rejection of the world or others change my day.

DAY 194
Man, Not Completed On
The Sixth Day

*God saw all that He had made, and behold, it was very
good. And there was evening and there was morning,
the sixth day.*

—GENESIS 1:31

*Being confident of this, that He who began a good work
in you will carry it on to completion until
the day of Christ Jesus.*

—PHILIPPIANS 1:6 [NIV]

When God created the world, He concluded his six days
by creating man and saying, "He is good." Yes, he was
good, but he was not completed. A tree is a tree, water is
water, a cow is a cow, and so on—those will not become
something else. Everything was created complete except
for the one thing left incomplete! Man was the only thing
in all of creation still in the process of becoming complete.
Cool! All the rest of creation is under compulsion; the
caterpillar must become a butterfly. Man is different. Man
was in a process moving toward completion. Man can
become a vessel of doom or a vessel of blessing. This fallen
world will help make that determination.

I have said it before, but bear with me. The angels in the
book of Jude are under judgment for going after strange
flesh. Genesis 6 explains that angels were after earthly

women. Then Paul makes it clear in I Corinthians that those of different "flesh" are not to mingle. God wanted a bride for His Son but could neither pick something in heaven nor on the earth without going after something "strange." He did what angels longed to look into: He became a man, like Adam outwardly but inwardly with the very life of God. The world had so defeated the Adam inner life, but the proposal comes that Christ (the second Adam) has an inner life that wins, and the vessels that exchange lives at the cross become at that moment vessels of blessing; they also become complete men. "It is finished" means many things, but one thing is this: Man is finished and can become complete; he can now have an outer life of the world and an inner life from heaven, the Life that wins. He can become exactly like the Groom, and the wedding in heaven will go on. After thousands of years wherein all of creation was complete, man can now be complete. Beautiful, wonderful, and beyond imagination? Yes, and more!

DAY 195
Many Religions and One Faith

One Lord, one faith, one baptism, one God and Father of all who is over all and through all and in all.

—EPHESIANS 4:5, 6

While traveling in a remote area of India, we were passing by an estimated 500,000 pilgrims walking barefoot up to 500 miles toward the temple of Shiva that rested on top of a mountain. Many had bloodied and blistered feet. Once they reached the temple, their heads would be shaved and they would receive a bit of sandalwood paste that had fallen off of an idol. Drinking the paste in a mixture was said to secure the favor of Shiva, and they would get the desire of their heart.

Not long afterward I found myself in Tibet, where the pilgrims were falling forward to reach the great temples of Buddha. Some had come as far as 300 miles in this manner; they would stand, make a praying motion with their hands, and fall forward. While lying prostrate, they stretched out as far as they could and placed a piece of paper at the end of their fingertips; this was the marker for where they were to stand next and fall forward. Men, old women, and children alike were slowly working their way to Lhasa by the length of their bodies. Some even had callused foreheads. These types of activities are played out around the world.

We often look at the passage in Ephesians where Paul mentions that there is one Lord, one faith, one baptism and apply it to the Christian Church. However, it must be viewed in a broader sense. Taken as a whole, the world brandishes very many religions, but there is only one faith. Religion, as it is most easily defined, is success resting at the feet of man. All religions have this in common, even the Christian religion, for it becomes a religion when the enemy and the flesh of man move focus away from the work of God to the work of man.

I visited an Orthodox Religion "church" building in India after visiting several Hindu temples. I turned to my friend and said, "Do you think a Hindu would feel the least bit uncomfortable in this Orthodox religion?" He replied, "No, the Hindu would have everything he needs here: candles, icons, idols, a secret place for priests, gold altars, and more."

The common thread of religions—that success rests in man's effort—is often accompanied by the tantalizing hope for success through somehow twisting the arm of the false god to get a favor. In contrast, there is only one faith, so never let it be said that people belong to different faiths; they only belong to different religions. The one faith is faith in the only God, His only Son, Jesus Christ, and the Holy Spirit. The success of the one faith ends at the feet of God, who loved us and gave us His Son. God works in us, Christ moved into us and is our life, and the Holy Spirit makes the things of God and Jesus not only reasonable but also doable in His power. It is all about the accomplished and ongoing work of the Father, the Son, and the Holy Spirit. If we move from the one faith that believes in what God does, period, then we move into an obsession with self and what men must do and find one of the most miserable religions in the world, which is Christianity without Christ.

DAY 196
Marriage and Sex

Stop depriving one another, except by agreement for a time, so that you may devote yourselves to prayer, and come together again so that Satan will not tempt you because of your lack of self-control.

—I CORINTHIANS 7:5

While the average frequency of sexual encounters among functioning couples, depending on age, is said to be between three to ten times per month, it is not uncommon to talk to married couples having abstained from a sexual relationship for anywhere from seven to twenty-seven years. Generally two reasons are given for the life of celibacy. The wife explains how she simply lost interest in sex and has no intention of being an object to meet the physical needs of her husband. However, since for the husband sex equals acceptance, the wife's attitude equals rejection, so soon sex equals pain and control to the point that the husband's thinking goes like this: "If she thinks I have to have sex, I'll just show her by killing the desire and refusing to be controlled." The husband is now rejecting back, which confirms the wife's suspicion that she is nothing more than an object. The spiral tightens, and soon bitterness sets in.

I have discipled many couples not getting along and often vigorously fighting; however, in marriages with an equal amount of discord, I always find a softness toward one another in the couple that has continued along in the sexual relationship despite the misunderstandings and disagreements. This softness is not found in couples having withdrawn sexually. Why? Because, I believe, it is impossible to maintain the same level of bitterness when sex is part of the equation. A husband or wife attempting to stay bitter during the sex act will self-destruct. Bitterness and selfishness must be laid aside in this expression of oneness. I am not saying it is always enjoyable to deny self and express oneness. However, I will argue that it is much more enjoyable than to remain bitter and selfish, no matter how bad things are.

The complaint I hear is "No, no, I just don't enjoy it." Well, there are two problems with that. First, I do not know where the Bible says sex gives everything the constant onslaught of media tells us it gives. We Americans are an odd lot. We know so much about sex but enjoy it less. Why? Sex cannot give what too many of us think it promises. Only Christ meets that deeper need. Second, the issue is rarely that one can no longer tolerate sex; that would be very unnatural. Rather, the issue is that one no longer remembers how to live apart from bitterness and selfishness and therefore finds excuses to stay in the misery zone.

Paul deals with sex as a separate issue. We have a tendency to put all issues in a bucket, mix them up, and look for one answer, believing one area of failure is tied to other areas of failure. This thinking is in error, since we all grow in different revelations. The only common dynamic in defeat is the lack of abiding in Christ. There are "other" issues in marriage, all of which can be met in the particular way they are to be dealt with, so we are not saying nothing else matters; we are saying those things that do matter are separate issues. A wife's failure in a particular area does not justify a husband's failure in another area. The purpose of this article is not to sweep under the carpet all marriage issues and have the husband or wife run to the other mate saying, "See what the article says? We should be having more sex!" Sex, unkind words, unloving attitudes, lack of forgiveness, help with the kids, and finances are all separate issues addressed in Scripture in different ways. Sex is dealt with specifically with one injunction: "Stop depriving one another."

DAY 197
Marriage Counseling, A Waste of Time?

I can do all things through Him who strengthens me.
—PHILIPPIANS 4:13

So then do not be foolish, but understand what the will of the Lord is.

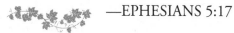
—EPHESIANS 5:17

There is a wall in marriage, and the majority of marriage counseling is an attempt to have success by skirting that wall instead of breaking it down. The wall consists of three things. First, each person must take responsibility for his own happiness. Second, each person is responsible for his own rebellion and must ask himself why he is not obeying the commandments of God. For instance, if the believer is called to love his enemies, why can he not love the spouse? Third, each person is responsible for embracing death to self. He must attend his own funeral and return alive in the ALIVE. That is, he must stop living for himself.

DAY 198
Marriage Problems

You blind guides, who strain out a gnat and swallow a camel!
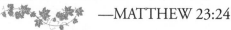 —MATTHEW 23:24

The problem revealed by a problem is the real problem! I am starting to garble a bit like a certain Irish brother. However, it is true that we focus on what we consider to be the problem, while avoiding the real problem that has been revealed to us.

For example, with the exception of a special call of God, men need women and women need men. This has been proven over and over again. Someone gets a divorce, proclaiming, "I will never get married again," and then almost immediately begins looking for a new mate. Some are in situations where abuse is obviously the problem and needs to be addressed, but short of that, the general belief among the majority of married people that their spouse is the problem simply is not true. The question is, how does the problem created by the mate reveal a more significant problem? Until the significant problem is dealt with, no one can expect the minor problem to disappear.

Paul mentions some of the major problems believers can experience: enmities, strife, jealousy, outbursts of anger, disputes, dissensions, factions, and envying. He also mentions the lack of compassion, kindness, lowliness, meekness, patience, forgiveness, and forbearance. Major problems are revealed through minor problems. Once the majors are taken care of, the minors appear as insignificant as they truly are.

An important distinction must be made: minor problems are those created outside of a person, while major problems are those created within. For example, war is considered a major problem, and yet what war creates within a man is far more consequential. Man is called to war by the fear that if something is not done, his people will be oppressed.

However, government oppression does not deplete the spirit and soul of a believer, but nourishes. Count the great men of God produced in comfort and those produced in persecution and oppression, and the numbers will be lopsided. Government oppression can only create in us something greater than the oppression. In the same way, problems in marriage can create something greater within.

At issue is not that our mates said something rude, left the gas tank empty, have not supported us, or enjoy pointing out our faults. None of those are major detractions making life uncomfortable. How we respond to those occurrences will determine our misery. If we respond angrily, disputing or lacking compassion, kindness, patience, and forgiveness, then we will be unhappy. We must get it fixed in our minds to love, forgive, and forget an offense primarily for our own good, not just for the good of the offender. Do you ever get sick of punishing yourself with self-righteousness, anger, unforgiveness, and the remembrance of offenses? Our responses to others have made us much sicker than their behavior ever did.

Apart from God's gifting, you need a mate. The mate you presently have is the best person you will ever be married to. The minor problems you have had together have revealed your major problems. Do not run from your mate; do not fantasize about another; turn and face the major problem. Now face the Lord, resolve to abide, and the life that overcame every major problem will flow through you. You will find yourself more than a conqueror and happy with the mate you have been given.

DAY 199
Marriage Under Attack

I do not ask Thee to take them out of the world, but to keep them from the evil one. They are not of the world, even as I am not of the world. . . . that they may all be one; even as Thou, Father, art in Me, and I in Thee, that they also may be in Us, that the world may believe that Thou didst send Me.

—JOHN 17:15, 16, 21

Submit therefore to God. Resist the devil and he will flee from you.

—JAMES 4:7

Nothing in the Bible is said about marriage's being under attack, the struggle of marriage, or the conflict in marriage; nor is anything said about marriage and regret, marriage and happiness, or marriage and fulfillment. Basically, the main theme concerning marriage is that the two will become one flesh. Biblically, flesh is the part of man—who is made somewhat in the image of God—that wants to be God. This means that two "fleshly" people become one "flesh" and will attempt to be God. Well, only God could think of that! Two people who could be yielding to God but are wanting to be God and working to make the other spouse into his or her image! Wow! At that point I can only say that the purpose of marriage is to make a person miserable and to reveal both self-centeredness and the desire to be God and rule over others. While that is unfolding, he is denying any blame as he casts himself and others into a living hell. Sounds like what I have been seeing; I have recently encountered many, many more Christian marriages under attack than in previous years. I am not totally objective, I realize that, nor am I the answer man; Jesus is the Way to every answer. However, it amazes me that I could spend time with a husband and enjoy the fellowship or visit with his wife and enjoy the fellowship, but they cannot seem to spend one content hour together. Satan has so clouded the eyes of the believers that they only see the negatives and cannot see God. Amen, I understand the grief in women when they are living with a drunk, drug addict, child abuser, physical abuser, adulterer, and more (things Paul says that we ought not even talk about, and I am thankful that the Lord lets me sleep at night after some of the things I have heard). However, the things I am hearing lately are completely petty. "You did not support me! You did not initiate intimacy, you do not court me, you only pick out the negatives, you do not support me with the children, you are someone different when we are out with others than at home, you are a fake as a believer, you do not pray with me, and you will not do what I ask you to do." Amen, every issue has some validity, but not grounds for bitterness, anger, hatred, emotional walls, and everything else the believer is not to have! Is anyone ever ashamed of this behavior?

There seems to be a genuine lack of communication among Christian couples; it has been replaced by a series of reactions. The world already offers us financial, social, and physical strain; do we want discord at home, too? Are we asking God, "What is the deal? What do You want me to do? Maybe I should hit the guy, and maybe I should love him." I do not know what God knows. I have been asking people to write, once each day for thirty days, something they love about their mate. They might last about ten days before coming up blank. However, they can write for sixty days all that is wrong with their mate.

Attitude is everything. I believe that Jesus is coming, and therefore, no matter what happens in world politics, I am comforted. Do you believe that God brought your mate to reveal something in you? Let Him reveal your selfishness, the lack of love, the list keeping, the dissatisfaction the flesh always harbors, and turn to Him. Get on your knees and say, "Jesus, what do You have for us? We are finished; we need a Source that lives outside us and inside us." He is God, it is His responsibility, and He will come. "God so loved the world that He gave His only begotten Son" (John 3:16). Do you think He does not love your mate? He has more than enough pure love to give your mate through you.

Listen, His coming is near, and there are three things a marriage needs: communication, common goals, and intimacy. Ask Him to show you where you have gone astray. Honestly, you did not marry your mate because he/she was a complete ass! You did not take vows while looking forward to the day when you would despise seeing the other entering the room. Intimacy in communication and in the physical will break down all barriers. One deathblow to self-will brings a refreshing rain on the garden of your relationship. Please follow Christ, take up the cross, deny yourself, and let your marriage flourish.

Brothers and Sisters, we are in a battle with a voice that just will not shut up. We will win, and we are those who conquer because of our Lord who already won.

DAY 200
Married To An Unbeliever?
You Are Blessed!

But to the rest I say, not the Lord, that if any brother has a wife who is an unbeliever, and she consents to live with him, let him not send her away. And a woman who has an unbelieving husband, and he consents to live with her, let her not send her husband away.

—I CORINTHIANS 7:12, 13

In the course of this ministry I have met many people married to unbelievers. A unique set of circumstances goes along with being "unequally yoked." However, there are two primary deceptions into which a believer may fall that can make the situation nearly intolerable.

The first deception is to believe that a mistake of the past will forever taint the future. On your wedding day, perhaps you recognized you were doing something wrong, not unlike the rest of us who, in the day of our sin, knew we were wrong. Yes, it may be true that you should not have gotten married. Yes, your peace left you and in the back of your mind there was the gnawing 'no' of the Holy Spirit. Yes, you did disobey and you did sin. However, we must add one more yes: God does cause all things to work together for good. He is not fighting our bad decisions but using them. What I am going to say next takes a big God. If your God is little, you cannot receive what I say; if He is big, you can. Also, once the decision to have a big God is made, do not expect every Christian to agree with you! Many have a vested interest in encouraging you to believe you made a mistake of such magnitude that abundant life in Christ will be diminished your lifetime through. In the mind of the carnal believer who has not made the same mistake, you are inferior in life and situation.

"When [Peter] came into the house, Jesus spoke to him first, saying, 'What do you think, Simon? From whom do the kings of the earth collect customs or poll-tax, from their sons or from strangers?' When Peter said, 'From strangers,' Jesus said to him, 'Then the sons are exempt. However, so that we do not offend them, go to the sea and throw in a hook, and take the first fish that comes up; and when you open its mouth, you will find a shekel. Take that and give it to them for you and Me.'" [Matthew 17:25-27]

Jesus was talking to the disciples about paying taxes. Of course the sons of God would not pay tax. However, so no one was offended, Peter was instructed to go fishing! The first fish he caught would possess exactly what Peter needed. Among the millions of fish in the sea, God sent the exact fish, to the exact line, to the exact man, to meet an exact need! Do you believe God sent the exact mate to the exact place, to the exact person, to meet an exact need in you? I believe it! How big is your God? The enemy would have you in fantasy dreaming of what it would be like to have a believing mate. However, if the goal of our lives is the revelation of Christ in us, then we need experiences where His life can be manifested.

Let me illustrate. I know a woman who has continued to grow in grace, mercy, and love, all because of her husband's sinful behavior. Many times she has wanted to leave him, and many in ministry encouraged her to do just that. However, God comes to her, reveals Himself, His love, and His safe-keeping. In the end she lives out of His strength and stays. One day I said, "Sister, when we get to heaven you will be way ahead of me. I have only told you what to do, but you have done it. You have excelled in the attributes of heaven. When you stand before God, what will you ask Him to do to your husband?" I knew the turmoil this sister had endured at the hands of her husband. Her response was beautiful. "I will ask God to bless my husband, for had it not been for his behavior, I would not be standing there!" She truly has caught on! Trouble is not in the trouble but in the heart's attitude toward the trouble. If the goal of marriage is comfort, then believers married to unbelievers will always find themselves uncomfortable. However, if the purpose of marriage is the realization and release of the attributes of Christ in a person, the one married to an unbeliever actually has a clearer opportunity for a head start. Some would say I am teaching "sin so grace will abound." Those who say it forget "God causes all things to work together for good," have the goal of comfort, and enjoy seeing others suffer the consequences of their mistakes.

The second thing that can happen to believers is to fall into the deception of discouragement and hopelessness. They love and love, perform and perform, and watch every word and behavior in the hope of seeing their unbelieving spouses saved. Articles are placed conspicuously where such a spouse might read them. Situations are manipulated to bring the unbeliever in touch with a believer who might be able to say the right thing. Yet after years of work and prayer nothing happens. The enemy then comes to taunt,

"Is this how you were meant to live? Is this abundant life? Do you realize how much better life would be had you married a believer? You should leave!" All of these feelings are compounded when the "perfect" couple in church stands hand in hand describing how they prayed for a child, how God made them a team, and how they confessed their faults to one another and prayed for one another. All of this breeds a deepening feeling that the consequences of a bad choice will continue to bear fruit even after the believers are dead and gone.

If you have fallen victim to this deception, get up and press on, for God is with you in a special way. You are in the most blessed of all places and in contact with the exact situation God lives with every day. You are sharing in the fellowship of His sufferings. In this exact situation you can expect all of His help, for you are only experiencing a minute measure of what God goes through every day with the unbeliever. To love an unbeliever is to live as God lives! He loves you for that, and all of His comfort is available to you. You are not an inferior believer, but you are in a superior position to receive grace and mercy. You have done so much yet done nothing compared to what God does in sticking with the unbelieving one. "For God so loved the world that He gave His only begotten Son (John 3:16)." You have not gone that far to reach the unsaved mate. I want you to know that if your goal—the revelation of Christ in you, the knowledge of His grace and mercy, His outworking through you, and the conviction of weakness—is right, then you are in the perfect place and married to the exact person who will meet an exact need in you. Do not keep trying to avoid the unbelieving mate and all the things this unique situation brings. God does not avoid fallen man; He jumped into the very middle of the situation and became man.

Let me use a different example. David and Job both say that God blessed them because they were fathers to the fatherless. God wants to be our Father so we will not be fatherless. When David and Job adopted God's attitude toward the fatherless, God blessed them. Since they were right in line with His heart, blessing naturally came. If you will lay down your life for an unbelieving mate, you have adopted God's attitude, and His entire blessing will come. If the mate never gets saved, it will not matter to you; you are one of the "others" of Hebrews 11 who believed, did not receive, and kept believing! It is said that the world was not worthy of them. If you are married to an unbeliever, have this attitude in yourself. You have the perfect mate to move you perfectly in line with God's heart, to reveal the perfect love of Christ, and to live in the glory of God.

"For the unbelieving husband is sanctified through his wife, and the unbelieving wife is sanctified through her believing husband; for otherwise your children are unclean, but now they are holy" (I Corinthians 7:14). Oneness is not two individuals trying to live together as one. Oneness is blending, like mixing milk and flour in a bowl. Once mixed it cannot be separated. Once married, you are blended together in God's mixing bowl. If food coloring is added when the mixer is on, the whole mixture changes its color. If you allow Christ to work His goal in your life, it will spread to your unbelieving mate's life. Again, is your goal comfort or the revelation of Christ in you? If it is the latter, you are in the most blessed of situations.

DAY 201
Ministering His Presence

Why are you in despair, O my soul? And why have you become disturbed within me? Hope in God, for I shall again praise Him for the help of His presence.

—PSALM 42:5

What is to be said about the presence of God? Only this: Things are worked out in His presence! There is nothing the presence of the Lord will not cure! His presence is all that matters; therefore, we must minister from, through, and into His presence. His presence helps us. We, as disciple-makers, are to minister His presence to others. Jesus said, "Destroy this temple, and in three days I will raise it up." The word Jesus used for temple literally meant the Holy of Holies, where God Himself dwelt. Of course, we know Jesus was speaking of Himself, for He was the very dwelling place of God. Paul uses the same term for temple when addressing the believers: "Do you not know that you are a temple of God and that the Spirit of God dwells in you?" (I Corinthians 3:16) The Holy of Holies held the presence of God; now the believer is the Holy of Holies and ministers the presence of God. In His presence, things are worked out.

Arthur Burt gave this advice, "Never minister to the people before God, but minister to God before the people." Then he told the story of a great pianist who, upon completing a concert, was overwhelmed by reporters asking how it felt to be so famous. The pianist pointed to an old man leaving the balcony and said, "That old man was my first piano teacher. He knows more than I ever will, and one nod from him means more than the praise of all the world." The pianist was not playing for the crowds but for one man in the balcony.

The believer is not ministering to the crowd but ministering to Him before the crowd, and it is true that one smile from our Father in heaven means more than all the approval of man. Preaching is very simple. Many have anxiety attacks from the thought of speaking to others. I remember driving to a church for my first preaching experience and the many stops along the way caused by a nervous stomach. I was nervous because I wanted to come up with something to say to the people. I wanted to speak to the people a blessing. However, preaching is not speaking to the people, it is speaking to God before the people. The easiest way to preach is to stand before God and tell Him the things for which you are grateful in front of the people. In a sermon I am talking to one person—God. I talk to Him about His mercy, love, compassion, forgiveness, help in time of need, and the blessing of my marriage. As I speak in His presence, His presence ministers to others, and things get worked out in His presence. Have a personal conversation with God in front of the people.

As we move into His presence, things are worked out. Often those in the Church move to doctrine, creeds, thoughts, or Scripture, and yet nothing is worked out. Why? They have not moved to His presence. Many a counseling session has analyzed the past, personalities, coping, denial, and co-dependency of the couple, and yet nothing is worked out. Why? Life is worked out in God's presence.

DAY 202
Miracles That Curse?

As the crowds were increasing, He began to say, "This generation is a wicked generation; it seeks for a sign, and yet no sign will be given to it but the sign of Jonah."

—LUKE 11:29

Many were questioning Jesus and seeking for a miracle they really did not want, because once they saw one, they were forced to a place of making a decision for which they were not ready. The decision was to accept what Jesus said He was or deny it. They had played a clever game in their minds and emotions; as long as they could ask Jesus questions, they could be unbelieving without condemnation. However, once seeing, they had to choose. The problem was that they could not choose, and the only thing left to do was rid themselves of the One who performed the miracle and forced the decision. The miracle was actually a curse. Believer, do you really want a miracle before God is ready to give it to you? It will demand a response and call for an action of faith on your part. Has your faith come to the place where you can so act? If not, the miracle will be a curse. To simplify things, seek Christ and not the miracle, so when the miracle comes, He will have prepared you for it.

DAY 203
Missing The Will Of God

As he neared Damascus on his journey,
suddenly a light from heaven flashed around him.
He fell to the ground and heard a voice say to him,
"Saul, Saul, why do you persecute me?"

—ACTS 9:3, 4 [NIV]

We need to stop and think about most things for a minute, and this passage is no exception. We know that God does not show partiality; it is not within the capacity of love to do so. Paul, as an unbeliever, was missing the will of God and so was stopped by Him and set on the proper way. When Paul was missing the will of God as a believer, an angel was sent to redirect him. If God did not allow Paul to miss the will of God, and God does not show partiality, then how could He let any of us? Therefore, if a believer were able to miss the will of God, it would be God's fault. Now, I am not talking about sins; all sins are missing the will of God. All have sinned, and therefore all have missed the will of God. No, what I am talking about is the ultimate will of God for life's calling and vocation. It is impossible to miss it.

Paul became content with whatever state he was in. Many in the Church have fed discontent into the lives of others. Some constantly meddle in the lives of God's people and define what the will of God is. It is evil to make someone discontented with where he is. A woman is struggling in her marriage, and the first thing the evil, meddling Christian says is, "You should go!" Another is barely coping at work with a condemning boss who makes him feel trapped. The meddler adds to the turmoil by saying, "God is calling you into fulltime ministry." How do these meddling people know the mind of God? Included in the love of God is the assurance that daily we are getting what we need, and that today we are in the perfect will of God. His will for us today may simply be changing diapers as we care for a new little life!

DAY 204
Money

Do not store up for yourselves treasures on earth, where moth and rust destroy, and where thieves break in and steal. But store up for yourselves treasures in heaven, where moth and rust do not destroy, and where thieves do not break in and steal. For where your treasure is, there your heart will be also.

—MATTHEW 6:19-21 [NIV]

I have been learning more about money lately. I know the topic of money is not evil, though sometimes while listening to certain appeals I have felt the world would be better off without it. Money is neither good nor evil, but money will often expose good and evil. How we use our money will reveal our values; giving makes known that in which our hearts ultimately trust. We tend to give our money to what we give our lives to. I find it amazing that Jesus used money to expose hearts. In the temple He went right past those who opposed God through all of the absurdities they brought in and straightway went over to observe the people as they were giving. God is not interested in our money, for He gave it to us to begin with. His contention is that generosity comes not from a bank balance but from the attitude of the heart. People do not need more money to change the heart's attitude; what they need is Jesus to transform their hearts to the extent that giving brings them a shout of joy. We must see money for what it really is. To me a most interesting aspect of money is how it represents our life in exchangeable form. We work, giving our time, talent, and energy; in exchange we are given money, which is not just a collection of paper and metal; it represents sacrifice and the expenditure of our lives. In giving we are presenting ourselves to God as a living sacrifice; giving is a form of our worship. Money is our servant; we are not to be its slaves (something we should remember when pulling out the credit card and indebting ourselves to others).

Money given in the Kingdom, although invisible in many ways, materializes in concrete ways through evangelism, helping others, provision for the needy, etc. It can make dreams a reality. The Tabernacle was built from the gold jewelry that was brought to the Lord. I marvel at what ALMI has been able to accomplish over the years. We stay with a Christian worker and pay. This is passed on to those who work with him; his food is purchased from a believer, the bricks are bought from a Christian's factory, and his employees are paid. How far does the money go? How greatly is it multiplied? God is in charge of that! True ministries receive donations because they are about people being blessed, His kingdom growing in tangible ways, and the revelation of hearts. I want all of us to use our wealth to serve God's eternal purposes on this earth while we have the opportunity. Giving leads to the expansion of our hearts. "Not that I seek the gift itself, but I seek for the profit which increases to your account. But I have received everything in full, and have an abundance; I am amply supplied, having received from Epaphroditus what you have sent, a fragrant aroma, an acceptable sacrifice, well-pleasing to God. And my God will supply all your needs according to His riches in glory in Christ Jesus" (Philippians 4:17-19).

DAY 205
My Sheep Hear My Voice

My sheep hear My voice, and I know them,
and they follow Me.

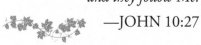

—JOHN 10:27

A friend formerly in the Navy told me of a game they played during training. One man would be blindfolded, and the object of the game was to direct the man to a chair and get him to sit down without touching it. Only one person had the man's interest in mind; all the rest were deceivers shouting the wrong directions. The goal of the truthful man was to get the blindfolded man to trust his voice and listen only to it. All others shouted bogus directions, wanting him to sit down with no chair under him! The men attempting to influence the sightless one could do anything but touch him. My friend told me it was amazing to watch the blindfolded person pick out the voice of the one who was truly his friend and not listen to the others. The blindfolded man would sit to find a chair under him.

Another friend tells me that man is never deceived unless he willingly wants to be deceived, and therefore he is not truly deceived. In part I believe this, for "My sheep hear My voice." The Lord is always speaking to us. There is a difference between His voice and all the deceiving voices, and though it may start out being difficult to discern, in the end it is unmistakably the one making our heart leap with assurance. His voice is the only one we need to heed.

DAY 206
New Titles For Old Problems

And no one puts new wine into old wineskins; otherwise the new wine will burst the skins and it will be spilled out, and the skins will be ruined.

 —LUKE 5:37

Americans have an interesting habit of taking old problems and giving them new, more palatable titles. For example, I remember the time I was talking to a woman who was struggling with an indiscreet rendezvous. I questioned her as to what exactly was an indiscreet rendezvous and discovered she was involved in adultery. I then explained how giving a new title to an old sin did not make the sin any more acceptable, but in fact made the sin more dangerous, for in the Bible we find forgiveness for adultery but nowhere discover forgiveness for indiscreet rendezvous.

In the same way, much is written today on the topic of shame, and indeed, many are struggling with shame issues such as might be created by an alcoholic parent, embarrassing events from the past, humiliating circumstances, or abuse of one kind or another. Some are happy to point out shame in the life of others, but of course when they are questioned as to how deliverance comes, the response is a hearty, "Learn to deal with it!" When questioned further as to how one might "deal with it," the answer becomes very vague or calls upon a personal strength not possessed by the person who landed in the counselor's office. No one really, absolutely knows how to deal with shame until we begin to dissect shame as another name for pride. It is impossible to have shame where there is not pride, for shame's roots are in pride. By giving pride the new title of shame, it does not sound so bad. In fact, it sounds like those struggling with shame are actually victims. But this new name not only allows for escape from personal responsibility but also makes an answer to the problem elusive. Stick to the proper name of shame and the Bible has plenty of advice to offer. Pride is not from God, and He is all too happy for us to receive His love that overcomes it (I John 2:15, 16). Shame is dishonor, but that is what pride brings, dishonor. "When pride comes, then comes dishonor, but with the humble is wisdom" (Proverbs 11:2).

Life is Jesus! Life is not increased or decreased by what has happened to us. When we look for life in a place other than Jesus, we will find shame. Why? Because of pride.

We must be alert as believers. The unbelieving world continues to introduce concepts to us through the back door. Psychologists do not believe in the concept of sin and therefore busy themselves retitling it so man will have excuses. However, God has an answer for sin and retitling excludes His answers. It simply is not true that Jesus died in 32 AD and no one was helped until Freud came along!

DAY 207
Nobody Has It All

And He gave some as apostles, and some as prophets, and some as evangelists, and some as pastors and teachers.

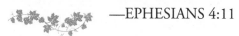

—EPHESIANS 4:11

In our uniqueness we express the things of God differently. I am once again reminded of how I prayed for the Father to give me all the revelation of Christ that is possible for man. I was given a vision of a room so large that none of the walls could be seen, but gold chests were all around, and on each chest was the name of a different believer. God spoke: "It would take every believer to begin to express who I am. Each is given his own revelation. There is a chest with your name on it. You will have what I give from within that chest, but all of Christ cannot be expressed in one man." Amen, I have seen Christ in, learned of Him from, and received revelations of Him from very different people, ranging from what the world and religion would call the upper and lower classes or castes. I understand

I am only a thread in this Christian life, my message is simple, and what I say is not intended to be the last word for the Christian life. Yet sometimes I am taken aback by the complaints.

I remember getting traditional East Indian treatments consisting of beautifully textured, wonderfully smelling botanical oils. The interesting thing about those doing the massages was that though their hands were constantly in oil and rubbing soft skin, the palms of their hands were covered with huge, hard calluses. As with everything in life, we can learn something about Life, and I could see how even in ministry in the Holy Spirit and touching the souls of believers where they hurt, there must be a little protection. If I reacted every time someone criticized me or sent an angry e-mail, I would never get around to ministering. I must glance at the complaint and gaze at the Christ within the person.

More than once I have heard this testimony from a believer who invited me to his church: "The pastor said he wants me to remain involved, but I am not to advance the 'Christ in you, the hope of glory' teaching that Abiding Life Ministries brought." This baffles me, for even if I were to look at the very worst in teaching I have ever delivered, I find no doctrine that would deter someone from a focus on Jesus, because it is the best teaching when the goal is Christ. However, I realize that the teaching of Christ in you does equalize all believers, and those in the Christian religion have worked very hard to be exclusive and appear superior. I thought I would have my throat cut in Asia when before a large crowd I said, "If the men in robes and collars have not admitted to you any of their weaknesses, you should stop attending their church." For it had, in fact, become "their" church, the self-serving domain of the higher-ups.

We must look at teaching and judge its goal. Is the goal the revelation of Christ in you? If not, then what is the goal? God was so depressed with man, so to speak, that He sent His Son. If the goal is man, then you will get depressed. However, I am a great supporter of the Christian religion and the legalism to which it gives birth. Why? Because we need it! We must pass through it to discover that the man who is now in Christ is just as weak as he was before Christ. Once this is accomplished, we will look in dependence to the Christ who is in us for everything needed.

Well, no matter what treasure chest is yours to open, you will know it is the golden one when "your message," or rather, as Paul called it, "my gospel," is pointing others to Christ.

DAY 208
No Condemnation

There is therefore now no condemnation for those who are in Christ Jesus.

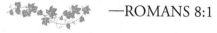

—ROMANS 8:1

I was ministering to a fellow whose particular area of defeat was drugs. Upon believing in Christ, he discovered that the life of Christ is free from drugs, and when Christ became his life, he was naturally free. For some time he lived quite happily in this newfound freedom. With the passing of time I lost track of this brother. One day I decided to call; I left a message, but my call was not returned. I knew what had happened; this brother was back into drugs. After a time I persuaded him to meet with me, and when he entered my office I said, "Don't say a word until I have finished."

I went to my whiteboard and began to explain what happened to him. "First, you turned your back on God; I know this is true, for you must always turn away from God to turn toward sin. God is always there; you cannot lose Him, but you can avoid Him. So the first problem is that you turned away from God. Second, that makes sin easier, for victory is only natural when you are turned toward Him. You know that to be true, for it has been your experience in the past, and truth is not only preached but experienced. The third thing that happened is in many ways the worst! Satan does not care so much if a believer sins, because sin lasts for an instant. What Satan wants is the self-condemnation that can last for a lifetime. Brother, you made a big mistake; you entered into condemnation! It moves your eyes completely to self by bringing obsession with the sin, self-hatred, guilt, fear, and a constant running from Him. Satan knows you cannot be free from the thing on which you focus, and what you focus on, you worship. Drugs have become the object of worship because of condemnation. You are in a Satanic spiral consisting of condemnation that makes you turn from God and avoidance of God that allows sin to dominate. This leads to more condemnation and a tightening spiral."

I finished, and with wide eyes he gave only an "Uh-huh!" So I continued.

"Brother, when you came to Christ you were carrying a bag called 'drugs.' Did God accept you with that bag?"

Yes, he knew that to be true.

"Well, do you think God has changed? If He accepted you with the bag when you came, do you think that now He rejects you with that bag?"

"Well, no, maybe," was his uncertain response.

"Brother, dwell on this. God knew what you would be at your worst, and still He wanted you." Then I dropped the bombshell. "Brother, you and I are designing a new discipleship program. For the next few months I want you to take drugs every morning and evening. God will accept you! Now, that being said, you no longer have an excuse not to read the Bible, not to fellowship with God, not to pray, or not to fellowship with other believers. I will expect you to continue on in all those things, for the drugs that brought the separation you perceived in your mind have been approved."

Guess what? He did not start taking drugs again! Why? Because moving out of condemnation and back to the Father naturally subjugated the drug habit. He was once again abiding! A lesser truth must always give way to a greater truth; once he possessed the greater truth, all lesser truth was his. Our top priority of what God wants fixed—in this case drugs—is rarely God's, which in this case was turning back to God. God's way never seems to be the way of man!

DAY 209
No-hopers?

Therefore if anyone is in Christ, he is a new creature.

 —II CORINTHIANS 5:17

Yes, we have become something new, different, and unique. We have received a new nature, and old desires have passed away. Our lives as Christians now naturally follow the commands of Christ without effort. We know this to be true, but has it been the experience of the average believer? Has it been our experience? Or is such a life—a daily following of Christ without effort—only reserved for the lucky few?

So often, by all appearances, the normal Christian life is not one of new desire but a constant battle against the old, one in which dissatisfaction over our inability to "be Christian" increases. Yet we are still told that we are new creations. How can we born-again, new creatures, with our old men crucified with Christ, continue to struggle with the habits, failures, sins, depression, and frustrations of the past? Does our struggle reveal something wrong with us or with our conversion? Does it show we need something else? Are we lacking a particular "spiritual experience"? Are we truly committed? Do we spend enough time in the Word?

On the contrary, take heart. The struggle reveals something right in you! It proves you are a new creation with new desires! Struggle is the proof of being born again!

Praise God that you struggle! Let me explain.

I met with a small group of men from varying denominations and opened the meeting with a question. "Would you be comfortable wearing a dress, high-heels, nylons, and a wig for one week? What if you had no choice in the matter?" I jokingly stated that if they were comfortable in women's clothes, I was taking appointments for individual counseling sessions. However, all the men agreed they would be uncomfortable…very uncomfortable! Why? Their wives were not uncomfortable in such attire. The answer was really quite simple. For a man to wear women's clothes goes against the male nature, causing a struggle and great discomfort. The fact is, we learn much more about our nature from what we struggle against than from our victories. The struggle against temptation says more about our nature than what we do daily without thinking about it.

Before you accepted Christ as Savior, did you struggle with immorality, lying, slander, and sedatives, or were these things quite natural for you? Before I became a Christian the greatest struggle I had concerning sin was the nagging thought that I may not get as much of it as I wanted. After Christ entered my life, I began to struggle with what at one time was perfectly natural for me. The struggle revealed a change. In fact, *the depth of conversion is revealed by the intensity of struggles*. Many assert that the proof of conversion comes in the form of feelings, voices, and miracles. Yet often overlooked is struggle as an absolute standard for conversion and commitment.

You can know, then, if your nature has changed by observing the behavior, attitudes, and sin against which you struggle. Most believe the opposite, that if they have struggled since their new birth, it is proof positive something is wrong with them. Struggle instead reveals that something is right with you, that you have been changed.

DAY 210
Obedience Learned

He learned obedience from the things which He suffered.

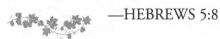

—HEBREWS 5:8

The most amazing things about this passage are the first two words, "He learned." It is not easy to wrap our minds around the fact that the God who became a man proceeded to learn. We thought God knew everything, past, present, and future! The secret is that if God can do anything, He can choose not to know and to learn. Christ, by becoming a man, chose to empty Himself, to know less, and to learn. Beautiful! I have met some very spiritual people in my life that did not know very much. Though they were in complete communion with God, there was much to learn. Learning through revelation is something that adds a yearned-for dimension to life; the excitement of enlightenment is beyond description. Jesus maximized His experience of what it means to be a man by not knowing and having to learn, and thus He learned obedience through the things He suffered. Our difficulty in understanding this verse comes from our knowledge that we all suffered through sin, failure, and pride in order to learn obedience. We learned the hard way what is not the Way before finally repenting and deciding to enjoy the Way as we walked obediently. We project this experience on to the passage and are confused as we think Jesus could have sinned in order to learn it was better to obey. However, the distinction is that He never sinned, He was the spotless Lamb of God, and He remained a perfect sacrifice. Obedience cannot be learned without suffering. Our suffering was self-imposed, and we learned obedience. His suffering was others-imposed, and He learned obedience. How could He be obedient to love an enemy until He had an enemy? How could He pray for those who persecute Him until He was persecuted? How would He be obedient unto death for the sins of the whole world if the sins of the whole world were not cast upon Him? To be perfectly obedient, there must be particular situations for which certain actions or behaviors are implicitly required. One cannot say, "I obey the command to love my enemy," if he has not yet had an enemy. He can have the willingness to obey, but he has not as yet obeyed, since obedience arises only when a situation calls for it. All that Jesus taught, He did. Therefore, suffering provided the situations that called for His obedience; out of those situations, as a man, He proved the joy of obedience. "He learned obedience through the things that He suffered." So will you! Wonderful!

DAY 211
Obedience That Blesses

For this is the love of God, that we keep His commandments; and His commandments are not burdensome. For whatever is born of God overcomes he world; and this is the victory that has overcome the world—our faith.

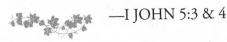

—I JOHN 5:3 & 4

Why is the topic of obedience a constant emphasis? Why are the people elevated in other believers' opinions and viewed as accomplishing the nearly impossible when they are perceived to be obedient? Obedience, after all, is not difficult. We either obey or we do not. We are slaves of righteousness, so every believer can choose to obey. The reason it is perceived as being a big deal is that legalism has found a way into the Christian life through the topic of obedience, just as sin found a way in through the law. Legalists find a way through obedience to manipulate and control believers' lives. We hear, "God blessed me because I obeyed." In reality, God blessed because of Jesus, and Jesus has set us free to obey. In every religion but Christianity obedience and blessing are tied at the hip; in Christianity we are tied at the hip to Jesus, hence, tied to many blessings. All believers are blessed, even though we do not always obey, because Jesus is a blessing and He dwells in us.

I was watching a man advertising holy spring water by claiming fantastic testimonies that came from its use. He told of one woman who won a $1,200,000 judgment against a man because she used the holy spring water. "Blessings" tied to spring water! As believers, obedience is one way we can bless ourselves as well as others. However, we must never forget that blessings come not from our behavior but His. Our obedience does not change God's view of us; Jesus changed God's view of us.

DAY 212
One and Yet Many

Hear, O Israel! The Lord is our God, the Lord is one!
—DEUTERONOMY 6:4

Then God said, "Let Us make man in Our image, according to Our likeness . . ."
—GENESIS 1:26

God is One and yet He is many. "The Lord thy God is One," and yet, "Let Us make man." We are made in His image; therefore we can gain understanding into Him by looking at ourselves. Draw a circle that represents you; you are one. Yet in that circle are mind, will, emotions, body, and heart. As we look at all the words in the circle, we discover that we are also many. These many elements do not often agree. We are in chaos and cannot say, "Let us do" anything. Mind is not in agreement with emotions, body wars with mind, and will keeps eating sugar when it knows body will suffer. We are in conflict.

Now draw another circle that represents God. The Lord is One. In the circle are His judgments, His names,

His provision, His love, His will, His Wisdom, and His Word (Jesus). They all agree perfectly; they are One. Do you believe that His judgments and His love agree? He gives the death sentence for certain behaviors in the Old Testament; is that love? We too often think of judgment as punishment. It is not. Sin and punishment are one and the same. Punishment happens at the very moment sin occurs. Judgment is God with an IQ of 999 trillion+ telling us how to make the best of a bad situation. Sin is not a created thing but a result of natural created things acting in an unnatural way. A mule is not a created being but the result of the coming together of two created beings, a horse and a donkey. Death will not change the nature of the mule, but it will take the reality of a mule out of sight, in which case the thought of making more mules is not overtly present. Judgments take a result out of sight so the sin is not overtly present and covertly encouraged. Judgments agree with love and do what is best for us.

DAY 213
Oneness

In the beginning was the Word, and the Word was with God, and the Word was God.

 —JOHN 1:1

There is a phrase often taken lightly and rarely understood by the speaker, but one which stirs God's compassion, love, His loss, His gain, His forgiveness, His hopes, His desires, and His pain. This one phrase can do all of the above. It is a sacred phrase! It gives the speaker the benefit of all of God's goodness, His fellowship, His constant care, His listening ear, and His loving heart. The phrase that does all of this is: *the blood of Jesus*! When we ask in the blood of Jesus all that is within God is stirred. This phrase calls to our attention the very character of God. He is reminded of His great love and oneness with the Son, the loss of His Son, judgment, and finally, new birth. Is not this phrase sacred? Should not the believer be careful when invoking it? Should we not expect great things when asked in the blood of Jesus? This one phrase reminds God of the condition of His creatures, their failure, their sin, their self-centeredness, their need for Him to do something, the sending of His Son, the crucifixion, the jeering mob, the denial of a nation, a city, and even the Son's followers. Be careful how you use this phrase, but do use it! "And they overcame him because of the blood of the Lamb" (Revelation 12:11).

DAY 214
Only His Death

For Christ also died for sins once for all, the just for the unjust, so that He might bring us to God, having been put to death in the flesh, but made alive in the spirit.

—I PETER 3:18

I begin every morning the same way, "Thank You, Jesus, that You became my separation from God, and therefore I can never be separated from Him." It is a beautiful revelation. His mercies are new every morning! Every single morning! Christ was my separation and that settles it all. I have often heard it taught that it should have been me hanging on the cross and not Jesus, but here is the problem. Let us assume it was me hanging on the cross for my own sins; how can a sinner bear his own sin? Had it been me and not Him, nothing would have happened to elevate my sins. Thousands were crucified for their sins; Jesus had a thief on both sides. One was invited into paradise by Jesus, but not because the thief suffered for his own sins. The thief's death on a cross did nothing to redeem him, but rather it was his recognition of Christ that redeemed him. My point is that if Christ had not taken my sins on the cross, then going to the cross myself would have accomplished nothing. In this regard it was a substitution, for if I refuse the substitution, I might die on a cross but I could never be a sacrifice for my sins; I would have a just death for my sins. What Jesus did was wonderful. Being sinless and blameless, He was actually able to take my sin out of me, have it placed on Him, and then become a substitution that redeemed me and set me free. His was the only death that could have accomplished such a feat, and He did it for all men. This is not religious dogma but faith in the Son of God who has loved me and was delivered up for me.

Today we say, "Thank You that because of the cross, that because You were my separation from God, that because You took my sins upon yourself, I have no obstacle between God and me. I will be heard today, helped today, shown compassion today, and You will treat me as David, a man after Your heart that will do all of Your will. All because of You, Jesus!" Amen, what a confidence.

DAY 215
Only One Faith

There is one body and one Spirit, just as also you were called in one hope of your calling; one Lord, one faith, one baptism, one God and Father of all who is over all and through all and in all.

—EPHESIANS 4:4-6

For years I would read the passage in Ephesians and attempt to discern what was the "one faith" of the Christians. I think I had read the passage so many times with a religious pair of glasses that I was missing the context. The "one faith" referred to is not the one faith among the many faiths in the world, but a statement of fact that there is but one faith, and everything else is a religion. The basic difference between faith and religion is that religion's success will somehow end at the feet of the worshipper, whereas the success of faith ends at the feet of God. Hence, religion is all about man, and faith is all about God. Religious people are not exercising faith in God; just listen to them talk to realize that life for them revolves around their behavior, knowledge, or attitudes. Whether it be the piety of the Buddhist, the meditation of the Hindu, the gyrations of the Voodoo priest, the Law keeper, the candle or incense lighter, the kingdom builder, the "cutting edge" preacher, or the doctrinally correct, there exists between them the fellowship of the religious. Among them, too, a great lie is perpetrated that the exercise of their religion somehow either alters the very flesh of man or the plane of flesh on which all men live. Religious people have an appearance of godliness, as described by Paul to Timothy: "For men will be lovers of self . . . lovers of pleasure rather than lovers of God, holding to a form of godliness, although they have denied its power; avoid such men as these" [II Timothy 3:2-5]. Interestingly, religious people will focus on certain aspects of religion that most cannot achieve in order to maintain their "position" in their manmade religion; they define what form the godliness will take, so oddly enough they succeed at their own definition! Honestly, I have no vested interest in stating the obvious, but all religious people are failures.

The adherents of humanism—which is one great competitor of faith—continue to take human beings' less than 1% success at playing God and amplify it in their minds and communications until it looks more like 100%. Any of us could come up with a lengthy list of famous people who have been sainted beyond human recognition. Christians have done the same general distortion through stories and images of believers to the point that they would be unrecognizable to those who actually knew, lived, and worked with them. The saddest thing is that many, upon hearing of the exaggerated portrayal of a spectacular spiritual life, begin a lifelong journey to emulate the Christian, who in reality is non-existent. This imitating leads to the disastrous consequences of "acting religious" as they flesh out phony copies of the exalted. "For all have sinned and fall short of the glory of God" [Romans 3:23]. Religious people, no matter what the religion, have fallen short of the glory of God. Amen!

There is one faith, and in that one faith God deals with man by putting success at His own feet. He gives an attainable faith, for God's goal is to bring in as many as possible, while religion's goal is to be as exclusive as possible. "But what does it say? 'THE WORD IS NEAR YOU, in your mouth and in your heart'—that is, the word of faith which we are preaching, that if you confess with your mouth Jesus as Lord, and believe in your heart that God raised Him from the dead, you will be saved; for with the heart a person believes, resulting in righteousness, and with the mouth he confesses, resulting in salvation. For the Scripture says, 'WHOEVER BELIEVES IN HIM WILL NOT BE DISAPPOINTED'" [Romans 10:8-11]. Paul, seeing the difference between the efforts of man that lead to religion and the work of God that leads to the one faith, rightly says, "Where then is the boasting?" "But by His doing you are in Christ Jesus, who became to us wisdom from God, and righteousness and sanctification, and redemption, so that, just as it is written, 'LET HIM WHO BOASTS, BOAST IN THE LORD'" [I Corinthians 1:30, 31]. Religious people are like shadows that do not exist in the manner in which they would like to portray themselves.

In this one faith, there will be times of discouragement, failure, doubt, bewilderment, rebellious children, loneliness, outbursts of anger, walking in the flesh, and more. There will also be times of unspeakable joy, fulfillment, satisfaction, encouragement, faith that is mountain moving, and unwavering focus. We are unique creatures, half spirit and half flesh. Just as we walk on two legs we must, for now, walk in two realities, that of the flesh and that of the spirit. Religious people seem to want to go through life hopping, either on the leg called flesh and wanting everything the visible world might offer, or on the leg called spirit, living a life of avoidance of the world. Did you know no revival has ever taken place around a monastery, whether Buddhist or Christian?

We must be of the one faith, of those who see this physical world as one in which life with a small "l" will reveal and perfect Life with a capital "L." The human being is not an accident but is exactly what God wanted, for the physical must come before the spiritual. This earth, our bodies, our souls, and our spirits have a common goal: the revelation and choice of the Way, the Truth, and the Life. Just as we bring a bit of heaven to earth, we will also take a bit of earth with us to heaven. Our minds will not go blank when we enter heaven. When we enter heaven, we will remember and rejoice all the more in the Lamb that was slain.

"But we have this treasure in earthen vessels, so that the surpassing greatness of the power may be of God and not from ourselves; we are afflicted in every way, but not crushed; perplexed, but not despairing; persecuted, but not forsaken; struck down, but not destroyed; always carrying about in the body the dying of Jesus, so that the life of Jesus also may be manifested in our body. For we who live are constantly being delivered over to death for Jesus' sake, so that the life of Jesus also may be manifested in our mortal flesh. So death works in us, but life in you" [II Corinthians 4:7-12].

DAY 216
Others Need To Change

Be of the same mind toward one another; do not be
haughty in mind, but associate with the lowly. Do not be
wise in your own estimation.

—ROMANS 12:16

Often we see irritating behavior in a mate, a friend, a coworker, or a child. We point it out, either covertly or overtly, in hopes of seeing what we believe is a much-needed change. If change does not come, irritation gives way to resentment. We blame the person for purposely continuing to do what we dislike, just to annoy us.

Here are two things to keep in mind when examining the behavior of others. First, one of the things that makes ALMI discipleship different is that when discipling someone who is discouraged, we emphasize gifting rather than understanding. I go into each session with an empty bag, knowing I can only give as He gives to me. Every morning I have asked God for the gifts needed so His people are filled with the Spirit, are in fellowship with the Son of God, and are living in His presence. In this context, the one thing for which I constantly beseech Him is discernment, to save time in getting to the deepest level of need. I say this because on occasion God has revealed a problem to me He did not want me sharing with the person who had the problem. Why? I believe the problem I was seeing was way down on God's priority list, and, as with everything God reveals to us in the fullness of time, with eventual revelation will come His power to overcome it. I have never grown bored with the Christian experience! I believe His work will continue throughout our lives. Are we willing to wait for God to reveal a problem in another's life and bring His healing? I am not talking about outright sin, but rather the annoying mannerisms and characteristics of others. Rarely will any person change for another man, but will, in the light of His love, drop everything that hinders in order to lay hold of Him. Not being able to rest and wait on God for the changes in others brings us to our second point. Often we want others to change for our own comfort, to make life easier, to free us from our struggles; we want them to be loving toward us when offended, to meet our needs, to allow us to be spiritual. When this is the case, the other persons' problems are exposing more about us than them, revealing how we have placed ourselves on the throne and how our happiness is more important to us than God's work or His satisfaction. God will in no way allow our revelation of another's problems to bring us freedom.

DAY 217
Our Source

Keep watching and praying that you may not enter into temptation; the spirit is willing, but the flesh is weak.

—MATTHEW 26:41

When spirit dwells in flesh, the spirit will either be perfected or destroyed. In heaven, without hindrances, spirit never really sees its limitations. This is partially the problem Satan had, thinking he was equal to God. Putting spirit in flesh is redeeming for the spirit, the short course in revealing weakness. Once spirit has lived in flesh and found it is conquered by flesh (the spirit is willing but the flesh is weak), spirit enters into the realm of humility, where—clinging to and empowered by God—spirit perceives something it never would have if not presented with that new level of need: a deeper experience of the glory of God as He meets the need. Revelation comes through contrast; self-righteousness will always mask and hide the true nature of God, but spirit as it lives and is being perfected in flesh reveals the glory of God. Having descended and ascended, does Jesus see the Father differently? If so, is it gain? Jesus was made perfect through suffering (Hebrews 2:10). Was there an advantage to His becoming a man? " . . . and, once made perfect, He became the source of eternal salvation for all who obey Him and was designated by God to be high priest in the order of Melchizedek" (Hebrews 5:9-10, NIV).

DAY 218
Overcoming Food

You were taught, with regard to your former way of life, to put off your old self, which is being corrupted by its deceitful desires; to be made new in the attitude of your minds; and to put on the new self, created to be like God in true righteousness and holiness.

 —EPHESIANS 4:22-24 [NIV]

How often we have seen a child with an imaginary friend until, with growth, the day comes when the child lays aside the pretend friend for a real one. The idols we hold such as withdrawal, bitterness, people pleasing, depression, and more are merely pretend gods. With growth we will lay them aside for truly God. Some idols—coping mechanisms—present themselves uniquely, such as food. A drug addict who decides to stop taking drugs can withdraw from the drug scene and never have anything to do with it again. How successful would that addict be if it were impossible to withdraw from the drug scene? What if man's body were created in such a way that it had to have drugs every day, and drugs were freely available? He could walk up to the table three times a day and take all he wanted. It was up to him to take only the amount needed for survival. He would have to discipline himself not to take so much that he derived any pleasure from drugs, just staying at maintenance level. Pleasure could be obtained easily by taking just a little extra three times a day, but he must not. This illustration somewhat helps us see the daily struggle of the overeater. It would be easier to conquer overeating if it were possible to walk away from food altogether. If you cannot relate to what I am saying, then please feel free to move on to another article. This article is for overeaters, those among us who have a skinny person within screaming to get out!

How does the abiding life apply to overeating? We will peer deeper into the problem. An interesting array of feelings can come from food, such as wellbeing, reward, and security. However, after eating too much and looking in the mirror, euphoria is replaced by worthlessness, punishment, disgust, self-hatred, and self-rejection. Food for the overeater carries three messages with each bite: maintenance, pleasure, and worthlessness. Often the worthless feeling is followed by obsessing on not eating, though obsession will without fail increase the desire for food, for it is impossible to be free from something when constantly thinking about it! Since attempting to stop the spiral by focusing on food is not productive, why not focus on the feelings of worthlessness, countering them with truth? "The worthless me was crucified with Christ. What is true of Him is true of me. I take up the cross daily, keeping dead, worthless me in the grave." When food comes into our minds, we determine neither to think of getting food nor staying away from food. Instead, we say to our mind, "I will not go there," and change direction to pray and think of something else.

DAY 219
Passing On the Good News

And the word of the Lord was being spread through the whole region.

And the disciples were continually filled with joy and with the Holy Spirit.

—ACTS 13:49 & 52

I see that one day I will become irrelevant. I was at a Bible college when the elderly founder was speaking, and his message was as dead as Nelson. The students fell out of the lecture hall with glazed eyes, happy the torture had ended. Fifty years ago this man was a great blessing to the Body of Christ. I related my observation to one of the other teachers, and he heartily but reluctantly agreed. I explained that I was not criticizing but making a point; this teacher had read the founder's books, taken notes, and lectured the same material. So I asked him, "What was the response from your lectures?" He replied, "Oh, it was great, and the students really understood it!" That proved my point. We must pass on to each generation the TRUTH for them to process, make it their own, and then relate it to others in terms their generation understands. This is how the TRUTH remains relevant and is also why no person should apologize for using an idea he initially heard from another believer. Anyone who gets the witness has gotten the revelation, and this whole issue of copyrighting is foul in the Body. What one hears, what witnesses to a person, is given to him by God. He can rework it, spread it, and then the Lord will give more. Do not ever be bothered with the false guilt and lying emotions that say we must be original. The drivel of original men is not of interest to anyone, but the word from an inspired man, the thoughts God has given him, are of interest. Those words if copyrighted are actually the copyrighting of words of another, Jesus, and breaking the very law with which he is trying to saddle others. I understand a publisher wants things copyrighted in order to avoid being sued, but beyond that, it needs to be given a rest!

DAY 220
Peace and Power (Victory)

Now I make known to you, brethren, the gospel which I preached to you, which also you received, in which also you stand, by which also you are saved, if you hold fast the word which I preached to you, unless you believed in vain. For I delivered to you as of first importance what I also received, that Christ died for our sins according to the Scriptures, and that He was buried, and that He was raised on the third day according to the Scriptures . . .

 —I CORINTHIANS 15:1-4

All of creation looks for stability, peace. The body can be in climates with temperatures from 31 to 120 Fahrenheit (dry heat), and the blood remains the same. Spiritually we would like that kind of stability, not to be controlled by the things outside of us. As spiritual creatures we tend to be either warm-blooded or cold-blooded. The cold-blooded need a meeting outside of them that will whip them up to get them moving again. The spiritual man is warm-blooded, more than a conqueror when it comes to the things outside of him.

The body has an order; it will protect the heart and brain and sacrifice all else. We should have a spiritual order that delineates the divine and moral things we refuse to sacrifice. Look at things people today get passionate about protecting, such as the right to abortion and the right for same-sex marriages. People like this are protecting what is less significant in life and are dying.

DAY 221
Pegs and Relationships

Be devoted to one another in brotherly love; give
preference to one another in honor.

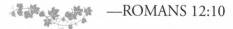 —ROMANS 12:10

I remember as a child being given a toy hammer and pegs sticking out of holes in a piece of wood. I would beat on each peg until it was even with the surface, turn the board over, and do the same again. Many see their relationships this way, full of pegs to be driven down before moving on to the next task. However, a relationship is not a task but something living, something that is never "accomplished." There is an old proverb about how one can know he (or she) is ready for marriage if first he manages to keep a plant living for one year, then a fish in a bowl alive for a year, and finally a dog or cat thriving for a year. If that can be done and nothing living around him suffers, he is ready for a relationship.

DAY 222
Permitting Versus Preventing

And His voice shook the earth then, but now He has promised, saying, "Yet once more I will shake not only the earth, but also the heaven." And this expression, "Yet once more," denotes the removing of those things which can be shaken, as of created things, in order that those things which cannot be shaken may remain.

—HEBREWS 12:26, 27

I am fascinated by and enjoying the amazing move toward 3-D movies. My first real experience with this technology was at the World's Fair in Seoul, Korea. I remember the little old women in traditional dress waving their hands in front of themselves to push away the images that appeared to be coming toward their faces. As an aside, I did make a mistake on that trip, in that there were few Westerners visiting and somehow the word spread among the crowd that I was Dustin Hoffman, the American actor. Out of politeness, I started signing autographs for the non-English-speaking spectators who had waited for me to emerge from an exhibit. It was people-pleasing gone mad, and it spiraled out of control when hundreds began to wait, and in the end I was exited out the back door of the fair! By the way, I am happy just being me. Well, back to the theater, where we are given glasses that allow us to see what the producer wants us to see, which are things that do not really exist.

In a like manner we are given "theological glasses" so that we will see what the giver wants us to see. Often it simply is not there. From our youth denominations have given us glasses to see what they desired to be seen. Something that must be twisted and distorted to be seen is rarely something true. Man is intent on knowing and systematizing God, which brings comfort to those who lack faith. Honestly, the mind of the created will never fully understand the mind of the Creator; it is not possible. The end result is the categorizing of believers. Are you Calvinist, Armenian, pre-tribulation, covenant, freewill, sovereignty, full-gospel, Spirit-filled, or more? When we hear a speaker, the glasses go on and we try to pigeonhole him. Often this is merely done to discount what is being said. Many actually are comforted by the thought that denominational leaders have already addressed all the pertinent issues, and therefore they do not need to. Of course, in all of this is the pride of man that makes him unteachable because of blindness and deafness. Why say all of this? Simply because I do not believe that the people of God are so stupid, unenlightened, ignorant, or "sheepish" (in the negative sense of the term) that the panic button needs to be hit when they hear something outside the denomination's theological box. Denominational leaders generally hate and oppose the teaching of the equality of believers. After all, they have sat through countless meaningless meetings and kissed up to hordes of self-important men to get to the place of wearing a robe or in other ways being "recognized." If all men and women were equal in Christ, they would have to admit to a wasted life. In fact, I have noticed that the truth of the equality of believers in revelation, relationship, and understanding of Christ creates a jealousy in those who have jumped through the hoops to gain some church-styled superiority.

Amen. I do not believe I know a thing more than any other believer, I have a special dispensation, I have a special handle on the truth, or others' insights into Jesus are any less important than mine, period. This is the foundation for looking at permission and preventing. I am not speaking in Calvinistic, Armenian, freewill, foreknowledge, or any other terms. I am just posing a question to a fellow believer, to a brother or sister in Christ. Ready? Does God permit what He could prevent? To bring this question quickly into black and white, I will add suicide to my question. Does God permit some to commit suicide while He prevents others? If the answer is no, then we should stop praising God for situations in which a believer was delivered. I have heard hundreds of such testimonies.

"My son was to take the bus, we got him there late, the bus ended up going off a cliff, and everyone died. Praise God that my son was not on the bus."

"There was a huge traffic accident, and if my daughter had been there one second earlier, she would not be here, praise God."

"My husband, praise God, at the last minute was sent to a different unit; his former unit was attacked, and no one survived."

"My wife overdosed, and her aunt she had not seen for years was in town, came to the house, called the police, and today my wife is alive, praise God."

Now, if God did not prevent these things, we must just label them as fate, and fate must be praised. On the other hand, if we are to thank God for preventing a death, we must admit that He has permitted others to die. For some reason that thought is quite objectionable to believers. It seems to lead to questions, justifications, and accusations, such as, "What kind of a God permits wars, death, and accidents?" This begs for an answer to the turnaround question, "Well, what do you believe in: Buddha, Krishna, spirits, the government? How can you keep believing when those 'gods' permit wars, death, and accidents?" Wars, deaths, and accidents are all absolutes; however, preventing and permitting is not to be equated with causing. The worship of false gods does cause those things, sin in human beings does cause those things, but the Creator does not cause them. If I let the dominoes fall in the direction of saying that God does not permit and prevent, the end is chaos, and there is really no need to have a God but just press on in chaos and fate.

Therefore, I must say I believe God will both permit and prevent. This is not a stretch on two counts. First, I believe what the Scripture teaches, "Flesh and blood cannot inherit the Kingdom of God; nor does the perishable inherit the imperishable" (I Corinthians 15:50). This establishes an absolute: Man must die. This then leads to another Biblical truth: The days of man are numbered. If God numbers our days, then can a drunken driver shorten them? Could a war shorten them? Can cancer shorten them? Could suicide shorten them? I do not believe it is accurate to say that a murderer took a life; instead, he was the "means" by which the life was taken; he was not permitted to take the life until the fullness of time, for flesh and blood cannot enter the Kingdom of God. I do not believe that cancer took the life of someone's mate. I believe that flesh and blood do not enter the Kingdom of God and cancer was the means by which God permitted the loved one to exit.

To recap, God has numbered our days, we must exit, there must be a means of our exiting, and God permits or prevents the "means" according to His will and the number of our days already set. Therefore, if the means of exiting is suicide, murder, war, disease, or old age (which is technically a disease), what is the difference? Here is how I see it. God permits the perfect means to accomplish the most in His will. For example, look at murder, which did not happen without permission, His permitting. However, the means will accomplish much. For those who have a heart for the Lord, hearing the news will break them. My children attended Columbine High School, famous for the mass murders. Hundreds of students turned their hearts toward Christ. Those who were killed only exited by permission. Those who did the killing by permission had their hearts revealed also; they were murderers. The glory of God is in choice. He permits choice, but choice is within His parameters, so man chooses, but God, in a sense, restrains the choice until the perfect time, when the choice will either reveal the soft hearts of people or their hard hearts; they will receive a blessing or a curse. Their judgment will be "good and faithful servant" or "depart from Me." Pharaoh's heart was hardened by both the good God had provided for him and the curses brought to his land and people. Is that not amazing to see? Some have pitted themselves against God, and any occurrence not proving their assessment of Him must be twisted and distorted in their minds to continue to support their position. At that point God is condemned by them if He helps and condemned if He does not. Even the blessings of God prove to them that God is to be rejected. One day I will die. I do not know the means, but I believe those means will be perfect, and some will recognize Jesus, and others will have the cup of judgment filled as they refuse to see Jesus. God is really incredible!

Now, if God has permitted something unpleasant into our life, it was done out of love. He only permits in the believer's life the things that will build the believer. I know so many people who would never have come to Christ had they not been abused. Does this mean God condones abuse? Never! It means He allows wicked men to choose, wicked men choose to do something wicked to victims, and those wicked men will be judged. However, it also means that God permitted the wicked to act in a believer's life only because it would ultimately drive him to Jesus. Had it not driven him toward Christ, He would have prevented it. This takes revelation, but it will set the believer free and keep him from living in regret concerning an event in time; the enemy only knows the past and therefore comes to whisper, "If that had not happened to you, if God had prevented it, you would be fulfilled and happy." It is a lie. The fact is that had the event not happened, the believer might never have come to know Christ. No doubt the wicked meant it to destroy the person, but God meant it to build him, and He has the last word.

Now, having established the above—that we must exit, there must be a means to our exit, and God will maximize the means of our exit—I will revisit my question. Is there a difference between exiting through old age or suicide? No! Many of us have had to experience a suicide in our families. I know the questions left unanswered. God permits. I have more stories from those who wanted to commit suicide and it did not work out than I do notes from families who had to deal with a suicide. God has both permitted and prevented. In our minds, the consequences of the "means" of exiting are much different. I must agree. Suicide is the most hurtful thing anyone can do to those he loves. It is much easier to blame a war or a drunk driver for a death than to blame the person who killed himself. However, I believe God did permit. Many "victims" of suicide have gone as far as they were going to go in this life concerning the revelation of Christ. God permits their exit in order to avoid many negatives that might come their way in the future. This is hard to grasp, since we only see someone's exiting as missing out on blessings. This is deception, because we all know the daily struggles of life with a small "l" as we discover life with a capital "L." I believe the God of LOVE permits a teenager to die in an accident because the revelation he needed was attained, and to remain on the earth would actually send him in reverse. I believe the same of the person who commits suicide.

I began all of this by saying that you have Christ, Christ is teaching you, and we believers are equal. This is my assessment, my gospel, and I have shared it with you. Amen.

DAY 223
Prayer

Then David the king went in and sat before the LORD, and he said, "Who am I, O Lord GOD, and what is my house, that You have brought me this far? And yet this was insignificant in Your eyes, O Lord GOD, for You have spoken also of the house of Your servant concerning the distant future. And this is the custom of man, O Lord GOD. Again what more can David say to You? For You know Your servant, O Lord GOD! For the sake of Your word, and according to Your own heart, You have done all this greatness to let Your servant know. For this reason You are great, O Lord GOD; for there is none like You, and there is no God besides You, according to all that we have heard with our ears."

—II SAMUEL 7:18-22

Prayer is a wonderful thing, for in it we can express the greatness of our God—the only God—and our gratitude toward Him. Prayer is a relationship builder . . . that is, from our perspective; God has had a relationship with us before the foundations of the world. I have often pondered prayer and have a few observations. Again, everything I say is not absolute, but I trust that I am pointing to the One who is absolute, the sum total of resolution and truth, fixed eternally in the universe.

To begin with, I do not think that the purpose of prayer is to direct God. We have a God, and that statement says it all, for the very confession of that designation proclaims that He does not need directing. Only those with a small god need to direct him; our God knows all and is directed by no one, but we are to listen to His direction. So many who entitle themselves "Prayer Warriors" believe they will change the course of God by countless repetitions. Jesus spoke to this very attitude: "And when you are praying, do not use meaningless repetition, as the Gentiles do, for they suppose that they will be heard for their many words. So do not be like them; for your Father knows what you need before you ask Him" (Matthew 6:7, 8). I have never understood the emphasis on going to a city to walk around it and pray. In a city near where I live there is even a huge building around which fly the flags of differing countries, positioned in the direction the country lies from there; the goal is to stand at the flagpole representing the country for which one has a burden and pray. I cannot get anyone to explain to me why we would have to go to a country or point toward it to pray. Can we not enter our closet and pray? Amen, if believers want to travel and see a place, they should go without spiritualizing it. God does not really care if they go to Israel for curiosity or enjoyment.

I believe there are several purposeful bases for prayer. First, it is the recognition of the constant unbroken relationship we as believers have with the Father, a relationship not dependent on time, place, or our present condition. "For in Him we live and move and exist" (Acts 17:28); it is so good to recognize that and not feel the need to create it. Second, the intent of prayer is not to change the mind of God but to come to peace with the will of God. This is of utmost importance in this present day. We must remember that God is permitting what He could prevent for the revelation of hearts. We will not change an evil person's choice. God permits man to have choice for the revelation of hearts. In the final judgment, a heart will be judged as it was revealed to be in this life. In prayer, we find peace with what God does, allows, prevents, and denies. Finally, prayer permits us to participate in the work of God. For example, I am awakened in the middle of the night and told to pray for someone. It is not as though if I turn over and go back to sleep, God will not act; it is merely a matter of my missing the blessing of participating in what God is going to do. Later, when I hear that the person was under attack, in a near accident, or had family struggles, I rejoice in the awareness that God came at the exact moment to deliver, and I am blessed that He allowed me to participate in what He was doing. In fact, any time we experience answered prayer we can boast in the Lord that He enlightened us to pray for what He was going to do; He allowed us to take part in His kingdom doings.

In short, prayer is very easy and enjoyable. In the recognition of His presence within and without, we rest, participate, and enjoy our life in Him; we want nothing but His will, which is the overriding affirmation of our prayer life. Have we not all had our fill of our own will, since we have never enjoyed it?

DAY 224
Predestination, Foreknowledge, or Choice?

What shall we say then? There is no injustice with God, is there? May it never be! For He says to Moses, "I WILL HAVE MERCY ON WHOM I HAVE MERCY, AND I WILL HAVE COMPASSION ON WHOM I HAVE COMPASSION." So then it does not depend on the man who wills or the man who runs, but on God who has mercy. For the Scripture says to Pharaoh, "FOR THIS VERY PURPOSE I RAISED YOU UP, TO DEMONSTRATE MY POWER IN YOU, AND THAT MY NAME MIGHT BE PROCLAIMED THROUGHOUT THE WHOLE EARTH." So then He has mercy on whom He desires, and He hardens whom He desires. You will say to me then, "Why does He still find fault? For who resists His will?" On the contrary, who are you, O man, who answers back to God? The thing molded will not say to the molder, "Why did you make me like this," will it? Or does not the potter have a right over the clay, to make from the same lump one vessel for honorable use and another for common use? What if God, although willing to demonstrate His wrath and to make His power known, endured with much patience vessels of wrath prepared for destruction? And He did so to make known the riches of His glory upon vessels of mercy, which He prepared beforehand for glory . . .

—ROMANS 9:14-23

What a topic to weigh in on! I still stand on the side of the train of thought expressed like this: "The way that leads to Life is narrow, and there is a wall on both sides to bump into as you move along making forward progress. One wall is predestination and the other is free will." I believe both are needed. Beyond that, the topic can quickly degenerate into man's wisdom and speculation, for systematizing God is dodgy business, as is thinking that one can know all there is to know about God. Where did God come from, anyway? Does a simple "I AM" not suffice? Does it not have to suffice? However, some things are worth a cursory look. A dilemma for many is that if God predestines, then what is the point? If it is all choice, then who ultimately gets the glory? Besides, we have found ourselves too weak to make the right choices. To be more succinct, what is it that man must do because God refuses to do it for him? At the same time, what is it that only God can do and man cannot? I believe God has a responsibility, and so does man. We are made in His image, and we see every family operating on that same principle: the parents have responsibilities, and so do the children. Some things only the parent can do, but there are also things only the children can do. Understanding our earthly relationship will take us a long way toward comprehending our heavenly one.

Romans 9:16 is an amazing passage and contains enough dynamite to blow to pieces 95% of all of those discipleship and church programs that proclaim what the Christian must do to be pleasing to God. The Amplified Bible states it in this way: "So then [God's gift] is not a question of human will and human effort, but of God's mercy. [It depends not on one's own willingness nor on his strenuous exertion as in running a race, but on God's having mercy on him.]" This passage and more make it abundantly clear that God is in charge of gift giving, yet there is hardly a chapter in the Bible not dealing, at least on some level, with man's free will or choice. Joshua 24:15, "If it is disagreeable in your sight to serve the LORD, choose for yourselves today whom you will serve: whether the gods which your fathers served which were beyond the River, or the gods of the Amorites in whose land you are living; but as for me and my house, we will serve the LORD." Then there is the foreknowledge of God. I Peter 1:1 & 2, "who are chosen according to the foreknowledge of God the Father, by the sanctifying work of the Spirit, to obey Jesus Christ and be sprinkled with His blood: May grace and peace be yours in the fullest measure."

First, definitions must be addressed, for we stand and fall by our definitions. Mine are as follows:

Predestination: pre-determined, planned beforehand

Foreknowledge: omnipotence, omnipresence, omniscience

Free will: the ability to choose

There are two categories within the concept of predestination. There are those in Christ predestined for heaven, and there are those outside of Christ predestined for hell. This cannot be argued, for there are no other classifications. Those who are in Christ will receive mercy, and those outside of Christ will receive wrath, so it cannot be disputed that God did, in fact, make vessels of mercy and vessels of wrath. The question that arises is whether a person can choose which predestined group he is going to be in. First, lesser truths must be seen in the light of greater truths, such as "God so loved the world" and desires "that none should perish"; "I take no pleasure in the death of the wicked." If we know the heart of God, we can understand, in part, how He is acting.

Imagine two rooms adjoined by one door. In one room are those predestined to heaven, and in the other, those predestined to hell. The door is Jesus. God wishes that "all" men be saved. As those in the room for the damned attempt to escape through every window, God is gently latching those windows, not wanting any to escape except through the one Mediator, Jesus. He will not make the choice for anyone, but He will do all He can to make Jesus the only choice. In this, another greater truth is revealed, which is that God does not show partiality. In the room for the damned, God both hardens hearts and softens hearts of people that go through the same event. I know two fellows who broke their necks and are now confined to wheelchairs. Assuming that God permitted what He could have prevented, God permitted both accidents. Why? God, knowing every intimate detail about the men, understood how this particular type of accident for these particular men was the best option to move them into the room for those predestined in Christ. One man was broken, his heart softened and revealed, and he gave his life to Jesus. The other man was hardened, his unyielding heart revealed, and he is strongly anti-Christ. Did God harden one heart and soften the other? Yes, for He permitted the accident. God's actions in permitting did not create the hard heart or the soft heart; His actions brought them to the light. So some might ask, "Who, then, made the heart that would be broken and the heart that is hardened?"

Man, in the image of God, is also an "i am," but in all lower-case letters! This does not mean that man is God, or even a god. But there are things about the creation of man no man knows. Some might ask, "Why does one man have a hard heart?" My reply is, "That man is an 'i am,' period." No answer beyond needs to be given, since no man knows everything about his creation.

Here is another greater truth: God is love, and His love compels Him to continue to work and give everyone in the room for the damned the best chance possible to make the choice to move into the other room. This He does, even knowing those who will not respond. Who among us can grasp that kind of love? In His foreknowledge, He knows who will be hardened, and yet He will not give up on them until the very end. Beautiful love! In my life, I came to the place where there was only one option other than Jesus, and that was suicide. God had been breaking me and softening my heart. My pride had been dealt a deathblow, and I was ready to move over and let someone else take over. I chose to believe in Jesus. Do I now have something in which to boast? No! First, He did the work of bringing me to the doorway. Second, man is not born again through effort inwardly or outwardly, but only from above. Even if I chose to believe in Jesus, God had to choose to give me a new birth, graft me into the Vine, and give me the Holy Spirit. James 1:18, "And it was of His own [free] will that He gave us birth [as sons] by [His] Word of Truth, so that we should be a kind of first fruits of His creatures [a sample of what He created to be consecrated to Himself]." To be locked up in jail and to choose to be free does no good; someone amenable to that choice must come along with the key. Here is where we need to see the limits of free will. I can choose to go to the airport, but only the plane can take me away.

Once we have passed from death to life through rebirth, God will permit those in the room of the damned to throw bricks into the room housing those of us who have received mercy. However, He will only permit those bricks that will work for Him in furthering the revelation of His Son. A wicked man may take our job so God can reveal His provision, and so on. Romans 8:29 & 30, "For those whom He foreknew, He also predestined to become conformed to the image of His Son, so that He would be the firstborn among many brethren; and these whom He predestined, He also called; and these whom He called, He also justified; and these whom He justified, He also glorified."

Back to the family, as parents we do all we can to see that our children make the right choices. Parents who have put themselves in the place of making all the right choices for their offspring are slowly going mad, and their children are not far behind them. Even when a parent sees his child making a wrong choice, the parent will not give up, even with foreknowledge of what is going to happen. I have seen parents outwardly give up on a rebellious child who is addicted to drugs, and yet all the parents' lives they will secretly hope beyond hope for a turnaround in the child's life. They will covertly work toward that conversion experience. Take a parent's love, multiply it by untold billions, and see why God is constantly at work in the room of the damned!

DAY 225
Procrastination

And tomorrow will be like today, only more so.

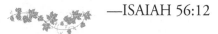
—ISAIAH 56:12

This could be the lifelong verse of the procrastinator, who never enjoys the moment, for the moment is a constant interruption. Some might ask what is being interrupted. Well, whatever is happening is an interruption to what the procrastinator is "going" to do. Since the procrastinator lives in the fantasy world of thinking he will do in the next hour what has not been done in the previous months, he is always too busy to take time out for the joys of life. Yes, he really would like to hike, to read a book, to go bicycling, to go to the movie, or even to take a small vacation, but, alas! "There is so much needing to get done." In fact, so many things remain undone that supposedly are going to get done that the postponing one is actually angry at the interruption and whoever brings it. "How am I supposed to get everything done if you keep interrupting me?" Again, the procrastinator would feel guilty taking any time out, because he could not allow diversion from the job he had planned. Comically—though sadly—the procrastinator does not actually get to the job. The exhaustion at the end of the day comes not from overwork but from falling into bed full of frustration and self-hatred, believing tomorrow is going to be different. A schedule is in mind. If everything goes according to plan, he will actually finish the task a few days early. But let's not forget, "And tomorrow will be like today, only more so."

What is at the root of all this needless delaying? Just to mention a few possibilities, it can be fear of failure, boredom, an unreachable standard, and inferiority. Any of these, coupled with self-deception, keep the procrastinator from getting started; he continues procrastinating until he must work night and day just to catch up. This time, he really cannot allow others to tempt him away from the job at hand, because he must isolate himself to get the job done. Try to reach him by phone and he will not answer; he must complete the task. He is not rejecting others but is merely the victim of his own procrastination. The end result is a procrastinator's diminished enjoyment of life.

If you are afflicted with the tendency to behave in this manner, here are a couple of suggestions. Stop fighting the fact that you procrastinate, admit it, own it, and embrace it. Actually, you can make it work for you by admitting you are not going to do the job until the last minute, then going ahead and enjoying all those interruptions in the meantime without getting frustrated about how you should be doing something else. Second, take up the cross and deny the feeling of inferiority. Third, lower your standard, remember that your 80% is like another person's 110%, for most procrastinators are perfectionist Thinkers by temperament. Fourth, realize that you can take on much more work than you thought you could. You are actually only productive, at best, 50% of the time, so take on more work. Fifth, start enjoying life! You will never be a "disciplined" person as defined by the "disciplined." You are what God made you.

DAY 226
Personal Freedom

But the fruit of the Spirit is love, joy, peace, patience, kindness, goodness, faithfulness, gentleness, self-control; against such things there is no law.

—GALATIANS 5:22 & 23

The other day I was noticing the similarities between cigarette smoking and philosophy. When one is addicted to smoking, his ten preceding smokes do not seem to relieve the need for the eleventh. The tenth cigarette did seem to give an immediate pleasure, but it left the participant immaculately unchanged in satiating his craving for the eleventh, which also will not alleviate the need for the next twenty. Having never been addicted to cigarettes, I understand it is an esoteric experience that looks odd to those who are unaffected.

Philosophy is like the tenth cigarette. For a moment it sets one on a throne and allows him to look down on others and give opinions, but it leaves the participant unchanged and merely waiting for another observation to make. A sick, morbid satisfaction can come from analyzing the flaws in others' ideologies and the shortcomings in others' logic. It feeds pride and somehow justifies lazy living. A person thus employed will do nothing to help fix the problem; instead he will move on to what he considers another case of inferior human reasoning, maintaining his lofty position. Philosophy is an addiction just like smoking; in both cases the participants die through not doing anything beneficial with what they know.

DAY 227
Pigs

Faithful are the wounds of a friend.
—PROVERBS 27:6

My grandfather told me of the time a neighbor invited him over to see how well his litter of pigs was doing. My grandfather noticed one pig had a large boil on its cheek making it squeal in pain when it tried to eat. He grabbed the pig, who squirmed and protested the whole time, and lanced the boil. Immediately the pig became quiet and audibly sighed; the pain of the cut was nothing compared to the relief the pig received.

The wounds we receive from true friends and from our Father above release poison and bring relief. These are to be distinguished from infectious wounds received from false friends and the enemy that produce only pain. When we receive a wound, we can ask ourselves if it expels poison and replaces it with life from above, or if it merely points out error to hinder us through guilt and deliver more condemnation. Too often believers have been told they must do better, and yet when they get one heel and two fingertips on the ledge out of the pit of despair, the same person who told them to improve appears to step on their fingers.

DAY 228
Poor Creation!

For the anxious longing of the creation waits eagerly
for the revealing of the sons of God. For the creation was
subjected to futility, not willingly, but because of Him who
subjected it, in hope that the creation itself also will be set
free from its slavery to corruption into the freedom of the
glory of the children of God. For we know that the
whole creation groans and suffers the pains of
childbirth together until now.

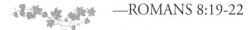
—ROMANS 8:19-22

I feel sorry for creation, from the cows and chickens forced by man to be cannibals, to the fish having industrial waste dumped on them, to the forests that are destroyed. Putting genetic material from one entity into another leads not to improvement but to distortion. All things created have an awareness of their Creator, for in Him all things are held together. The trees and mountains proclaim Him. Jesus said that even the rocks would shout out His name. God never intended us to mess with His artwork the way we do. To destroy anything mindlessly is a sin against Jesus. No wonder creation longs for the revelation of the sons of God.

There is nothing wrong with need; we are free to eat a cow and eat the calf, but the law stated not to boil the calf in the mother's milk. As a child I remember killing a small bird, not to eat, but for nothing. It haunted me and still does. I know my coming to Christ changed the way I view and treat creation. Just as it would not be right to visit one's earthly father and break everything he has made around the house, it is not right for man callously to break what the Father in heaven has made. The abuse of creation is most obvious in countries without a Christian base. Where abuse of man is tolerated or encouraged, imagine the abuse of creation. I am not a "greenie"; I just love what my Father has made and know it has suffered untold injustices. Come quickly, Lord Jesus.

DAY 229
Precious Teaching

Do not give what is holy to dogs, and do not throw your pearls before swine, lest they trample them under their feet, and turn and tear you to pieces.

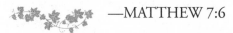 —MATTHEW 7:6

I was watching the neighbor children play with a toy called a "soaker"; it certainly lived up to its name. Two tanks mounted on a child's back were filled with water. A large pump applied the pressure, a geyser gushed from the nozzle, and any victim within reach of the spray ended up soaked.

No one puts perfume in a "soaker." Perfume is too expensive. Living water, like perfume, is too costly to be thrown on the ground and trampled underfoot. In the last several years I can honestly say I have not tried to pressure anyone against his will into believing in Christ. I am content to walk away, with and in the Lord, when a person is not receptive to Him.

What we present to a dying world is very unique, special, and holy. I always mention to those I disciple that they are hearing not what they pay for, but what Christ paid for. What He paid for is very precious. He replaced the old sinful life with His life. He does the work, He gives the blessing, and He provides mercy and grace. We believers do not wrap our lives around a belief system and then walk around in the frantic hope that others will validate our religion by demonstrating interest in Christ. We are people who have been purchased by a Person who walks with us, and those who meet us come in contact with Him.

DAY 230
Precious Waiting

But when the fullness of the time came,
God sent forth His Son.

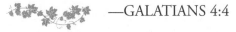

—GALATIANS 4:4

When I was young I waited and worked to purchase a car, and my grandfather told me that working for the car would be more fun than possessing it. He was right! There was more enjoyment from waiting, thinking, and imagining than from the actual possessing. Waiting maximizes enjoyment. When a child is given everything he wants and not made to wait, the parent is actually cheating the child out of a blessing. We are made in the image of God, and God enjoys waiting. He waited for the fullness of time to send His Son. Why did He not send the Son the instant Adam and Eve fell? Waiting adds maximum enjoyment and benefit to the gift of the Son. He still sends the Son in the fullness of time into hearts of men today. So wait in faith for the salvation of your child or husband or for personal freedom.

DAY 231
Problem Is Not The Problem

Behold, the Lamb of God, who takes away the sin of the world!

—JOHN 1:29

Jesus answered them, "Truly, truly, I say to you, everyone who commits sin is the slave of sin. The slave does not remain in the house forever; the son does remain forever. If therefore the Son shall make you free, you shall be free indeed."

—JOHN 8:34-36

A problem is not really the issue if you have said there was a time when it bothered you and you tried to stop, but now you do not want to stop. We hear the cry of your heart every time you mention it; it shows you really do hate what you are doing. Deep in your heart is the desire to stop. As I said, the problem is not the issue. What we want to look at is the heart behind why you know there is a problem.

Whether you are looking at the problem or not looking at it, it still owns you. But now that you feel dead to it, with no remorse or regret, you surely feel scared.

All of this is working for you, not against you. You seem to be saying that you have no strength left, that you feel a real indifference to the whole thing. By your own words, I see that you know God has the solution to this. The problem is, you feel you are cut off from God, so now you cannot ask Him, or if you do, He will not listen to you. That is where the real problem lies. The only block in your fellowship with Jesus is your belief there is a block; this keeps you from turning to Him. Jesus clearly says that He accepts you unconditionally where you are. You may not think or feel that He does, but He does. Will you take a step of faith and believe it in spite of what you think, feel, or do? Will you believe that He meant what He said?

One of the most freeing things I ever discovered was asking Jesus to give me the desire for the desire. It sounds like this, "I know what I am doing is wrong. I cannot change it; I have tried, but I cannot. I do not even want it to change. If You want this area in my life to change, then You are going to have to do it. If you want me to have the desire, then You will have to give it to me. I am totally dependent upon You to do it." This is not a magic prayer by any means. If a prayer like this does not seem to fit you, then simply ask Him to tell you what to pray. Speak to Him about the issue. Believe that He has heard you no matter what you feel. Then wait on Him to do the work.

DAY 232
Problems and Obstacles

And while being reviled, He did not revile in return;
while suffering, He uttered no threats, but kept entrusting
Himself to Him who judges righteously.

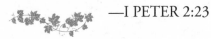

—I PETER 2:23

Christ has overcome every problem and obstacle. Christ is in me. If He is allowed to meet the problem and obstacle head on, it is not even a battle; He is immediately the conqueror! There is just one obstacle to His overcoming power: me! I stand between Him and the problem. Therefore, I must first be removed, so here is what God does. The problem is first used to break me; like a sledgehammer, upon striking, it breaks me to pieces. The problem then believes it has won; however, it has merely been used and permitted by God to break me. Why? In order that I might be removed! I have nothing left but utter dependence on Him. Once I am out of the way there is nothing between the Christ within me and the problem. He immediately breaks the problem and obstacle to pieces. It is quite beautiful. The problem breaks me and then He breaks it.

DAY 233
Prophets

And I fell at his feet to worship him. And he said to me,
"Do not do that; I am a fellow servant of yours and your
brethren who hold the testimony of Jesus; worship God.
For the testimony of Jesus is the spirit of prophecy."

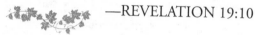
—REVELATION 19:10

I have constantly run into prophets in the course of traveling these many years. In these times prophets are increasing, and I wanted to pass on to you some observations.

1. **The real deal.** I love those guys; they are purely Christ-centered and point to Jesus in a Spirit-empowered way. They would not let someone spend one second talking about them, for they are pointing to another, Jesus. Many times I cannot remember the names of these brothers who have impacted my life in so many ways, because they were consumed with Christ. Just as with Jesus, there is nothing psychopathic about them! They are not into dreams or visions, their teaching is in the realm of real life, and they are very natural. Also like Jesus, they are defined by their refusals. They refuse to proclaim themselves, to crush anyone, or to further discourage the already downhearted. There are relatively very few of these, but they have been a great source of encouragement to me.

2. **False prophets.** I have met only a couple. They were shocking in that they were actually "speaking on behalf of

God" and leading people away from Jesus into blatant sin. Found often in mainline and orthodox type churches, they are authoritarians who present to believers spiritual and intellectual contentions that right is wrong and wrong is right. These fellows will consistently be trouble.

3. **Those who enjoy the title of Prophet.** Certain developing countries are full of these brothers wanting a title, like an American might want to flash around a Ph.D. They generally do some ministry but want to be set apart as having a higher calling and a perceived authority. Many times I do not think they have any idea of what a prophet is; it just sounds better than being a servant. I do not mind these fellows. Generally once they have introduced themselves they do get on with the work of sharing Christ.

4. **The neurotic.** The "prophets" with whom I have had the misfortune of having the most dealing, these are quite common in the West. Generally speaking they have had heaps of childhood rejection, everything from a vicious father to no father. Most often their temperament is Thinker, and at some point they committed suicide of the personality. They do not like who they are in real life, they have had very few successes, and they are not the kind of persons others would naturally gravitate toward. In short, no one would put them in charge of a company. These rejection cases have found a form of Christian religion enabling them to impose, for the first time in their lives, some power and influence over weak believers. They have a deep self-hatred and attempt to manipulate through their special "prophetic" gifting to attract followers. They need followers to validate their existence, and so to keep followers on the hook, they dispense "secrets" slowly; they create

a dependency on themselves as opposed to dependence on Christ. They claim to be hearing God personally for their followers or having visions of heaven that really are of no help to the struggling believer other than to be a short diversion from the realities of life. If questioned or starting to feel deserted, there will be veiled or overt threats concerning God's judgment and what will happen to the followers if they abandon the "teaching." Usually there is an obsession with repentance and revelation; often they say they have been given a date for the Lord's return. The book of Revelation is open to nearly any interpretation, and therefore these "prophets" like to camp there. Remember, a neurotic person builds castles in the sky and a psychotic person moves in. The whole thing can easily become psychotic when the new identity is put in the hub of the wheel and every spoke made to feed it. If people call these deluded people prophets, that proves they are; if people disagree with their proclaimed status as prophets, then that refusal to be recognized by man also proves they are. I do not discuss with psychotics their "prophetic call"; I direct them, and therefore I refuse to ask them obvious questions like, "Why is God telling you things about me and He is not telling me Himself?" or "How does the revelation move out of heaven into my home?" These they would immediately use in some distorted way to prove their prophetic gift. It does not help to discuss in any way the prophetic gifting, for in so doing, the beast is being fed. It is best to stick to Jesus and the real need a rejected person has: the revelation of Christ. The psychotic prophet only sees two options: remain a prophet or move back to being a rejected nobody. Our goal is for him to embrace a third option: Become a child of God and glory in the Christ who dwells within. I have seen the Lord break through and get people out of varieties of psychoses.

In the end, let Christ be the Prophet. He will speak truth, lead, guide, intercede, and be the mediator. I believe Jesus will send real prophets our way, and when He does, we will walk away with our heart singing and our eyes on all that Jesus is doing for us.

DAY 234
Purchased With a Price

Or do you not know that your body is a temple of the Holy Spirit who is in you, whom you have from God, and that you are not your own? For you have been bought with a price; therefore glorify God in your body.

 —I CORINTHIANS 6:19, 20

There is an old saying: "I have rededicated until my rededicater is worn out." We all know the meaning. We are sick and tired of rededicating. We go to the meeting, get inspired, encouraged, and often even condemned, and then we rededicate, pledging that tomorrow we are going to be different. Are we? With the passing of time the habits of the flesh return. We wallow, we wait, we attend another meeting, and we rededicate.

Let me tell you a secret: You do not need to rededicate. You never need to rededicate again. You need merely recognize, realize, and confess that you are dedicated already. Romans 12:1, "I urge you therefore, brethren, by the mercies of God, to present your bodies a living and holy sacrifice, acceptable to God, which is your spiritual service of worship." Do you realize that the reason you are miserable is because you are totally and absolutely dedicated to Jesus? I can prove it to you. Go try to live anti-Christ. You will come apart, fall to pieces, and sink into depression and despair. Why? You are dedicated to Jesus. However, you have yet to admit it. Normally a man wearing women's clothes is not comfortable. The discomfort is a message to the man that he is not a woman! You are uncomfortable in the world because you are not of the world; you are already dedicated to Him. Stop looking any other place. Only Jesus will make you happy.

DAY 235
Pushed God Too Far?

For if we died with Him, we shall also live with Him; if we endure, we shall also reign with Him; if we deny Him, He also will deny us; if we are faithless, He remains faithful, for He cannot deny Himself.

 —II TIMOTHY 2:11-13

It is no secret that Abiding Life Ministries International is interested in seeing discouraged believers encouraged, something accomplished when Christ is the focus of their lives. We have a firm conviction that there is nothing His nearness will not cure! However, many of the defeated have trouble returning to strongly finish the race because the enemy has convinced them that their willful sin has cut them off permanently from God's grace. They come to my office with an arsenal of passages to prove God has cut them off, such as Hebrews 12:16, "that there be no immoral or godless person like Esau, who sold his own birthright for a single meal." Hebrews 6:6, "and then have fallen away, it is impossible to renew them again to repentance, since they again crucify to themselves the Son of God and put Him to open shame." Or Psalm 101:3, "I will set no worthless thing before my eyes; I hate the work of those who fall away." Whatever Scripture says is true; however, the aforementioned passages and many more like them do not apply to the discouraged believers' condition. The proof that the birthright *has not* been sold, that the Son of God *has not* been crucified anew, and that a condition of falling away *does not* exist is evident in the fact the broken believer is sitting in my office bemoaning his sin, undone by guilt, and wanting a restored relationship with God. These are all the characteristics of a believer who has fallen but not fallen away. When an unbeliever sins he often busies himself looking for another opportunity to do the same thing, but when a believer fails he is full of sorrow, fear, and depression; he is undone. Sorrow over failure is proof of being born again; it is a sorrow according to God's will. "For the sorrow that is according to the will of God produces a repentance without regret, leading to salvation, but the sorrow of the world produces death" (II Corinthians 7:10). Godly sorrow leads to life, while sorrow the world produces leads a believer deeper into death and despair. "Why are you in despair, O my soul? And why have you become disturbed within me? Hope in God, for

I shall yet praise Him, the help of my countenance, and my God" (Psalm 42:11).

Why, when believers are promised forgiveness in the name of the marred Jesus, would a believer remain in depression, rejecting the forgiveness on the basis of feelings? The argument is that he simply does not feel forgiven, near to God, or acceptable to Him. Two fundamental problems are revealed in depression following failure and the refusal to accept forgiveness. The first problem revealed is self-righteousness, the root of unrighteousness. Self-righteousness will always manifest itself in unrighteousness. Therefore, to stop unrighteousness we must always examine self-righteousness, which shows that a person has put trust in his own ability. God is never surprised when the self-righteous sin, only the self-righteous are! Some go so far as to be angry with God for not stopping them from sinning, an attitude again revealing their position on the throne. They believe God is working for them! A self-righteous person lives out of self-strength, not weakness, succumbing to the enticement of supposing he can march into a temptation and leave unscathed. The self-righteous examine God's simple way and opt for their own elaborate schemes of deliverance, coping with life, living with a mate, raising their children, or working with others. The depression of the self-righteous is simply anger over not being able to perform satisfactorily according to their own standards without God.

This leads to the second problem revealed, unbelief. "However, when the Son of Man comes, will He find faith on the earth?" (Luke 18:8) Many desire to be people of faith, and yet few want the experiences that will produce faith. How do you feel after confession? Do you feel unforgiven, cut off, lonely, or depressed, like God has had it with you because you finally pushed Him too far? What God says about your condition will often contrast with your feelings. He has not left you undone! "I will lead the blind by a way they do not know, in paths they do not know I will guide them. I will make darkness into light before them and rugged places into plains. These are the things I will do, and I will not leave them undone" (Isaiah 42:16). He has not left you unforgiven! "If we confess our sins, He is faithful and righteous to forgive us our sins and to cleanse us from all unrighteousness" (I John 1:9). He has not left you in a pit of despair! "Who redeems your life from the pit, who crowns you with lovingkindness and compassion" (Psalm 103:4). However, to most, what God says is not as significant as their own feelings. True feelings will always bring freedom, for the truth sets people free. Feelings with their source in a lie will put us in bondage.

Does feeling *cut off* after confession and repentance, then, have its roots in truth or error? The only way to move from lying emotions to truth is by faith! "Now faith is the assurance of things hoped for, the conviction of things not seen" (Hebrews 11:1). Assurance that forgiveness has come is desired by all who repent, but such assurance can come only through faith. Unbelief sent you on your own path and only faith will put you on His path. You must choose to walk where every great believer has walked, in faith. Faith will primarily be exercised through feeling one thing and believing another, and there is no other way. How did Joseph feel after being told the sun, moon, and eleven stars would bow down to him, and then finding himself in a pit stripped naked? Next, it was servitude, then off to prison! At that how did he feel? Do you feel any worse? You have been told you are a new creation, a child of God, and holy, but now you are in the pit of despair. Having acted the opposite of your newness, you now feel the opposite of what God says. I have been there myself but I do not believe what I feel or even my own behavior; I believe Him. He is greater than my feelings and I am becoming a faith man, and so are you! All that is not of faith is beginning to drop off naturally.

I remember talking to a couple after they had rebuked their son for some of his activities and attitudes, and the son silently withdrew to the basement, loaded a gun, and shot himself. The parents were undone, for the rebuke was intended to lead to life, not death. Can you imagine being this couple after such a tragedy? Our Father in heaven is the most loving of any father; the desired end result of His pointing out sin is not death, nor is it guilt, withdrawal, or depression. The end is to be life that comes via faith. You must now begin to be a faith person. Examine what you feel and the bondage emanating from it, next examine what God is saying, and finally as your emotions once again begin to move to the place you have allowed them to call home for so long (bondage), simply say out loud, "I am not going there, period! If I never feel, yet I will believe, for I cannot trust a lie; I must trust God." In so doing you admit your weakness and confess your faith. Now we have what God wanted to be the RESULT of your failure: life, not death.

DAY 236
Putting Your Head In the Sand Concerning Others

Therefore do not go on passing judgment before the time, but wait until the Lord comes who will both bring to light the things hidden in the darkness and disclose the motives of men's hearts; and then each man's praise will come to him from God.

—I CORINTHIANS 4:5

As I have grown older, I have often found myself in a faith crisis. I used to be one of the most judgmental people one could ever meet. I could, and would, find fault in nearly everyone and everything, despite the fact that all judgments are a waste of time and energy, for knowledge of something wrong without the power to change it is useless. However, one day I had a revelation of myself and could see that what I hated in others was also in me, which meant I hated a lot of myself. Since that day I have still made my share of false judgments—since I do not abide perfectly—but I recognize when the peace of God is leaving me. This has caused new behavior in me, and when I am told how terrible this or that person is, I can choose to remain quiet. One day I was told point blank, "I know your position on judging, but you are just putting your head in the sand and refusing to acknowledge the problem." I understand what was being said, and I have been there and done that. But here is my faith crisis: I can either put my head in the sand concerning others, or I can put my head in the sand concerning the Lord, for He is the One Who has commanded the impossible by saying, "Love your enemies, and pray for those that persecute you; bless those who curse you" [Matthew 5:44, Luke 6:28]. I would rather have my head in the sand concerning men and my head in the clouds with Jesus. It has been said that if we glance at men and gaze at Jesus, we will be eternal optimists. If we glance at Jesus, but gaze at men, we will be eternal pessimists. We make our own heaven and hell on this earth, and only God, not man, deserves our attention (worship).

DAY 237
Racism

For He Himself is our peace, who made both groups into one and broke down the barrier of the dividing wall.

 —EPHESIANS 2:14

Racism: discrimination based on the belief that some races are by nature superior [Webster's Dictionary].

I must be clear about my goal, which is not to abolish racism but to heighten the revelation of Christ in the hearts of men. The greater truth will include the lesser.

The sin of racism has been elevated above others. It is a great issue in the United States, where the Constitution specifically forbids it and yet it is practiced. However, from my traveling observations, be assured that racism is alive and well in every country. It is generally overlooked in other countries, because those on both sides of the fence openly admit it as a way of life and do not have a subculture that condemns it. In short, the majority of mankind practices it and sees nothing wrong with it.

I am allowed my opinion and it is this: Every single person on the planet has a racist attitude somewhere in a place deep within. Why? We look to the results of racism for the answer and not the cause. The cause is pride. Pride is the root of every form of racism. Even those prejudiced against racists have their cause rooted in pride, for the Bible tells us judgments reveal our heart. "You who judge practice the same things." When people busily describe so accurately the heart and mind of a racist, how can they do that? They know perfectly the heart of a racist, for they themselves have that heart and respond with reactionary racism as they keep pointing out the foul motives of the racists. Now we know their own motives.

Let me illustrate with true stories. A pastor friend was forced to leave his church in the Deep South because he wanted to allow Blacks to attend church! Another friend, from Australia, had the opportunity to visit a Black church in Canada. One member got up and prophesied that in the end times Jesus was going to allow the Black man to go to war with Whites and conquer them! The entire congregation exploded with approving shouts and clapping. My point is, "as it is written, THERE IS NONE RIGHTEOUS, NOT EVEN ONE" (Romans 3:10). Do you believe there is someone righteous in the area of racism? I do not, for every man has pride.

When I first started traveling around the world, there were many instances where the atrocities of the White man—specifically Americans—were brought to my attention. I really did not care, for I was there to preach Christ. However, as the accusations and condemnation continued, I would eventually find myself defending White people. What a stupid thing, to defend the flesh of another man. One day I came away saying to the Lord, "Jesus, I came to preach You, not defend man. I know it is stupid to get sucked in. Why do I let myself?" He was gracious to whisper the answer, "Pride." I have been in hundreds of homes around the world. Despite their color or lineage, every family worries about the same things: their relationship with God, their marriage, their children, and finances. We are not different, and the answer for all of us is Jesus. So it is vexing when there, in that place, with so much in common with my family in Christ, I find myself talking about something that could not matter a bit: White people!

How could any of us believe ourselves better than any others if not for pride? Why would we try to prove ourselves as good as others if not for pride? Pride makes us live to man in one way or another. It may keep us from inviting to our home the teenager whose style of dress, hairdo, and body adornment is different from our own. If he were invited, it could be discovered that the teen's home is a wreck, he has never been loved, he only knows how to hate, and he is full of self-protecting pride. Would we have done better growing up in his home? A Black man's son wants to marry a beautiful Christian who is White. At the family reunion, out of earshot, she is judged and condemned by the other women. Why? Pride! An elderly man in England often verbally abused me for years. One day he came to me, saying, "I just hated you because you are an American. The Americans came to World War II late." Pride!

The root of racism lies not so much in believing your color is better than another color; the root is believing you are better than another, any other! Are you? Are you better because of your understanding, your politics, your wealth, your health, your strength, your education, your intelligence, your color, your anti-racist stance, your looks, where you grew up, your national heritage, your family history, or your "open mindedness"? People really do not want equality; everyone in some shape or form wants to be better than and believe he is better than someone else. This attitude of pride is all the justification carnal man needs to abuse another. There is no need beating a dead horse; history is replete with examples of the results of pride. I do not believe it is possible to educate people out of their pride. It is interesting to note how we feed pride in people and then wonder why they think they are better than others.

Jesus comes and equalizes all men, but not in the way we think He should bring equality! He makes all men equal in two ways. First, as Romans 3:23 tells us, "for all have sinned and fall short of the glory of God." Oh, yes, all men are EXACTLY the same; all in their pride have sinned! More than anything else we have this in common with every person of every race: We are sinners. It is a greater title that includes the lesser, for if we can accept this, we have accepted our pride and are ready for embracing the second category of equality. "For He Himself is our peace, who made both groups into one . . ." (Ephesians 2:14). He has made us one! We are equal in Him, all sons, all gifted, all accepted, all holy, all righteous, and all humble.

Now, you must admit where you are to leave where you are. Are you willing to admit that you are a racist? For to be a racist you need have the attitude that you are better than only one other person. Are you willing to admit to pride? If so, then belly up to the bar and start preaching Christ; He is the cure for the cause.

One last thing, if you have been on the receiving end of racism, do not embrace the identity of a victim. Becoming a person with a victim mentality makes the victimizer your god, one who ultimately controls your life, happiness, and future. No one can truly live that way. You must see God in it. Jesus answered, "You would have no authority over Me, unless it had been given you from above; for this reason he who delivered Me up to you has the greater sin" (John 19:11). Bless those who curse you. God is not fighting wicked people; He is using them in our lives. You will have your reward in heaven when your oneness is revealed to all!

DAY 238
Reap What You Sow,
Unless There is a Drought

You will sow but you will not reap.

—MICAH 6:15

For they sow the wind and they reap the whirlwind.

—HOSEA 8:7

*He said to him, "By your own words I will judge you,
you worthless slave. Did you know that I am an exacting
man, taking up what I did not lay down and
reaping what I did not sow?"*

—LUKE 19:22

*For the one who sows to his own flesh will from the flesh
reap corruption, but the one who sows to the Spirit will
from the Spirit reap eternal life.*

 —GALATIANS 6:8

Some sow and do not reap, some sow and do reap, and others reap where they do not sow. Well, which is it? Actually all, in context, make perfect sense. However, I am looking at what it means to sow and reap. I believe there are three points. One, the person who sows to the flesh will reap (and reek) of the flesh. I have witnessed those who sow to the flesh and in the end are given over to it to the point that there is no distinction between them and their flesh. Sin and flesh are one, and the person merely manifests the sin. Secondly, some forget that sowing is for a season.

Every farmer would like it if he could sow once and reap for a lifetime. We can manipulate people by telling them that because of one mistake, they will be punished the rest of their lives. Third and finally, if one has sown to the flesh and repented, I believe God can send a drought leading to no reaping and no fruit. The drought, the winter, the isolation, and the awareness of failure are not pleasant, but they keep the crop from growing. A temporary pain delivers a person from a season of pain. God is extra good to the heart that turns to Him. Factor in repentance and a person need not reap what was sown. "'Return, O faithless sons,' declares the LORD; 'For I am a master to you, and I will take you one from a city and two from a family, and I will bring you to Zion. Then I will give you shepherds after My own heart, who will feed you on knowledge and understanding.'" Legalism wishes to control through fear, the fear of punishment before an act and the certainty of punishment after the act. However, God is not as interested in one's getting punished as He is in each individual. I Peter 3:9, "The Lord is not slow about His promise, as some count slowness, but is patient toward you, not wishing for any to perish but for all to come to repentance."

DAY 239
Receiving Honor

They love the place of honor at banquets and the chief seats in the synagogues, and respectful greetings in the market places, and being called by men, Rabbi.

—MATTHEW 23:6, 7

It is amazing how much is said in the Bible about receiving honor from men and interesting that the one thing I believe holds much of Asia from revival is honor, which is desired, sought, and dispensed to one another where so much is woven into the culture about saving face. Yet, we must lose face. "For I know that nothing good dwells in me, that is, in my flesh; for the wishing is present in me, but the doing of the good is not" (Romans 7:18). Honor is a good example of good's being the enemy of the best. Where there is such an emphasis on being a person of honor, the achievement of honor hardens the heart to the Lord. We will one day receive honor from Him, period. In the meantime, He is the honor and His is the honor.

DAY 240
Recognizing God

The God who made the world and all things in it, since He is Lord of heaven and earth, does not dwell in temples made with hands; neither is He served by human hands, as though He needed anything, since He Himself gives to all life and breath and all things; and He made from one every nation of mankind to live on all the face of the earth, having determined their appointed times, and the boundaries of their habitation, that they would seek God, if perhaps they might grope for Him and find Him, though He is not far from each one of us; for in Him we live and move and exist . . .

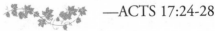

—ACTS 17:24-28

The Son wanted a bride, and that led to the creation of man, made in God's image but not God. Man will fall into much sin, but he can become a child of God in the room of contrast. The only thing that will make all of this work is the Love of God and the sacrifice of the Son.

God is I AM, the source, and the source is Love, not hard love or soft love, no qualifiers. He will forever remain Love. He will forever hope in man, believe in man, endure with man, and more. Forever.

People look for the supernatural in order to see God, having arbitrarily divided the world into the natural, unnatural, and supernatural. Were we to recognize that everything about and in this life, all things around us and in us, are quite supernatural, we need only divide the world into the natural and the unnatural. We are blind and do not recognize God in our daily supernatural lives. Have you ever witnessed a woman giving birth? The scene is like something out of an alien movie; a little human being pops out of a big human being. Supernatural. The sun, the moon, breathing, walking, balance, sight, and more are all supernatural. However, we do not recognize those things as supernatural; hence, we do not recognize God. God is not proven merely by the spectacular; His proof is all around us, but we do not see it. We are blind. We have to recognize that God is all around us and in Him we move and breathe and have our being. We must accept that there is no place we can go to flee from His love. One of the deepest revelations any man can have is this one: Even if I walk in the valley of the shadow of death, I will fear not, for YOU ARE WITH ME (Psalm 23).

Could we agree that if you recognized that God was all around you, the moment you lost your job, had to talk to your child about the drugs you found, heard news of a loved one having cancer, or found out about an unfaithful mate, those events, though painful, would be viewed in a different light? What if you could really recognize God standing right beside you when thinking about how to pay the medical bills, provide for a child's education, or purchase a house? Would that change things? When you are confronting a neighbor or being confronted, what if you see God standing right beside you with His hand on both your shoulder and the neighbor's? Imagine a dangerous journey in a distant land, and while traveling, recognizing Him and seeing Him holding your hand. Would you have a different attitude toward the world? Or if in a hospital bed, believing and receiving that He is with you, nothing would be frightening. Let me tell you a secret: He *is* in all those places and our lives *are* supernatural!

The little fish said to the big fish, "One day when I grow up, I want to see the big ocean." To that the big fish stated, "You are in the big ocean." The little fish, looking around, said, "Is this it?" We are like that little fish in that we are immersed in the supernatural, immersed in God, and yet we do not see Him. The little fish was blind to the truth, and things were about to happen to make him recognize his "real" world. We are born blind, not recognizing God. This is what Jesus meant when He spoke of the blind guides and the blind leading the blind (Matthew 15:14). People who did not recognize God were leading others who likewise did not recognize God. Jesus recognized God: "And He lifted his eyes to heaven and spoke" (John 17:1). How could Jesus speak to God at any and every moment? It is because He was not blind, He could see. The blind man said, "I see, I see." I know how he felt. "If the eye is dark, then how great is the darkness, but if light, how great the light" (Luke 11:34).

Here is a deception: The Christian life is not one of devotion, prayer, and work until God finally comes to a person. The Christian life is one of either recognizing God or not recognizing God. The Christian does not worship to make God appear; he worships because of the awareness of God's being all around him and in him. Psalm 139:7, "Where can I go from Thy Presence?" For years I read material from the mystics and sought for what they had: the presence of God, hearing God, the spectacular, God's sign of approval through miracles, fillings, and visions. In hindsight I see I went left when I should have taken the road to the right, for one day I realized my daily life was immersed in God. I recognized Him in nature, in a baby, in heavy breathing, in a conversation, in quiet times and loud times, in arguments and affection. My world became supernatural, completely immersed in Him, and I did not have to memorize a single Scripture, whip up any emotions, experience specific miracles, tell a mountain to move to prove I had faith, pray for hours, follow a program, or any other of the hundreds of distractions offered. I had an awakening, a recognizing! God was in everything, throughout my being, in the deepest recesses of my heart to the tip of my hair. I was just walking along, apparently doing nothing, and I shouted to Jesus, "I see, I see, I see!" I saw that He was everywhere, I was floating in the arms of love, and my world was what it always had been, supernatural! It is not just Truth for me, but was and is Truth for everyone.

The world attempts to create an environment for people wherein they can remain blind and yet live comfortably.

This hinders us from recognizing God to the degree that we recognize man, not Him. If we recognize God all around us even when we are in prison, then man cannot hold over us the fear of prison. We can say, "You meant it for evil, but God meant it for good." We would do well to avoid environments that attempt to blind us, and I believe this is one reason Jesus said so little about governments. The discussion of governments recognizes man and credits power to him while blinding us to God, the source of power. Getting caught up in a political discussion leads to our recognizing the stupidity of man, but not necessarily to turning to God. The various Christian clubs are all about recognizing man, his wants, his excesses, his guilt, his failures, successes, and more. I no longer believe in addictions. For too long Christians have accepted the diagnoses and remedies offered by lost man. Honestly, this must be questioned. What the world calls an addiction, God calls recognizing man. Alcohol, drugs, sex, food, and mind all have their God-given, God-created place. Drugs are a beautiful thing when man recognizes God in illness and in the drug He created. Taken for its appropriate use, the miracle of the drug's beneficial nature can be enjoyed. However, when in blindness man takes the drug, he recognizes only man in it and becomes more self-aware through physical pleasure; thus he takes more. Before long he is self-aware on a level not pleasurable; he is aware of the fact that he cannot control himself. This self-awareness brings self-hatred, and with it the need to sedate. By this process the man is creating an environment where the recognition of God fades. In a completely self-absorbed state of man-recognition, he cries out, "Where is God? Why does God not do something? It is all God's fault!"

This is akin to gouging out one's own eyes and asking, "Where did the light go?"

"All things are lawful but not all things are profitable" (I Cor. 10:23). It is lawful to drink, but when drink takes a man out of God-recognition and into man-recognition, it is not profitable. Many environments in the world are unprofitable for the one simple reason that they blind and keep us from God-recognition. Toy stores, electronics shops, and mega malls deaden us to God-recognition, for we leave those places with the feeling of want. We create places between our ears that make recognizing Him nearly impossible through self-absorption, fantasy, and obsession. Bitterness, judging, examining the flaws of others, debates, doctrines, replaying the pain others have caused, liberal talk vs. conservative, and economies all conspire to make us recognize man and go blind concerning God. I have done them all and speak from experience. Would you agree that recognition of God in the aforementioned would give peace? What is the highest potential Christian life on this earth? Your life, if you could recognize Him! This fact brings a deathblow to all religious structures, programs, plans, efforts, assignments, educations, abilities, and caste, for these things are attempts to create something man-based concerning the believer and his God. I am saying you do not have to create anything, you cannot do anything, and everything has been done. I, we, you are on equal footing with any of the Apostles when I, we, and you recognize God in everything.

In the Garden man wanted to know, create, and clothe himself. God's goal is for man not to know, not to create, and to let God clothe him. Faith is not knowing, recognizing is not creating, and resting is not clothing oneself. "Let God be true and every man the liar" (Romans 3:4). Is it true you are free from all things (John 8:36)? Is it true that "all things work together for the good" (Romans 8:28)? Is it true He is leading you (Psalm 31:3)? Yes, but in our man-hearts we say no and therefore continue to work to make it so, and we listen to those who tell us how to make it so, the blind leading the blind (Luke 6:39). There is a direct correlation between lack of the recognition of God and a need for a miracle or sign. Once we recognize God, we have no need for miracles or signs, for everything surrounding us is recognized as supernatural and of God.

"Give us this day our daily bread" (Matthew 6:11). I see eating as something supernatural, from the seed that dies to give life, through the yeast that makes it rise, to the hands that knead the dough, and with the fire that bakes it. Amazing! It is all God. I like those environments that seem to push me along in the progressive recognition of God, such as watching a baby be born, an eagle soaring, a nursing calf, majestic mountains, and the fellowship of the saints. When I see God standing by me in the interruptions, then my day is a delight. I read, I work, and I rejoice. When I recognize man in the interruptions, I go through the day angry, upset, distorted, and non-productive. God has created the perfect world for allowing man to get sick of being man-aware and walking in the darkness. What does it mean that man's greatest potential is to become a "living soul"? An animal has mind, will, and emotion but does not have a soul. What makes a "living soul" is mind, will, and emotions made aware by God in order that the soul can recognize God. Again, the world works against this. How many things were thrown at you today to steal your recognition of God? Was it the lady at the airline counter, sharp words of criticism from your mate, a glance at the bank account, or a distracted driver cutting in front of you? Whatever it was, its goal was to steal the recognition of God. Our goal at Abiding Life Ministries is recognizing God. We are not attempting to dismantle the problems every person has. Instead, we want believers to recognize that God is there, walking with them in the midst of the problems. That attitude changes everything and is at the core of the Christian walk.

We end where we began: If you had recognized Him encompassing you and holding all things together, would you have seen the situation differently? The peace of God is the barometer, for His peace only leaves when you are not recognizing Him. "In Him we live and move and have our being" (Acts 17:28, NIV). It must not be an impersonal fact.

DAY 241
Recognizing God Is a Gift From God

Search me, O God, and know my heart.
—PSALM 139:23

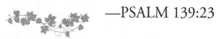

To recognize God in your situation is a gift from God and proof He is working in the situation. We would agree that all revelation from Him as well as all recognition of God must come directly from Him. "When they had come into Samaria, Elisha said, 'O Lord, open the eyes of these men, that they may see.' So the Lord opened their eyes and they saw!" (II Kings 6:20) If you are in a bad relationship, with rebellious children, untamed flesh patterns, unemployment, or health issues that have dragged on and on and on, the only thing that will bring a lift in your spirit, an expectation for the future, or hope is when the Lord opens your eyes and you see Jesus in it all.

A man had suffered in oppression and darkness for three years. What broke the darkness is when the Lord opened his eyes and he could see that the whole situation was God. He proclaimed, "I no longer care about my situation, because I see that He cares, and there is no need for two of us to care! All that has happened is for my good." The next day he got a job and declared, "I am not happy about the job! I do not care, because Jesus cares for me. He knew it was good for me not to have a job, and now it must be good for me to have the job. He does what is best always, so I do not have to be concerned. He carries me, and I can live like a sparrow!"

One day I drew a diagram of a pit, and inside the pit I drew a picture of the couple to whom I was talking. I said, "I must be honest; you truly are in a pit. Your life is in the sewer. You deal with sickness, teenagers, both of you working two jobs, the marriage, family relationships, and many emotional disturbances. I cannot tell you that none of this is true and you should be of good cheer, for you know the pit is real. However, Joseph's pit, too, was real, but his eyes were opened by God for a revelation that changed everything. He could see that God meant it for good. My advice to you is for the next thirty days, every time you think of the pit invite Jesus into it with you. What you give to Him, He takes responsibility for. Ask Him to open your eyes so you can see."

I counsel two people in wheelchairs, both Christians, but one is angry and the other is glowing. The difference? One sees God in his circumstances and the other does not. It is said of Charles Wesley that he preached with blackened eyes given to him by his wife. How? Though outer eyes were beaten closed, the inner eyes had seen God in it. I often ask people in terrible marriages, "Do you believe God is in this situation, He is teaching you something, and you are learning something you will take to heaven with you?" If the answer is yes, I know their eyes are opened and they are to stay. Upon the death of Rockefeller, his accountant was asked, "How much did he leave?" The accountant stoically replied, "He left it all!" We are going to leave it all, except for the things of God, which we will get to take with us.

You can see the difference the opening of the eyes makes when viewing life's events. This brings me to the final thought. What about those who have not had their eyes opened by God? We must agree that it is God's work to open eyes. I am graciously brought back to that awareness every day. I talk to some who have their eyes opened by God, and I talk to many more who have not had their eyes opened by God. To date, I have never opened the eyes of anyone's heart. Oh, occasionally I have watched the effects of my words open the mind, but that only turns into information not acted upon. We cannot open men's eyes. God must do it, just as He opened the Apostle Paul's eyes. I sometimes conclude that it is not the fullness of time for "eye opening." Jesus knows the right time, the time that will bear the most fruit. I also believe that if people cannot see God in their situation, maybe God no longer wants them in that situation. Situations are like stations, each one preparing us for the next station, with the revelation of Christ at the end having been something toward which we had to build. I meet believers who are abused in their marriage, do not see God in it, and in keeping the one command to stay married are breaking ten other more significant commands each day. (Do not shut down and take this as a blanket endorsement of divorce.) We all agree we need God's grace to stay in any given situation. In absence of such grace to stay, our staying would be in the power of flesh. When people cannot see God, they will only see the situation, others, and self. All of this becomes an obsession, which hides God even more. In the end, I know how helpless we are if we cannot witness to the work of God. "'Oh LORD, open the eyes of these believers, that they may see.' So the Lord opened their eyes, and they saw!"

DAY 242
Recognizing God Is Key

The God who made the world and everything in it is the Lord of heaven and earth and does not live in temples built by hands. And He is not served by human hands, as if He needed anything, because He Himself gives all men life and breath and everything else. From one man He made every nation of men, that they should inhabit the whole earth; and He determined the times set for them and the exact places where they should live. God did this so that men would seek Him and perhaps reach out for Him and find Him, though He is not far from each one of us. For in Him we live and move and have our being. As some of your own poets have said, "We are His offspring."

—ACTS 17:24-28 [NIV]

I am writing this in Australia, and my age is showing. I forgot my Bible and rely on my electronic Bible in my computer. However, the Gideons continue to be a blessing by putting a Bible in every hotel room; hence, the passage above could be typed out. Over the years, from my personal-life experiences to my First-World experiences to my Third-World experiences, I will forever delight in the sight of a nursing baby. There is nothing like watching the child's eyes examine the mother as he determines just exactly who is this person bringing such provision, such care, and such love. One day the child realizes it is a very intimate person with a name; it is not some vague being but a specific individual named Mommy. The young one has a revelation; this heretofore unknown recipient of his gaze now has a name and becomes personalized, and not only is that unknown entity loved, but the baby cannot help but be drawn to his mother.

So is the world. God is providing for every single creature; He is loving them, watching over them, listening to them, protecting them, and caring for them. It is the hope of God that in the will of man, he will look up and begin to recognize the One who cares for him. This was Paul's point in the sermon on the hill in Acts: God has cared for all of them no matter how pagan, no matter how lost, and no matter how sinful. It is Paul's desire that they might recognize and call Him by His proper name, Father.

In this life there are many situations God will not fight but use to make us look to Him and discover the One who maintains us. We must point people to the One and continue to point them to the One, no matter how exhausting, in the hope that they might see the One who maintains them.

DAY 243
Rejection

Love your enemies and pray for those who persecute you.
—MATTHEW 5:44

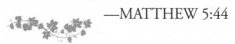

Throughout our lives we will find those who think very little of us. Often their assessments are valid, but often they are invalid. We must be realistic in admitting we are not perfect but are growing in perfection. Who we are in Christ is continually unfolding. For our purposes here let us assume every bit of the negative we have heard is true. What is our response to be? Our options are actually very limited: either sink into despair with all its accompanying woes or love. Yes, we can love the one who sees so many things wrong with us, and here is a secret! If our response is love, care, forgiveness, and service, those very actions elevate us above even the justifiably critical one. Once again, the Way, Christ's way of treating others, makes the last first.

Do not despair; do not allow the assessments of others to create their very behavior in you. In Him rise above it, humble yourself and love, remembering love covers a multitude of sins. Love perfects you! Love unfolds the true life that exists within you. As this happens, you will sense an awareness of exaltation, freedom, and encouragement. You will sense that even though much is lacking in your life, the foundation of new life within is being laid, and soon everything mature and perfect will begin to build upon this foundation of love.

Once a believer began to recount all the mistreatment doled out from another Christian and to condemn the other believer's attitude. I asked a simple question: "What is the minimum acceptable behavior of a Christian toward an enemy?"

He properly answered, "Love and prayer."

My next question was, "Have you been loving and praying?"

"No," he responded.

I then explained that he was in error, for if Christianity had not grasped his heart at the very root of love, it had not grasped him at all. He had not reached the foundation of life, and if this were the case, he was not fit to be in the ministry.

You see, the behavior of another is never the issue for us. The issue is our response to the one who, whether legitimately or not, confronts us. We give our best to people, and all that is needed is Christ.

DAY 244
Relative Sin?

"Woe to me!" I cried. "I am ruined! For I am a man of unclean lips, and I live among a people of unclean lips, and my eyes have seen the King, the LORD Almighty."

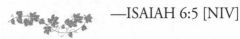

—ISAIAH 6:5 [NIV]

Sin is absolute, but the weight we give particular sins is relative to a culture. Simply put, on a scale of 1 to 10, what an American considers a 10 is different from what an Asian would consider a 10. I am surprised that in Asia, Africa, or the Philippines, an extramarital affair is not a 10. Losing face is a 10 in China. Being naked in front of men is not an issue in Africa, but being naked with a particular piece of string around the waist is shocking and is a 10. All men know of sin, all men sin, and the law reveals sin. We all have our own list of 10's, and as long as we are not engaged in those, we do not feel condemned. Yet others have a different list, and some of what we do is a 10 to them; they cannot understand how we could do those things. I know a man who so strongly believed it was wrong that he could not wear a tie, and I know other men who simply could not go to church without one. We all have a list of priorities and think we are doing well because of our list. Yet when one of the most holy men, in terms of behavior, is caught up into heaven, he is undone, recognizing he is a man of unclean lips. Why? He experienced God's holiness and His list. Once the true scale is seen, we are undone.

What is my point? There are none righteous, no, not one. Jesus made it simple. No list, no scale, just believe in Him. Walk in emptiness and dependence and let Him live through us in an abiding relationship. He knows what is truly a ten, and He will live it through us.

DAY 245
Repent!

Or do you think lightly of the riches of His kindness and forbearance and patience, not knowing that the kindness of God leads you to repentance?

—ROMANS 2:4

Many say they are called to exhort people to repent, but their call so often is exhibited as something of a one-off from how we know it was viewed by the Old Testament prophets, for whom repentance centered more in the root than the fruit as they sought to bring people back to God. Today the call to repentance seems to take the form of spreading a rebuke, such as this tirade: "'You think you are saved, but you are not! You call yourselves My children but do not act like My own. If you would have loved Me you would have kept My word. I am going to cut you off and give your portion to those that obey Me,' thus says the Lord." It is fairly consistent and only ends in condemnation, even though we know that "there is therefore now no condemnation for those who are in Christ Jesus" (Romans 8:1). Men instruct on the topic of discipline with a similar approach and fervor, and that, too, ends in condemnation. The offenders' sin is pointed out, coupled with a threat to punish. Because of such teaching by the religious who wrongly present God's judgment, one fellow said, "I wish I would have waited to accept Christ until the last minute, got baptized, and had someone shoot me as I came up out of the water. At least that way I would not have accumulated so much of the judgment of God as a believer." This man expressed a common feeling that has occurred among Christians throughout the centuries, but this kind of view of judgment is not dealing with the root but rather the behavior, the fruit.

There are two types of discipline: one is punishment, which reaps few benefits and is rarely successful, and the other is a self-discipline that takes a person back to Christ. A Christian who finds himself continually in the deeds of the flesh does need discipline, but it is of the type found within himself that can enable him to begin and end each day recognizing the presence of Christ. It is our job as disciple-makers to pull such a person aside and urge him to go to the Lord and abide. The subsequent awareness of the fact of Christ's indwelling living through him will free him from the deeds of the flesh. ("If perhaps God may grant them repentance leading to the knowledge of the truth," II Timothy 2:25.) Continually emphasizing a person's deeds of the flesh will never set him free from the flesh; that has been proven. ("But the sorrow of the world produces death," II Corinthians 7:10.) Believers ought to be disciplined in recognizing Christ. It does take time to teach that understanding; Jesus spent three-and-a-half years with his disciples. However, the fruit of taking this approach is verifiable, for Jesus said that the Father prunes.

To say it another way, when we abide, the deeds of the flesh fall off of us. Unfortunately, there are those who will refuse this discipline; they willingly continue in the deeds of the flesh, making themselves an unhealthy leaven in the Body, and at this point to disfellowship them is appropriate.

As for the call to spread the message of repentance, it generally is meant to be a call to stop a particular behavior, and repentance is seen as different from forgiveness. The hiccup enters in when Christians do repent and subsequently continue in the same behavior. This is again where Jesus is tying the hands of man and forcing us to a life of abiding, for only the living Christ within can make a permanent change in behavior. Therefore, the message of repentance without the message of the indwelling Christ is incomplete and will not be attainable.

DAY 246
Repentance

For the sorrow that is according to the will of God produces a repentance without regret, leading to salvation, but the sorrow of the world produces death.

 —II CORINTHIANS 7:10

Repentance is something often talked about but rarely understood. After all these years in the people-helping profession, I am wondering if I really understand repentance. It seems to me that too much repentance is done only after discovery; the believers are caught in sin before the repentance comes. An obvious question comes to mind: Had they not been caught, would they be repenting? I doubt it. Repentance to most represents a way to acknowledge the fact after the act. We have already determined that to say "I will never do such-and-such again" is idiotic, for it would be the same as asserting that the flesh changes and will improve. Therefore, when repentance includes those words, it smacks of an attempt to avoid the consequences and to say, in essence, "Had I known I would be caught and all this trouble would come out of it [the loss of glory, righteousness, pride, and strength], I would never have done it."

Well, amen. What is true repentance? I believe it is the revelation of how God sees things in my life. It can be something unrighteous, such as anger, or something self-righteous, like image protection; it is something I am allowed to see somewhat from His perspective. Our initial repentance (change in thinking) at salvation came from a revelation of our own being, the sin it produced, and the impending judgment. However, many more similar repentances must occur. Being caught may cause me to be sorry, but it does not necessarily produce real repentance, as revelation does. In truth, I want repentance in my own life. I want the revelation of what I am doing, how it affects others and my relationships, and most importantly, how it impacts my walk with the Lord. Last summer I had just such an experience. Those who would observe from the outside often do not see the significance of what God reveals, but those who experience it firsthand find revelation. (Remember, revelation is not a knowing in the mind but in the spirit.) I asked the Lord, "What at this time do You choose to reveal as the one thing of which I most need to repent?" I am sure that, if given the opportunity, those who know me could offer a whole host of things of which I need to repent. What He said, as usual, surprised me, and yet it cut to the deepest part of my being. "You do not know My love and discount it." All I could say was "Amen." After spending a day pondering what it meant, I repented; I had a change in thinking. Not because I was caught in my unbelief, but because I could see it. "Lord, I have sinned. I have forgotten Your love. Everything You ask me to do is based in Your love. You love me. I love You. I will obey what comes next." Revelation brought repentance.

I do not think believers walking in the flesh intend to hurt those around them. They are truly sorry. But repentance is allowing your behavior to come under His light, to see it as He sees it, and to change your thinking about the behavior without outside influences. Now, here is where admitting where you are can help. I do not believe in making others wear our problems. If He is revealing your flesh in revelation (the enemy reveals it only to condemn), then repent. It should be in private. Then listen to Him; if there is more you must do, the peace of God will tell you. I have repented of wrong attitudes, assumed I was to go tell others, and watched the self-righteous smirks on their faces. The look communicated what was intended: "I bested you. I got you to admit your shortcomings!" I have actually watched people gloat as I told my failures. In the end, I wished I had said nothing. However, perhaps a humble, contrite admission of error is just the contrast a prideful person needs to see, and a deathblow to my own pride never hurts, either.

DAY 247
Resurrected Truth

So Jesus then said to them plainly, "Lazarus is dead."
—JOHN 11:14

The man who had died came forth, bound hand and foot with wrappings, and his face was wrapped around with a cloth. Jesus said to them, "Unbind him, and let him go."
—JOHN 11:44

A friend recently called to tell me how something I had written changed his life. He then said, "Why is it that God tells you things and not me? Why do I have to read it before I understand it?" I asked him to imagine a picture of a heart in which were thousands of tombs. Within each tomb was a truth, bound and dead. In the fullness of time Jesus comes, giving life to the truth and raising it from the dead. The day we believed in Jesus, all truths were put in our heart, but in a dormant, dead state. In the fullness of time for a truth in the life of a believer, when He plans to raise it from the dead and quicken it, He sends a witness. You see, teaching does not put truth into a believer; in the fullness of time, in the power of the Holy Spirit, it can be used as an instrument to raise a truth from the dead. Many Holy-Spirit-inspired witnesses besides teaching can come at the perfect time to precipitate the raising of a truth, witnesses such as the Bible, a person saying or doing something, nature, experience, pressure, worry, need, vocation, circumstance, and more.

People wanted Jesus to come earlier, for, they reasoned, if He had, Lazarus would not have died. Yet Jesus waited until he was dead for the glory of God to be revealed. In the same way, we might want a truth—such as casting our anxiety upon the Lord—to be alive in us immediately. Yet He waits! He knows the perfect moment for maximizing our joy, the moment that will bear the most fruit in our lives, the moment when God will get all of the glory. In just such a perfect moment He raises the truth that had been dead and bound, and we rejoice. He simply says, "Unbind him, and let him go." The friends and family of Lazarus had given up; they did not have the power to raise him from the dead. Much of what we read in the Bible we cannot do, because though the truth is in us, it is still in its dead state. Often we give up on a truth's ever coming alive in us, but He will come when we need it. The crowd around Lazarus wept over their inability and rejoiced at Christ's ability. We will do the very same thing. As believers we all have the fullness of Christ already within, and as we walk in Him, truths upon truths will come alive in us, but only He knows how and when to bring vitality to them.

DAY 248
Retirement

And whatever you do in word or deed, do all in the name of the Lord Jesus, giving thanks through Him to God the Father.

 —COLOSSIANS 3:17

The term work is used 355 times in the Bible. God works, man works, animals work, and the Son of God works. Work is a wonderful thing, characteristic of being created in His image. God contributes to man's work; it is to be an expression of Him. The only time work becomes a hindrance is when we do the work that is specifically God's. How many of us have hurried in to help prepare for a grand family gathering only to find that we were in the way and a hindrance? There are some things with which God does not want any of man's help—our salvation, acceptance, new birth, and holiness, just to mention a few.

Even the most menial of jobs will heighten life. We always feel better after working, and when it is to provide for someone other than ourselves, even more joy comes as a bonus. The shallowest people I have ever met are those who through poverty or wealth refuse to work.

With all that is said concerning work in the Scriptures, from where does the concept of retirement come? Many are waiting for the great someday when they no longer work but just sit under the magnolia tree sipping mint julep, basking in security, and dying! The significance of the job we perform is in displaying the life within us. Life is something that always expands, for it comes from God. We may move from that job to another, but the purpose will remain the same. In whatever work we are involved, we will display God.

In Australia a man quit after working 40+ years. He then began to take troubled youths to his house, and together they made complex models out of Popsicle sticks. He infused the gospel into work times. The boys took the models to school, and then others wanted to get involved.

The fellow recruited more "retired" men to help. He has shipped as many as 10,000 popsicle-stick models out in one year. By the way, he feels great.

If a 90-year-old man were talking to Methuselah, lamenting his life and wondering at his inability to make a difference, what would Methuselah say? I imagine he would say something like, "You are only a kid! There is much more to know of the Lord and much more to do. Now get on with it!"

DAY 249
Revelation

But we have this treasure in earthen vessels, so that the surpassing greatness of the power will be of God and not from ourselves.

—II CORINTHIANS 4:7

Often I used to pray, "Lord, I want all of the revelation of You possible for a human being to have in this life." Over and over and over again I prayed it. Then one day God spoke: "The revelation of My Son is like a roomful of treasure chests. There is one chest for every one of My children, but no child will receive them all. There is one for you, and that one you can have." I more fully understood the body of Christ and His love for each and every one of us. Just as the body needs countless cells to express a human being, it takes countless believers to begin to express everything Jesus is. He is way too big for one person, and any one person who believes he possesses it all is deluded.

Paul himself said we are like members of the body; he refused to see himself as the whole body. I am afraid many believers have succumbed to the Christian caste system, wherein a particular believer or a certain expression of the body becomes the norm or standard for everyone else. In my early days of being a believer I remember attempting to copy another person's expression of Christ. It was error then and it is error now. I have often said that if I could change anything in my Christian life as it developed, it would be one thing: I would have taken all of the "great" people of God and kept them on the fringe of my life where they belong, leaving Jesus in the center. No one person has it all, and we each have what He has given to us as He determined what was best.

DAY 250
Rewards

Behold, I am coming quickly, and My reward is with Me,
to render to every man according to what he has done.

—REVELATION 22:12

We are fearful, for when we see Him, will He say, "Well . . ." or "Well done"? The whole topic of rewards is frightening to all but the self-righteous, though they will be most surprised at their reward. Like most topics, the one of rewards is used by the carnal to manipulate the goodhearted. However, it can be a worthwhile discussion. In fact, I find it most amazing.

Did you know that our rewards are actually going to be based on doing nothing? The rewards will not be for what we have done directly, but what we have done indirectly. Did we let Jesus live through us? Jesus experienced separation from the Father, suffering, and death for the opportunity of living through us. The Father knows full well that the heart's desire of the Son is to live through others. It pleases the Father so much that He rewards those who allow Christ's expression. He honors us for honoring Christ. The reward is not based on what we did, which is hay, wood, and stubble; it is based on what we allowed Him to do through us. Imagine! We get the reward for what Jesus did! His love is too good, His ways too high, and His rewards unmerited. We get a crown, but when we see why we get it, we will be just like the elders in Revelation 4:10: "The twenty-four elders will fall down before Him who sits on the throne, and will worship Him who lives forever and ever, and will cast their crowns before the throne . . ." We can begin to see that when man does something on his own, out of his own strength, building his own glory, he has his reward already. Think of when you entered a room and said, "Jesus, I can't love that person; come and be my love," or when you said, "Jesus, I no longer want to go to work; I hate that job. Come and be my strength." Did you imagine that in all those things you would reap a reward? Amazing!

DAY 251
Running On Instinct

But these men revile the things which they do not understand; and the things which they know by instinct, like unreasoning animals, by these things they are destroyed.

—JUDE 10

I looked out the window to watch a huge black bear sit up, paws in the air, sniffing and watching as two little cubs ate out of the deer feeder. The cubs ate until stuffed and spent until 3:00 AM rolling around on the deck, chasing each other. So cute! But I remembered my grandfather's words. No way was I going outside with them. I do not believe a person can reason with a wild animal; the mother's instinct would kick in and she would protect the cubs, even though she was actually protecting them from nothing, since I would mean no harm.

When someone is being carnal, he is being animal, living by instinct. It is difficult to reason with him, nor do I know what he will do next. I try to remember to avoid the person in words, actions, and interaction, for how quickly I, too, can be pushed into a carnal state. At that point there are two unreasoning people in the room; pride in me has welled up within, so I will move into instinctive self-protection and give a defense. Then he reacts, I react to him, he reacts to me, and so on. The only thing accomplished is that now there are two carnal men standing where there had been one! The next morning I think how I did not even care what the man thought, so why in the world did I spend that much time arguing?

When you are making excuses, defending self, defending creditability, clarifying position, getting another on your side, or trying to gain approval, you are the same as a carnal, unreasoning beast! Think for just a minute about the contentious relative, neighbors, teacher, or leader to whom you made a defense. What you really wanted was for them to understand your position, and you wanted them to know your real motive. Do you really want them to think so well of you that they stay around all the time judging you? I promise if you fix one issue with the carnal, another will arise. When someone finishes chewing (harsh, critical, condemning, judgmental) me up, I often say, "Given that, you would be well advised to stay as far away from me as you can! If you see me coming you should turn and run!" After all, if I won that person as a friend, what would I have won?

Do not enter into others' carnality; let it work for you to push them away. Jesus did not try to reason with the carnal. "And after the morsel, Satan then entered into him. Jesus, therefore, said to him, 'What you do, do quickly'" (John 13:27). I am not begging people to let Christ live through them. It is a privilege!

DAY 252
Running On Reserve

If anyone does not abide in Me, he is thrown away as a branch and dries up; and they gather them, and cast them into the fire, and they are burned.

—JOHN 15:6

I remember purchasing my first motorcycle. My best friend, who was an expert at taking the machines apart, took me through the basics of how the motorbike worked. The thing I was most taken with was the reserve tank. To that point I had only owned automobiles with no such thing as a reserve, and being short of cash, I had often found myself out of fuel. But now I had a reserve tank; if I ran out of gas, I simply turned the switch and kept going. However, increasingly I kept finding myself stranded; the reserve was a great idea if fellows like me had not decided to make it the main tank.

It is very difficult to disciple someone who is not personally talking to God. Some go years without acknowledging they are, in fact, abiding in Him. They are operating on reserve. Believers who have turned their reserve tanks into their main tanks find themselves stranded in self.

There will be times when the world so overpowers us that we forget all about the Lord and rely on reserve. We may be overwhelmed—stranded—for a day or two, but can immediately return to a state of being full.

Think of the times you were full of power and confidence. Return, with the words of your mouth, to a full tank with the simple acknowledgment that you are in His presence. "Jesus, thank You that today I abide in You, because You have placed me in You and have given me Your life."

Day 253
Running With The Horses

If you have raced with men on foot and they have worn you out, how can you compete with horses? If you stumble in safe country, how will you manage in the thickets?

—JEREMIAH 12:5 [NIV]

What are the thickets? I can already tell you I like hiking and I hate thickets. There is never a clean way through them; they are perfect places for rabbits to hide. I have forged through lots of thickets around the world and never emerged unscathed without scratches, cuts, and torn clothes. My advice is to stay low, close to the roots, head down, single minded, and take the shortest route. Two things I cannot understand are why thickets and mosquitoes were created. Thickets keep people out. Out from what? Out of the top of the mountain, from the beautiful view, from the land that is good. Fires are the best possible solution for a thicket.

There are many thickets in life. The judgments, control, slander, and complaints of the carnal, the bickering over minutia, details that could not matter, chasing rabbits, comparisons, competitiveness, empty complaints, and prideful defense of doctrines. I have done them all and have even been a thicket to others. I sometimes see people as though they are trees, and basically, I see a thicket as people with a Judas ministry. Men as trees can sometimes be thickets; they are unavoidable. I understand that our encounter with thickets will leave us scarred; I do not expect anything different. However, if we stay close to the root, Jesus, we can avoid many of the entanglements that come further up. If we remind ourselves this is the carnal world, a world we once belonged to, and refuse the entrapment that comes from moving above the root, we need not respond as we move forward without stopping toward the light of His presence, and we can shorten this unpleasant experience. Any seed planted in a thicket will be snuffed out; legalism is the proof.

Jesus is the clear path through the thicket. After passing through, you will run with the horses.

DAY 254
Satan And His Children

, , , the father of lies.

—JOHN 8:44

I was being told of many people in Africa, believers and unbelievers alike, who suffered afflictions put on them by demons. I can understand a demon's dwelling in an unbeliever; however, nowhere does any writer of the New Testament—despite dealing with a variety of sins, behaviors, and problems—refer to the casting out of demons as a way of deliverance for a believer. In ministry Paul had to deal with immorality, idol worship, and all the deeds of the flesh. His solution was to point people back to Jesus. In some countries there are visible signs of demonic attack among many of the believers: wounds, sores, and a variety of ailments "having beset them because of the demonic." However, I do not think Satan is the primary cause of such oppression. Satan is the father of lies. When a father and mother divorce, the father is given a piece of paper that gives him the legal right to visit his children. A lie is Satan's child; if you invite in a lie, Satan has the legal right to come visit it. A lie can produce physical symptoms in a person. This is most obvious in the Aboriginal culture of Australia, wherein a witch doctor can "point the bone" at a man and the bone will start to grow in the man until it kills him. Doctors, though, have found a solution; they will give the recipient of this curse a local anesthesia, make a large cut, put on butterfly stitches, and give the man some unrelated random piece of bone as if it had been removed. At that the man will begin to get well. Before he had received a lie that manifested itself in physical symptoms which could lead to death, simply because he believed they would. The same takes place in Africa. Remove the lie and both Satan and the physical symptoms will leave. The lie needing to be removed is that Satan has more power than God. The people have been taught this through parents, culture, and experience, and they have received it. Because of this false concept of God, the lie received is that Satan can harm the elect, a lie used by the enemy to steal joy, confidence, and victory. I would recommend all this type of focus on Satan be removed and all such lies invited out, so the Christ within can flow freely to fill the void, and the father of lies can have no legal right to visit. Some believers focus on Satan and deliverance for the removal of the symptoms, and it is better to get deliverance from the source of all freedom, which is Christ. It is important for us all to guard against any part of the lie that Christ is weak. Again, the revelation of the truth of Christ will fill the void left when the lie leaves, and the symptoms will go.

DAY 255
Satan Never Shuts Up!

*Then he showed me Joshua the high priest standing before
the angel of the Lord, and Satan standing
at his right hand to accuse him.*

—ZECHARIAH 3:1

I remember as a university student taking a cross-country trip with a fellow student I barely knew; he was catching a ride with me to a city some distance away. I did not know the fellow had no capacity ever to quit talking, but rather there appeared to be a random firing in the brain that connected to the tongue. What made it even more frustrating is that he presumed to know everything about nothing in particular. Like the doll that could start talking when a child pulled a string in its chest, he prattled endlessly as if pulling his own string. When he did stay on a topic, the longer he talked, the more it sounded like he might know what he was talking about, but I was probably just getting brainwashed. I began to look for a blowhole in the top of his head that enabled him to keep talking without seemingly ever taking a breath. The monologue just went on and on and on.

I have only had a similar experience with one other being, the devil. He never shuts up, never. If he followed Jesus into the wilderness in order to get on a topic and not let up, how much will he do to us? A brother told me one day of the appearance of a demon who spoke to him, and he asked what I thought about it. All I said was: "Do not talk back, because the longer it talks, the more sense it makes."

One day a friend sent a letter, and after I read it, I was really frustrated. He was judging everything I was doing. I put it aside and refused to answer immediately. For the next two weeks all my thoughts were harsh, critical, driving, and condemning toward the brother. Oh, it made me mad. Finally I got the letter back out and prepared to respond (or, actually, react). I reread his letter only to find that it said nothing of what I had thought it said! It was completely supportive and positive! Satan had twisted the whole meaning of the letter.

Satan gets on to our flaws, the things that make us safe for God to work through us, the things that brought us to Christ, and the things of the flesh that do not change apart from abiding; and he harps, and harps, and harps until we are left wondering why God does not just kill us, or we ask God to take our life. He also talks through others; we all have had a share of that. How he loves to play off of our self-life through the offense of another, a failure, a disapproving glance from someone, a criticism, and more. He knows everything about nothing; he is a liar that never shuts up! According to him we are all hypocrites, hopeless, in terrible relationships, and being constantly abused; we are the unhappiest people around, surrounded by a world conquering us at the whim of wicked men. He never shuts up. He is a liar, the father of lies, and just as a judge grants visitation rights to a man with his children, if we receive a lie, Satan will have the legal right to visit it in us. Once he has gained access to us in that way, he torments us.

We must for the sake of our own sanity bring every thought captive to Christ. Christ knew us at our worst and yet chose us. We have been stupid, and yet look at how, because of Jesus, we continue to be blessed. God is nothing like what Satan is attempting to tell us. God has not judged us, wiped us, punished us, or killed people we love just to see us weep! God is love, and Satan is the liar who never shuts up; he is a noisy being, and those following him on earth are noisy. When all the noise gets to be too much, first of all, do not give the enemy your attention by starting to do battle. Jesus showed us how to handle him by saying, "The Lord rebuke you!" That is enough; any more and things will get worse. Second, go to I Corinthians 13, read what Love/God is, and let His peace and Truth flood over you. "The God of peace will soon crush Satan under your feet. The grace of our Lord Jesus be with you" (Romans 16:20).

DAY 256
Satisfaction

Now may the God of peace Himself sanctify you entirely;
and may your spirit and soul and body be
preserved complete, without blame at
the coming of our Lord Jesus Christ.

—I THESSALONIANS 5:23

At the very least, we see man is made up of a spirit, soul, and body; all three have their own respective needs. In listing the body's needs we would find things such as food, sex, touch, and sunlight. Needs of the soul would include understanding, choice, and a variety of feelings. Spiritual needs come in the form of love, acceptance, assurance, security, and commitment. Each unique part of our being must be specifically satisfied. The desires of spirit, soul, and body may influence one another but are not transferable from one to the other. Many today experience spiritual emptiness and attempt to fill the need of the spirit through activities in the body or soul. Having someone hug a person's body will not fill his spiritual need for security. Reading a book will not help a body in need of food. Conversely, eating will not help anyone pass his driving exam.

One reason psychology has been a bust is simply because it refuses to acknowledge the existence of the spirit and its accompanying needs. When attempts to fill the needs of the spirit through activities of body and soul fail, we are left feeling depleted and dissatisfied. At this point we are requiring out of the body and soul what they simply cannot give us.

One thing advertised today as a cure-all by secular and Christian writers is the pursuit of *right relationships*. If we have right relationships we purportedly will have security, happiness, sexual satisfaction, blessings, romance, kind conversations, and total commitment. The problem is that the Bible does not tell us right relationships will give all of these things. Right relationships often squeeze us, since they are calling us to forgive, not hold grudges, not complain, and to grow in Christ. I enjoy my relationships, but I do not require from them what they cannot give. The same can be said of life. So many are looking for more out of life. When asked to define *more*, they say satisfaction, job fulfillment, security, excitement, pleasure, and comfort, but life does not give these things. We are looking for what advertisers and the lost have told us will bring satisfaction to our being, but the activities of the body and soul will never meet the true desires of the spirit.

Many in relationships sense a measure of lacking fulfillment and assume this feeling must be coming from something wrong in the relationship. Next begins the odyssey of attempting to give more and milk more out of their mates. At the same time, many who are single feel something is missing in their lives and are quickly told the cause of the emptiness stems from not having a mate. The obsession begins to find a mate or to rationalize why one will never be found. In the end both camps are still found lacking. Why?

The deepest satisfaction in life cannot come from the fulfilled desires of body or mind; satisfaction comes from the spirit. We are looking for the right things in the wrong places. Genesis 25:8, "Abraham breathed his last and died in a ripe old age, an old man and **satisfied** with life; and he was gathered to his people."

Psalm 63:5, "My soul is **satisfied** as with marrow and fatness, and my mouth offers praises with joyful lips."

Here is the secret: When the spirit is satisfied, the fullness of body and soul immediately follow; as the emptiness disappears, cravings of the body diminish and thirst for knowing is replaced by faith.

You can prove it to yourself. The next time you find yourself distraught over what the future might bring, get up thirty minutes early, open your Bible to Psalm 139, and read. Stop and drink in every word, be quiet and listen, and experience the lightness in your heart. You are satisfied because your spirit is satisfied with Him.

DAY 257
Seeing Jesus In Others

And the King will answer and say to them, "Truly I say to you, to the extent that you did it to one of these brothers of Mine, even the least of them, you did it to Me."

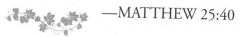

—MATTHEW 25:40

As I travel I have occasion to see Scripture in a different light. I have often been frustrated at what someone can do to me as a stranger. It seems I am under a constant attack of lies, manipulations, and harassments. Often I do not feel like a human being, but more like a Christmas tree having its ornaments plucked off one by one. This is a necessary evil in the work. Recently a fellow told me he had to talk to me after the conference. The Lord, he said, had really touched him, so I made the time; of course I would find some time to talk about Jesus! We met and he said, "I need money for a ticket to Australia; can you help me?" Another fellow, the head of a ministry, invited me to his country a few years back. He wanted to pay my way there, and I agreed to come. After I organized the trip, he said he could not pay my ticket or his, but everything else was ready. I agreed to pay his ticket. After the tickets were purchased, he announced that he could not take the time away from his "busy" schedule to interpret unless he was paid. I did not have another interpreter, and because I had invited others to come to that country with me, I agreed. Then I needed to pay all of his expenses, and on top of it all, I discovered he had paid another to do my book's translation, lied about the cost, and pocketed eighty percent of the money. This was no small ministry he had going, and so much of it involved deception. He meant it for evil, but God used it for good, and because of the young men I met on that trip and later trained, ALMI conferences are being done all over his country. Then there are the numbers of police and customs and immigration officials who have held me up, kept my bags, and refused to allow me to leave without paying them. I used to get frustrated, but now I remember the passage that begins this article. They will all be surprised one day to discover it was not from me they abused or stole money, but from Jesus. The $40 yanked out of my hands by the police at the last minute before they would allow me to board the plane was not actually yanked out of my hand. It came from the hand of Jesus, from whom we receive everything we have and who cautioned us to beware of every form of greed. I believe it will prove to be a very expensive $40 for those men. In fact, I have started something new. When someone is taking advantage of me, I do not protest by saying, "That is my money!" Rather, I say, "This is not my money; it belongs to my Master. Are you sure you want it?" Jesus said something interesting when having the Roman coin examined: "Whose image is on it?" It was Caesar's. "Then give to Caesar what is his and give to God what is His."

Let the dead steal from you. After all, if everyone has to give account for what they have done to Jesus, they have done nothing but stolen a curse. "Never take your own revenge, beloved, but leave room for the wrath of God, for it is written, 'Vengeance is Mine, I will repay,' says the Lord" (Romans 12:19). Then to further prove the point of the freedom in which we are to live, "But if your enemy is hungry, feed him, and if he is thirsty, give him a drink; for in so doing you will heap burning coals upon his head" (Romans 12:20). I see that we are free to be abused.

DAY 258
Seeing Things Differently

*Consider it all joy, my brethren, when you encounter
various trials, knowing that the testing of your faith
produces endurance. And let endurance have its perfect
result, that you may be perfect and complete,
lacking in nothing.*

—JAMES 1:2-4

I have had such a shift in my theology. It is Truth. For the facts of earthly life and the faith of heaven meet in a man named Jesus. I see the consequence of the fall as being "Christ in you." I see suffering as God's greatest evangelistic tool. I believe that nothing works against me. I know the earth is the womb in which the child of God is birthed. I also see that a situation does not create problems but reveals them.

A man said his wife had made him so angry, vindictive, and bitter. I stopped him, explained the purpose of life on earth (which is the loss of glory, pride, righteousness, strength, and kingdoms), and then said, "How can you tell me your wife made you angry, vindictive, and bitter? She did not make you that way. She is God's shovel digging down and finding it in you. You have been angry, vindictive, and bitter since other children started calling you a Snipe many years ago."

There was a long pause and tears before his response of, "Yes."

I said, "You want one answer for several issues." I then pointed out thirteen things with which he was dealing, and the last was the most important. "You do not really believe God is love. If you did, you would know it is love allowing this in your life. You believe God shows partiality. You do not believe this situation is the best for you. Under your ID photo should be the name 'Unlovable.'" More tears. We continued until I saw the lift in the countenance of this suffering person that only comes as the Holy Spirit brings the revelation of the work of God. It was hope I was seeing on his face. We discussed how he could mourn, take action, and have peace all at the same time. We finished close to midnight and discussed many more things.

DAY 259
Self and Manipulation

Truly, truly, I say to you, he who hears My word, and believes Him who sent Me, has eternal life, and does not come into judgment, but has passed out of death into life.

 —JOHN 5:24

I once knew a man who had the most ridiculous dog for a pet; it was kept on a chain tied to a tree in the back yard and was so mean that at feeding time, the dish had to be placed on the ground just short of where the aggressive dog could get to it with the chain stretched its full length. Then the dish was pushed with a broom handle until it was within range to be eaten! All the while, the dog would be snarling and biting at the air. This dinner scene would at times be witnessed by the nephew of the owner, a young boy of five, who naturally wanted nothing to do with that dog. One day the boy was walking hand-in-hand with his grandfather toward the garage to ride in the pickup truck. When they opened the garage door, to their surprise, there stood the dog, without chain or barrier, just teeth! The boy climbed straight up his grandfather's leg into his arms, yelling, "The dog! The dog!" The grandfather never flinched, paused, or changed direction; he only said, "Today I think I will kill that dog." All fear drained out of the boy as he looked from dog to grandfather. He knew his grandpa meant it, and obviously, so did the dog. The grandfather never wavered as he calmly headed toward the dog, who jumped out of the window, ran off, and was never heard of again.

There simply is nothing to fear when we are in God's arms. It would have been ridiculous for the young boy, upon seeing the dog, to run anyplace other than straight up Grandpa's leg into his arms. Unfortunately, unbelief renders our God small, too small to have arms into which we could climb. God appears so small that we must decide what to do on our own. We must analyze past action, the performance required, the resources available, and then we have to act. Of course, we generally lack whatever is needed to act on the strength of our acquired knowledge.

So much effort and strain is involved in daily living when our God is too small. A small God leaves the requirements for daily living in the hands of persons too weak to do anything of substance. The formula of studying to know the will of God, doing it to bring honor to Him, and being pleasing is accompanied by the problem of follow-through.

We all know more than we are doing. The end result yields individuals attempting to manipulate calm into every area of life—circumstances, people around them, finances—but failing at it and all the while being depleted.

The root of manipulation is unbelief. As the believer keeps his eyes on Christ, he is kept in perfect peace that passes understanding. Often a Christian will comment to me how he does not even understand how he could have peace in the midst of his situation, and yet he does! A believer is comfortable in every situation in which God is comforting him.

God's goal for our lives is accomplished through choices. There are two ingredients to decision-making. First, God moves through the natural (our likes, dislikes, economy, opportunities, and lack of opportunity). The second component is based on what we cannot see, faith. For example, I may not like my job (God is moving in the natural), and yet I must make a decision to leave and go somewhere else, which takes faith, for I ultimately do not know if I will find other work. Since choice has these two ambient factors, it is easy to see why so many stay at the job they hate. The only thing that can help us in this life of choices, that can relieve the pressure, that can lighten the load, is a big God! I need a God who is bigger than my circumstances, my understanding, my ability, my government, and my economy. I need a God who is in everything, holding all things together, and causing all things to work for good. I need to know that when I quit my job, I have a God bigger than my fears and insecurity.

Once the revelation comes that I do, in fact, have a big God, the life of manipulating can cease. I do not have to make sure I am never cheated or have followed every detail of the conference speaker's recipe for success. I need not be undone by my failure. I have a God, a big God, a God even greater than my failure.

On a practical note, how do we get this big God? We do not get Him through effort; we cannot manipulate God to our side. Many seek to gain the attention of God through works; others through constantly telling God what miserable creatures they are, in hopes He will draw near and show pity; and others through long petitionary prayers and Scripture memory. However, if His presence could be obtained through what we say and do, then He is under our control, His actions are determined by our actions, and in the end we have once again delineated confines for a small God. The secret is to obtain a big God simply by acknowledging we have a big God! He is at our side, and this understanding is the deepest level of faith. He *has* drawn near to us because He has desired to do so, and our belief in that is faith.

Every religion gives the followers something to do that will force the hand of their god to act in a predetermined way. Now, if a god can be forced into action because of my behavior, then I am greater than that god. The emphasis will be on the greater. This is why the emphasis in every religion is on the activity of the worshippers. In contrast, the Christian emphasis is on the One worshipped! His action for good on my behalf, when I have not merited it, solely embedded in His own nature, is mercy defined. Mercy is a unique attribute of Christianity. "For God has shut up all in disobedience so that He may show mercy to all" (Romans 11:32). "For He says to Moses, 'I WILL HAVE MERCY ON WHOM I HAVE MERCY, AND

I WILL HAVE COMPASSION ON WHOM I HAVE COMPASSION.' So then He has mercy on whom He desires . . ." (Rom. 9:15 & 18).

Often we do stupid things; we find ourselves in the fires of life burning up or in the waters of life drowning. All efforts to redeem ourselves are of no benefit. Our actions appear all the more deranged when we acknowledge this is not the first time we have done the very same thing and have once again brought misery. Given our history, we have absolutely nothing in our pot to merit a second look from God. What is to be done? Actually, it is only a very simple thing. "Lord, have mercy on my son, for he is a lunatic and is very ill; for he often falls into the fire and often into the water" (Matthew 17:15). Simply appeal to the mercy of God with the words of your mouth. Stupidity, sin, and weakness do not hinder the mercy of God; they reveal it. As Christians it is our luxury to be weak and defeated, to have nothing to offer, and yet to be delivered and strengthened to the point that we can soar like eagles, all because of the mercy of God. Our Father in heaven has such compassion for our condition of defeat that in our weakness, He comes. Manipulation can give way to praise! "In all their affliction He was afflicted, and the angel of His presence saved them; in His love and in His mercy He redeemed them; and He lifted them and carried them all the days of old" (Isaiah 63:9).

DAY 260
Self-effort Or Mercy?

He who did not spare His own Son, but delivered Him
up for us all, how will He not also with
Him freely give us all things?

—ROMANS 8:32

It is interesting to note how often any teaching on mercy (not getting what I deserve) and grace (getting what I do not deserve) is accused of spreading liberalism. The Scripture does say, "Are we to continue in sin that grace might increase?" If the Bible says it once, it is eternally important. However, in several thousand hours of discipling discouraged believers in dozens of countries, I personally have never met anyone who actually believed that to sin would be a benefit which allowed grace to abound. Scripture mentions it, so it must happen somewhere to someone. My experience with defeated Christians raises a practical question. Why is the occurrence of liberalism (sin so grace might abound, cheap grace, etc.) minimal while the fear of its happening enormous? It has been my experience that those who react most aggressively against the mercy and grace teaching of God are those who have worked the hardest to merit God's favor. It is the legalists who are so disturbed, for after having given so much time to performance, they are exhausted, angry, and repulsed over the thought of a "nobody" receiving freely that for which they have worked so hard. This attitude of legalism—believing performance equals acceptance—is confronted more than once in Scripture, and nearly any believer can name himself or an acquaintance as having been sidetracked through legalism. We see this failing in the elder brother of the Prodigal Son, not to mention in the whole book of Galatians.

This brings us to a second observation. If we are to rate teaching by its propensity to being misunderstood, then which would be the more dangerous teaching, the mercy and grace of God or the work a believer does? The flesh of man immediately distorts the work he does as a believer into something deserving merit, glory, and favor. The nature of the flesh is to find something in which to boast; hence the warnings against legalism are more numerous. The pride in flesh cannot boast in the mercy of God, for to discover the mercy and grace of God, the flesh had to fail; consequently, the warnings of liberalism are fewer! Both are important! "It was for freedom that Christ set us free; therefore keep standing firm and do not be subject again to a yoke of slavery," Galatians 5:1.

Mercy is a central theme in the Old and New Testaments, for God the Father is the subject, and He is mercy. To have our God, the one true God, is to have mercy; the two cannot be separated. When the believer asks Christ into his life, mercy and grace come, not through manipulation and work, but as a free gift.

A primary school teacher made an interesting observation: "All children have a heart for God." It is true! Children come naturally to loving Jesus, and then they are taught to fear and also, to a measure, to fail Him. If children could stick with the theme of loving Him, they would discover throughout adulthood that being in His loving arms is the easiest place to please Him. Good behavior is not the cause of holiness, mercy, or grace; a change in behavior is the result of holiness, mercy, and grace. "For the grace of God has appeared, bringing salvation to all men" (Titus 2:11). Salvation is a change in behavior, not just a ticket to heaven. "Christ Jesus, who gave Himself for us, that He might redeem us from every lawless deed and purify for Himself a people for His own possession, zealous for good deeds" (Titus 2:13, 14). Again, we do not clean ourselves up to go to God, we go to God and He cleans us up! Jesus did not come to make bad men good; He came to give all dead men life. Life is Jesus! "He saved us, not on the basis of deeds which we have done in righteousness, but according to His mercy, by the washing of regeneration and renewing by the Holy Spirit" (Titus 3:5).

DAY 261
Self-righteousness

But the Lord said to him, "Now you Pharisees clean the outside of the cup and of the platter; but inside of you, you are full of robbery and wickedness."

—LUKE 11:39

Self-righteousness is simply my imitating the fruit of the Holy Spirit. If in my own strength I am acting out love, joy, peace, patience, kindness, goodness, faithfulness, gentleness, and self-control, I am self-righteous. Believers spend so much time describing the unrighteous, but self-righteousness is worse and much more insidious.

Imitating the fruit of the Spirit will not give you a standing with God; it only gives a standing with the devil. It is for your glory, for its roots are in wanting to be seen, and it will fail you when you least expect it. Recognize abiding and true fruit will be yours naturally.

DAY 262
Separating the Issues

Who is the man who fears the Lord? He will instruct him in the way he should choose.

—PSALM 25:12

As I have often pointed out, we must learn to separate the issues. One answer will not fit all the issues. Some people use the turmoil in the world to build themselves an image. In order to do this they must go to places where people will listen to them. Hence, they will go where there are Christians, who will respond to the news of injustices and hope to help. When the Christians work on making the change, the image-builders take the credit. However, when anyone takes the information given him and effects changes, he alone should get the credit for the change. A faith teacher cannot take the credit when a person activates faith after the teacher has told him such-and-such will happen "if you have the faith," for if the person did not activate faith, the faith teacher would never take the blame. A "peacemaker" talks to two groups, one of which accepts the information and makes the change (they did it by an act of choosing of their free will), but the other group refuses. The peacemaker gets the award on the basis of the group that acted. People are given awards for the successes of others; it is just amazing how the world works.

In preaching we witness to what God is doing in people; we do not create it. If people change, THEY change. Releasing them to choice releases us. The preachers can never take the credit. It is dodgy business to take the credit for the grace of God and the choice of another person. No one can point to any Christian and tell me my message failed. Why? My message affirms that a person must choose Jesus at every point. When he does not, then he will probably sin. If he does, he will experience the life of Christ flowing through him. In the message of abiding in Christ, results rest not in a method but in the freewill choice of the believer. Therefore, the message is Truth, but its outworking is up to the individual. However, when a message is presented as absolute and as having the ability to change lives with no consideration of choice in a person, then that message is responsible for all those who do not make a choice. When we hear that a method or teaching has produced a positive result and covertly the teacher and the message are given the credit, then personal choice has been stripped away and the teacher and the message must likewise be accountable for all those who have gone back or refused to go forward. I know a man who takes credit for the changes in every person he has ever met, and yet when confronted with the subsequent failures of those same people, he simply goes into denial. Christian disciplers are simply witnessing to Truth, and believers themselves must decide whether or not to receive it and reap the rewards.

DAY 263
Separating the Issues In Your Life

And behold, one came to Him and said, "Teacher, what good thing shall I do that I may obtain eternal life?" And He said to him, "Why are you asking Me about what is good? There is only One who is good; but if you wish to enter into life, keep the commandments." Then he said to Him, "Which ones?" And Jesus said, "YOU SHALL NOT COMMIT MURDER; YOU SHALL NOT COMMIT ADULTERY; YOU SHALL NOT STEAL; YOU SHALL NOT BEAR FALSE WITNESS; HONOR YOUR FATHER AND MOTHER; and YOU SHALL LOVE YOUR NEIGHBOR AS YOURSELF." The young man said to Him, "All these things I have kept; what am I still lacking?" Jesus said to him, "If you wish to be complete, go and sell your possessions and give to the poor, and you will have treasure in heaven; and come, follow Me." But when the young man heard this statement, he went away grieved; for he was one who owned much property.

 —MATTHEW 19:16-22

We see in this discourse that Jesus is separating the issues in the rich young ruler's life. What the young man thought was the issue was not the only issue. We think there is only one issue in our life to be resolved, and even if we discover there are actually several, the mistake is made of looking for the one thing that will fix all of the issues at once. The same tool will not fix a flat tire, a sink, a bicycle spoke, and a computer; they all have separate problems requiring different tools for repair. One answer does not work for every situation, and any one event carries with it several issues, each with a separate answer. The sign that a believer is looking for the magic elixir to fix every issue is confusion. Therefore, the issues must be separated and dealt with individually, such as when an injustice occurs and spawns the need for blessing those who curse, loving the enemy, forgiveness, and the process of reconciliation that will bring closure. Let us take a look at those issues and break them down one by one.

1. We must bless those that curse us or they live in our heads and pay no rent.

2. Loving our enemies is commanded, for He makes His sun to shine on the just and the unjust. He takes no pleasure in the death of the wicked (Ezekiel 33:11).

3. Forgiveness is a package. Just as a person cannot hold a tire and tell me he owns an automobile, since a car is made up of many parts, so forgiveness has many parts. There is an offense, a break in relationship, confession by the offender, forgiveness given by the offended (necessary since there is no forgiveness for unforgiveness), all ending in restoration. Due to its very nature, there is no forgiveness without confession, since the purpose of forgiveness is restoration. "If we confess our sins," "repent for forgiveness of sins," and "as often as your brother comes to you" all show the context of the giving of forgiveness. We must carry a heart of forgiveness so that when it is asked for, we can dispense it freely. Does God forgive without confession? (I am not teaching here about the common concern of, "What if I die and I forgot to confess a sin?" Once a person is in Christ, Jesus died for all of his sins.) Confession for man

is cleansing and releasing, but there is a common teaching that believers should go to an offender and offer forgiveness without any acknowledgement from the wrongdoer that a sin was committed. Instructing a young woman who has been abused to go and tell the uncle, "I forgive you," when the uncle has not asked for forgiveness usually has a detrimental outcome. I have heard many stories of believers who went to someone to forgive him when it was not in the offender's heart to ask for it; the offender actually denied it, walked off, and/or condemned the hurt person for making such an accusation. This is soul-killing anew for an injured believer. Many will argue that forgiveness is unconditional, but those two words do not go together, for "unconditional" implies that there is no sin, and if no sin, there is no forgiveness. Yet all have sinned, and through confession, "He is faithful and just to forgive our sins and cleanse us from all unrighteousness" (I John 1:9). The Prodigal Son asked for forgiveness and was restored. Today there seems to be more emphasis on the need for the offended to forgive when it is not asked for, thus loading responsibility on the victim. Why not draw attention to the offender's confession as something cleansing and restoring? Those who have sinned against another are cheated when there is no mention of confession. Confession and forgiveness are two words that should remain together, inseparable. However, the victim is not stuck; there is something to do when confession has not and may never come. "Bless those that curse you," "do good to those that harm you," and "pray for those that persecute you." All of these things set us free and make us all the more excited about forgiving, should the occasion arise.

4. Forgiveness must be given when asked for. "Forgive us (See? We are asking) as we forgive our debtors." However, there is a process after forgiveness that brings closure. Let me explain. A man has an affair; once it is over, for three years he is tormented. He repents before God and then tells his wife, asking, naturally, for forgiveness. She must forgive. However, this has taken her completely by surprise, and she is extremely hurt. Yet, if she asks any further questions or gets angry in the future, he accuses her of walking in unforgiveness, which covertly shifts the load of the whole event to her shoulders. The children have been hurt, the wife has been embarrassed and betrayed, there is a break in trust, and she has many unanswered questions; she needs closure. Though I do not want the couple to camp at the event and do want them to move forward, a few things need to be said about forgiveness. Talking will help bring closure. Yes, she must move on, but talking and getting a few answers will help her do so. The same is true for the believer who has lost a loved one due to an injustice such as murder. We hear many stories about murderers asking for forgiveness, which must be granted by the family. However, normal questions ensue, such as, "How did (s)he die? Where did you put the body?" (This was the question asked by the women at the grave of Jesus.) Some believers use an injustice and the lack of repentance to get stuck at a point of hatred and condemnation; there is no profit in that. Hearts are revealed through injustices, confession, and forgiveness.

5. We must and will forgive. However, that does not mean that a lawbreaker should not go to prison. I Peter 3:17, "For it is better, if God should will it so, that you suffer for doing what is right rather than for doing what is wrong." A

couple told me of a man who killed their daughter. From prison the criminal sincerely confessed what he had done and asked for forgiveness. The parents asked what they should do. I told them they must forgive and must also let the man serve his prison sentence. Forgiveness and staying in prison are separate issues. Judging the man and putting him in prison is the job of government in order to protect the populace. "For (governments) are a minister of God to you for good. But if you do what is evil, be afraid; for it does not bear the sword for nothing; for it is a minister of God, an avenger who brings wrath on the one who practices evil. Therefore it is necessary to be in subjection, not only because of wrath, but also for the sake of conscience" (Romans 13:4 & 5). The thief on the cross was forgiven but not taken off the cross. Lawbreakers are not victims, but it does amaze me to watch the news and see how the world is consequence conscious and not cause conscious. It seems as though the treatment of those who have caused atrocities (consequence of their actions) is more important than the cause of their being treated that way! The victims of their crimes are looking for assurances it will not happen again, a security not likely to come as long as those who violated them do not ask for forgiveness. (Of course, the opposing danger is that victimization is a religion; it is very addictive.) It reminds me of the Great Depression. Because of its great impact on my grandmother, she still saved newspaper, jars, rubber bands, bread wrappers, and more. She never forgot what it was like and never, looking at unrepentant government, regained the confidence that it would not happen again.

6. Facts do not oppose each other. It is a fact that birds fly and a fact that I cannot. We separate the facts. It is a fact

that I love my enemy, a fact that I bless my enemy, a fact my enemy must ask for forgiveness, a fact when I am asked I must forgive my enemy, and it is a fact that wounds do take time to heal. Each of these facts will come to fullness in our daily lives as He makes them alive according to His own timing.

DAY 264
Settled In Being Unsettled

Now faith is the assurance of things hoped for, the conviction of things not seen.

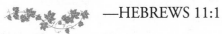 —HEBREWS 11:1

Where am I going? What is to be my vocation? Will I get married? What about kids, and should I get a pet?

Are you unsettled? If you are, then you are in good company! Most believers are unsettled or have been a good part of their lives. We agree that if Jesus ceased to exist, so would we. "Yet for us there is but one God, the Father, from whom are all things, and we exist for Him; and one Lord, Jesus Christ, by whom are all things, and we exist through Him" (I Corinthians 8:6). Jesus holds the physical world together; therefore, He is in everything. I am not teaching pantheism, which essentially views the creation as the Creator. I am saying the Creator is revealed in the creation He holds together. This is why Paul could say, "And we know that God causes all things to work together for good to those who love God, to those who are called according to His purpose" (Romans 8:28). God uses the natural things and events of the world He holds together to make us supernatural!

To be unsettled is a natural thing that reaps a supernatural result. In being unsettled, we are forced to make faith decisions, have assurance of things not naturally seen, and act on convictions based in Him. Incredibly, all things are used by Him, even the unsettling areas. Therefore, we can do ourselves a favor by becoming settled in being unsettled. Everything is moving along according to His plan; we just do not know the plan. I have found that His plans are generally revealed on a *need-to-know basis*!

DAY 265
Show Us the Message
In the Messenger?

But you, beloved, building yourselves up on your most holy faith, praying in the Holy Spirit, keep yourselves in the love of God, waiting anxiously for the mercy of our Lord Jesus Christ to eternal life. Have mercy on some, who are doubting; save others, snatching them out of the fire; and on some have mercy with fear, hating even the garment polluted by the flesh.

—JUDE 20-23

Should a Christian listen to the music or read the book by a believer who has fallen? For me this question actually has two answers. First, our responsibility is to judge the message, for it always takes precedence over the messenger. Paul makes this point repeatedly, such as in Galatians 1:8, saying no matter how beautiful the messenger is, the message is what counts. "But even if we, or an angel from heaven, should preach to you a gospel contrary to what we have preached to you, he is to be accursed!" Paul sees the message as being much more important than himself: "What then is Apollos? And what is Paul? Servants through whom you believed, even as the Lord gave *opportunity* to each one" (I Corinthians 3:5). Even when it came to having a messenger with wrong motives, Paul remained interested primarily in the message, as when he wrote, "the former proclaim Christ out of selfish ambition rather than from pure motives, thinking to cause me distress in my imprisonment. What then? Only that in every way, whether in pretense or in truth, Christ is proclaimed; and in this I rejoice" (Philippians 1:17, 18). Therefore, if the message was correct when the writer or performer was walking with Jesus, the message is still valid today, and I will not throw it out. David had a moral failure; I will not throw out what God had clearly given him before his failure. It would be my loss. When one takes the position of seeking to discredit everything ever said by a fallen believer, he is walking on thin ice, for God may define for him anew what fallen means. In Galatians 5:19-21, Paul gives a description of the flesh; none of us can boast that at some time in our life we have not fallen into some of these things. Who can rightly judge the messenger?

Now to the second answer, which is that some have not promoted the message but rather promote themselves. Their plan is that whenever we hear their music or read a particular paragraph, their picture, not Christ's, flashes into our minds. Paul talks about such people. "For we do not preach ourselves but Christ Jesus as Lord, and ourselves as your bond-servants for Jesus' sake. For God, who said, 'Light shall shine out of darkness,' is the One who has shone in our hearts to give the Light of the knowledge of the glory of God in the face of Christ" (II Cor. 4:5, 6). There are those in the business of riding on the back of Christ to create an image for themselves; they do not make a distinction between the message and themselves. They are the proof of their message. They, in fact, believe they are propping up Jesus. The focus is constantly on them and their faith, their talent, and their cleverness. Their formula, writing, or music and how it makes them stand out is one with their image. "For Christ did not send me to baptize, but to preach the gospel, not in cleverness of speech, so that the cross of Christ would not be made void" (I Cor. 1:17). When such a believer falls, it is impossible to separate him from his message, for in reality he was the message, and with such a high standard set for himself and others he will have trouble finding grace. Such a one is left having to clean up the mess on his own. In interview after interview he will try to separate himself from the message, so that the message can retain its integrity, but it is too late. It becomes impossible to defend his message when it is revealed that it was not THE message of Christ. People quickly abandon him. The books and the music will find their way to the trash bin, but though his reputation is also in the trash bin, the person is not! The blessing in all of this is that God will use it to move him into clinging to the proper message. In the grace of God, we see him rise from the ashes with a new message, THE message of Christ. Well, amen!

DAY 266
Showing Up

And it came about when the vessels were full, that she said to her son, "Bring me another vessel." And he said to her, "There is not one vessel more." And the oil stopped.

—II KINGS 4:6

What does it mean to let go and let God? I must do something, but what? There is so much I try to do but cannot. Where does my activity begin and end? Where does God's activity begin and end? What must I do for myself because God will refuse to do it for me? What must I not do, since God alone can do it? All are valid questions! Put another way, where do God's sovereignty and my responsibility meet?

The prophet Elisha was going along and met a woman who explained how after the death of her husband, the creditors had come to take her two children. The prophet asked if she had anything. "Only a jar of oil." She was then told to go borrow vessels, shut the door behind her, and fill them from her jar of oil. In the end when she told her son, "Bring me another vessel," he said, "There are no more," and at that the oil stopped. Can God be limited? Of course not! Can God be limited? Of course He can! If they had continued to find and bring more vessels, would the oil have ceased? No. However, when they ceased to bring them, the oil did stop. I wonder if the son really did find all the vessels in the whole neighborhood. Why did they quit borrowing? Were they tired or discouraged?

Did they question the wisdom of the exercise? Were they weary of listening to a stressed mother, or were they just unbelieving? Suffice it to say that God's activity was to fill the vessels, and human responsibility was to bring the vessels. God's activity and human responsibility met at a place called choice.

There is only one thing we must choose, and it is a simple thing. It is our human responsibility, our activity, the one thing God will not do for us, the thing we must do for ourselves. We must show up to be filled. Each morning we must show up! God does the rest! The expression of *showing up* is different for each person. Some open the Bible, others turn on a praise hymn, and still others awaken with praise on their lips. I stop for a moment and utter a few things, "Holy Spirit, You are welcome here today. Thy will be done, and let everything I see today preach Jesus to me." It matters not what is our own individual way, just so we show up!

DAY 267
Simple Failures In Marriage

Wives, be subject to your own husbands, as to the Lord.
. . . Husbands, love your wives, just as Christ also loved the
church and gave Himself up for her.

 —EPHESIANS 5:22, 25

When it comes to wives in dealing with submission and to men as regards love, I believe there are two major sources of confusion: pride and unbelief. We do not believe God can lead us through a mediator, such as a husband. Unbelief gives way to the fear of what will happen if we do not have our way. Pride simply says, "I want it my way." Then there is a third problem: We do not see the commands as being given to make us happy. Because of these three things, I believe we hear thousands of "concerns" about submission and love that only stem from wanting to rule them out.

There is an obvious point to be made about submission. When the general enters the room, I stop listening to the captain. Jesus can at any time override a husband's wishes. Concerning how submission works, I really believe that is the cart before the horse. Many are asking the details of how this will all work out before having done the first things. If the first things were done, they would not be asking these questions; they would be hearing from God. It is important for counselors not to get trapped into giving the details of how something works out, for it all works out in the Way. Jesus is the Way. There are five billion people, and we cannot be responsible for answering five billion separate situations. However, we can point every person to Jesus, for as everyone draws near to learn from Him, they will receive a perfect answer. I am purposely vague. The majority wants answers, not Jesus, but I cannot make a general statement which would prove to be absolute on leadership, submission, and love. We remember that God says to kill the prostitutes and then tells Hosea to marry one. I love this great problem with the Bible: Try to be absolute, and there will always be a passage that will not fit in. It makes us run to Jesus in dependence and trust.

Having said that, I say, "Are the people questioning submission free from pride, offense, kingdom building, righteousness, and strength? Do they know who Jesus is?

Can they hear His voice personally? Are they working *from* His Life or *for* His acceptance?" The other day I was speaking in a church and asked how many would like to be close to Jesus. The whole crowd raised their hands. Before they could put them down, I said, "No, keep your hands up. I am counting all the unbelievers, for we are already close to Jesus." They really got it. Submission is not an issue when the above foundational issues are addressed and dealt with.

DAY 268
Simplicity

And He said: "I tell you the truth, unless you change and become like little children, you will never enter the kingdom of heaven. Whoever humbles himself like this child is the greatest in the kingdom of heaven."

—MATTHEW 18:3 [NIV]

Recently I spent a couple of days with a good friend who amazes me by living an unencumbered life. How healthy someone can remain when he determines to live life for others. He finds delight in the simplest of things: a pancake in the morning, children petting a dog, or a small, delicate girl wanting to touch the hand of another. All this he takes in with wide-eyed excitement. His childlike ways help me understand the observation of Jesus, "Unless we become as little children."

In a world of empty people looking for life but not living it, I find this man refreshing. Men today walk around like zombies, attempting to drown out the emptiness with music blaring in their ears. They are Swiss-cheese people with holes throughout their lives.

DAY 269
Singing Birds

*And they sang the song of Moses the bond-servant of God
and the song of the Lamb, saying,
"Great and marvelous are Thy works,
O Lord God, the Almighty.
Righteous and true are Thy ways,
Thou King of the nations.
Who will not fear, O Lord,
and glorify Thy name?
For Thou alone art holy.
For all the nations will come
and worship before Thee.
For Thy righteous acts have been revealed."*

—REVELATION 15:3, 4

Of all the animals on earth, only two sing: man and the songbirds. Of approximately 9,000 species of birds, about half of them are songbirds. This is unlike the chicken and the frog with hardwired sounds they can make, even if deaf, for chickens do not have to hear to make their repetitive sound. Many birds have a simple vocalization with very little variety, if any, in their patterns. In contrast, the songbirds can often follow an instrument note for note. One fellow reports going to an aviary and playing his instrument to a white-crested laughing thrush; the bird began to follow along with the song.

Carnal persons, like the chickens, seem to make the same noise day after day. They are deaf to the life of God, and their droning is monotonous. The carnal show very little breadth or depth in what is said. Get them together and the sound is even more annoying. They are always an echo and never a voice. The spiritual, like the songbird, listen, become excited at the music, and begin to sing along with the One who started the singing. The spiritual move with Christ, and He will speak into their hearts a new song. Psalm 40:3, "He put a new song in my mouth, a hymn of praise to our God." The sound of the spiritual is a balm for the broken and hurting heart. Isaiah 52:7, "How beautiful on the mountains are the feet of those who bring good news, who proclaim peace, who bring good tidings, who proclaim salvation, who say to Zion, 'Your God reigns!'"

In the end, it is good to be a follower of the One who is leading us, to listen to His voice and to follow what He is speaking. In so doing, make a beautiful sound for the rest of the world to hear.

DAY 270
Situations Reveal,
Situations Do Not Create

For nothing is hidden, except to be revealed; nor has anything been secret, but that it should come to light.

—MARK 4:22

A woman once asked me, "Could you please talk to my husband? He had an automobile accident and is very angry and bitter." I agreed to talk to him but said, "Be assured the accident did not create his anger, it merely revealed it. Your husband has always been an angry man." She thought for a minute and said, "It is true; he has always been angry."

To my mind one of my friends has suffered much in this life, fleeing a war in his country to another country of unrest, and departing yet again to a different country. He has been a pastor and suffered much at the hands of believers. To support himself in ministry he has taken job after job below his skill level. He really is topnotch. I could never understand it. He is more qualified than I, more spiritual, more everything! Then recently he fell out of a tree and broke his back, so he is paralyzed. Many would think this to be the final straw and finally this man, like Job, would complain against God. Yet he did not! To the amazement of so many of us he has remained very sweet. How? It is because he has always been sweet and a man of integrity. The accident has brought to the forefront what all of his close friends have always known, that he is a beautiful man and Christ is his life. We at Abiding Life embrace the teaching that we are broken so we will accept Christ, and then we are broken for all the world to see the Christ within us. This man proves it.

Here is another example. I had the privilege of meeting a ninety-five-year-old Welsh preacher. At age eighteen he noticed he could not see properly. Upon further examination, it was discovered that he was going blind. At the time he was studying to be in the ministry. He told his pastor he had to quit because of the ailment, to which the pastor retorted, "Hogwash! That does not change your call." He continued and has ministered all these years. He even tells of preaching in a whiskey town where the pulpit was made of discarded whiskey barrels. Upon discovering that, he had it torn down. He, too, had suffered much at the hands of believers and yet remained sweet. I asked his daughter what it was like to have a blind father. "Oh, to this day I have never heard him complain." He even told me he was grateful he was blind, for if he had been seeing, he might have fallen into the temptations David did.

Again, the breaking of a man by a situation reveals what is within, whether the great treasure of life in Christ or the piffle of self-love.

DAY 271
Sour Dating Relationships

And He who searches the hearts knows what the mind of the Spirit is, because He intercedes for the saints according to the will of God.

—ROMANS 8:27

For God sees not as man sees, for man looks at the outward appearance, but the Lord looks at the heart.

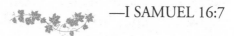

—I SAMUEL 16:7

I would like to share a couple of thoughts with you on broken relationships. When it comes to the topic of relationships, it is really easy to take three or four issues, put them in a pot, stir them all up, and look for one answer to the whole mess. However, I have found what seem to be three main issues in relationships.

First, when a relationship ceases, a normal Christian, no matter how spiritually attuned, will spend a good bit of time mourning. Being distraught over the loss of someone speaks well of a person; it is a sign of commitment, maturity, and of the emotional vested interest. I am always suspicious of the person who breaks up and experiences no turmoil whatsoever; if a person is not upset over the closure of a relationship, then I probably do not want that one as a friend. There is no easy answer or quick fix for grief; God takes us through the hurt one day at a time.

Second, I have been amazed when a relationship is not working and both people acknowledge it. However, the first one to break up always feels better, while the other feels rejection, with its accompanying messages unrelated to the event. It is somewhat like a kite with a long tail. Capture the kite and you discover all that is attached to it. The kite is like the initial issue (a couple is no longer going to see each other); the tail holds all other issues that the enemy stirs up through feelings of rejection. "You really messed up." "You should have acted differently." "You are a worthless person." "Who else would want you?" "That was your last chance for happiness." Often a spiral begins that simply does not have any valid basis in the context of what has happened. Maybe we have some problems, but rarely are our problems connected to the rejection of another. This can be a perfect opportunity to learn what it means to renew the mind.

Third, and most important, there is no such thing as the natural world and the supernatural world; there is only the supernatural world. God has created all things through Christ; therefore, all things are supernatural. The only thing existing outside of the supernatural is the unnatural, what takes place when the supernatural is distorted under the power of man's flesh as it yields to sin. What does this have to do with dating? God creates the individual as He wishes. Attraction to certain attributes in the opposite sex is God-given and natural. Man does not create those desires; rather, they are created by God. The preferences for a particular color of hair, personality, form, etc. come from Him. Therefore, when attraction is lost for a person, we find God at work in that situation. We do not set out to possess a mate; God gives a mate as He gives the desire for one another. Without His working, no one could love one another. This is great news! The weight of the foundation for a working relationship is not on our backs, but His. We cannot create in someone else a desire for us, but rather we receive from Him the gift of desire He has placed in another person's form. When a relationship does not work out, it is not because one or the other is defective or has not done enough to create desire. It is because God has withdrawn desire. The question can then be asked, "Why did God give the initial desire to get me involved, so that now I have to deal with the pain of rejection?" Quite simply, it is through experience that we learn how to maintain a relationship He gives. In dating we learn how to communicate, work through issues, love sacrificially, and more. These things will not create desire, but they will maintain it. We would like to learn how to be Christian in a book; however, it will never happen. We learn what Christ in us is through experience. Likewise, we can never learn the art of developing relationships in the text of a book; it is within the context of relationships that we learn to love, forgive, encourage, confront, and minister.

All of life teaches faith. Even unbelievers have been learning the lessons of faith, such as when there were ten things they wanted to know before purchasing a car, at best they only knew nine, and buying the car became a faith decision. When it comes to a faith decision, we can either trust ourselves or trust Him. Trusting God makes a faith decision easy. Anxiety, questioning, fear, depression, worry, and doubt are all signs we have trusted ourselves. After a relationship is over, if we sit around thinking, "I could have done this or that," "I could have moved right instead of left," "I should have seen this coming," or "I could have made better decisions," all this is a sign of trusting ourselves. When we trust in God as He works in the natural—holding it together, giving and taking desire—then we do not have to have all the preceding regrets. We rest, trust, and wait on Him. The relationship went exactly as it was supposed to. No mistakes were made. Some will say, "No, I remember saying something I should not have." True, but the problem with that thinking is it regards a relationship as based on performance, and no such relationship could last, for eventually someone would not perform and the whole thing would fall apart. It is better to recognize the relationship is based in God-given desire. Also, if God causes all things to work together for His glory and our good, does a breakup not fit into His "all things" category?

I have never had anything go wrong in my life. Not one single thing. God has caused all things for His glory and my good. The problem arose when I have gone wrong with things and resisted or even rebelled against them. As Christians we never have to spend one day looking back in regret, for God was working.

I am not going to say there is a better person for you; God does not have "better persons." But I will say there is another person God is going to give you, and you to him or her, in a relationship based in desire, and everything you learn in previous dating relationships will be used to maintain it.

DAY 272
Sowing What You Reap

For the one who sows to his own flesh shall from the flesh reap corruption, but the one who sows to the Spirit shall from the Spirit reap eternal life.

—GALATIANS 6:8

The topic of sowing and reaping often comes up when talking about the grace of God. How can one sow unrighteousness and not reap it? I am often confronted with this teaching when I make the point that God is not as interested in consequences as He is in results. A spiritual abuser will use the sow-and-reap theology to control those who fail. Their reasoning goes like this: "You have failed. God has forgiven you, but you must now bear the consequences the rest of your life." Aside from the fact that consequences are not absolute (one man gets drunk, drives, and kills an innocent driver, while another gets drunk and drives home safely), there is another problem with the sowing-and-reaping theology. It is a fact that if a person sows to the flesh he will reap to the flesh, but here is my problem. I come from a farm, so I understand how every farmer would love it if he could sow just one time and reap for a lifetime. However, sowing is an annual affair, requiring plowing, planting, cultivating, and harvest. This annual cycle never ends. I believe when someone sows to the flesh (mind you, it is a heap of work) and maybe sows some more, the sowing is for one season only. The sowing and reaping of the Bible allows for repentance, stopping the sowing to the flesh, resuming sowing to the Spirit, and then reaping of the Spirit. The legalist will never mention that. Sowing is only for a season, and a believer can change what he is sowing at any moment.

DAY 273
Spiritual Attack or Spiritual Oppression?

Submit therefore to God. Resist the devil and he will flee from you. Draw near to God and He will draw near to you. Cleanse your hands, you sinners; and purify your hearts, you double-minded.

—JAMES 4:7, 8

In earlier years of being a believer, there seemed to be a certain appeal to someone's saying he was under spiritual attack; it was generally described in terms that appeal to the flesh. "God wants to use me and my ministry, and therefore the enemy wants to stop me!" Basically, the whole concept of spiritual attack held the possibility of a person's possessing an extra measure of grace and power and therefore being feared by the enemy. Spiritual attack could be used to insinuate that a ministry's effectiveness was about to explode, and the enemy was trying everything to stop this great expression, as if the kingdom of God were dependent on a man or a ministry! Well, we are growing up. Jesus said this: "I will not speak much more with you, for the ruler of the world is coming, and he has nothing in Me." When we look at the temptations of Christ, we can see they follow a pattern described by John as, "All that is in the world, the lust of the flesh, and the lust of the eyes, and the boastful pride of life." Satan was looking for a toehold of lust and pride in Jesus from which to launch his attack, yet he found nothing. When Satan launches an attack on any of us, he is looking for a foothold, a place from which to base his offensive. "Your adversary, the devil, prowls around like a roaring lion, seeking someone to devour" (I Peter 5:8). For what kind of "someone" is he looking? He hunts anyone who has the lust of the eyes, the lust of the flesh, and the boastful pride of life. In short, the enemy cannot start an invasion without having a foothold in the flesh. I used to believe that a great struggle with the enemy revealed a great heart for God, when actually, a great struggle with the enemy reveals a wrong heart. It reveals flesh. It reveals a stronghold. Christ's struggle with Satan did not last for days or even hours, since nothing in Christ found the temptations appealing.

It is very difficult for an enemy to mount an attack against a person who is not moved or intimidated by the threats. For example, someone can say a person is actually a woman parading as a man, but with no truth to the statement, the attack falls dead and the attacker looks like an idiot. However, someone can say, "You are a liar," and to the degree a person does lie, the attack will haunt him. God is using the attacks and not fighting them, but we must be honest and ask ourselves what the attacks reveal. Man has a thousand ways of hiding the lust of the eyes, the lust of the flesh, and the boastful pride of life. These complicated schemes to feed the flesh and yet appear to be spiritual are revealed in the rich young ruler. "The young man said to Him, 'All these things I have kept; what am I still lacking?' Jesus said to him, 'If you wish to be complete, go *and* sell your possessions and give to *the* poor, and you will have treasure in heaven; and come, follow Me.' But when the young man heard this statement, he went away grieving; for he was one who owned much property" (Matthew 19:20-22). The young man "appeared" to be quite spiritual; however, behind the mask of spirituality hid a secret, the lust of the eyes, the lust of the flesh, and the boastful pride of life. Behind the spiritual front was his heart's desire.

To drive the point deeper, we need only look at our response to the enemy when he has found something in us. If we go into despair, fear, anxiety, worry, and insecurity, it is further proof there is something in us we hate to have revealed, something in us we have been fueling and, by so doing, have in some measure permitted the attack. The first step is always to admit where we are so we can leave where we are. Take whatever desire of the flesh we have, lay it on the table, admit it, and stop making provision for it. "All things" have been given to Him, and He has set us free from "all things." The problem is we do not want to be free from our little precious thing feeding the flesh, even though this gives the enemy the right to attack and oppress. An attack is different from a temptation. Temptations come and go and will reveal there is nothing like that in us. An attack comes and reveals there is something amiss in us, and oppression proves it. We do not need a counselor to reveal to us what it is we are holding on to. We know the ways we have made provision for the flesh. When we give it to Him, at the same moment we have invited Him to participate in our freedom from it. We need not bemoan attacks; they are only the fruit and not the root. The root is whatever we have allowed to remain within.

DAY 274
Spiritual Frankenstein!

Then one of the seven angels who had the seven bowls
full of the seven last plagues came and spoke with me,
saying, "Come here, I will show you the bride,
the wife of the Lamb."

—REVELATION 21:9

Shelley's novel, *Frankenstein; or, the Modern Prometheus* (1818), is a combination of Gothic horror story and science fiction. The book tells the story of a Swiss student of natural science, Victor Frankenstein, who created an artificial man from pieces of corpses and brought his creature to life. Though it initially seeks affection, the monster inspires loathing in everyone who meets it. Lonely and miserable, the monster turns upon its creator, who eventually loses his life. I think Shelley was on to something as a low, worldly contrast to the picture of a spiritual reality. God at this very moment is putting together the Bride of Christ. It will be a beautiful combination of all the believers from around the world in every era. It will not resemble the hodgepodge Frankenstein but a beautiful Bride needing every believer to make it the most stunning bride ever. You are needed, period!

As I mentioned before, one day I was talking to the Lord and made a request (remember, all of His sheep hear His voice, and one day we discover that our thoughts of Light and Life actually came from Him). "I want to know all there is to know about Jesus in this life. I want to know all a man can know." He spoke, and at first I was not happy with His remarks. "In My house are many treasure chests; none of them are exclusive to one man. There is a chest with your name on it, which you will open, but you will not open all the others. I am too big for one man, and each man will have his own chest. My treasure is too much for one man to describe, so it will take millions to do that. My bride is not made up of one but of many, and it will take all of those who love Me to describe Me." Well, I was discouraged; I wanted everything for myself. Yet, I could easily see He is way bigger than what I could describe, and we needed every member of the body of Christ to begin to express Him. There are no great men of God, but only weak men and women with a great God.

There is something about Jesus that can only be expressed through you. Beautiful! Press on, for the rest of us desperately need to know what you know of Jesus in heaven.

DAY 275
Spiritual Pregnancy

And she was with child; and she cried out, being in labor and in pain to give birth.

—REVELATION 12:2

Believers are pregnant with the great truth of Christ in us; we are carrying something eternal within. We must give birth to it. Has anyone told you what a spiritual pregnancy will look like? There are many symptoms, and here is one: You must have continued revelations of your self-life, your flesh, in order to have continued revelations of Him, which come from need. You must see your need for Him in an area before He will be your life in that area. You must see yourself as selfish before He can become your selflessness. Do not be discouraged but be realistic. You can easily think of three things the people at work do to annoy you, three things your mate does, three things the children do, and three things done at church. But can you think of three things *you* do in all these areas? Do you really believe yourself to be so pleasant and perfect to live with? Stop examining others, come under His light ("Search me, oh God"), see your weakness, accept His strength, and have a move in God, a revelation of Jesus.

DAY 276
Staying On Point

I am amazed that you are so quickly deserting Him who called you by the grace of Christ, for a different gospel; which is really not another; only there are some who are disturbing you and want to distort the gospel of Christ. But even if we, or an angel from heaven, should preach to you a gospel contrary to what we have preached to you, let him be accursed! As we have said before, so I say again now, if any man is preaching to you a gospel contrary to what you received, let him be accursed!

 —GALATIANS 1:6-9

I was presented a list to follow which purportedly would assure any believer's deliverance from the enemy. Looking at the list I began thinking to myself how everything in these steps to freedom could be done by an unbeliever. That being the case, how could the list be Christ-centered? Jesus was not mentioned in even one of the ten steps. Any list calling for the flesh to do something to improve itself is ultimately doomed to failure. There may be initial success, but in the long term, there will be none. Steps taken in the power of the flesh would have to eradicate flesh, and the flesh will have none of that! It will not participate in destroying or hindering itself! (The odd thing about Satan is that he loves to stir the flesh, but he is at the same time an enemy of the flesh, since he is involved in every suicide and murder to destroy man.)

In these times there are myriad methods for club growth, personal growth, financial growth, family growth, and spiritual growth. Be alert and ask the question, "Could this method apply to an unbeliever? Could an unbeliever follow the same steps?" If so, Christ has been left out and we are fixing to be sidetracked. Start with what He has already done for us, get a firm grasp of that, and then move to more of what He has done for us. It is a struggle. I often find myself headed down a track I do not want to take. I get a check in my spirit and stop talking about the latest book, method, miracle, experience, and doctrine and move back to Him. I have prayed during the nearly forty decades of being a believer that God would be gracious to me and not allow me to move from Jesus, add to Jesus, subtract from Jesus, or stop lifting Him up. It is true that He is our sufficiency. I cannot count all the programs going around today, and few believers ask why the last program did not produce what it promised it would when introduced two years ago. Why are those who were so involved in the latest "move" of God back in the same place? Let hearts and minds dwell on the Man who did everything and yet did nothing, for it was the Father doing it through Him. Then ask for testimonies of growth and God's faithfulness at the end of two years of that.

DAY 277

Stop! Point To Jesus, and You Won't Have a Crowd

And I, if I am lifted up from the earth, will draw all men to Myself.

 —JOHN 12:32

In the West we find so many popular programs for building churches, with the idea in mind that more is better and is proof we are on track with Jesus. Of course, Jesus emphasized the few and not the many. There is also a clamoring to see something spectacular outside of man, because too often there is so little reality of the relationship with the Lord going on inside man. A fellow I know was talking to his pastor and said, "I know a way to grow the church; it is a simple program that will not cost much." The pastor responded, "Have you noticed that the parking lot for both services is full?" My friend replied, "I noticed that the parking lot at Walmart is always full on Sundays, also! My program is better; it is this, 'If I be lifted up, I will draw all men unto Me!'" At that, the pastor walked off. However, the fellow's point was made. When we stop pointing to Jesus, we may have a crowd, but what are they crowding in to hear?

If you are teaching, preaching, or sharing and you feel the thing dying, just stop and start talking about Jesus. You will have a significant crowd, even if it is just one person.

DAY 278
Strange Flesh

Now I desire to remind you, though you know all things once for all, that the Lord, after saving a people out of the land of Egypt, subsequently destroyed those who did not believe. And angels who did not keep their own domain, but abandoned their proper abode, He has kept in eternal bonds under darkness for the judgment of the great day. Just as Sodom and Gomorrah and the cities around them, since they in the same way as these indulged in gross immorality and went after strange flesh, are exhibited as an example, in undergoing the punishment of eternal fire.

—JUDE 5-7

Given the state of our present world, it is important to keep such passages in mind. Incredibly, quoting from Romans or Jude is increasingly considered to be a hate crime in the "aware" Western countries. Along that line, there is a converted Muslim who became a pastor in Australia and spoke one evening on understanding Islam.

Two Muslims in the audience reported to authorities that they felt threatened, and the police arrested the pastor. The pastor refused to admit he had done anything wrong, since he was only quoting from the Koran!

The world is upside down. However, the passage from Jude reminds me of something else. All flesh is created, and each is called to its own. God has set boundaries beyond which no one is to pass without a judgment both swift as it destroys today and slow in its effects for eternity. God will bind Himself by His own judgments and will not go after strange flesh, either. This is why God became a man and the God/man will one day have a man/child-of-God bride. Believers compose the bride of Christ, and we are not something strange because we are born again of His Spirit. Looking ahead, it will be so much fun to discover what we really are and how He has made us like Himself. It takes revelation to glimpse it in this body, but one day we will see it clearly. "Beloved, now we are children of God, and it has not appeared as yet what we will be. We know that when He appears, we will be like Him, because we will see Him just as He is. And everyone who has this hope fixed on Him purifies himself, just as He is pure." —I John 3:2 & 3

DAY 279
Suicide

Elijah was afraid and ran for his life. When he came to Beersheba in Judah, he left his servant there, while he himself went a day's journey into the desert. He came to a broom tree, sat down under it and prayed that he might die. "I have had enough, LORD," he said. "Take my life; I am no better than my ancestors." Then he lay down under the tree and fell asleep. All at once an angel touched him and said, "Get up and eat."

—I KINGS 19:3-5 [NIV]

The Jews would actually publish a book, the Mishna, in the form of a man, for they believed that on Mount Sinai, God gave both the written law for all men and the oral law only for the Jews. In the same way, I have seen that God publishes men and women of God as books, working particular topics into a person's life. In the book called "Michael Wells," there would have to be a chapter on suicide.

Apart from the distress it causes, suicide is an interesting topic. Many consider it the unforgivable sin, a thought with roots in Catholicism, a religion lacking in hope and strong in legalism. Catholicism brought people in and then through fear was always threatening to put them out. So many of its members decided to take themselves out, having been driven to suicide as a legitimate option to a lifetime of penance, that the hierarchy had to issue an edict declaring suicide as an unforgivable sin. However, in many religions suicide was and is viewed as an honorable exit. I would be opposed to suicide, of course, because it is based in deception. The point I would make is that many have had a loved one commit suicide, and they immediately assume the person was not a believer and is therefore condemned to hell. This is a false assumption. Not everyone who commits suicide goes to hell, for a lesser truth must give way to the greatest TRUTH. If suicide can take one out of heaven, then it stands to reason it is stronger than the grace of God. Absurd! "Who shall separate us from the love of Christ?" (Romans 8:35)

First I want to establish that suicide does not nullify the new birth in Christ. Next I want to look at the two groups of individuals most affected by suicide, those who have committed suicide and their loved ones left behind.

The rate of teen suicide in America is a tragic fact. From my experience (much of it personal), I have realized that the suicidal are often the most sensitive and yet the most self-centered of all people. Often I use the example of looking at a pencil on the desk. From a distance the pencil is quite small, but pick it up, move it toward the eye, and soon the small object is blocking the view to everything else. Sensitive people notice the pencil (their failures, deficiencies, rejections, procrastinations, embarrassments, hurts, and even pain they may have caused others), but it is the self-centeredness that makes them pick up the pencil and move it to the eye, thus making it their obsession. All of life becomes centered in them, their image, failures, success, wants, disappointments, relationships, and more. One missionary noticed just how selfish those in an asylum in Spain were during World War II. He had asked the depressed if they could tear up sheets to make bandages for the wounded. Though they had the mental and physical capacity to do the work, they refused, because the wounds of others did not have anything to do with their wounds. This, too, is a characteristic of the suicidal, that the word *others* does not seem to be within their emotional scope (remember, I am preaching my own funeral, having been suicidal myself for years).

Well, look without and we will be discouraged, look within and be depressed, but look up and be impressed. The suicidal look within and without instead of up. Man is not created to give himself to himself, and when that happens, depression sets in, for he sees his inability to be godlike and despairs of his humanity. In this state of self-absorption, suicide makes its move. Suicide reminds me of the angel who appears as a human being and walks among us; suicide is a spirit that takes form and, though never seen, makes its presence known. As the suicidal person begins to obsess on himself and the pain of his failure, suicide goes to work, just like a young man wooing a girl with promises and images. Suicide begins to whisper, "Come and go away with me, and I will take away all your pain." At first the suicidal person is repulsed by the thought. Everything within him (Jesus is the glue that holds man together) struggles against death. However, suicide continues its onslaught. With each passing day, as he looks to himself, the phone calls to the brain increase, saying, "Meet with me! I will take away all your pain. Others will no longer have to worry about your being a failure, people will not have to put up with you, you will not have to suffer further, you will be free from the sin to which you are in bondage, and you can punish those who have criticized and offended you. All you have to do is meet with me!" At first the self-centered one hangs up the phone, but with the passing of time, Suicide, the intruder into the mind, is allowed to talk longer and longer, building its case for a long-term relationship. The battle is in the mind and the emotions. The longer Suicide is allowed to talk, the more it makes sense, and yet life continues to rebel against the death sentence it has been given. The conflict rages so greatly, and it becomes easier to fall victim to the fantasies of what suicide will supposedly bring: no more struggle, no more conflicts, no more day-to-day working, no more merely existing. The thought of Job forms anew, "Why did I not die at birth, come forth from the womb and expire?" (Job 3:11) The enemy has great wiles to accomplish the unthinkable. Suicide convinces the child of God—the only person in the world with hope, the one who can cast all his anxieties on Him, and the one with life abundant—that life is not worth living. Amazing.

I must mention a few more weapons in Suicide's arsenal: the side effects of medications, drugs, and alcohol, and the insane behavior of others. As I said to a fellow, "If you want to commit suicide, think it through and do it because you want to, but don't do it because of the actions of a carnal person. Not only have you let this person hurt you, you are letting him dictate if you are going to live or not." I was not advocating suicide, I just wanted him to open his eyes to how he was letting someone else be his god. Suicide will also use the things that are true but not the TRUTH to oppress and gain ground in the "logic" of suicide. It is true we have trials, and if we stop there, what is the point of life? However, we are not fatalists who cannot find a purpose in trials; we are optimists who believe trials will reap fruit, fullness, faith, and life. The existence of trials is not merely something true; trials for us are TRUTH, encompassed by our trust in Jesus. As I write this, the ploys of the enemy and his friend, Suicide, appear to be very obvious; but from experience I must say that when I am in the midst of the oppression, the constant phone calls, the whispering, the fantasies, and the self-centeredness, clarity blurs and they can all begin to make sense.

I remember going past a bridge in Melbourne, Australia. I was told how many hundreds of people had jumped off the bridge. To man, being born with the fear of heights, jumping off a bridge would be quite a frightening experience, and yet to the suicidal, the bridge is not as frightening as living one more day! Many succumb to that hellish fear. I know saints commit suicide for what seem to be absolutely absurd reasons, such as having a restraining order issued, being told their mate was divorcing them, losing a job, being made to feel foolish, procrastinating, being rejected, personal failure, a recurring sin, the discovery of betrayal, not meeting one's own standard, being too short, and even being told to kill themselves by someone else. It takes some maneuvering by the enemy to make the events of life lead to suicide instead of to Jesus. Many who have unsuccessfully tried suicide talk about the days or moments before making the attempt as a time when false peace descended upon them and they were without conflict. I believe them, for at that moment their will surrendered to suicide, the struggle against it over.

What is there to do if you are suicidal? I have a few suggestions.

First, settle it in your mind that you are not going to commit suicide. After years of struggle, that is exactly what

I did. I finally said, "Suicide, I listen when you talk, even though I would not let anyone else say things like that to me. Today I am through with you. I will not commit suicide. I will not entertain the thoughts you send my way. I will no longer answer your phone calls to my mind. Today we are breaking up. Satan, you will have to find something new with which to tempt me, because no longer will I be tempted by suicide. I have settled it with God." From that day I have refused to entertain the thoughts of suicide; I just do not allow my mind to go there.

Second, "Death and life are in the power of the tongue" (Proverbs 18:21). Say out loud, "I will not commit suicide." Well, truth is not merely preached but demonstrated. Say it out loud and see what will happen. I have a friend who practices this regularly. When someone comes into his office and says, "I am going to commit suicide," he immediately stops them and says, "You are not leaving here with that on my floor. You pick it up immediately by saying that you are never going to commit suicide."

Third, when someone tells me he is going to commit suicide, I immediately ask him to play a little game with me: I will pretend to be him, and he will be the thing Suicide. I then ask, "Suicide, why do you want to kill me?"

Most often the response will be, "Because you are worthless and a failure!"

I then ask, "How am I worthless and a failure?"

The response: "You just are!" I have found that the suicidal are never specific in the beginning. This is a sign of demonic oppression.

Next I say, "You have given me the death sentence for being worthless. I am sorry, but in order for me to kill myself, you will have to be more specific than just telling me I am worthless." As I continue to press, some specifics will come out, such as, "I keep sinning," "I am a bad parent," "I can't please God," and more. I then address each of those issues. It is interesting to see the veil of deception slowly lift as the person begins to realize he has been duped.

Fourth, stop dating suicide. The illusion of what an abusive person can GIVE keeps an abused person involved. The only way to break up from any bad relationship is to stop being self-centered and seeking the attention the abuser (in this case suicide) places on your self-life. Stop being a person who spends all day and all night thinking about yourself. You are not that interesting. In fact, when comparing yourself to Jesus, you are quite boring. Again, I challenge every believer—not just the suicidal—to spend one hour, then one day, and finally one week without thinking about yourself. You will be surprised at how much better you will feel by the end of the week. Do something for someone else. Stop fighting life, see Jesus in it, and yield to Him.

Now, what is to be the response of those who have been left behind by a loved one's suicide? First, remember that the believer can have two different emotions at the same time, but these emotions are not to run on the same railroad track. A woman told me she was feeling guilty for mourning the death of her husband of fifty years. I asked why, and she said, "The Christian is to have a joyful and glad heart." I explained that was true, but the Christian was also to mourn. She had put mourning and joy on the same track headed toward one another; a collision was imminent. Instead we are to mourn and have joy at the same time, just as two trains can pass one another if they are on different tracks. I have had friends commit suicide; they were believers I had known for years and we had worked through many issues, and yet they could never rise above the oppression. Though some will react to what I am about to say, I am joyful those friends are with Jesus. On the other hand, I am vexed because they did not have the revelation of LIFE in this earthly existence, and I mourn because they are missed and were much more of a blessing than they ever knew or could see. Those of you who have lost a loved one will have both emotions, joy and grief. I despise the saying that time heals all wounds; it so cheapens our relationships. To think time will make me forget a loved one is unthinkable. Rather, the first year the pain of the loss will stand on your head, crushing you. The second year the pain will walk beside you, making you feel as though you have the flu; the third year you will stand on the pain. Yes, stand on the pain. The pain will never leave you and is a constant memorial to that person, but the love in your heart makes the person a permanent part of your life and ministry.

So first, we establish that we will have pain. Second, we establish what we will not do; namely, we will not wear the choice of another person, for ultimately the choice to commit suicide was his. Choice belongs to man; not even God believes that man's choice is His. As my friend says, "There is a God, and He is not you." How true. When we believe we are in charge of someone else's choice, we believe we are God, and yet not even God will take responsibility for choice.

A woman kept crying as I spoke at a conference. At the end I invited her to my office. She unloaded and shared that her daughter had committed suicide in another country.

I said to her, "I always wanted to commit suicide, and yet God was always in the room and would not allow me to. When your daughter wanted to commit suicide, God was in the room and He permitted her to. Why? Could it be that I am worth more than your daughter?"

She responded, "No, I don't think you are better than my daughter, and I don't know why He didn't let you and allowed her."

I agreed and then made my point. "Sister, God was in the room. God permitted what He could have prevented, and yet for the last nine months you have imagined yourself in that room, floating above your daughter and thinking, *If only I had not let her move away, if only I had visited her, if only I had called that night, if only I had sent her uncle to visit her, if only she had gone to a doctor.* See, Sister, you are playing God, and the throne is getting very crowded. Please, step down. You do not want to play God." It is important when someone has committed suicide that we never presume to play God, pretending we could be in charge of another's choice.

Third, we are not to live in the past. Just to show you how ruthless the enemy is, he will not let the suffering moments pass without taking a shot at you. He will whisper in a voice sounding very much like yours, "If only I were a better parent. If only I had taken more time with him. If only I could have seen this coming. If only I would have grounded him. If only I would have put him in an institution. If only I had kept him from the harm that caused depression. If only I had affirmed him more." Now, I want to make a very strong point. If you want to talk about your failures as a parent, mate, or friend, I would be very happy to do that with you. However, it will be on a separate occasion at another time; it is a separate issue. If you were a bad parent, we can talk about it sometime, but your being a bad parent did not lead your child to make the decision to commit suicide. Not to be rude, but you do not have that kind of authority over someone else's life. Again, you are not God. There were things you could have done differently as a friend, mate, or parent. Amen! But the enemy is the one attaching your behavior to the choice of the suicidal. Honestly, I have seen people who came out of the worst families, with the worst parents, who married the worst persons, and yet they are filled with joy. In contrast, I have seen people come out of the best families, with the best parents, and marry the best persons, and then commit suicide. The two are not related. Do not let the enemy tie the two together; they are and will remain separate topics. I am not saying this to try to make you, as a survivor, feel better, but to point out the facts. Your behavior could never take choice away from a person. Again, truth is demonstrated. Have you been able to choose for your mate, friend, or child when that one is away at school, work, or the mall? Of course not! Then how can you be in control of choice in the deepest, hidden part of a person? You cannot wear it, you simply cannot. Let me warn you that if you believe your behavior could change the choice of another, then you will believe those around you, too, could have changed the suicidal person's choice through their behavior. This will lead to judging and blaming your mate and others when a loved one commits suicide.

It would be foolishness on my part to think I understand the pain you are experiencing. However, the Lord has shown me if I had the revelation of His love, I could sleep perfectly well no matter what the situation. It does not mean that if people are close to Jesus, they feel no pain. It just means that being close to Jesus allows us to rest in Him through the pain.

DAY 280
Symbols Or Spiritual Reality

Or who has first given to Him that it might be paid back to Him again? For from Him and through Him and to Him are all things. To Him be the glory forever. Amen.

—ROMANS 11:35, 36

I have a question: Did the sins of the people actually go onto the goat set loose into the wilderness (Lev. 16:20-22)? Was the death of a bull actually for sin? Was sin placed on the bull, or was it all symbolic? These are important questions. Are there acts done in the physical realm that affect the spiritual realm? Does sex with a person actually make you one with him or her, or is that symbolism? Are earthly things separate from spiritual things? It would appear that in Jesus, the things on earth and the things of heaven meet, and nothing in Him is symbolic. Outside of Him things may be symbolic, for only in Him do the two meet. Now, is Communion symbolic, as many teach, or is it actually the transformation of bread to flesh, as others teach? No, it cannot be discussed on that level. It is something in Him, and therefore the two (act of the physical with an effect on the spiritual) meet. If this were not so, how could some in Corinth be sick and dying from taking

Communion wrongly? Can we apply this argument to the other "sacraments"? Obviously, being dunked in water will not make a person become born again. If that were the case, we could dunk a Hindu and he would be born again. But is baptism just a symbol, or is it a physical act with true spiritual reality and meaning? Many are confused by Peter's statement, "Baptism now saves you, yet not the washing of water." First, *saved* refers to daily living. Second, Peter does not believe it is the water doing something, but Jesus. Paul says, "I am glad I baptized none of you!" "I was not sent to baptize!" Does Peter think baptism important and Paul not? No, Paul is simply saying to make the physical act with water out to be something is casting Christ aside. Any physical act outside of the Jesus in whom the physical and spiritual meet is useless. But in Him does it have a spiritual significance? I am only asking the question because it is odd that Communion and baptism are so often called symbols. I cannot find in Scripture where God asks for symbols. However, there seems to be indication that some spiritual realities have become symbols to us and therefore are now rejected by Him: "What good is circumcision?" Maybe the secret is the danger involved in neglecting the Jesus (where physical meets spiritual) in our physical acts, so they become nothing more than symbolic and are then repulsive to God. The carnal mind seems to see only the physical and stand fast in the assertion that water cannot save someone. Well, amen. But I am talking about seeing things with a spiritual mind, which for me brings up a broader question beyond the "sacraments." When anything becomes just symbolic to man, does that thing become an abomination? God said He was repulsed by Israel's sacrifices. He wanted their hearts to be right in the sacrifices. A lesser gave way to a greater, and the heart was the greater issue.

Do we view abiding, Christ as the door, victory, and more as mere symbolic statements of Jesus? Do we just see the vine and branch as symbols and lose the heart of the issue? It is not symbolic for the spiritually-minded; it is a fact in Jesus. It is truth, where fact and faith meet. Fact and faith only meet in Jesus; He is the way, the truth, and the life, and this is not a symbolic statement. Thinking inside the box leads to seeing only the physical or the spiritual, not adjusting to seeing both meet in Jesus, and that limits the attachment of spiritual significance to something like baptism, which would make baptism a work. If it were a work, then it would be an abomination, but it would only be a work in our minds. I am wondering what it would mean to us if we could see something like Communion as a spiritual reality.

DAY 281
Thank You For Keeping My Baby Safe

Trust in the LORD with all your heart, and do not lean on your own understanding.

—PROVERBS 3:5

It is beautiful every day a new mother holds her baby and says, "Thank you, Jesus, for keeping my baby safe and healthy." However, there can be a problem in that the mother is holding, nurturing, and protecting the baby as she says it. The day will come when the mother cannot hold the baby, keeping it safe even as she speaks. At that time there will come either revelation or stress, all depending on her belief system. If the mother possesses a small God, that time will be very stressful. If she knows she is the possession of a big God, in faith there will be a sense of relief and rest. What do you think went through the mind of Moses' mother as she watched the baby drift down the river of the world, to be found by the world and ultimately raised in the heart of the world? Either she possessed the baby or the baby and mother alike were possessed by God. In a sense every mother must replay the life of Moses' mother.

Recognize that you and the child, too, are possessed by Christ, and then say as the child is taken from your arms, "Thank You, Jesus, for keeping my baby safe and healthy in Your loving care."

DAY 282
The Answer

. . . always learning and never able to come to the knowledge of the truth.
—II TIMOTHY 3:7

Since we have a great priest over the house of God, let us draw near with a sincere heart in full assurance of faith, having our hearts sprinkled clean from an evil conscience and our bodies washed with pure water.
—HEBREWS 10:21, 22

I find interesting the volumes written and forthcoming on the topic of marriage and childrearing, when the Scriptures give only a couple of verses on each topic. Christian psychologists have provided us with countless books on coping, destructive behavior, and relational problems; many of the topics are never even mentioned in Scripture. Why? Some would say it is because man is evolving in his thought process, or that Paul simply did not have to deal with such problems as molestation, co-dependency, or addictive behavior. Many attempt to validate and Christianize what they present as all-important information on man's behavior with an obscure passage from the Bible.

I once told a Christian psychology student to imagine a seminar begun with prayer and conducted by a leading Christian Psychologist who discussed the symptoms and treatment of depression. What would happen, I asked him, if at the end of the seminar I stood up and said, "I think depressed believers need to draw near to Jesus"? What would those in attendance think about me and my statement? The student immediately answered that they would think I was ignorant, insensitive, unrealistic, out of touch, and shallow. Yes, I knew that would be their response, but why?

It is really quite simple! When Jesus—who is the Way, the Truth, and the Life—is not considered to be the answer, then questions immediately increase. In giving Christ, God gave us something on which to focus. In giving us this one thing, Jesus, as the answer to every question, life would become quite simple. When Jesus is taken out of the equation and no longer considered as the answer, man lives in chaos. I often meet men who live in chaos with a thousand questions and a thousand answers; they do not have *the* answer and refuse to look to Jesus. I can prove that Christ is the answer for every man, for once He is found, chaos disappears, life makes sense, and man lives in harmony. No man who remains steeped in inner chaos truly has Christ, the Divine Answer.

No wonder man is hostile and frustrated when ignoring the basic dependent relationship on God he was created to enjoy. In a hundred lifetimes of searching he will not run out of possible answers. I liken it to a man standing on a shoebox facing millions of other shoeboxes, each one hoped to be the one holding the answer but yielding nothing. The man spends his life searching through each box, when the answer is in the box on which he stands, where he refuses to look. Given the choice, would a person grope day after day in a cave looking for light, or would he opt to walk through the cave with a light? We can grope through life's myriad unanswered questions looking for the answer or have the answer before approaching any question. The believer is able to approach every question with the answer—Jesus! Leave Him out and confusion abounds on all sides; finding answers is extremely difficult, calling for patience and self-effort.

Why are there only a few Biblical statements concerning how we are to raise children, have a pleasant marriage, and carry on relationships with those around us? Because the writers of the New Testament assumed we were doing the basics of keeping Christ in the center of life, making Him the answer, and simply abiding in Him. When our focus is the Divine Answer, we need very little else. Many avoid this simple answer for the obvious reason that they have not personally found Him to be the answer, so they look elsewhere. They cannot lead where they have not been. Those who have found Christ to be the answer to depression will give a hearty *Amen* to the statement, "Draw near." Those who have not found Him as their all conclude that since Jesus did not "work" for them, He will not for others.

We want to enter each problem and question with a light, with the answer to guide us through. When this is done, there will often be accusing screams that we are in denial, as though we are refusing to recognize real issues, problems, questions, man's condition, and past hurts. To this we answer, "Deny self or deny the Lord!" Most of our issues, problems, and questions have their roots in the self-life, the desire for man to be his own god and source of enjoyment. That self-life wants to remain in control and alive; therefore, it uses every situation and question to maintain control of man's focus. Hundreds of believers will testify that after weeks, months, and years of looking for answers to their problems and to past and present issues, they are not one bit closer to the peace Jesus gives to all who are His. Why? It is because He is not considered to be the answer. Answers lying *outside* of Christ are sought, and there is only peace *in* Christ.

As believers we must not be intimidated by those who insist we must *know more*, for we *know Him*, the Divine Answer! Draw near! We do not serve a dead God, but One who is living; in His light we see light.

Once a reincarnationist told me all religions possess some element of truth. This, of course, we have all heard before and must acknowledge, since every major religion has some element of the Ten Commandments. His next statement built upon the first: "All men possess a measure of truth, but no one has the complete truth. Therefore, it is up to man to determine what is truth for himself." So we are to pick and choose what is right for us. Following this logic would lead to chaos, characterized by the Biblical warning about men doing what is right in their own eyes. Presuming every man can have his own truth is ultimately to believe there is no truth. Once I explained this, the fellow made another common statement: "The annoying thing about you Christians is that you believe you have the absolute truth." I told him that was exactly right; I possessed absolute truth! This angered him, and he said the large variety of denominations all read the same Bible, and yet all perceive truth differently, condemning those who do not see truth as they do, and this proved his belief that all men must find their individual truth. Many, I admit, have wondered at that very phenomenon. Once I was told of the division beginning among believers in the former Soviet bloc; while persecuted they were in agreement, but now with the introduction of so many different and opposing doctrines from the West, they are separating themselves one from the other. This, to the unbeliever, proves each man perceives truth differently. The next step is quite logical. If believers do not agree, then what if someone wanted to accept only that Jesus was a good teacher for His time as others were for their time, and man is left deciding what is best for him.

The problem is the definition of truth. Man considers truth to be a system of thought, action, and belief, which is right. Therefore, when truth is argued, each individual defends his system. The reincarnationist falsely believed I was attempting to persuade him to follow my system, just as he was attempting to do to me. We as believers are not attempting to lead others to the truth of our denomination! We are leading others to truth, the divine truth, the correct definition of absolute truth—Jesus. Jesus is the Way, the Truth, and the Life. We never lead to a system but rather to Christ. If He is not possessed, then truth is not possessed. For all his years of study, the reincarnationist was no closer to truth, for He was no closer to Christ. Some falsely assume that at Abiding Life Ministries International we have a system of helping defeated believers and we would defend our method against other methods of counseling. Not so! Our goal is not to fit others into our system but rather to introduce them to absolute truth—Jesus. When men abide in the Truth, there is an absence of chaos and the presence of consistency. In dozens of countries and denominations I personally have observed abiding believers who act exactly the same way. Abiding in truth brings consistency. Abiding in systems and calling them "truth" brings division.

Therefore, when truth is properly defined, we can understand why we can know the Truth and the Truth will set us free. However, when truth is a system, we know the truth and the truth makes us mad and brings division; our system is an extension of self-centeredness, so for others to attack what we believe is tantamount to their attacking us. However, the Truth has freed us from self, and an attack releases His love through us. Also, if we love Truth we then love Him. As we grow in Him we will grow in our appreciation of Truth. It has taken me time to come to a place where I love truth. That is only because it has taken time to move from liking Jesus to loving Jesus. Once Truth (Jesus) is accepted, then truth can be received, and both bring freedom. Once the Truth (Jesus) is received, it is interesting to note how a person responds to truth, which, although it may be upsetting and cut to the bone, is received with gladness. At Alcoholics Anonymous meetings the first step is to admit the truth, "I am an alcoholic." This brings some relief. However, when this statement is accompanied with The Truth (Jesus), it can bring absolute freedom. Note how those who have no regard for truth (such as the adolescent) have very little love for Christ but much appreciation for themselves and their desires. Those who love Christ despise falsehood and self's wayward independence from Him. Therefore, when an unbeliever states that he searches for and loves truth but rejects Christ, he is lying, the truth is not in him, he exalts piety in his own eyes, and his desire is for a truth which will not upset a well-planned system to feed the flesh.

DAY 283
The Basics

Fill your horn with oil and go.

—I SAMUEL 16:1

The horn of oil in the temple was always to be filled as part of the service to the Lord. Samuel was mourning, and God told him to go and first fill the horn. He had neglected the basics and could not go until he did the basics. I am thinking more and more about the basics. Christ within us is knocking to get out, to express His life through us. With the door closed through pride, we attempt to "do Christian things" and find them a struggle. With it open, those same things are quite natural. That is basic.

Samuel was looking for the next anointed king. Jesse brought to him all the best, assuming that God wanted the best. Samuel said, "Are these all your sons?" The weak thing Jesse had hidden in the fields was exactly what God wanted. We never hide our weaknesses; they are the very things He can use.

DAY 284
The Believer's Cycle

Not that I have already obtained it or have already become perfect, but I press on in order that I may lay hold of that for which also I was laid hold of by Christ Jesus. Brethren, I do not regard myself as having laid hold of it yet; but one thing I do: forgetting what lies behind and reaching forward to what lies ahead, I press on toward the goal for the prize of the upward call of God in Christ Jesus. Let us therefore, as many as are mature, have this attitude; and if in anything you have a different attitude, God will reveal that also to you.

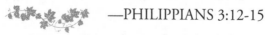 —PHILIPPIANS 3:12-15

Often I receive phone calls from committed believers vexed by new revelations of their self-centeredness. God has shown them a new area of their life in which He would like them to freely walk. Instead of greeting the prospect of Christ's life doing a deeper work as He reveals and heals, the believers heed the voice of the enemy that immediately whispers, "How could you be so selfish? Look at how your behavior has affected your children. Most of your Christian life is a joke; your hypocrisy is finally being revealed." The excitement we should have anticipating Christ's deeper work is replaced with regret, depression, frustration, and a looking within that makes us all the more carnal.

As you twist a screw into a piece of wood, each new thread builds upon the previous thread to allow the screw to go deeper and deeper. Your life moving deeper and deeper into Christ is like that screw. Each thread is a cycle building upon the previous cycle, taking you deeper into the abiding life. Each cycle in life goes something like this. First, because you have given Christ control of all known areas of your life, He now reveals where you are maintaining control in new, hidden areas of the heart, such as self-centeredness, materialism, lack of love, lack of joy, self-consumption, judgment, critical thinking, and on the list goes. But remember it is only because you have been placed in Him that the screw is turning to allow for deeper realizations. Second, upon seeing the problem, you might immediately say, "I can fix it." You attempt to clean yourself up so you and others can feel better. As these attempts fail, you give up in despair. Third, you recognize, "I can't fix it, but He can." You just then moved another thread deeper into His life. There is release, faith, and joy. You are now prepared for the next revelation. As you go through the cycle, you continue to decrease, and the life in you is revealed, causing Him to increase.

This cycle, I hope, goes on my whole life. I am not vexed by it. Many want to know all, experience all, and instantly be free from all. Not me! I enjoy the unfolding of Christianity, of just how deep the Lord's work is, and of the gradual replacement of the flesh-life with His life. Without this aspect of life, the unfolding, life could become very boring. Just as the meaning of marriage, being a father, and being a son constantly unfolds before me and causes excitement and anticipation, so does my life in Christ. Whatever He reveals tomorrow can only be revealed because of all His work in me in the past. Paul says, in essence, I am mature but not yet mature. I am where I ought to be today, but there is more for tomorrow. Life in Christ is never boring.

DAY 285
The Believer's Death

Blessed are the dead who die in the Lord from now on!
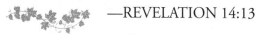 —REVELATION 14:13

We are all dying, some sooner than others, and that is not the issue; the issue is what is learned in our days. Some are taught more quickly than others and have learned all they needed to learn. The ultimate lesson for us in this life is what we cannot do. We cannot overcome sickness, we cannot overcome lying emotions, we cannot overcome the enemy, we cannot overcome suicidal thoughts, and more and more. Did we learn this? We did not fix our emotions, our habits, our addictions, and there were so many more things. Without God's deliverance, we were stuck. Job learned to loathe life on earth during his crushing trials. Any of us who live here long enough will loathe it also. It is not our permanent home.

When it comes to the believer, blessed are those who die in the Lord. What about premature deaths, sickness, overdose, suicide, and accidents? The passage still stands. There are no premature deaths, because our days are numbered and this is absolute (Psalm 139:16). We are to die; it is the way of things, but our death of the body is entrance to more Life. "I am the resurrection and the life; he who believes in Me shall live even if he dies, and everyone who lives and believes in Me shall never die. Do you believe this?" [John 11:25, 26] "But we do see Him who has been made for a little while lower than the angels, namely, Jesus, because of the suffering of death crowned with glory and honor, that by the grace of God He might taste death for everyone" (Hebrews 2:9). We begin to see the excitement of the Prodigal's Father as he sees his son again and are reminded that our failure will be forgotten (washed as white as snow) when we see our Lord face to face.

When I die, please, please do not pray to have me raised from the dead. I know a man who was killed twice in Nepal for preaching and tells of the glory of heaven and the strong desire he had both times not to return to the earth.

Death is an absolute. There is no way to prepare ourselves for it. However, when it comes it will thrust us into the presence of the One who has conquered death, and there we will find peace.

DAY 286
The Believer's Grief

For not one of us lives for himself, and not one dies for himself; for if we live, we live for the Lord, or if we die, we die for the Lord; therefore whether we live or die, we are the Lord's. For to this end Christ died and lived again, that He might be Lord both of the dead and of the living.

—ROMANS 14:7-9

Death impacts the dying and has great meaning for the loved ones left behind. Even those who do not question the why or the how of death will make these statements: "Yes, I know my loved one is with Jesus, but this morning I fell and my husband was not there to pick me up, my child was not there to hold and laugh with, my friend was not there to call and share my good news, there was no child to tuck into bed at night, my grandfather was not there to open my heart to, my son was not there to share my vision with, there is no hand holding my hand, no smile to be greeted with, and I experience a void. Oh, there were down times, but the good far outweighed the bad, and I miss my loved one." Samuel was very angry with Saul for interrupting his time in heaven. Well, like Saul we would call back the one we love if only we could. However, the experience of being a survivor is intended for every person who lives long enough. God understands being a survivor; He knew His Son was the Slain Lamb from the foundations of the world, and yet I believe God nearly delivered Him, for on the cross Jesus looked up and said, "Father, forgive them for they know not what they do!" Perhaps it was a close call for mankind.

At times I have watched as those around a dying person begin to die themselves. They die physically, emotionally by sinking into regret, socially as in hatred they accuse others of causing the death or of not understanding their pain, they die in self-pity and anger, others die with the sedatives used to deaden the pain of the loss, and they welcome this false type of death, refusing to return to normalcy. In one place, a tribal region, only one out of five children live. Understandably the women have attachment disorders. The one child who does live feels completely rejected as the mother refuses to risk loving again. Why would God make us one with a spouse, or give us a child from our own bodies, or permit very special people in our lives loving us, when they are only to be ripped away from us? We wish we did not grieve at all, but what kind of world would it be if men did not grieve, did not have regret, did not have guilt, and had no emotion or sense of loss? Immediately two men come to mind, Stalin and Hitler, and what if we had a world of Stalins and Hitlers?

We see a lesson in David. His son is dying and David mourns by fasting and praying (we all mourn in our own unique way and must never allow someone else to tell us how to mourn) until the child dies and David gives the revelation, "I shall go to him, but he will not return to me" (II Samuel 12:23). Next, David is able to get up, wash himself, and move forward. Through revelation the loss was settled and he yielded to God's will. We see the steps of grief in David. First we are undone, driven to God hoping we might undo death, and finally, in His presence, we come in line with the revelation of God, since permanent life on earth is not the will of God.

Some might complain that God went from the death of His Son to a joyful reunion in three days, while we must wait thirty years or more. However, "do not let this one fact escape your notice, beloved, that with the Lord one day is as a thousand years, and a thousand years as one day" (II Peter 3:8). Those three days did not pass quickly for God. God creates by His word. The Word became flesh. The Word is Jesus. Cutting Christ off while the sins of the whole world were poured upon Him was likened to God's taking out His vocal cords and crushing them with a hammer. God has thought, the thought becomes Word (Jesus), and something happens (creation). To take away the Word is for God to have thought and yet no possible creative action. For three days God waited, handcuffed, like a stroke victim who can think but not communicate. My point is I believe God suffered greatly at the death of His Son. He understands all of our suffering in separation.

The death of Jesus did something to God. For all eternity Jesus will be the Slain Lamb in heaven, a marred man. He did not go back to his previous state. This fact changes how God sees man. The death of a loved one makes permanent changes in us. For that reason I dislike the statement, "Time heals all wounds!" Does it? In time the pain of the loss will move from standing on you, to walking beside you, to your standing on it. However, the wound never leaves, for the pain of the loss is to change something permanently in you to keep the person alive in your soul and in daily experiences.

There is the thought that no one can ever meet the same need in your life as the departed loved one. That is true but not the TRUTH. In reality the one who was meeting your needs was God through the other person. The person you loved was made in the image of God and you were seeing God through him or her. It is only God who loves, listens, gives a tender touch, rejoices with you, and meets your needs. He was working through this person He gave you, but it was God who met your needs. You can still go to God and He can meet those same needs through another unique expression (another person) or He can meet them directly. From the testimonies of many we know there are those who find themselves alone and lonely and those who find they are alone but never lonely, because God Himself filled up the lack. If you lost your son, find another; there are plenty of lonely men in need of a father. No, they cannot be an exact replacement, but you are in the image of God and you must love, and they are in the image of God and desire your love. When you bond to a person, what is it to which you are really bonding? The attraction is to the unique expression of their being made in the image of God. God, as I said, was always meeting your needs. In his grief David bonded to the source of what his son had given him. David was thus alone but not lonely.

Therefore, when we discover in our grief the comfort of the Christ within, it will not just be comfort in our discomfort but an actual victory over death. Looking at the thing death from afar may be frightening; we feel its sting as it takes those we love. We desire some comfort, and more than comfort comes to us in The Life that has conquered death, a life that death fears, a life that has raised the ones we love to the presence of the Father.

In Africa I had one of the strangest experiences I ever had. In a vision during my time of devotion I was caught up to heaven, and all I could hear was God's weeping. I believe God's emotions are multi-faceted. Right now His anger is close to overflowing, and yet He is love. We attach, we weep, and we have joy and hope . . . and we do it all at the same time. He is God and can go through grief without a disorder, and that is why it is so important that I invite Him into my grief, to live it through me, or I will have a disorder. This is another place where He is the I AM and I am not. He will be for me what I am not, but first I must admit what I am not. I am not able to go through grief without becoming distorted, so I must invite Him: "Jesus, come and be my grief, come and be my attachment. Come and be for me all that I am not." It is easy to tell when I have moved into disorder, for there is guilt, regret, anger, blame-giving, depression, reliving the past, withdrawal, alcohol, sedatives, and more. Why allow the drama when we all will die? It does not honor the dead to become a disrupted individual.

DAY 287
The Believer's Love and Grief, Made In His Image

Then God said, "Let Us make man in Our image, according to Our likeness; and let them rule over the fish of the sea and over the birds of the sky and over the cattle and over all the earth, and over every creeping thing that creeps on the earth." And God created man in His own image, in the image of God He created him; male and female He created them.

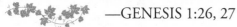

—GENESIS 1:26, 27

Man is made in the image of God, and that is not to be denied. Many are attempting to deny it by not feeling, not loving, not laying down their lives. We are in His image. Our sex drive is a picture of His drive for intimacy, our desire for food is His desire to feed the spirit, our desire for water is His desire for living water, our desire for emotion is His desire for peace. The self-will that would destroy ourselves and others is used by Him to bless man. To live outside in any other image than of our being made in His image is chaos.

We are slow to come into agreement with Him. We must believe what He is telling us or He will prove it in our lives. He says we have joy and we disagree, He says He will provide and we distrust, He says we are free from every sin and we disbelieve. We hate our jobs and He says do everything as unto the Lord. We say we hate slavery and He says serve our masters with respect. We say, "How can we be thankful?" and He says, "In everything give thanks." He says to deny self and we suppose we must feed it. He says give freely for freely we have received, and yet we hoard. We say we are not one with Him or our mates or the family of God, and He says we are. We call ourselves addicts, and yet He says we are free from bondage. He says we have no need of anyone to teach us, and yet we constantly seek to be taught. He says we are His beloved, and we say we are worthless with no value. We list our worries, and He tells us not to worry.

Every one of us are made in the image of God and tempted to be God, but we are not God, and this desire must be denied. We should be told at birth that we must give ourselves to something much bigger than ourselves, for we are not God but we are in His image. Then we should be told what we should expect. There are some things we desire from being made in His image: to build, to create, to love another, and more. Yet other things we want that we are to deny, all stemming from the desire to play God; however, we are not to deny the fact that we are made in the image of God. We can be selfish and avoid the evidence of being in His image, and one selfish act is to hang on to those who must die (as we all must). To deny love, to deny laying down our lives, to deny grieving, to deny sorrow, or to deny anger is to deny our being made in the image of God. We must suffer loss. We must grieve. He witnesses and suffers seeing the death of those He loves, and so must we. We are made in His image, and therefore we must love. Love builds a cross, and the one we love will hang us on it. It is the way of things, the way of life! It is predetermined. On this cross something in us will die, will be buried, and we will then find His resurrection power, for only the life of Christ has overcome the thing death.

It is a fact that you are not God and must deny the desire to be God, but it is an equal fact that you are in the image of God and cannot deny it. As surely as waves come to the shores, death and grief are coming to you and all of us. These waves of grief can push you closer to the One who made you in His image, and in Him you can find everything you have looked for—and sometimes thought you had found—in other places.

Actually, what are our options? No care, no concern, and a life without love? We are in His image and we attach. Think of the pain of detachment when a loved one dies. Now take that pain times a billion and you will begin to understand God's attachment to us. He is so attached that He gave His Son to have us and to keep us from an eternal death. We are made in the image of God, though sin distorts the image to one degree or another. Do we realize when we do not attach to those who may or will die it is a distortion of how we are made? In some places where four out of every five children will die, the parents stop attaching to the children who do live; they have an attachment disorder, and the whole family then suffers from this distortion. Attachment is the way of our being, the way we were created. There is no other option. We do not need an attachment disorder, and I am happy God does not have one. He is attached and desires for none to be lost, He takes no pleasure in the death of the wicked, and therefore, He takes no pleasure in death. "For He must reign until He has put all His enemies under His feet. The last enemy that will be abolished is death" (I Corinthians 15:25, 26).

You are in His image, so you do have attachments. What is attachment? Love! What is love? I Corinthians 13. Attachment means pain when there is a loss.

DAY 288
The Blood

And they overcame him because of the blood of the Lamb.
—REVELATION 12:11

When communicating with someone who has experienced the loss of a loved one, we soon learn just what we are not to mention. Because the loss is so deep, certain questions, phrases, and recollections immediately call the absent person to mind and cause great pain. For example, we are cautious around someone who has lost a child through violent means, because the very mention of children will cause a flood of past remembrances, stirred emotions, and immediate suffering.

There is a phrase which, when mentioned by the believer, causes a much more widely encompassing reaction in God. This phrase is often taken lightly and is rarely understood by the speaker, but it stirs God's compassion, love, hopes, desires, His loss, His gain, His forgiveness, and His pain. This one sacred phrase can do all of the above and also give the speaker the benefit of all of God's goodness, His fellowship, His constant care, His listening ear, and His loving heart. The phrase that does all of this is "the blood of Jesus"! When we ask in the blood of Jesus, everything within God is stirred. He is reminded of His great love and oneness with the Son, the loss of His Son, judgment, and finally, a new birth. Is this phrase not sacred? Should the believer not be careful when invoking it? Should we not expect great things when asked in the blood of Jesus? This one phrase reminds God of the condition of His creatures: their failure, their sin, their self-centeredness, their need for Him to do something, the sending of His Son, the crucifixion, the jeering mob, the denial of a nation, a city, and even the Son's followers. Be careful how you use this phrase, but do use it!

DAY 289
The Bridge

And we know that God causes all things to work together for good to those who love God, to those who are called according to His purpose.

—ROMANS 8:28

There is a divine bridge on which the believer is privileged to stand, the bridge between God's perfect will—the revelation of Christ in us and the hope of glory—and His permissive will, including all of the evil man is allowed to produce through choice. The airplane crashes, the earthquake hits, or the disease strikes for believers and unbelievers alike. It is not God's perfect will, but it is permitted. However, the believer has the perspective from the bridge and need not despair, for God will cause all things to work together for good. At their point of suffering, many complain that such knowledge is useless. However, were they to try to stand in such a situation without this hope, they would immediately be overcome. I have been to funerals and also observed starving, dying people firsthand. Hopelessness is worse than the disaster that precipitated it. When we live in Him, a comfort comes in the midst of pain that cannot be described with words, for it is attached to the peace of God. All those who have experienced it will testify to it. It is the bridge we stand on, and it serves us so well in the time of need.

DAY 290
The Chosen

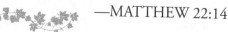

For many are called, but few are chosen.
—MATTHEW 22:14

The chosen will allow the place they are in to be the tool that brings the revelation of Christ. I had an amazing experience; something I had not expected occurred. When it happened, the Lord brought to my remembrance that over twenty-five years ago I had prayed for the very thing. The memory was crystal clear. I had prayed for it, but I had only prayed once. He then spoke to me: "See? I never forget!" It made my heart sing! He never forgets! He does hear! He does act, all according to His timetable! He gives at the perfect time to accomplish something perfect. I could see more clearly that my life was perfect. So is yours.

Again, the chosen allow the place they are in to be the tool bringing the revelation of Christ. Have you ever prayed to ask God to give you the revelation of Jesus? Even if prayed only one time, once it is uttered all events begin to push you toward moments of revelation. Everything in life will be a tool to bring it.

A woman in my office was suffering greatly with an unbelieving husband. He had many affairs. However, I discerned that she was one of the chosen. I did not try to comfort her. Instead, I pressed her. Do you want to know Jesus? Have you asked to know Him? Do you know how He will prepare you for the revelation of Him? Will you deny the tools He uses for the revelation? She answered each question properly. I knew she would; she was chosen. I then told her, "Your husband is the tool! All of us want to know Christ's forgiveness without having to forgive. We want to lay down our life for a friend but never want to be offended by the friend. Sister, the enemy means it for your destruction, but God intends to use it for your perfection. Will you cast away the tool?" Again, my heart sang at what she said, "I will not! I will let Jesus be my love. I will let Jesus be my comfort! I will not seek temporary comfort!" Nothing is better than being chosen!

DAY 291
The Christian Club Revisited

Be on guard for yourselves and for all the flock, among which the Holy Spirit has made you overseers, to shepherd the church of God which He purchased with His own blood.

—ACTS 20:28

Once again we will examine the "Christian Club," which is how I have come to regard a building which houses the gathering of believers, as opposed to speaking of the corporate Church, the Body of Christ. Actually, the club reminds me of a cruise ship, where there is an activity for everyone, and the talk of the day may be how big the ship is compared to a bigger one with even more amenities soon to be sailing. So much goes on that is not Biblical in the club, and it is interesting watching people maneuver around that fact. They remind me of researchers at the university slowly starting to build a teaching based upon nothing. Next something is added to the nothing, and inevitably there are additions to the additions of the nothing. The whole purpose is to distance themselves from the nothingness at the base and to appear to be logical and Biblical. The desired end result is a very "firm" teaching with strict "Biblical" rules for how "spiritual dancing," "falling down in the Spirit," "worship," "inner healing prayers," and "casting out demons" is to be done, still with no Biblical foundation. Then brother Mike comes along and asks the obvious question, "Where is this in the Bible?" Of course, in their minds every question was laid to rest long ago, and the "fact" they are in the truth is proven by a multitude of experiences. The goal is to have enough positive, irrefutable experiences to outweigh the dearth of evidence for those "manifestations" in the Bible. Again I ask for Biblical evidence. This is met with blank stares, lengthy examples of "their experiences," and sympathy for such a poor person as me who has not had the revelation. However, I kept asking, "But where is it in the Bible? Would Paul cheat us by giving no instructions?" Finally, we shift to a different topic, and they go on building the system with their experiences.

Is it possible for a club to transition to the expression of the Church? For a church is to be an expression of Life. It will make that transition when it no longer goes about the activity of creating Christians, but recognizes them. When it is no longer consumed with having every stick in place without a spark, but it is old wood drenched in water, yet ablaze. It will make the transition when the goal is lifting up Jesus, not just in word but in fact. This will be revealed by certain attitudes. It will not live to numbers, having the attitude that another group is "doing" something to bring in more people, or the accompanying attitude of "we lost one." It will not imitate anther branch but participate in the Life expressed through its own branch. It will not send out surveys to see what the people want but will stand in the conviction that it already knows the need, and the need is Jesus. It will not view itself as the machine being the mechanism for folks to come to Christ. Pentecost killed religion; Church is in any place at any time the Lord comes "where two or more are gathered." I remember in South Africa when He came in response to prayer and a slave girl's reading.

Jesus is silent about the strategy of making a "successful church," because the plan of action was always to be connected with His Life and leading. A machine takes strategy, but the Vine is Life, producing not plastic fruit but living grapes.

Do I have a strategy? Yes! Go where the people are, lift up Jesus, and see what it is to which He witnesses. It has worked, if "worked" is the word people want to hear. It works in "dead" churches, "live" churches; it works over a coffee table or at a bus stop. I have never been limited by environment. If Christ were to be limited by the environment, then the environment is greater than He. The clubs today are full of formulas: sit, sing, sit, sing, pray. It is enough. Something could look like a club and not be. Something could look like a bus station and be a Church. Something could be invisible and be a Church. We must throw out our definitions, for we hear "church life" and think "program in a big building"; we do not think "invisible." Is the purpose of the program to touch the inner man's needs, or is it calculated to touch the needs of the outer man and move the flesh? Could the program operate without Christ? Was Pentecost an expression of Christ, or did it create His coming? Is the Holy Spirit waiting for a program before He acts? Is the Holy Spirit waiting for me to act, or is the Holy Spirit waiting for me to receive Life and move and breathe, and then He will move me to where I need to be?

It is interesting to look at Christian Companies; have they created a "Christian environment"? What is a Christian environment? What about the Church Company, the Christian Club? How does building an entertainment center for the youth balance with needs of the unemployed? Generally speaking, the plan to purchase new curtains will never give way to a need like someone's cancer-treatment payments, and the bricks will be more important than the unemployed. How could the Church in China grow without any of the externals? Where have we seen the early Church joking around in order to have something relevant? The Life they expressed was relevant. If, for argument's sake, it is possible to move out of the Spirit and into the flesh, what would a fleshly program look like, and what would a spiritual program look like? How do statistics help? Are the statistics we get relevant to the needs of the inner man? What avenues into a man's heart are legitimate? Is what makes a strategy good or bad the goal? Which is easier to follow, the strategy or the Spirit? If we install a program, can we be creative, or does a program by its very nature kill creativity? If creativity is copied, is it still creativity? Why are there people who really do love God—and the Spirit witnesses to it—and yet are sick and tired of the club? We cannot say they are just trying to cause strife. If they could hear something about Jesus and how He works outside the box of religion, then even in the worst setting they would come alive. Where is there such a thing as a minister of music in the Bible? Why does a church hire outside the congregation for its staff? Is there something wrong with making the statement that "We are the Church" instead of asking, "How are we to be the Church"? Are there more believers this year and last year because of the new programs? Amen, a Christian carpenter will hammer a nail pretty much the same way a non-Christian does.

DAY 292
The Christian Club Strategized

The life was manifested, and we have seen and bear witness and proclaim to you the eternal life, which was with the Father and was manifested to us—what we have seen and heard we proclaim to you also, that you also may have fellowship with us; and indeed our fellowship is with the Father, and with His Son Jesus Christ.

 —I JOHN 1:2, 3

Just as a man can go to GM and work because it is where God has Him and the place God will bring people to him, the building and the programs are not church but the club. When we are looking at the club, we should go easy, for we do not know how God has led, worked, or brought people to this vision. Still, somehow the building has come to be the place of a seeker service for unbelievers, a fellowship of unbelievers, so that cannot be the Church. I am thinking we should separate in our minds the difference between having a Christian club where people come to hear the gospel and the recognition of the Church as the invisible fellowship without walls that all believers belong to. A club can be a valid form of outreach; hundreds of places are valid forms of outreach. However, Jesus did not bring people in, but He sent the disciples out, and church was the gathering of believers. What we call "church" is a transvestite, a method of outreach dressed up in clothes and called the "church." It is confusing because the clothes do not fit what is underneath. A believer will often have trouble in this dating relationship.

Where is Jesus giving a strategy of expansion or how is Pentecost a strategy of expansion? This is the Western mindset, and experience proves that lining up the dominos does not guarantee they will all fall in the right direction. Are you where you planned to be a year ago with your kids, your marriage, or your vocation? Is the club reflecting the condition where the program promised to take the congregation? A program gives us a sense we are doing something, but are we really doing anything? Does life prove it? I listen to the strategy and it is based in "people need," needing a certain environment, particular setting, and on and on. I thought people needed Jesus. I have trouble with a strategy if it offers an absolute it cannot deliver. The difference is that without Christ a strategy will still work; the Church will not work without Christ. Strategies are without LIFE, and we need Life as the witness, too.

Now, to those building a club, it will be utilized; it can be legitimate to build the club. But the Church is not in need! It has Christ. He did not die; He is multiplied. Jesus did not have a business plan. He had an organic human plan including death, contrast, rest, trust, God's leading, and more. He did not offer a program with the veiled promise of absolute results. How does the parable of the Sower and the Seeds fit into these new club plans? We have to stop and separate the club and the desire for its expansion from the Church Jesus is in charge of and responsible for. I cannot get through my head how a program to get men to talk could be a substitute for Jesus. In the club, amen. In the Church, no. The Church offers what people cannot get anywhere else, Jesus.

I appreciate the club; it does give believers a place to share. Some are better than others, but what makes up the club does not make up the Church. The goal of the club is membership; the goal of the Church is Christ. Still, there are those who come alive and get interested in Christ because of the Church program. God is able to touch us with His Life in any situation.

DAY 293
The Company Of the Unknowns

Now as they observed the confidence of Peter and John and understood that they were uneducated and untrained men, they were marveling, and began to recognize them as having been with Jesus.

—ACTS 4:13

Are we happy to be in the company of the Unknowns? To go into the ministry of the unknown, ministering to the Unknowns? This is the true ministry of faith. Jesus came, God in Man, unknown! He did not attempt to make Himself known; He wanted the Father to be known. Divine humility! Amazing! We, too, are to be unknown. We are making Him known.

Why are we unknown? Being unknown keeps us safe. Being unknown will keep the elect from kingdom building, self-righteousness, glory, and image. All of these things must be broken at His feet, for they are of the kind of wealth we do not need when we belong to Him. We must lose everything to discover the power of the life within. It is crucial that we are unknowns. Amazingly, we are entrusted with the greatest message and kingdom, and no one wants to know us! We represent Him, we have direct access to Him, and no one wants to know us. We will judge angels and no one wants to know us.

A ministry of the Unknowns, a company of the Unknowns, all with the same vision to remain attached to the Life of the Vine and allow the Life of the Vine to flow out of the Unknowns. We are all one, yet all different, all tapped into the same Life, none of us a branch clinging to a branch but a branch attached to the Vine. The ministry of the Unknowns is a WITH ministry. Unknowns band together. Unknowns are not recognized. We work without recognition.

This world's system is not an accident. It is all permitted. It is all in the plan of God. It is all there for a purpose: the breaking of kingdoms, righteousness, pride, strength, glory. Again, it is all in the plan of God. Permitted. It is, well, nice that He is using man's stupidity. It all works to His end. Nothing is bad. This is the best possible life. How do we judge different things as good or bad? The soulish judge them on the basis of their outer life, their soul life; they do not like their outer life broken. They fight against being unknown. However, everything must go that hinders the release of the Life in the believer. Nothing is bad when it accomplishes that. Being unknown accomplishes that, and remember, we are forever known by Him!

DAY 294
The Curse Of Self-Centeredness

Woe to you, scribes and Pharisees, hypocrites! For you clean the outside of the cup and of the dish, but inside they are full of robbery and self-indulgence. You blind Pharisee, first clean the inside of the cup and of the dish, so that the outside of it may become clean also.

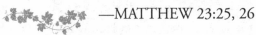

—MATTHEW 23:25, 26

Who among us has not experienced self-centeredness? By the very nature of man, we were created to be other-centered, but we are self-centered. As we look at the creation of the world and God's desire for man as a bride for His Son, we see selflessness. We are made in His image, and nothing but selflessness will suit us.

I remember a frightening experience in Malaysia when I went to pray on a walk, and the "pray" was to play much more into the day than the walk itself. I went close to the shipyards and stumbled across over thirty dogs that encircled me with the intent to attack. As I slowly backed out of the place and surrounded myself with people, the dogs retreated. The point is that though there is nothing positive in the Bible said about dogs or men, most people love a dog, but it is only a blessing when it gives itself to something greater. Dogs are made to give themselves to man and thus become a blessing. Man is made to give himself to God and in that way be a blessing. Man simply is not made to be self-centered, which causes him to shrink and become animal-like; he is meant to be God-centered.

Often I have challenged the oppressed to go find someone in great need and help him. The results have been consistent: The helper grows happy! The world says there is a way and freely offers it, and Jesus says that He is the Way, a Way of giving, of sacrifice, of loving. Those who follow Him on the Way can become so happy as to feel they might explode. There is no happiness in building for one's self. We need to realize we will die, and so for what will we live? Our life can be given to something greater than ourselves, to our loving Father and His people, not exalting self-centeredness, but preferring to despise it.

DAY 295
The Curse Of the Christian Caste System

The scribes and the Pharisees have seated themselves in the chair of Moses; therefore all that they tell you, do and observe, but do not do according to their deeds; for they say things and do not do them. They tie up heavy burdens and lay them on men's shoulders, but they themselves are unwilling to move them with so much as a finger. But they do all their deeds to be noticed by men; for they broaden their phylacteries and lengthen the tassels of their garments. They love the place of honor at banquets and the chief seats in the synagogues, and respectful greetings in the market places, and being called Rabbi by men. But do not be called Rabbi; for One is your Teacher, and you are all brothers. Do not call anyone on earth your father; for One is your Father, He who is in heaven. Do not be called leaders; for One is your Leader, that is, Christ.

 —MATTHEW 23:2-10

India is mocked because of its caste system. Though illegal since 1947, I have found it is alive and well in practice. The flesh of man enjoys the caste system. It is like bigotry in that it seems to be abhorred only by those who cannot practice it! Well, amen! As my Indian teacher says, "The world continues to be the world!" However, what about the Church? Should it be riddled with bigotry and a caste system of its own? It is, have no doubt about it. The messages may not be overt (it would nearly be more palatable if they were), but the covert message is quite clear. Many in the "churches" have convinced those who join that they will never, in this life, arrive to a stature and standing which would allow access into the deepest revelations of Christ. I do not just preach, but I also listen to heaps of preaching, and what I hear are things such as how those who are single, those who have experienced a divorce, those who do not have children, those who have not been in "fulltime" ministry, and those who have rebellious children will never arrive as successful Christians. Blah, blah, and more blah! Many believe the deception, which simply put is that life with a small "l" translates into life with a capital "L." There is a perceived disparity in life, one good example being that there is such a huge difference between those married to unbelievers and those married to believers, and those who lack marriage to believers are to take their rightful place in the sub-Christian caste. When it comes to life (with a lower case "l," as in the world), there is minimal difference between living with an unbeliever or a believer; however, when it comes to the thing of Life (with a capital "L," the Life of Jesus within us), there is no difference. People successful in the world's eyes—educated, famous, or having millions of dollars and prestige—are far more likely to commit suicide than those who have little. Jesus is using all of life—indeed, He holds all of life together—to teach us the things of the kingdom within us and the kingdom to come. He is not fighting divorce, singleness, and failure but using those to bring man to the revelation of Himself.

If you fit into any of the above categories and have been led by man to feel inferior in your walk with God, please, please do not let a Pharisee define your spiritual condition. God is using everything in your life to bring you to Life.

Philippians 3:7-11, "But whatever things were gain to me, those things I have counted as loss for the sake of Christ. More than that, I count all things to be loss in view of the surpassing value of knowing Christ Jesus my Lord, for whom I have suffered the loss of all things, and count them but rubbish so that I may gain Christ, and may be found in Him, not having a righteousness of my own derived from the Law, but that which is through faith in Christ, the righteousness which comes from God on the basis of faith, that I may know Him and the power of His resurrection and the fellowship of His sufferings, being conformed to His death; in order that I may attain to the resurrection from the dead."

If you have had struggles, failures, and calamity in the things of "life," do not let anyone tell you it translates into failure in "Life." You have come to Him; you do not dwell in a lower level of the Christian life; you are blessed. Is the world living according to His standards? No! Not to worry: He is not fighting the world but using it. He has used it in your life to bring you to Him. Rejoice!

DAY 296
The Dealer

For the time will come when they will not endure sound doctrine; but wanting to have their ears tickled, they will accumulate for themselves teachers in accordance to their own desires.

—II TIMOTHY 4:3

As a youth working in the inner city of Chicago, I was always mystified by the drug dealer. He would stand next to an expensive convertible, have on a fur coat and big hat, flash gold teeth, and usually be accompanied by more than one woman dressed to the nines. He exuded all the deeds of the flesh. There was always a demeaning air about him as he dealt with those lining up to make their purchases. He had something they wanted (or had to have, in some cases), which gave him the upper hand; he could be as rude as he wanted to be. It was vexing to watch the twisted, worn, and toothless come to make their purchases. Even then I knew that a lesser gave way to a greater, and the reason he so despised those pathetic creatures was because he needed them to maintain his lifestyle. Something in him knew he was the lesser and they the greater, and this he disliked.

I am seeing something disturbing and similar today. The "spiritual" dealer is nearly a mirror of the drug dealer. I have heard the sermon on "seed money" so many times from the "spiritual" dealer as he admonishes believers to give and it will come back to them. The "spiritual" dealer may own three twenty-million-dollar homes, a jet, designer clothes, a multitude of luxury cars, and jewelry. This is all justified, because Jesus deserves the best. But Jesus is not living in the houses. Jesus had a robe with no pockets for collecting things; His Kingdom was not of this earth. Yet believers line up to give to such foolishness, even though the "spiritual" dealer talks about his followers with disdain, due to the clear separation between "us and them." I watched a hidden camera catching the "spiritual" dealers sweep up the donations, put them in trash bags, laugh, and gad about town on a shopping spree. I have to say that these things are good, because God has permitted them for the revelation of many hearts. In the context of His will, He gives the desire of the heart; and if it is health, wealth, security, and fame, it may be given. However, if the heart's desire is to know Him in this short life, that also will be given. We are not to peddle or promote ourselves, but we are to lift up Christ.

The best way to stay away from a drug dealer is never to let what he has stir something in our flesh. The best way to avoid the "spiritual" dealer is never to let his appearance stir some flesh in us. Finally, we can ask for the grace of God to accomplish in this life our never being sidetracked by giving attention to something that may surround Him, but is not Him.

DAY 297
The Destruction Of the Flesh

I have decided to deliver such a one to Satan for the destruction of his flesh, so that his spirit may be saved in the day of the Lord Jesus.

—I CORINTHIANS 5:5

I have often heard this verse used to justify giving up on an unrepentant believer. The idea communicated is to let the hedge of protection others have placed around a believer be lifted, so Satan can have his way and destroy the person before he does any more damage in this life. However, I would like to give a different twist to Paul's statement. God is not fighting Satan, but He is using him for the perfecting of the saints. Now, many believers are about the constant protection of other believers from Satan, and yet Satan has been used to destroy the flesh of many men. I am not talking about their physical being but their fleshly behaviors as described in Galatians 5. I watched a man for years plead with his wife, who was intent on having an affair. In the end he released her and stopped praying that she be protected from the flesh. Satan immediately went to work (for he works on a permit) and her flesh was given over to immorality. She had invited in a greater conflict than she could have ever imagined, for though the flesh was given over to immorality, the spirit remained the Lord's. Her life became increasingly complicated and the whole situation brought her into deep depression. In the end she was broken, her flesh life destroyed! She repented and returned to her husband. He had spent all those years of protecting her, and yet it was in the hands of Satan that her flesh life was destroyed. It is believed that the person Paul delivered over to Satan is the very same person (II Cor. 2:5-11) Paul subsequently entreats the people to allow back into the fellowship.

DAY 298
The Disciple and Motivation

Or do you think lightly of the riches of His kindness and forbearance and patience, not knowing that the kindness of God leads you to repentance?

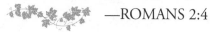 —ROMANS 2:4

The sermon began, "People are more loving in a pub than in the church." I knew immediately that we, the congregation, were going to receive an emotional beating. We were not loving enough, and this fellow was going to motivate us to love. On my notes I drew a wagon wheel; in the hub I wrote the phrase, "need to love," and then I began to write on each spoke a different emphasis the pastor was making. The unloving person was compared to the loving. An appeal was made to understanding; obviously, only ignorant people do not love. We were made to feel guilty for our lack of love. There was the fear of punishment and judgment if something did not change. It was apparent God had great expectations for us, we had let Him down, and we were just short of incurring His wrath. Finally came an entreaty: "Start loving; it is a command!" Very little was said about how loving people live, though the speaker seemed to know an awful lot about how unloving people act! The fear of God's rejection was definitely stirring something in me. I wanted to run. I knew I had failed God in more areas than just being unloving! The sermon did not encourage me one bit to love or leave me thinking about how better to be loving; I was actually encouraged to run from God!

We are not to question the clear commands of God, and therefore we are to love. "A new commandment I give to you, that you love one another, even as I have loved you, that you also love one another," John 13:34. Sin and punishment are one and the same; if we are not obedient, we pay. I am not questioning the command to love. What I would like to examine and question is how we are to motivate fellow disciples to keep a command.

Do we think greater understanding of the commands will empower? Do guilt, comparison, fear, wrath, and the fear of rejection represent how we are to motivate disciples? Does pointing out weakness actually encourage a disciple to get stronger? Do we impel disciples by demanding that they pull themselves up by their bootstraps and get going? Those in the discipleship ministry have recognized that pinning the hope for change on guilt, fear, judgment, condemnation, and rejection is completely unrealistic. It is not the experience of disciple-makers that a believer makes long-term life-changing directions because of fear. Is there anything that will successfully motivate a believer?

For a clue, we must look at what has motivated past believers, such as the acknowledgment of being helpless. "Immediately the boy's father cried out and began saying, 'I do believe; help my unbelief,'" Mark 9:24.

Mercy, and our awareness of our need for it, was identified as a motivator. "Let us therefore draw near with confidence to the throne of grace, that we may receive mercy and may find grace to help in time of need," Hebrews 4:16.

Disappointment over failure proved to be a great motivator. "And Peter remembered the word which Jesus had said, 'Before a cock crows, you will deny Me three times.' And he went out and wept bitterly," Matthew 26:75.

Loneliness and abandonment: "for you once were NOT A PEOPLE, but now you are THE PEOPLE OF GOD; you had NOT RECEIVED MERCY, but now you have RECEIVED MERCY," I Peter 2:10.

Significance: "fixing our eyes on Jesus, the author and perfecter of faith, who for the joy set before Him endured the cross, despising the shame, and has sat down at the right hand of the throne of God," Hebrews 12:2.

Forgiveness: "for this is My blood of the covenant, which is poured out for many for forgiveness of sins," Matthew 26:28.

Rebellion: "To the Lord our God belong compassion and forgiveness, for we have rebelled against Him," Daniel 9:9.

Liberty: "So speak and so act, as those who are to be judged by the law of liberty," James 2:12.

Weakness: "For indeed He was crucified because of weakness, yet He lives because of the power of God. For we also are weak in Him, yet we shall live with Him because of the power of God directed toward you," II Corinthians 13:4.

I have been motivated to love, forgive, give, and lay down my life for my brother through experiencing the Lord's love, mercy, kindness, liberty, grace, and forgiveness. I was only able to know of the mercy of God because I needed it. I experienced grace because it was imperative that I find it. I discovered the law of liberty because I required it. Why did I need grace, mercy, love, and forgiveness? Always it was because I failed. Without failure I would never have needed those things, learned of those things, or been motivated by them. What was shown to me, I want to exhibit to others.

Christianity is the only religion possessing a theology of failure; it has no place in the world's religions, where failure always excludes the practitioners. Not so for the disciple of Christ! Failure is a great tool in the hand of God as one method for moving spiritual truth from our heads to our hearts. A spiritual man comes to spiritual truth through weakness. Our weakness works for God. I will repeat what I have said before, nothing is against the Christian, since God causes all things to work for the good. Allowing failure to work for the Christian is not encouraging failure. As a pastor has said, "Worldliness will not taint true Godliness." A disciple-maker is not one who withdraws from those who have sinned; we stand by them, relating the mercy and grace of God which will free them up. We maintain a simple attitude, which is if a person hates his sin, the door is always open; for the one who loves it, the door is closed.

We must teach and motivate disciples to be obedient. However, fleshly motivation of guilt, competition, insecurity, and punishment will only increase fleshly behavior. When the flesh draws a believer to disobedience, exercising the tools of the flesh will bring the flesh into a strengthened state, not a spiritual state. Mercy and grace are received when the weakness of the flesh is recognized and completely set aside. "For what the Law could not do, weak as it was through the flesh, God did: sending His own Son in the likeness of sinful flesh and as an offering for sin, He condemned sin in the flesh, in order that the requirement of the Law might be fulfilled in us, who do not walk according to the flesh but according to the Spirit. For those who are according to the flesh set their minds on the things of the flesh, but those who are according to the Spirit, the things of the Spirit. For the mind set on the flesh is death, but the mind set on the Spirit is life and peace, because the mind set on the flesh is hostile toward God; for it does not subject itself to the law of God, for it is not even able to do so, and those who are in the flesh cannot please God" (Romans 8:3-8).

DAY 299
The Disciple and Rest

*You did not choose Me but I chose you, and appointed
you that you should go and bear fruit, and that your fruit
should remain, that whatever you ask of the Father
in My name He may give to you.*

—JOHN 15:16

Which one of you, when he wants to build a tower, does not first sit down and calculate the cost, to see if he has enough to complete it? We know whatever advice Jesus gives is true to His nature. We can then assume that if Jesus were building anything, He would first count the cost. We know from the gospel that the most costly building project He began was the one that included us. As living stones, we "are being built up as a spiritual house for a holy priesthood, to offer up spiritual sacrifices acceptable to God through Jesus Christ" (I Peter 2:5).

Jesus has started a building project that is taking place in you. Day by day, moment by moment, He is working to reveal the extent of the free gift of His life in you. He counted the cost before He chose. You have done nothing that has surprised Him. He knew what you would be at your very worst, and still He chose you. God chose me and He chose you to reveal His Son in us, that we "might preach Him among the Gentiles" (Galatians 1:16). If we have made any progress today, it is not because we have been leading, but because of following His leading. It is not because of right decisions, but His decision. It is not because of our building, but His investment in us. He has kept building and investing even when we were not agreeable to it.

I have lived in a home when it was being remodeled, and I have also moved into a home already completed. The word that best describes the contrast is rest. In a remodel there is never any rest, just constant rearranging and frustration. In a home built to suit, we move in with several boxes and a lot to organize, but we know there is an end to it. Remodels never seem to end.

We are not being remodeled. God is not attempting to put new clothes on the old man. He has provided a new man; the old man is gone, and He is working with all the raw materials that will reveal what it is to be a child of God. As God builds us, we must have an attitude of rest. He has counted the cost and will complete what He began.

DAY 300
The Divine Janitor

Surely goodness and lovingkindness will follow me
all the days of my life.

—PSALM 23:6

I remember my days as a janitor. I had completed most of my studies, had amassed a few degrees, moved to a new state, and found myself unemployed. I was grateful to be given a job as a janitor at a federal building. It was definitely a change from the management job I came from while completing seemingly endless schooling, but I enjoyed the fellowship there and my weekly Bible study with the FBI agent. I was surprised to see how happy people could be if things were kept clean. It seems that one person's leaving a dirty toilet stall in the morning could affect the mood of many by midday. There was a simple fix: I could just return to clean the toilet throughout the day. Apparently workers do not mind a coworker who is messy if there is someone to clean up the mess. People do not mind the snow if someone is there to shovel it for them. A janitor's job is a very important one.

Now this brings me to my topic. "Surely goodness and lovingkindness will follow me all the days of my life." Why would this goodness and lovingkindness following him excite the psalmist? Would it not be much nicer if goodness and lovingkindness went ahead of him? Well, they come after him to clean up the messes he made. If I look objectively at my behavior toward those I love in my personal family and the family of God, there is no plausible reason why anyone talks to me, prays for me, or ministers with me. The only thing I can come up with is that goodness and lovingkindess came behind and cleaned up the messes I made of relationships, jobs, promises, and more. Goodness and lovingkindness have made my relationships possible. Therefore I, like the psalmist, will sing with joy, "Surely goodness and lovingkindness will follow me all the days of my life!"

DAY 301
The Eighteen-Inch Journey

For though we walk in the flesh, we do not war according to the flesh, for the weapons of our warfare are not of the flesh, but divinely powerful for the destruction of fortresses. We are destroying speculations and every lofty thing raised up against the knowledge of God, and we are taking every thought captive to the obedience of Christ.

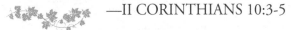

—II CORINTHIANS 10:3-5

The journey to become aware that struggle reveals something right within us is twofold. The first segment of the journey usually takes the longest time; this is the eighteen-inch journey from head to heart. The second journey is from the heart to our shoes.

The first journey comes through revelation. God alone must take what we know and make it something we believe and embrace. Our lack of faith is the obstacle in every teaching. We are often under the deception (thanks to the tree of the knowledge of good and evil) that understanding equals change. However, since humanity understands the error of its way but continues in it, this logic is discounted. Knowing only equals doing when faith exists between the two. Often I hear that the Bible is the manual for living. How true! Yet the majority of believers already know more than they are doing. Is memorizing much Scripture (a great work) better than doing what is already known from Scripture (an act of faith)? Here is where most believers get stuck when it comes to the fulfilled promises of God: they *know* but do not *believe*. To know *and* believe is revelation. It is light with might and confidence, for Jesus is both the teacher and the power from heaven.

To the person of faith, accepting Christ is not just an eventual going to heaven; it is becoming something he never was before—a child of God. He now has a new nature, identity, and life as a new person with new desires. Christ's life is now his life (Colossians 3:4). He is dead to sin. He has power over sin, Satan, and the world, for he has resurrection power. Heaven does not exist only in the future, for the Kingdom of God is within him.

It is true whether or not you believe it. I cannot prove it to you, but you can prove it to yourself! How? Your struggles prove it! What you struggle with proves your true nature! Struggle comes first as the bud, the prophecy of the bloom and the coming fruit. Abundant life does not end at struggle but begins there. All along through your misery God has been speaking, "My child, sinning no longer suits you. You are not made for sin; you are something new. Your desire is not for sin, and your struggle with sin proves it." Hallelujah! You are not a "no-hoper"! You can faintly start to see that you must be something new!

I love Jesus. One significant reason for this statement is that Jesus has consistently ministered to my desire, not my behavior. Often my behavior has been disastrous, and yet I can honestly say that the desire of my heart has remained constant throughout the years. When Jesus met the woman at the well, the disciples wanted nothing to do with her. They made an assessment of the woman from examining her lifestyle, and all believed the woman to be a "no hoper." Yet Jesus looked beyond the behavior to the woman's desire, recognized that she was the one woman to carry the message of salvation to Samaria, and thus dealt with her. Her desire must have been to serve God. On the contrary, many looked at the behavior of the Pharisees and believed them to be holy. Once again Jesus looked past behavior to desire and pronounced them "white-washed tombs . . . full of dead men's bones" (Matthew 23:27). Therefore, desire means more than behavior. Many illustrations in Scripture embody this point; from Abraham to Peter we see desire carrying the hearts of believers and forming the basis of God's continued work in their lives despite regressions in behavior.

In my personal discipleship ministry it is my constant prayer for God to reveal the desire of the person with whom I am talking. It has been an absolute that despite present behavior, if his or her desire is for the Lord, this right desire will bring the believer to the experience of deliverance that was given already on the day of salvation.

This leads us to the most important question: How can we know if we have the right desire in our lives necessary for God's continued work to carry us past the behavior making us so miserable? The answer, again, is struggles. What we struggle with reveals not only the existence of a new nature, but also the new desire that came with it.

A woman was vexed by her obsessive jealousy, a man vexed with his appetite for pornography, a father with rejecting his children, a pastor with his bitterness, a young man with the lie he had told, a mother with a past abortion, an employee with a theft, a father with his drug addiction, an elder with his lust, and a missionary with his inactivity. All vexed, feeling stupid, foolish, ashamed, and uncomfortable. Why? No one knew of their failures, for I was the first to hear of them. Why were they all tormented? Because they have new natures! Their behavior does not suit them, they are not made for it, and the struggle reveals the truth of the depth of their conversion.

This brings us to the second journey of allowing revelation to move into our shoes, not by dead works, vain attempts to be holy, or trying to gain God's acceptance through improved behavior, but by the action faith always brings. Every morning the believer can get up and ponder his sin, failure, past, worries, fears, depression, anxiety, anger, and every other deed of the flesh and simply say, "I could traffic in those things today and know I would still go to heaven, but they simply would not suit me."

In an airport in London I was standing beside several businessmen when a young woman walked by in very skimpy attire. The majority of the men had something to say after the woman passed; one actually turned to me and asked, "How would you like to spend the night with *her*?" I commented that the woman was attractive; however, "It wouldn't suit me." It would not make me happy, it would not bring a lift into my spirit, and such behavior would go against my nature, making me miserable and uncomfortable in the end. I went on my way feeling very comfortable and happy.

The Christian life—the life of Christ—suits believers. We were made for it. Nothing makes us as comfortable as something like the Sermon on the Mount. There is no struggle involved in expressing the life of Christ within. Struggle comes from anything outside of Him and is a gentle reminder that no longer are we made for the lust of the eyes, the lust of the flesh, or the boastful pride of life.

We Christians are suited for a world created by God. He made all that we feel, see, touch, taste, and experience. He made His children to live in this world. We enjoy it the most. We are not in a constant fret to get out of the world. We own it, we inherit it, we can move in it, and we conquer it. When we walk in our new nature with Christ's life within, even the flowers seem to nudge us along our way. Those who are not born again have everything pitted against them. The Christian life is the most natural life. It must be natural, for we are in Christ, Christ is in us, and all the world is held together by Him. If anything is non-Christian, it is at the same time unnatural. Christian living is natural living. We need not prove it, for life itself proves it to us daily. The experience of Christ as our life is not for the chosen few in the faith, but rather is where all believers are being driven.

DAY 302
The Emotional Snowdrift

Be devoted to one another in brotherly love; give preference to one another in honor; not lagging behind in diligence, fervent in spirit, serving the Lord; rejoicing in hope, persevering in tribulation, devoted to prayer, contributing to the needs of the saints, practicing hospitality. Bless those who persecute you; bless and curse not.

—ROMANS 12:10-14

Often in early spring I like to go four-wheeling on some magnificent trails in the Rocky Mountains, many of which are rarely traveled. The trails are just wide enough for a Jeep, and on the open areas, the sun has done its job of melting away all the snow, making for uneventful driving. However, there are always areas of snow on the shadowy side of a mountain that have not had the opportunity to thaw. The road is clear up to these snowdrifts and beyond, so I am confronted with a couple of options. First, go in reverse, find a place to turn around, and abandon the trip. Second, go in reverse a certain distance in order to pick up forward speed and momentum to burst through the drift! I prefer the second method, for once I have broken through, I can continue on unhindered.

Relationships are like trails in the mountains. Once God's path is discovered, the map located, directions written down for resolution, and the way clearly marked, a snowdrift can reveal itself right in the middle of the path! Emotional snowdrifts are interesting things; they may represent only a small part of the trail, yet if not broken through, the whole trail might just as well be packed with snow. These drifts are hurts caused by others—harsh words from the past, offenses, breeches of trust, lies, unmet needs, criticism, uncaring or not listening ears, indifference, opposition, and/or lack of support, respect, or love—made, so often, more significant by the fact that others do not see them or even care to confess them. For all practical purposes, the offended have to remain offended with mountains of self blocking the heat of the sun and impeding all progress.

An elderly brother in Christ ended his conversation with me by saying, "You know, Mike, every time you have been offended, upset, insulted, wounded, incensed, angry, aggravated, exasperated, irritated, or disgusted, I want you to know it was all your fault!" What a list, what a conclusion, and yet he was right! "So although I wrote to you, it was not for the sake of the offender nor for the sake of the one offended, but that your earnestness on our behalf might be made known to you in the sight of God" (II Corinthians 7:12). Mike's response to an offense is much more a revelation of Mike than of the one doing the offending. I exhibit my fragile self when I cannot allow any offense (a state in which I have often found myself). I must be earnest concerning God; it does me no good to allow the Son to shine on all but one area of the trail, for even that halts forward progress.

Unfortunately, we derive a sick satisfaction from hanging on to offense. We think it justifies us when we can quickly recount the nature of the hurt to any who will listen. However, most are fed up with listening! Well, all of it is our fault! We must back up and break through the snowdrift in order to continue on. We must hug an enemy, take two steps forward and talk to one who has offended us, forgive indifference, move back into the house, begin to communicate again, initiate sex with our mate, allow affection to be initiated, and love with Christ's love. In so doing, the only thing that will be lost is self, that miserable servant of only itself, wanting its own way; it would turn us around on the trail to happiness and keep us shrouded in a cave of self-pity. Do not think for one minute it is too difficult to plow through the drift. It is much more difficult after having completed the journey thus far to retrace our steps and find ourselves, after so much time, at the beginning place.

DAY 303
The Faith Hub

Now faith is the assurance of things hoped for, the conviction of things not seen. For by it the men of old gained approval. By faith we understand that the worlds were prepared by the word of God, so that what is seen was not made out of things which are visible.

—HEBREWS 11:1-3

I have always found systematic theology to be a bit of an enigma, since I do not see how man (the lesser) with his minimal intellect is able to systematize, or rather, put God (the greater) in a category or a box. At its best these attempts reveal a Western mindset and at their worst reveal unbelief, for the one who lacks faith is the one who must try to figure out God to know what He is going to do next. I find it interesting that the vast majority of splits in the church/Christian club do not come from a disagreement over what Jesus says in the Gospels but rather a dispute over what the Apostles said in the rest of the New Testament. The gyrations that take place among the differing theological camps are, sadly, comical, for no matter what systematized framework is developed, there will always be a number of passages that do not fit neatly into the arrangement. This leads to the twisting and distortion of unfortunate passages, with proofs from what the "original" Greek actually says, until they fit the system. Of course, Jesus is lost in all of these systems in which right doctrine is the goal. Just as God divided the people because of the tower of Babel, He also scatters believers at the tower of systematic theology. There are many examples, but I will pick some of the more obvious.

—God said that a prostitute must die. That is absolute. Then He tells Hosea to marry one! He says an adulterer must die; that, too, is absolute. Then He tells Hosea to go bring home his adulterous wife.

—Jonah was commanded to say, "Yet forty days and Nineveh will be overthrown." Again, this was an absolute statement; Nineveh was going to be overthrown. Jonah knew the test of a false prophet was whether or not what the prophet said came about. When Nineveh repented and turned to the Lord, Nineveh did something that went against what God had told Jonah. This made Jonah out to be false, and he was angry because God had broken out of the system. Jonah is more concerned about the system and his own reputation than the wonderful fact that Nineveh repented.

—God provides, but I am commanded to work.
—Grace is free but truth is purchased.
—We are predestined but we must choose.

Now all of this brings me to the central point. Many truths in the Scriptures, from an intellectual standpoint, oppose one another. Some passages do not agree, period. What I am suggesting is for us to move from a Theological (the very term is filled with presumption) system to a faith-based system where everything agrees. For example, if we view the attributes of God, He is Love and yet judgment. Well, how can this be? Think of Theological systems as square wheels and think of a faith system as a round wheel with spokes and a hub that allows the believer to move forward. The spokes (Scriptural truths) at the fringe appear far apart, as though they do not agree. However, looking down the spokes it is easy to see the truths getting closer and closer until finally they meet at the very center of the hub. This center—called faith in the Father, Son, and Holy Spirit—is what holds all opposing truths together. It is faith allowing us to believe and rest in them even though we cannot systematize them. Persons of faith do not need a system, for we have a faith in what is greater. All of us, I suppose, have had experiences as believers that baffle us. However, abiding in Him we find no fault when we examine Him. We do not have to spiritualize or understand the "reasons" for the experience. All we need do is rest and trust Him, in faith.

DAY 304
The Faith Of Jesus

For we who live are constantly being delivered over to death for Jesus' sake, that the life of Jesus also may be manifested in our mortal flesh.

—II CORINTHIANS 4:11

Often I read with amazement the stories of the great men of faith: Abraham and the willingness to sacrifice Isaac, Moses and the parting of the Red Sea, and Noah and the building of the ark. How could these men stand? How did they have the faith that could be counted to them as righteousness? Simply to think of obeying and building an ark when there had never been a flood boggles the mind. I must admit that after close examination, I just do not have that kind of faith. The recognition of my lack of faith makes Galatians 2:20 mean so much to me. I like Darby's translation, which gets closer to the meaning of the original, "I am crucified with Christ and no longer live, *I*, but Christ lives in me; but [in] that I now live in flesh, I live by faith, **the [faith] of the Son of God**, who has loved me and given himself for me. I do not set aside the grace of God; for if righteousness [is] by law, then Christ has died for nothing." What a blessing to know I can live out of His faith, far superior to the faith we saw in Abraham, Moses, and Noah. Again, the lesser truth will give way to the greater truth. He is the greater truth. If I move in my recognition of being in Him and He in me, His faith will be the faith out of which I live. He is the Vine, I am a branch, and if that is true, then the faith of the Vine must flow into the branch, allowing me to live out of His faith. It is refreshing to know I do not have to generate faith and can simply live out of His. Amen!

DAY 305
The Flesh Is That Hostile Voice

Because the mind set on the flesh is hostile toward God; for it does not subject itself to the law of God, for it is not even able to do so.

 —ROMANS 8:7

Beware of the voice of the flesh. A good working definition of flesh is this: man's soul and body under the rule or influence of anything other than Christ. The flesh is of the dust and fights for its independence to indulge in things of the dust. Flesh calls to flesh, and the flesh hates subjection to Christ.

Were it not for the damage done in the flesh, we could almost find it comical. Our flesh has a voice! Few have discerned it, but it is very distinctive. An animal has mind, will, emotions, body, and desires. Watch as the animal works situations to get fulfillment. It is thinking and reasoning to fulfill the desires of the flesh. I had two dogs; when they were fed, the female would quickly eat her food and then rush to the fence barking as though someone were there. The male would quickly run to the fence to see what was going on. While he was looking about, she would run back and eat his food. The flesh, the carnal, has a voice of reason, but does it ever really make sense?

God is love, and to come under love is to nullify the flesh. Love is a deathblow to the flesh. Therefore, the flesh loves conflict and can actually feed on and grow through conflict, like yeast in dough. In conflict flesh feeds on flesh, ever expanding and making its presence known. As in dough there must be starter yeast, so, too, the flesh needs a starter. Let's look at some typical starters.

For no reason you are thinking about the neighbors, when next comes a thought, "What if they came over and told me to move our car?" This is followed by a thought in response to something that has not even happened: "I would tell them I will park my car wherever I want." Once accustomed to its characteristics the mind of the flesh is easy to spot, for there is never a center to things.

At work your mind drifts to the boss and then to an imaginary meeting in which he indicates you are not meeting the quota. Next you are telling him, "I am working twice as hard as anyone else in this office, and if you watched the people better you would not be talking to me!" Again, it is comical to stew over something when no meeting has taken place.

Then there are all the imaginary conversations we have had with our relatives.

I actually had a fellow take me out to lunch to tell me I had disfellowshipped him. I stared in amazement, disbelief, and silence as he told me each point on which I had taken issue with him and then his response. It had all been imagined. Once he finished talking, I told him I had not been thinking any of those things, nor had I disfellowshiped him. He never even heard me and just said, "Well, that's it. I won't have anything to do with you, either." Honestly, I was as clueless when I left as I was when I went in. It was laughable except for the fact that I really did like the fellow. Well, amen. I, too, have listened to the flesh and have to stop and say, "What is the point?" The flesh stirs and stirs to try to get the "starter" going.

The flesh needs a foothold. It needs the residue of the old "I" to be stirred. I have mentioned before how when someone you have lived with dies, he is gone, but his baggage remains. Go stir in the baggage and the feelings of his presence will follow. The flesh looks for events that will similarly stir up the baggage of the old "I." If your father was critical and now you hear your husband being critical, the feelings of the old "I" are stirred. I need to be clear here, the flesh does not need the old "I" to be activated, and, indeed, it cannot be activated, because it was crucified with Christ. What the flesh can use instead are the old attitudes of the "I," the baggage resident in your head. When we are fighting the expression of the flesh (Galatians 5), we are wrong. We must fight the attitude of the old "I" that has crept in. Go back to the root. The attitude is what gave the flesh a stronghold from which to work.

I intensely and immensely enjoyed my grandfather. His policy was always to do what is right! I remember selling a pickup and the fellow, because of his driving, blew the engine the next day and brought the truck back to me. My grandfather said, "Do what is right!" I bought the man another engine. Later my grandfather told me he was happy I did that. He was from the old school; when something needed to get done, a person just did it. He never really caught on to all the government agencies producing laws and paperwork seemingly just to hinder people from being able to get on. One day he decided to burn down an old barn. As he was getting ready to burn it a neighbor informed us we needed a permit. "A permit for what, to burn down my own barn? Who cares if I burn my barn? Who would have the time to produce such a permit?" In the end, he yielded and attempted to get the permit. This led to a series of phone messages, number punching, being put on hold, and question answering. In the end he hung up, only to emerge from the barn with a five-gallon can of gasoline. He told me to get in the truck. I asked, "What are we doing?" He responded, "We are going to start an accidental fire!" That day the barn burned with no permit. After the fire started I was thinking of how I would tell off the neighbor, the government, or the fire department if they came by to question us. I was in the flesh. The foothold was the fact that I was doing something illegal; whether it ought to be illegal and behavior needs to be regulated to that degree is another topic. Honestly, in ten thousand years of human history, ours is the first generation apparently lacking the sense to know whether or not an old barn should be burned. If I had not been told it was illegal, I would not have had a problem; once I knew it was and what I was doing was wrong, it stirred the residue of the old dead "I" which purposely engaged in doing wrong. See, it is illegal for me to be offended. When I allow an attitude permitting offense, the flesh quickly goes to work manufacturing varieties of the deeds of the flesh. The deeds would not be possible without the attitude. It is illegal for the Christian to be proud; it is the residue of the old independent "I" that was crucified. However, once the flesh becomes proud, it has a stronghold from which to set up its manufacturing process.

Why would God give us flesh? Adam and Eve had flesh, and what was proven in them is also proven in us: "The flesh is hostile toward God." Remember, we are made in His image. When we want to be like God we make a mess of things, for we are not Love. He can be trusted, we cannot. He put our spirit in flesh to keep us in check, remind us who we are, and cause us to lose our glory and pride. It really is not that bad. All we have to do is acknowledge the Jesus within, invite Him to flow out, and the flesh is immediately subdued.

DAY 306
The Fleshly Marriage

So then, brethren, we are under obligation, not to the flesh, to live according to the flesh—for if you are living according to the flesh, you must die; but if by the Spirit you are putting to death the deeds of the body, you will live.

—ROMANS 8:12, 13

Before discussing a fleshly or spiritual approach to marriage, a basic foundation must be laid, for I often hear lists of expectations of godly marriages, and they include things only God Himself can provide. So our foundational basis for discussion is that marriage will not give what only Christ gives.

When there is disturbing behavior in our spouses, the most popular approach among Christians is to eat from the tree of good and evil and decide what to do to get the desired response, which is to make our own flesh comfortable by soothing the flesh of our mates. Obstacles to fleshly comfort are removed by us as we watch what we say, leap to attention at the sound of a raised or stressed voice, agree with all excuses for carnal behavior, and jump through every hoop, all in the hope of receiving a crumb of reward. However, this whole approach will turn around and bite us, because flesh always calls out to be the center of its universe and becomes ever stronger when it is. Subsequently, then, one minus after a long list of positives will draw the negative response of anger, strife, withdrawal, and rejection. The mate who has been working really hard in the flesh to appease the other's self-centeredness may simply give up.

Another approach is centered in Jesus, Who lived in a man's body. Matthew 5, 6, and 7 describe how the body was meant to operate with peace. All commandments are primarily given for the good of the persons obeying them and not for the benefit of others, though that is definitely a secondary result. For instance, the command to love a wife is not given to comfort the flesh of the wife, but to give a man joy. The command to respect the husband is not given to benefit the husband, so the common phrase, "You don't love me, so how could I respect you?" reveals a tit-for-tat attitude, as though the command exists for the benefit of the receiver rather than the doer. The false assumption that the behavior of believers is to make the flesh of others comfortable is simply an error that, when believed, prostitutes love and respect and gives fleshly people excuses for their behavior. A man who hates, punishes, and withdraws from his wife never has a countenance worth emulating; his lack of love punishes himself. Whether or not the wife respects means nothing to the spiritual man; the command to respect was not given to aid the man in his pursuits but to enable the woman to function properly. Once the spiritual person sees this, he or she is truly set free from the behavior of others and can enter into true inner contentment springing from Christ. How others respond to our love or respect is not the issue; we need to love and respect to be happy. In this way we set others free from their own flesh, and they can find themselves loving unconditionally and respecting in the absence of merit.

Is this a popular teaching? Not at all, for at its crux we find self-life continually being dealt deathblows. Yet, where there is death, His life is always manifested. Rubbing our two hands together as hard as we can, we can feel the heat, and that is a good picture of marriage as flesh rubs against flesh. Everyone thinks separation is the only option, but the other is to put at least one hand into a vat of oil, the Holy Spirit. Oil is the power, the lubricant, and it only comes by way of the death of the seed.

DAY 307
The Fork In the Road

Therefore, my beloved brethren, be steadfast, immovable, always abounding in the work of the Lord, knowing that your toil is not in vain in the Lord.

—I CORINTHIANS 15:58

I want to say something deserving of some thought, for a lot of teaching has come along the Christian downspout that though not necessarily true is rarely questioned.

We have been taught (covertly) that one of the main goals of Christianity is producing happy, fulfilled, and contented marriages. I do not see that emphasis in the Bible. "But if you should marry, you have not sinned; and if a virgin should marry, she has not sinned. **Yet such will have trouble in this life, and I am trying to spare you**" (I Corinthians 7:28).

If I said I was going to quit the ministry to collect gold, many would rebuke me. Why? Obviously because I cannot take gold to heaven with me; we are not to be consumed with something that cannot make the journey with us. Many things are useful on earth for God's purpose of revealing Christ, but they will not have value in heaven. There is no marriage in heaven! "For when they rise from the dead, they neither marry nor are given in marriage, but are like angels in heaven" (Mark 12:25). Marriage is used of God for His eternal purposes. The world does not have eternal purposes in mind but temporal. For the world, the goal of marriage is self-contentment, self-happiness, and self-satisfaction. A good marriage is not the goal of the Christian. The goal of Christianity is Christ within us, and marriage is a tool to bring about this revelation. When Christ in us is a reality, we will have the marriages that glorify Him.

Often a believer makes this observation: "Jesus didn't have to struggle through a marriage." That, of course, is true. But could it be that Jesus was not married because marriage is not all-important in the scope of the Christian life? I am still saying all of the following: God did ordain marriage, He does make us one, and He does speak of His Bride, the Church. I do not want to minimize marriage, but I do want to see it ascribed its proper place. Therefore, my observation, after thousands of hours spent with couples, is that marriage is not an end but a means of revealing God's end, the "revelation of Christ in you, the hope of glory." I believe the perfect life of Christ dwells in every believer and marriage works to reveal it. In the marriage relationship it is impossible to be consumed with self and have inner or outer peace. The only cure for self is to be selfless. Marriage is a tool in the hand of God to free us from self-absorption. Pride closes our eyes and ears to the voice of God; marriage continually chips away at pride. The flesh in all its manifestations keeps us from Life. Marriage makes us uncomfortable with our flesh. Is it reasonable to think that where there is a chipping and stripping away of things not of Him, there is not some conflict? I have noticed something. The world, through the media, constantly barrages the believer with ideas and images of what a perfect marriage should be: to like all the same things, do the same things, travel to the same places, think the same things, have everything in common, and have all the same goals. Well, I know couples like that, and generally speaking they appear shallowly consumed with their perfect little world. I believe there is something God would accomplish through marriage that is far beyond the world's impression of an ideal couple.

I have a diagram called the *Divine Marriage Y* that makes a case for what I am saying. In our frustration we approach the fork in the road of marriage, where we can turn to the right or the left. If we go down the road on the left, we begin to question our decision to get married. We examine the incompatibilities. We explore our definition of happiness, oneness, companionship, and relationship. We compare our situation with what others seem to have. We measure our marriage against what we have been told the Christian marriage is. In the end we determine that our marriage is lacking. This, of course, brings great frustration. With our emotions we run toward despair and the feeling of hopelessness. We wonder what could have been and what should have been. We begin to focus on the marriage and attempt to bring it up to a different level. In the end we grow weary, for it is just too hard to try any longer and we do not have the energy. We react and emotionally give up. It is just too hard to go on. Is it? We hate the feeling of being out of control, we feel we must do something, and so our chosen activity is to give up. Once we give up we have to justify our action by obsessing on our misery. Every day is spent in frustration and rebellion. I believe living this way is very hard, but another option is yielding to let the cross have its way and bring a deeper revelation of Christ in us. At first taking up the cross seems so difficult, but it always deals a clean deathblow immediately and then it is over. We get up and say, "Amen," to the situation, we love the perceived enemy, we decide to walk in faith, and we believe God knows what He is doing. This is the right-hand side of the fork in the road.

Going to the right is a different paradigm. On the right road we believe the purpose of marriage is not happiness but the revelation of Christ in us, the hope of glory. If He is revealed we will be joyous in any situation. A lesser truth must give way to a greater truth, and if we possess the Greater Truth, all lesser truths will be ours. We believe we need to be offended until we cannot be offended. We can say there are none who offend us because we cannot be offended. Others may say, "But there are offensive people." No, there are none, for we can no longer see them. On the right road we know we are disappointed only when we have stopped loving our mates and are actually living for them, not for Christ. On this road our frustration reveals that our belief system is too small. We want to shrink the situation rather than expand what we believe God can do in it, both for us and through others. In our interaction with our mates we find pride lingering in places we never thought imaginable, leading us to react rather than respond, to build an image outside of Him, and to keep our love on a short leash.

The entire Bible has to do with our relationships with God, ourselves, and others. What we are at our worst is the best anyone can get out of us, for when things are the worst, those around us need us to be at our best. The Father need not allow us to escape; no matter what has happened, He may whisper, "So what is your excuse for being disappointed, offended, and rejected, and why do you want to punish?" On this right road we believe God causes all things to work together for good and He is always the positive hidden in the negative. On this road we see the depth of despair revealing the height to which His life can take us. The marriage relationship perfects us, so we can be happy with ourselves, our situation, and all things. It is working out flesh, hacking and cutting away everything that does not look like Him, and all this is done alongside a spouse we love, we are one with, we cannot escape from . . . someone who loves us and does not always know how to show it. Marriage makes us deal with self in a situation from which we cannot run. When self is laid down, we are free. Next, the marriage takes the form God wants it to.

A woman who came to my office for twelve years had a husband who was consistently unfaithful. He hated what he would do and was always repentant; he truly loved his wife. This woman had every bit of pride, self, and image stripped away, and so she shined with His glory. One day I said to her, "Sister, you will stand ahead of me in heaven, for I have only told you what to do. I have never had to forgive an unfaithful mate. You have always done what I asked. You have forgiven and turned to Him. One day He will say to you, 'Well done, good and faithful servant! Enter into the joy of your Master.' When He says that, what would you have him do to your husband, who was the cause of your suffering?"

She spoke from her position on the right side of the Y, replying, "I would say, 'Father, bless him, for without his actions toward me, I would not be here!'"

All things work together for good for those who love Christ! We may only get out of our marriage a whispered, "Well done, good and faithful servant," but that whisper will be so beautiful and valuable! Few dare to travel on the *right* road and none could without His mercy, grace, and calling. My advice is to forget pursuing the goal of a good marriage, stop thinking about how miserable ours is, stop comparing, do not listen to others, stop feeling cheated, cursed, and inferior, and move on in Him.

One last thought. At some point every couple will need to gain a certain freedom from one another. It is important to say, "I love you but I do not live to you!" We live to God, and He is the One we must please. Many refuse to tell the truth to a mate because they are living to him or her. "One who is married is concerned about the things of the world, how he may please his wife, and his interests are divided" (I Corinthians 7:33, 34). I believe this speaks of the beginning of a Christian couple's togetherness, but not the end. The condition Paul talks about is what happens as the road on the left is chosen. However, when a couple chooses the road on the right, their interests are not divided and the revelation of Christ is central.

DAY 308
The Fullness Of Time

But when the fullness of the time came, God sent forth
His Son, born of a woman, born under the Law.

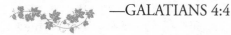

—GALATIANS 4:4

It is interesting that Jesus came at the perfect time in history, a time that included His people's being surrounded and suffocated by an occupying force. It was the perfect time because men would be less tempted to look around than up! He basically said little about the government, such as, "Give to Caesar what is Caesar's." Why?

In Pakistan I was scheduled to speak to a group of Muslims, but before the sermon I was asked, "What will you be saying about Islam?"

I responded, "I do not teach Islam."

Again came the question, "No, but what will you be saying against Islam?"

I said, "I do not preach Islam. Brothers, to teach against Islam is the same as teaching for it. Islam would still occupy my mind and the minds of the listeners. I do not have time. I will be teaching only Jesus." I spoke for two hours on the way to live and then Who was the Way. Over forty Muslims believed in Jesus. I do not believe those results would have occurred had my sermon been against Islam.

Jesus just did not have time for politics, which are of the world and will die when the world is destroyed. Why not talk about something permanent? Because of the expanded awareness of Christ in me, I am becoming more and more disinterested in the world of politics. To focus on it stirs my pride, angers me, makes me accuse men, fills me with fear, and has me debating facts—or, often, misinformation—and issues that in reality I do not know about. I have watched the evening news reporting on a place to which I have been going for enough years to know there is very little truth in what is being said. The Koreans once said to me, "Do you know when the man representing the media and the news is lying?"

I said, "No, tell me!"

Their response was, "When his lips are moving."

This is not the age of information but the age of misinformation, and perhaps there has never been a time in history when less truth was being broadcast throughout the world. Yet we possess the TRUTH. We can speak about Jesus and do not have to worry if we are lying or not. We can hear and read of Jesus and know it is the TRUTH. Jesus came at the perfect time, and the focus was on Him, the Father, and the Kingdom. We are finding ourselves in the perfect time for the focus to be on the same things.

DAY 309
The Glory Of Waiting

Do not leave Jerusalem, but wait for the gift my Father promised, which you have heard me speak about.

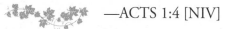 —ACTS 1:4 [NIV]

I recently made an interesting discovery. As we know, the word "faith" is rarely used in the Old Testament. The word "wait" is, a term in Hebrew used literally by those who made rope. If someone were "waiting," he was weaving a weak strand of rope into the strong strands. If someone were to visit Jack's Rope Shop and ask where Jack was, the response might be, "He is in the back waiting," or in the back room braiding a weak strand in with the strong. This gives a new meaning to "waiting on the Lord," for the longer one would "wait," the stronger the rope would become! The longer we wait on the Lord, allowing Him to braid our weak, pathetic lives into His, the stronger we become. A vine planted by itself in a field will wrap around itself; however, plant it by a mighty oak and it will climb as high as the tree itself. "They that wait upon the Lord will renew their strength." Amen! We believers need waiting, which reveals the true glory of our God.

DAY 310
The Grace To Turn

You shall not bow down to them or worship them; for I, the LORD your God, am a jealous God, punishing the children for the sin of the fathers to the third and fourth generation of those who hate Me, but showing love to a thousand generations of those who love Me and keep My commandments.

—DEUTERONOMY 5:9 & 10 [NIV]

Most of us are familiar with this passage because of the teachers of the generational curse. To understand Deuteronomy 5 we look at the culture of Eastern Religions, such as Judaism or Islam, in which children are not free to change religions; a person must follow the faith of his father. In Deuteronomy 5:9, the context in which God is speaking is one of the God-hater who has gone to idols to worship instead of to God. If the father is a God-hater, the son will be a God-hater, and God says that will happen up until the fourth generation—or rather, can happen up to the fourth generation—and He would oppose them. However, in the very next verse, God declares how He shows love to thousands of generations who love Him and keep His commandments. Once a person moves from hating God to loving God, he is shown love instead of punishment. To say that every generation springing from a God-hater is bound and has no choice to become anything other than what the forefather was would negate all evangelistic efforts. It would be just as wrong to use verse 10 as an absolute that if the first generation loves God, the following thousand will also love God. Therefore, using this passage as proof of why a Christian is having problems is, to me, ridiculous.

This passage also has to be viewed in the light of repentance, man's ability to choose, and the fact that when we are born again, we are brought into a new family with God as our Father; we now have a new history rooted in Christ Himself. Therefore, it is impossible for someone to believe in God and still suffer the effects of previous generations of God-haters. This point can be proven over and over again, and for one example we can look at India, where upon conversion the new believers' family members actually attempted and in many cases succeeded in killing those who accepted Christ; despite that, there have been 30,000,000 conversions. The converts' parents were God-haters, but their progeny became God-lovers. Obviously, the persons in the new generation of God-lovers were not cursed by the God who hated the idolatry of their fathers and mothers.

DAY 311
The Great Cloud

Not that I have already obtained it or have already become perfect, but I press on so that I may lay hold of that for which also I was laid hold of by Christ Jesus. Brethren, I do not regard myself as having laid hold of it yet; but one thing I do: forgetting what lies behind and reaching forward to what lies ahead, I press on toward the goal for the prize of the upward call of God in Christ Jesus.

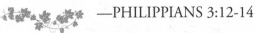

—PHILIPPIANS 3:12-14

The enemy whispers to us things from our past in order to waylay our thoughts and thereby force something onto the mountain of our heart with Christ. Soon we find our focus on performance, money, security, man-pleasing, etc., and as always, the accompanying cloud overshadows us. Next the enemy tells us that until all these issues crowding for a place are resolved, the cloud will not lift; that is, the issues must have our full and undivided attention. It is important to recognize that legitimate plus illegitimate does not equal legitimate. It is true there is a cloud with many issues (in fact, all the issues have become chaos), but freedom will come from neglecting all the issues and focusing on Christ. Give the issues neglect, not focus, and the cloud will lift. If Moses and Elijah could not remain on the mount with Christ, then neither should our mundane issues. It was God in a Man's body who said, "Each day has enough trouble of its own" (Matthew 6:34).

DAY 312
The Greatest Statement
Of Unbelief

And God said to Moses, "I AM WHO I AM"; and He said, "Thus you shall say to the sons of Israel, I AM has sent me to you."

—EXODUS 3:14

The greatest statement of unbelief, the thought from which all unbelief springs, is "Where did God come from?" This question is the mother of all sin and unbelief. Dwelling on it will cause a pit in the stomach, an aching in the brain, discomfort, and sleeplessness. It is the question not to be asked, because from it many wicked things will sprout. This one question embodies all that is wrong with man.

Conversely, the greatest statement of faith is this, "God is." It settles all issues and allows us to rest, have peace, and be confident about the future. When asked who He was, He said, "I AM." If that simple statement can be received in the innermost part of my being, I will have no worries.

To ask where He came from is to say we do not believe in God. He will not tell us where He came from. Why? For faith's sake! It is essential we not know, for not knowing yields faith. Knowing can only lead to unbelief and wickedness. Faith is the assurance of things hoped for, but we want to know, leading to our loss of conviction of Him. Settle it that He is the I AM and do not ask the question. After all, acknowledging the great I AM is the only history we need know in order to trust Him fully.

DAY 313
The Hatching

For if we have become united with Him in the likeness of His death, certainly we shall also be in the likeness of His resurrection.

—ROMANS 6:5

I remember the day my grandfather looked at me and said, "Mike, I am dying." We had just walked from the chicken coop and stopped for him to lean against the well house as he puffed in exhaustion. He looked at his body with bewilderment. "Mike, it is amazing that our bodies last as long as they do. I have done a lot of work with mine." As I stared at him, I was deeply vexed to see his unhealthy condition and uncomfortable witnessing any part of his physical breakdown. If only there were some way to stop it.

I then remembered waiting as a child for chicken eggs to hatch. After a few days of waiting, the eggs got plain boring! However, it was very exciting to see the chicks at last beginning to peck at the shell and to know the life within was soon to emerge. As I thought of my grandfather, it was as though the Lord were gently speaking, "Mike, did you ever put tape on the eggshells to keep them from hatching?" Of course not, for I anticipated the hatching. "Your grandfather's shell is cracking. Do not be vexed or attempt to put tape on it; he is only hatching out!" At that, I was comforted by the God of all comfort. There is no death for the believer, only a hatching. We are spiritual beings confined in a body. One day we will all hatch, and the beauty within will be fully, exquisitely revealed. With that I was at peace with my grandfather's passing!

DAY 314
The Heart

*But the one who joins himself to the
Lord is one spirit with Him.*
—I CORINTHIANS 6:17

I think a lot about the heart. Often we draw three concentric circles—to represent Body, Soul, and Spirit—as a feeble attempt to describe man's makeup. Perhaps we need a fourth circle representing the innermost part, the source of man's being, his heart. The heart must be converted before the spirit, soul, or body experience a conversion. "But thanks be to God that though you were slaves of sin, you became obedient from the heart . . ." (Romans 6:17). David longed for God to create in him a clean heart. The heart is deceitful above all things. Why? How? The heart has us believing that choice rests in mind, will, or emotions. I am meeting more and more believers who have lost hope in the mind's ability to choose. They have analyzed their problem to death and yet have no freedom. Too, there are those who have lost all hope in emotions to choose freedom; the emotional "high" and what it promises just does not last or change their condition. Some are sick and tired of feeling guilty, for all of the guilt in the world has not stopped their behavior. Finally, people are sick of whipping up the will in an attempt to choose. The basis of choice rests in the heart, and the day the heart chooses Jesus, God gives Jesus, the desire of the heart. The day God does not give the desire of the heart, man is no longer made in God's image.

Why do people continue to struggle with the past, drugs, self-hatred, eating disorders, and more? It is because their hearts desire such things. It is a big pill to swallow, but as far as our personal habits and inclinations are concerned, we all have the desire of our hearts. There really is no other option. I said to a fellow, "Be honest. You would rather take drugs and go into self-hatred than not take the drugs." In the end, he admitted that what I said had to be true. Everyone gets the desire of his or her heart. I do not question that the desire of the man's mind, will, and emotions is either a refusal to take drugs or a willingness to be in bondage to them, but this struggle does not represent the desire of the heart. Also, choosing with the heart is not something begun in the spirit and fulfilled in the flesh. That is, we do not choose with the heart and then make the desire of the heart happen through will, intellect, or emotion. Rather, the day we choose with the heart, God must give the desire of the heart. "The desire of the righteous will be granted," Proverbs 10:24. Again, the heart is deceptive in that it is telling us choice rests outside of itself, and in so doing, the heart (the source of our being) is choosing something outside of it to be its source. When the heart chooses Christ as the source, there is abiding.

How do we change the heart? I do not know. I do not think David knew, or he would not have said to God, "Create in me a clean heart." There is something we can do that God cannot do for us. We must acknowledge where we are and in honesty admit our condition to Him: "I would rather sin and struggle than not sin and not struggle. I would rather hate my mate and beat myself up over it than love my mate. I would rather be depressed than change the things that could be making me depressed." He will not confess for us; we must do the confessing. Then God will do what only God can do, which is to create a clean heart and give us the heart's desire. Think about behaviors we, as believers, did not like in ourselves, and over the years many of them merely dropped off. We never worked our way out of them. If God gets all the glory, then He must do all the work. Things just fell off as our heart turned to Him.

Let me give an example. A brother came to me undone by his homosexual "lifestyle." There was no need to make an appeal to his mind, for intellect had told him homosexuality was not the way. There was no need to make him feel guilty, since he had enough guilt for a thousand men. There was no need to tell him tomorrow could be different and he could will it to be so. Already there had been enough tomorrows to have dashed every hope. There was no need to talk about spiritual issues; he knew the spirit warred against the flesh. The brother was out of hope.

The source of his being, his heart, had found a source that, contrary to all logic, was homosexuality. Weeks later he returned, but all he talked about was the love of God; homosexuality was no longer the issue. I asked what had happened. He narrated his journey. He had been pulling homosexuality toward him with one hand (the heart) and pushing it away with the other hand (mind, will, and emotion, or soul power). Then one day his heart turned against homosexuality and God gave him the desire of his heart. He was free because freedom was something he desired in his heart. He was completely amazed at the transformation. God had given him the desire of his heart, and that desire was freedom.

God will not give me what I think about, what I feel about, or what I will, but God will give the desire of my heart.

I know there are several disagreements to this line of thinking. One disagreement is the issue with the heart's being a separate entity within man. The fact that the mind has intellect does not, in my understanding, nullify the fact that the heart has intellect. A mental IQ of 80 does not equate to a heart's IQ of 80. Also, there is the objection to the heart's converting before the spirit. The battle of spirit against flesh, or the Romans 7 conflict of doing what I do not want to do, does not change the issue of the heart's desire. The soul does war against the spirit, even in an unbeliever, but I am talking about heart desire. In the end, I am thinking we all get the desire of our hearts, "great inner battles" are glorified to keep the flesh alive, and if we simply turn to the Lord in our heart, there is a great conversion. There is much more to this life on earth, in the flesh, in the midst of failure, than I ever imagined. Our souls and bodies covertly want to give us their own desires. This is proven when God begins to give the desire of the heart and the body and soul rebel. There will be confusion in the mind, a rollercoaster of emotions, and the rising up of the will. The soul has been playing a deceitful game, working to have us identify with its own desires in order to remain in control. The soul does not mind working for good or bad desires, for the goal of the soul is simply to stay alive and in control.

When the heart chooses, the soul does not carry out the choice and make it happen. Can what is begun in the spirit be perfected in the flesh? Many think when we choose, willpower makes it happen. No, we choose in our heart and God makes it happen. Neither choice nor willpower makes something happen. We choose in the heart what God will make happen. God created the vanilla bean and the cocoa bean; we are free to choose one or the other, but we do not choose in order to create one or the other. Many are fearful to choose in the heart, for they think they must then set about creating what they have chosen. Willpower attempts to create what was chosen. The desires of the heart are things we choose and God gives. Choice is picking something we want but cannot create; "for with the heart a person believes, resulting in righteousness . . ." (Romans 10:10). We may choose to fly, but we cannot fly. Willpower is picking something we want and seeing its fulfillment by using something He has created. So, in a very real sense, willpower can only enable us to put together the pieces He has created in a way we would like to see them. God gives the desire of the heart; He does not give the focus of choice or will. Many choose victory; others try to create it through will and then wonder why God has not kept His promise to give the desire of the heart. It is quite simple. He does not give what we choose or will to make happen. He gives the desire of the heart.

I am attempting to make the point that choice and will are different from desire. An animal has choice and will, but an animal does not have the desire of the heart. We can choose things that exist. Christ exists. Choice is the acknowledgement of something that exists. To will is to make something visible that up to this point did not exist. We cannot will Christ, for that would give us the ability to create Christ. A person can say, "I will build the house" (make it visible from things God has created), or one can say, "I will choose a house." We can choose to ask God to create within us a clean heart and to give the desire of our heart. We cannot will to choose or have the desire of our heart. Now, faith is the blending of will and choice, and as such, we can choose the assurance of things hoped for and have a conviction of things not yet seen.

DAY 315
The Hurting Father

So he got up and came to his father. But while he was still a long way off, his father saw him, and felt compassion for him, and ran and embraced him and kissed him.

—LUKE 15:20

We all know the story of the younger son who, desiring to cast aside the restraints of his father, requested his freedom, went to a faraway land, squandered all he had, and found himself wishing he could at least devour what the swine were eating.

Something can be learned from this father. He let the boy go! He let the boy come to the end of his rope! This was a wise father, for a child who only keeps the rules because of force grows up to be a religious child, not a person of faith. Religion is all we can give a child by imposing values from without, while relationship comes from within and then expresses itself outwardly. But children can equate the expression of a Christian's relationship with a force that is attempting to be applied to them outwardly and rebel. Wanting to avoid the battle between the Old Nature within and the expression of Christ in their surroundings, they run. The son looked at his father's expression of faith and perceived it as confining. The expression of Christ is confining to one who has nothing but Adam-life within. Naturally, once Christ is living within, expression is natural and freeing.

The son was given his money and allowed to go. In short, the son was sent away from religion to discover a relationship. The father watched and looked every day for the return of his son, knowing that when and if his son returned, he would be changed, free from the conflict brought by religion and ready to be a part of the father's home. The father saw him coming from a far distance, felt compassion, ran toward him, and embraced him. This is a far cry from those who never send the rebellious son away to learn a relationship. Every time that son shows up, dread, fear, anger, frustration, and conflict come with him. The world can teach a child sent out what a parent cannot, that only a relationship with Jesus can bring peace.

When the child returns there will be excitement, not the dread of seeing someone daily who is in rebellion against the relationship.

DAY 316
The Idol Maker

How then shall they call upon Him in whom they have not believed? And how shall they believe in Him whom they have not heard? And how shall they hear without a preacher? So faith comes from hearing, and hearing by the word of Christ.

—ROMANS 10:14, 17

I was told of a man who was an idol maker. One day he thought to himself, "I will cut the head off one of the idols and see if anything happens to me." Nothing happened. Next he cut off a hand and nothing bad happened. In the end he cut the idol in two and nothing happened. He came to the realization that something made with hands could not be a god. This revelation led him on a journey that found him at the feet of Jesus.

I was told by one missionary that people can be born again through a clear conscience without having to hear the name of Jesus. I did not believe it. Truth is where fact and faith meet. He could not produce a single person able to say that God gave him a new life before he later discovered that the new life was Jesus. However, though an unbeliever in a remote area cannot be born again, he could have a conversion in his thinking, as did the idol maker. Revelation can lead someone to Jesus.

DAY 317
The Issues of Marriage

Just as the Father has loved Me, I have also loved you;
abide in My love. . . . This is My commandment, that you
love one another, just as I have loved you.

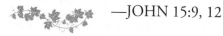

—JOHN 15:9, 12

Often I like to begin a discipleship session with a married couple by asking them to tell me everything a good marriage should give them. Their lists include fellowship, contentment, happiness, peace, joy, and companionship, just to mention a few. I then ask for Scripture to substantiate their claims and justify their complaints. The passage that most often comes to mind is Paul's admonition from Corinthians, "But I say to the unmarried and to widows that it is good for them if they remain even as I" (I Cor. 7:8). The point is not to discourage marriage but rather not to require out of marriage what only the Lord can give. An undercurrent in the Church today asserts that Christians whose marriages are not perfect are somehow second-class believers. I have seen faith in Christ work in a variety of areas but not in a systematic way. For some, faith first works in habits, for others in work relationships, some in attitudes, and still others in marriage. Yet He never seems to work according to our priorities and what we would believe to be of primary concern.

One of the main purposes of marriage, as I see it, is the destruction of self-centeredness. We simply cannot remain self-centered when there is someone else in the room. Having said that, I want to examine the four types of issues that present themselves and should be recognized in the marriage relationship: legitimate issues, issues of personality, Satanic issues, and issues of the flesh.

First, the legitimate issues, practical issues within a marriage. For example, I do not like being bound by a clock. However, it is not a major inconvenience for me to stop and call my wife when it appears I will be late. This is an issue of understanding how I operate and then making adjustments.

Second are issues of the personality. Thinkers, Feelers, and Doers all relate differently. Each shows love the differing way he or she desires to be loved. The Thinker loves truth and can appear cutting when communicating. The Feeler goes on and on, taking too much time to get to the point. The Doer likes to force his opinion. However, none of the above can always be equated with a lack of love or respect. Neither a Doer nor a Feeler like being stared at, not spoken to, or ignored; yet if married to a Thinker, all three of these will occur, and the mistake of associating a motive with the behavior can be easily made. Again, understanding must be exercised.

Third are issues the enemy likes to use to drive wedges between mates. These issues have no center, are rooted in bitterness and anger, build over time, and cause obsession and withdrawal, especially sexually. I am not sure why believers are commanded not to withdraw sexually, except

I have noticed that those who do find it progressively easier to remain in bitterness. "Stop depriving one another, except by agreement for a time, so that you may devote yourselves to prayer, and come together again lest Satan tempt you because of your lack of self-control" (I Cor. 7:5). It is my conviction that prayer is intensely personal, something between the child of God and his Father. However, there is a place for agreement in prayer, and often couples miss this aspect of defense when they are being attacked. A simple prayer together can break the satanic efforts.

Fourth is the issue of the flesh. We each need to deal with our own peculiar flesh patterns: the insecurities, the inability to allow others to be themselves or to have a bad day, and the reactions to certain messages that stir up carnal behavior. All will go well if we operate under the simple principle that no matter what other people do, we do not have any excuses for our own negative behavior.

One last point to consider is communication style, or how you communicate to those you love. Simply ask yourself how you tell someone something is wrong. Do you wait until you are angry, thus causing an explosion? Do you heap on condemnation? Do you attack with a vested interest in showing others how rotten they are? We are admonished to tell the truth in love, not in hostility, anger, or frustration. When there is a legitimate issue, share it in love, and remember that their response to your sharing has nothing to do with you.

DAY 318
The Judas Ministry

While I was with them, I was keeping them in Thy name
which Thou hast given Me; and I guarded them and not one
of them perished but the son of perdition,
that the Scripture might be fulfilled.

—JOHN 17:12

What a title to be given, "son of perdition." The term perdition means, "a state of final spiritual ruin; loss of the soul; damnation, hell." It was prophesied that Jesus would be delivered over, and Judas was the guide to those who arrested Him (Acts 1:16). Judas, motivated by pride and greed and possessed by Satan, did something unthinkable. After three years of eating, working, and ministering with Jesus, he betrayed Him. Judas ended his ministry lying to himself and to the Son of Man. At the revelation of his actions, Judas showed great remorse; others who denied Jesus were filled with grief, but it is only of Judas we read, "he went away and hanged himself" (Matthew 27:5).

However, all was not lost through the actions of Judas. It was because of his betrayal and Christ's subsequent loss of life that so many millions have received life. Jesus appeared before the disciples with the marks of death, received at the hand of a friend and proof of resurrection power. "To these He also presented Himself alive after His suffering, by many convincing proofs, appearing to them over a period of forty days and speaking of the things concerning the kingdom of God" (Acts 1:3).

Believers suffer in order that they might manifest the same resurrection power of Christ; suffering produces positive results. "But we do see Him who was made for a little while lower than the angels, namely, Jesus, because of the suffering of death crowned with glory and honor, that by the grace of God He might taste death for everyone" (Hebrews 2:9). "While being reviled, He did not revile in return; while suffering, He uttered no threats, but kept entrusting Himself to Him who judges righteously" (I Peter 2:23).

If suffering is essential to the Christian life, then it is logical that we need those who bring the suffering, those with a "Judas" ministry. I have observed in every family, church, club, mission organization, and office someone with the "Judas" ministry, one who will set out to discredit, deceive, betray, stir, cause strife, and hand the spiritual man over to those who will destroy him, that one person who stirs up all the others against the believer. It is the one pastor, elder, deacon, or chairman who puts the spiritual person in his gun sights, the one disagreeable staff member, parishioner, or neighbor who has the believer under the microscope and who has the unpleasant behavior that cooperates with the plan to perfect, bring life out of death in, and earn rewards for the believer. This type of person pays a high price to harass God's people; he bears the full weight of his behavior. After all, Judas had a terrible job description, and I am grateful it was his and not ours.

We are not to judge a latter-day "Judas," for all of life is judging him and he plays a great part in our spirituality by revealing in us a hidden power. Those who put Corrie ten Boom in prison for her faith paid a heavy price personally and, in the end, catapulted her into a worldwide ministry from which thousands came to know Christ. How will we learn of the freedom we have in Christ to love an enemy until the enemy emerges? Paul caught on. His first response was not to run from those in the "Judas" ministry, but to bless them for the work they were accomplishing in his life. "Bless those who persecute you; bless and curse not" (Romans 12:14). Notice Paul does not tell us to react to those in the "Judas" ministry, but to bless them, which will set us free from them and yield the resurrection power.

Paul said something interesting about those in the "Judas" ministry. "I hear that divisions exist among you; and in part I believe it. For there must also be factions among you, in order that those who are approved may have become evident among you" (I Corinthians 11:18 & 19). The "Judas" ministry must come, and those who are walking in resurrection life will be revealed. There is ultimately nothing that stands against the believer.

DAY 319
The Law Of Liberty

And I will walk at liberty, for I seek Thy precepts.
—PSALM 119:45

Liberty is a wonderful thing; it is complete freedom to do what we want. We are told to "so speak and so act as those who are to be judged by the law of liberty" (James 2:12). I would like to examine this law under which every believer lives, because the "one who looks intently at the perfect law, the law of liberty, and abides by it, not having become a forgetful hearer but an effectual doer, this man shall be blessed in what he does" (James 1:25).

It is easiest to understand the law of liberty by examining parents and children. Children, for the most part, live under the law of liberty. If the monetary contributions a child makes to a family for his first sixteen years of life were compared with his expenses, in most cases the child would be greatly lacking. Even so, the child is welcomed without consideration of this great debt. Continually mentioning the deficit would rob the child of all joy and bring him under bondage. Not mentioning it brings freedom. The child does not have to contribute financially; the child is free! What should he do with this freedom? What brings more joy to a parent is not to badger a child over and over to get something done, but when he comes home and is surprised to find the child has voluntarily done some chore. We are thrilled when something is done without asking—so thrilled that other failures are forgotten. We judge the child with the law of liberty, which allows him to do nothing and yet remain ours, or to do something loving and receive a clean slate and even reward for what he should have done anyway. What a deal!

"If you then, being evil, know how to give good gifts to your children, how much more shall your Father who is in heaven give what is good to those who ask Him" (Matthew 7:11). The parent/child relationship is only an illustration of a greater truth. God judges us with the law of liberty; His mercy is greater than judgment. We are His children through birth; we are accepted with no strings attached because of the life within, His life. He has given more than we will ever be able to give in return. We are free! What will we do with our freedom?

DAY 320
The Life Of a Sparrow

Are not five sparrows sold for two cents?
Yet not one of them is forgotten before God.
Indeed, the very hairs of your head are all numbered.
Do not fear; you are more valuable than many sparrows.

 —LUKE 12:6, 7

I must live as a sparrow. I must have the simplicity, the freedom, the joy, and the song of the sparrow. I am really quite suited for such a life, for anything else depletes me. Fortunately, there is only one secret to being a sparrow; a sparrow does not sow but merely reaps! If a sparrow were responsible to provide for itself, we would see a nervous, flittering wreck, not the simple bird which sings so beautifully each morning, who weathers every storm, and whose life preaches to me of the provision, rest, and love of a Father in heaven. I have a God no less than does the sparrow. It is my birthright! I must live as a sparrow.

DAY 321
The Longest Journey In the World

Therefore, just as the Holy Spirit says,
"Today, if you hear his voice."

—HEBREWS 3:7

It is often said that the journey of a thousand miles begins with a single step. True, and with each step one will find he is that much closer to the goal at the end of the thousand miles. However, there is a journey wherein one step will lead to the next step, and the next, and the next, but with each passing day the traveler will discover he is no closer to the goal. Some have spent a lifetime on this journey only to realize at the end of their lives that they are no closer than when they began. This impossible journey is the one to our past, a place to which we are not to go, and therefore a destination made unattainable by God. Many spend their lifetimes attempting to get to the past to fix it up so their future might get brighter. The deception is that in journeying to the past one forfeits his present and future life. God is the God of the "now." We only have this moment, and if God wanted us dwelling on the past, He would have made it possible for us to go back there to sort things out. Great misery comes from protecting ourselves in the memories of yesterday's events or thinking about ourselves in the situations of the past. A life lived looking toward the past is a sad and dark life marked by the retelling of the same story and singing the same note; it can communicate regret or the recounting of a time in history when one was "so happy." Either way, the enemy has us back where he wants us, missing life today. The enemy need only mention some embarrassing event, a painful moment, the time of false peace, a rejection, an abuse, or more to initiate an attempt to journey to the past, even though it has great cost and no benefit.

The only viable option is to live today in His mercies that are new every morning. I was once told I was teaching "denial"; of course, this is another carnal term outsourced from the world with its tentacles now in religion. My response to the complaint was simply this, "I can deny the Lord or I can deny myself, so denial it is." Honor God and bless yourself by denying your self-life. We cannot take lightly what we are taught by those who have gone ahead of us in the faith. Philippians 3:13, "Brothers, I do not consider myself yet to have taken hold of it. But one thing I do: Forgetting what is behind and straining toward what is ahead . . ." Some good news is that though you may have spent years putting one foot in front of the other in the unending journey to the past, it does not take an equal amount of time to backtrack and return to the present. You can return to the place you belong in this very moment. "Jesus, today I heard Your voice! Today You have called me, and today I have returned to You. I embrace what You have for this day, and Holy Spirit, grant me the grace never to return to the past." Your heart will slowly begin to sing.

DAY 322
The Man Who Loved God

The Lord has sought out for Himself a man after His own heart.

—I SAMUEL 13:14

It was said of David that he was a man after God's own heart. Then he had an affair. However, what God said about David was true before, during, and after the affair. The problem was never that David did not love God; the problem was that David did not know how much God loved him! It is easy to say, "God loves me," when we are doing everything right. However, do everything wrong and see if we can still say it! In defeat we can realize the depth and the riches of God's stand-alone love that is not dependent on us, but is the very nature of God.

DAY 323
The Marriage Pain Stick

And the glory which Thou hast given Me I have given to them, that they may be one, just as We are one; I in them, and Thou in Me, that they may be perfected in unity, that the world may know that Thou didst send Me, and didst love them, even as Thou didst love Me.

—JOHN 17:22, 23

I often like to mention this particular stick in marriage counseling. The illustration goes like this: The day you get married, God gives you a twenty-inch pain stick to eat. You can only eat one inch per year, and every inch is quite painful, since it involves the dissolution of pride, self, the desire to be adored, and much, much more. At any point you can—and many do—give up and give the stick a heave; you have had it. Who needs it? You can live quite well without marriage, thanks. With the passing of time, loneliness comes to the forefront (man is a social creature), and you find someone so totally different from the past mate that you are willing to pick up a new pain stick. However, this pain stick is exactly the same length as the one given on your previous wedding day, twenty inches. You must start all over again!

I readily admit that during 25 years of counseling, I have seen people I felt never should have gotten married, period! They have no skills for an intimate relationship or any desire to grow and become something different. Amen, God has something for everyone involved in such a union. Even Jesus said that Moses allowed divorce because of "hardness of heart." Some are hard by choice, and they will have to wear it. However, in the course of normal marriage struggles a couple gets to glimpse just how deeply they can sink in selfishness and stupidity. As one man said, "I was going so well in the Lord until my mate entered the room." What an admission!

We are commanded to love our enemies, and yet we avoid loving our mates. Well, we are all on a journey down our own path to discover God is God and we are not, He is love and we are not, He holds all things together and we do not. It is a great trip. Marriage is death, death, death, and more death to the thing we hold dear, our self-lives.

DAY 324
The Most Negative Man
Ever To Live? Jesus!

But Jesus, on His part, was not entrusting Himself
to them, for He knew all men, and because
He did not need anyone to testify concerning man,
for He Himself knew what was in man.

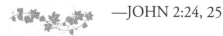

—JOHN 2:24, 25

Jesus was never a humanist who believed that man, given enough "education," would act in the proper manner. Therefore, He was not about broadcasting the suitable information on which man could act. The history of the human race has proven this one thing: man is inhumane, period. Paul echoed the same truth, "For I know that nothing good dwells in me, that is, in my flesh" (Romans 7:18). Jesus did not come to improve man through a system of religion; He came to remove the inner life of Adam (Romans 5) and replace it with His life (Colossians 3:4). He was not all gushy over mankind but rather was negative about man in his present condition. It was not until Pentecost that He would become positive about the second Adam, the new creation, the child of God, for man without Christ is nothing about whom to be optimistic. The first Adam was of the earth and the second from Heaven, and so we have the earthly and also the heavenly, says Paul, who had the revelation of what we truly are (I Corinthians 15:40-49). I can be positive about the believer and aloof from the delusions of the unbeliever. Even the great humanitarians display their foolishness with discussions concerning the goodness of man apart from Christ; their words fall flat and lose their appeal in the light of history.

DAY 325
The Move Of the Spirit

When the day of Pentecost had come, they were all together in one place. And suddenly there came from heaven a noise like a violent rushing wind, and it filled the whole house where they were sitting.

—ACTS 2:1, 2

Pentecost is worth enjoying. There was a time in the Church when Whitsunday (the coming of the Spirit) was celebrated more than Christmas (Christ among us). He is just as much in us as He is among us. In fact, what makes a person Pentecostal is not believing in gifts and miracles but in Jesus' residing within us. Pentecost gives a deathblow to religion by taking Christianity completely out of the realm of religion. The move of the Spirit was not generated from within but from without. In the same way, any move of the Spirit today would be initiated by the Spirit. If an expression is not initiated by the flesh, the proof comes when those who have the experience do not point others back to the experience, but will point them to the One who gave the experience. To say a particular expression is of the Spirit and then to point people to the expression is proof that it is not of God. In religion, the experience becomes the focal point and the experience is fought for. In Pentecost, Jesus is the issue; people are pointed to Him, where they will get what they need. Personally, I never understood how there could be a move of the Spirit, and yet for me to have it, I had to work and move my flesh. If He came to the original recipients without the initiation of man, then why would He not come to me without my instigating it? Why must I be convinced, be in the right place, and believe a certain thing? Can we all simply look to Jesus and let the Spirit initiate what He wants?

DAY 326
The "Mumble-Me"

And He summoned the multitude with His disciples, and said to them, "If anyone wishes to come after Me, let him deny himself, and take up his cross, and follow Me."

—MARK 8:34

I have said it before, but it bears repeating, and I am only telling you what I have done. I have joked with Betty and said, "The problem with our family is that everyone is too self-centered just to think about me." It gets to the heart of the issue. Sometimes I find believers who are "mumble-me's," like the bumblebee but instead of making that annoying buzzing sound, they continue to make a me-me-

me-me-me-me sound. Everything is about "me." "What did you do for me?" "How have you offended me?" "What about my needs?" "Why don't you respect me?" Always me! It is sickening, it gets old, and we just want them to go away. It is far more annoying than the bumblebee.

Remember, the cure to being selfish is to be selfless. Can you, as a mumble-me, take up the challenge to go one day without thinking about or mentioning yourself? I bet you cannot do it for twenty-four hours, but it wouldn't hurt you any to try, and it would be a great blessing to all of us! "Me, me, me!" Here is a newsflash: God is concerned about you. He loves you, but He loves the Son more. Everything is centered in the Son; the Son is the issue. Allow the Son to fill your thoughts; He is far and away more uplifting than self. Make a list of the Son's names and meditate on Him every time you want to mumble. It really will bless your life.

DAY 327
The Need For Suffering

And a woman who had been suffering from a hemorrhage
for twelve years, came up behind Him and
touched the fringe of His cloak.

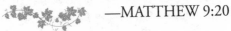

—MATTHEW 9:20

There are things learned in suffering that cannot be learned in comfort, and therefore man is in need of suffering! It is interesting to hear the stories from some of those who experienced prison in Siberia under the Soviet Union. The reported suffering was very severe, and in fact, many were purposely taken to Siberia to die. Despite no shelter, food, or clothing, some survived. Amid such intense suffering, it was possible to create a very small niche of comfort. Someone had the idea of making shoes out of potato sacks with paper placed in the bottom for insulation; that netted a little comfort. Others discovered how to catch the little snowbirds for an added protein delight, gaining a little more comfort. Some discovered how to make charcoal drawings from the ashes for a little creative comfort. Man simply cannot thrive with only suffering. Many witness to the fact that some simply lost the will to live without some comfort.

In the same way, however, there is a need for some suffering. Man cannot live in comfort alone. In fact, the comfortable Western world is in such need for suffering that it actually manufactures it. Because I travel where people do consistently suffer, it sometimes seems ridiculous to me to see what an American can call suffering. Many in the world would love to experience Americans' level of suffering. There are howls over the most vague injustices, the unending pictures of the homeless, the slightest perceived infractions of rights, and the inequities of society. The media is nearly comical in its pursuit of the discovery of some perceived suffering. It only confirms the inherent need man must have for some kind of suffering. Those who never suffer lack character. I often see kids who at age twenty are sitting around waiting for the perfect job. They do not want to suffer through something not perfect. Can the caste-born man in India imagine a twenty-something without a job because it would not be fun? We learn so much of what Christ can be in us by doing the things that are not fun. Was it fun for God to be in a human body? Was it fun for Him to help provide for His mother and siblings? Was it fun to have so little of a hearing among His contemporaries? Yet in all those non-fun activities we see a victorious Man we want living in us. The Western world in its shallow pursuit of comfort has lost character. Having an enemy is suffering, but learning that Jesus can love an enemy through us is sheer delight. We need suffering, and I will tell you something already known by many: Suffering is coming! It is coming to the West! It is not to be feared, for its purpose will be the perfecting of the hearts that are for Him. Remember when it comes that our brothers and sisters who live amid suffering in a multitude of countries witness to the fact that God is greater.

DAY 328
The "Now What?" Ministry

If we confess our sins, He is faithful and righteous to forgive us our sins and to cleanse us from all unrighteousness. If we say that we have not sinned, we make Him a liar and His word is not in us.

—I JOHN 1:9, 10

We constantly learn from others. All discipleship we have received—whether good or bad—passes through our Lord's hands and is a positive in our lives. From two men in particular I have learned greatly by their negative discipleship; both taught me through their example the folly of taking credit for the work of God in a believer's life and the stupidity of marching to one's own praise band, refusing any criticism. This awareness of negative discipleship's being a positive in me leaves me with the hope that my negatives can be a positive for others! It has also caused me not to place so much weight on criticism (which has often been mindless). However, here is a criticism I just do not understand; it is fairly consistent, so I have to take it to Jesus and ask if there is validity in it. There seem to be a bunch of believers who do not have in their paradigm the concept that a Christian who has failed can move forward in Christ and not have to suffer the consequences of his sins for the rest of his life. In their minds, his failure does and should make him a second-class Christian the rest of his life. I am accused of not being hard enough on sin, taking Christians' failure lightly, talking about mercy, and, in so doing, giving a passive consent to sin. I keep saying, "I do not," and I keep hearing, "Yes, you do." There is no evidence behind the accusations; I have never condoned sin, moral failures, self-righteousness, judgmental attitudes, spiritual exclusivity, or those who cause division. But in the world in which I live, I do meet believers who have fallen into all of the above categories and more; that is a fact. So my question after their repentance is, "Now what?" I have a "Now What?" ministry.

To a large extent the Epistles are written addressing the problems into which believers have fallen, having taken their focus off of Christ. It is not a stretch to say that every person who enjoys reading the Epistles is indebted to believers who on some level failed. In essence, we learn from their failures. Without these varied problems we would lack a good portion of the New Testament! We also must see the additional aspect of the writers' wanting the believers redeemed, pressing on, renewed in their love for Christ, and expressing the life of Jesus within them. There is no hint of a suggestion indicating that once their problem is addressed and they have repented, they must live a life of consequences in self-condemnation.

I remember when a prominent "evangelist" said, "Any man who has had an immoral thought is an outcast and can never minister." Three days later his photo was taken, amply showing his own immorality. No believer is a castaway. Christians fall, but we must let them see they can fall forward into the lap of love. They need not live in regret. I have often taught that it is not wise for a believer to marry an unbeliever, but the fact remains that some do. Now what? Repeatedly tell the believers they are out of the will of God, until we drive them away from God, and in so doing compound their problems? No, we tell them to keep moving forward in Christ and not to allow their decision to define them, to let Jesus, and Jesus alone, define them. You get the picture, and the list of shortcomings of believers goes on.

I have noticed a jealousy among the religious (defined as those who believe success rests in their hands with the many things they must do) when they see the freedom enjoyed by faith persons (defined as those believing in resting in Jesus and His Righteousness, for nothing is impossible for Jesus). It is easy for the religious to judge as hopeless someone when his flesh flows in a ravine theirs does not. Here is the warning: God can turn that same critical light on them, and they will not stand. Judgmental people are keeping their own list while failing at His list always. Having examined the options, I must line up on the side of faith and believe there is a glorious "Now what?" for every believer who has had a failure.

DAY 329
The Pain Of Recovery

As an example, brethren, of suffering and patience, take the prophets who spoke in the name of the Lord. We count those blessed who endured. You have heard of the endurance of Job and have seen the outcome of the Lord's dealings, that the Lord is full of compassion and is merciful.

—JAMES 5:10, 11

I remember my grandfather when his hip had become faulty. With each passing day his appearance deteriorated and he would look older, though he was a man who was strong through hard work and never retired. At any rate, I gradually grew accustomed to seeing the old man. At length came the point at age 80 when he could not farm, do mechanic work, or build as he used to. It was time for a new hip. I wanted to be with him for the operation and sat in the hall as the hip was replaced. After what seemed like an eternity, they let me go in his room, and I was shocked at what I saw. He looked twenty years younger! I had mistakenly thought his drawn face reflected who he was, but when the pain lifted, he was a new man. I could not believe he had grown so accustomed to the pain, especially since he never even took an aspirin and always said he felt great. The pain of the hip had been so much greater than the pain of recovery that he actually felt better already while still in recovery.

We may suffer pain for years, and in the end, there will be a pain associated with recovery, but we can remember it is not as great as the pain that preceded it! Whether a divorce from a marriage which had spiraled into abuse, a death of a loved one who struggled with addiction, or a departure from ongoing rejection, the recovery is much more pleasant than the constant daily pain that came before. Apparently we can become so accustomed to such situations that we get numb to the pain associated with them. The events leading up to the operations God performs in our lives are more hurtful than the stinging recovery that ensues. When any of us are suffering from recovery, remember that we have the witness of many believers who have gone ahead: There is life after suffering. Also, let our history with the Lord, as well as the encouraging history of others, carry us. Remember, the purpose of life is to know Him; that is an absolute. We will know Him in a good marriage, a bad marriage, divorce, and post marriage. We will learn of Him even after sin, for children who rebel return to walk with God. There is no waste in God. Everything is for our good.

DAY 330
The Peace Of God

And let the peace of Christ rule in your hearts, to which indeed you were called in one body; and be thankful.

—COLOSSIANS 3:15

One day while visiting the mountains I noticed the eagle between the great heights, suspended above all the world, stopping, observing, listening, watching, waiting, and resting. Perfect peace! This is like the peace of Jesus. In prayer we recognize we have been placed in Him, and He is in the great I AM. Not only does Christ dwell in us, but we dwell in Him as surely as the eagle is at home in the heights. We can take time to be quiet, settle our mind, and acknowledge by faith that we have entered into Him. In Him it is quiet; we float above earthly cares in rest and peace. With no effort we wait for a whisper from Him, the gentle blowing of the wind (His Spirit). The peace of God holds us. We are silent. We watch, observe, stop, and listen. We are in Him, suspended. In this place I call the peace of God we can pray for hundreds in seconds. We do not try to change His will; we see the wisdom of it and are comforted by it. We even rejoice in what others would say is bad. Oh, to be the eagle, to float in His peace. I have been there. It was only a visit, but one day I will reside there permanently.

DAY 331
The Pit

We have this treasure in jars of clay to show that this all-surpassing power is from God and not from us. We are hard pressed on every side, but not crushed; perplexed, but not in despair.

—II CORINTHIANS 4:7, 8 [NIV]

Often as a child I would watch a mystery movie. Typically a scene would show an unsuspecting victim opening a stairwell door to discover the thing he or she feared most. I remember silently screaming, "Don't open the door!" However, the door was always opened and the victim destroyed. Similarly, when discipling I perceive impending danger to a believer, such as the distinct possibilities of a destroyed relationship, overwhelming sin, and personal harm. Many times the warning is not heeded and the believer—with full understanding of the possibilities of the future—marches straight into danger and stupidity. In short, he opens the door that should remain closed and becomes a victim.

I have often pondered the enemy's ability to dig a pit for the unsuspecting. However, I stand in awe at God's ability to do something far greater. Yes, the enemy does dig the pit, but unknowingly, as he mounds up the dirt, he is building a ready access to God. How often I have witnessed a believer standing in a pit, the enemy believing the end is near, and then God speaks. The believer turns around toward the voice and there, in front of him, is a mountain reaching up to the presence of God. I have personally observed children in an alcoholic environment, women with unfaithful mates, individuals in bankruptcy, and people with dashed dreams all turn to find that the pit had actually become the vehicle for moving into the presence of God.

In every situation we must ask, "Is God with us?" "How is this pit to become a mountain?" "Do we not have a God?" Many times, upon seeing those we love standing at the edge of the pit, we panic, race to help, and attempt to fill the pit. We forget that we have a God greater than the pit, a God who will take all the effort of the enemy and with a word turn it into the vehicle by which our loved ones rediscover Him. In finding Him, they find life.

Many believers become frantic to ensure none of the unpleasant things that brought them to Christ ever happen to their own children. I will continue to warn about the pits, but I will also continue to trust in the living God to make the pit a mountain. We never need to be undone, for we have a great God.

DAY 332
The Races Of Man

Then God said, "Let Us make man in Our image, according to Our likeness; and let them rule over the fish of the sea and over the birds of the sky and over the cattle and over all the earth, and over every creeping thing that creeps on the earth." God created man in His own image, in the image of God He created him; male and female He created them. God blessed them; and God said to them, "Be fruitful and multiply, and fill the earth, and subdue it; and rule over the fish of the sea and over the birds of the sky, and over every living thing that moves on the face of the earth."

—GENESIS 1:26-28

What is discussed in different parts of the world is always interesting to me. I have often noted that I have a theological paradigm. Others do, as well, and sometimes what is important to me is not to them, and vice versa. This is easily settled by acknowledging each of us is only one thread in the tapestry of Christian life, and together we are, in fact, a body. Oneness does not come from agreeing on what we believe but in agreeing on Him in whom we trust, Christ. The topic of race seems to turn up everywhere, though there is a huge difference between the racism practiced in most countries—where one geographical group considers itself superior to another—and the racism that sees another people group as less human or even nonhuman. I suppose there is an element of racism that came with the Tower of

Babel as men separated into language groups. The pride of man came to the forefront, and instead of seeing the wickedness that caused the separation, man began to boast in the separation and view his people in his language group as superior; this would easily transfer to include his "race." Race has caused many wars; however, the majority of these wars did not stem from seeing others as not actually being human. This is my problem with evolution, since some races unavoidably are seen as "links" to the superior race, the survival of the fittest! The earlier diagrams from the Theory of Evolution are disturbing. I suppose in some way the Tower of Babel introduced an aspect of segregation, but it did not introduce the concept of dehumanizing man. That task has been left to the wicked around the world, and they do it in a variety of ways.

I am asked, "What do you think of interracial marriage?" What a question! First, I would want to know the purpose of the question and whether affirmation or denial is desired from the answer. Some in their flesh have a vested interest in a negative or a positive response. To these I really have nothing to say, for it is not what they are doing but the why that will condemn them. Amen. Presently I am thinking of some very big-hearted believers in other countries; they have asked the question in humility, honesty, and sincerity. On the other hand, those who dehumanize others often hide behind the argument that God separated the races at the Tower of Babel, one of the sons of Noah was cursed, or Cain was given a mark after he killed his brother. This is actually even believed by many in Africa. While the Biblical events are all true, none has a single thing to do with dehumanizing people.

Then there is a parallel drawn from nature in the suggestion that birds and fish stay within their "kind," and so people naturally segregate, and so on. Back to creation, God created man, singular, and He created fish and birds, plural. Within the fish of the sea, God put within them a boundary, and the same is true of all the birds of the air; if not, the uniqueness of the ocean and the skies would be at risk. In that spirit, Paul states that there are different kinds of flesh. I Corinthians 15:38, 39, "But God gives it a body just as He wished, and to each of the seeds a body of its own. All flesh is not the same flesh, but there is one flesh of men, and another flesh of beasts, and another flesh of birds, and another of fish." The flesh of animals (many KINDS) is different from the flesh of man (singular, in that it is one KIND). I agree with a point an African was making, a rather simple one. Each kind of fish was to remain within its kind. Man, too, is to remain within his kind, and his kind is human, notwithstanding some differences within mankind that are easily understood considering the dispersion of man after the expulsion from the garden, the flood, isolation, migration, and recessive and dominant genes within man. These are only differences in appearance within the group of man. Man is man, and man can only marry within his kind. (Of course, this excludes the notion of homosexual "marriage," which is not marriage, since the two cannot become one.) When man, who might appear different from someone of his own kind, marries, there is nothing in Scripture against that. Romans 2:10,11, "but glory and honor and peace to everyone who does good, to the Jew first and also to the Greek. For there is no partiality with God." The validity of interracial marriage is not up for debate. However, something else not up for debate that should be is the impropriety of scientists who break the commandment of God by mixing "kinds" in the laboratory.

DAY 333
The Result Of the Fall

She gave also to her husband with her, and he ate.
—GENESIS 3:6

Then the Lord said, "My Spirit shall not strive with man forever, because he also is flesh . . .

—GENESIS 6:3

I was riding with a professor of theology and asked, "Tell me, what is the main result of the fall?" He mentioned separation, death, sickness, depravity, and more. I then said, "I want to tell you something. If you receive it, it will shake your theological world and change everything—how you see God, how you see yourself, how you see others—and God will get bigger than He has ever been! The result of the fall is Christ in you, the hope of glory."

God had one Son in heaven; this Son needed a bride. God's plan was to have many sons in heaven to make a bride for the One Son. If man had not fallen, the world would be perfect and populated with perfect people, but there would be no sons in heaven. It means that Jesus was not Plan B. God is not playing catch-up to sin, Satan, and the world. Jesus was the lamb slain from the foundation of the world. The whole thing was in the mind of God from the beginning. Does this mean God is the author of sin? No, may it never be. Does it mean God knew putting man in a body of flesh would lead to sin? Yes. Think about it. Man is made in the image of God. What would make him submit to God? Therefore, God gives him what he wants: freedom to choose, freedom to have a kingdom, righteousness, and strength, and freedom to imitate God. The end result is that man, not God, messes the whole thing up. However, in messing the whole thing up, man is not willing to exercise his chooser to choose God's kingdom, glory, strength, and righteousness. This means the defective life of man will need to be replaced, which can only happen through a new birth and Christ in man, making more sons for heaven. Wonderful! Beautiful! Oh, the depth of the riches of the wisdom of God.

Instead of weeping over your failure, why don't you ask why you failed, then release yourself to God at the point of your why? The why is what He is dealing with. He knew there would be failures, and He is using them. He is not playing catch-up with Satan. If God is for us, then who can be against us?

DAY 334
The Revelation: He Does Not Hate Me!

And hope does not disappoint, because the love of God
has been poured out within our hearts through
the Holy Spirit who was given to us.

—ROMANS 5:5

"God so loved the world." Considering everything we know about the world, if we dwell on the thought of how God loves the world, we will be overwhelmed. We have all seen more than our share of wickedness, and yet He loved the world! Now, if God loves the wicked world, would it make sense to think He would not love His own children? No, we are not comparing our righteousness to the world's and coming out looking more deserving. We are just examining His love. The following are soul killers for a Christian to believe about God: He hates him, is disappointed with him, has decreed he has not measured up, or has had it with him. When we believe God hates us, we shut down, withdraw, wither, move into guilt and regret, and become resigned. Messages that tell us God is upset with us bombard us through sermons full of comparing, accusing, spreading guilt, condemning, and judging. We hear, "Will God know you? Will God say, 'Depart from Me, for I never knew you'? Will you put your hand to the plow and look back?" Legalists work so hard to get a person in the faith and then go into overdrive to kick him out by making it look like he has come up short. Simply put, we just will not approach a God we think is mad at us, but by avoiding Him, we avoid LIFE and the solutions to all our failures. See how important it is for us to know God really does love us and is not angry with us? To know God entered into our humanity, lived in a fleshly body, and is not surprised by what we have done?

Let me warn you to believe God loves you or you will have to prove it through nightmarish experiences. He will withdraw His grace until you cry "Uncle!" and admit you make no contribution or have any hope of being loved. In that spiritual fetal position you will then hear Him say, "I never stopped loving you."

I must know He loves me. I must be able to get up after a failure and not believe I need to work my way back to acceptance. I must have a God whose love is that big. I remember a blown day (actually, there are too many to remember). I blew the meeting, I blew the message, I blew my temper, I blew my judgments; it was a completely blown day. I went to sleep with those two haunting fears I have when I am feeling at my worst: first, that I would wake up still alive, and second, that I would make it through another day. However, in the morning I felt beautiful. I did not have a care. I did not have a hint of condemnation. I kept thinking how strange it was. Then I did the unthinkable and rationalized to myself that why, when I was having such a beautiful day, was I going to mention to God all of my failures from the previous day? Well, I did, and He said, "I do not want to talk about those. I love you. Let's move on." Yes!!! From the world we get the idea that when we fail, we are abandoned, cut off. This carnal trait of reacting is not to be transferred to the Father in heaven.

DAY 335
The Revelation Of Love

*And though you have not seen Him, you love Him, and
though you do not see Him now, but believe in Him, you
greatly rejoice with joy inexpressible and full of glory.*

—I PETER 1:8

Those in ministry would bring to our attention many
revelations, such as the revelations of our flesh, our sin, our
failure at being good parents, our attitudes, and our lies.
However, the most important revelation, greater than all
of these put together, is of how much you really love Jesus.
Why are you miserable when dabbling in the flesh, walking
in sin, being offended, pursuing material gain, and having
friendship with the world? I will tell you! It is because you
love Christ! In the deepest part of your being, you are in
love with Him. Manifestations of sin, Satan, the world,
and the flesh will always attempt to keep you from this
revelation, and though you find no satisfaction in them,
they whisper "more" at all times. If you can admit that you
truly love Him, can go nowhere else and want nothing
else, then all those things of the flesh must flee. I want to
be clear: We do not lay aside the flesh so we can love Jesus
more deeply; we lay it aside because we do love Him. Our
misery with the flesh is proof of our love for Him alone,
and nothing else. This takes revelation. He will permit the
flesh to take you to the bottom to prove it to you. Have
you had enough? You love Him. Shout it, "I love Him, I
love nothing else, nothing else will ever satisfy, and all of
life has been proving it to me!" Amen!

DAY 336
The Reversal

*Therefore humble yourselves under the mighty hand of
God, that He may exalt you at the proper time, casting all
your anxiety on Him, because He cares for you.*

—I PETER 5:6 & 7

We have mentioned it before, but it is worth noting
again how God gives a promise, but then comes the reversal
before finally the fulfillment. I have observed God's normal
way of working is to make us dissatisfied with where we
are before He opens another door. It makes sense, because
few would walk through a new door if they were totally
satisfied with where they were. However, after the open
door comes the reversal.

Joseph was given a promise about how the sun and moon
and eleven stars would bow down at his feet. After the
promise came a stripping, a deep pit, being sold as a slave,
false accusations, and prison, every one of which worked
together to make him the type of person who could handle
the fulfillment. One day from his throne he looked out
to see his eleven brothers bowing, and guess what? He
could handle it, for his deep trials had made him a man of
grace and mercy. Without the pit-to-prison preparation,
the throne would have been a curse and his undoing. As it
was, the throne became a place of salvation.

I will keep repeating myself until others can finish my
sentence. One "praise God" before we understand His
workings is worth a thousand "praise God's" later when
the trials are over.

DAY 337
The Right Road

"My grace is sufficient for you, for my power is make
perfect in weakness." Therefore I will boast all the more
gladly about my weaknesses,
so that Christ's power may rest on me.
—II CORINTHIANS 12:9 [NIV]

It is so important to be on the right road. For years you have been trying to do better. If only you could make a final, lasting decision to do better. But you have not been able to. Why? Doing better was the wrong goal. Giving up and trusting Him is the right decision. Once you see the difference, you will see that God permitted you to live in defeat for a reason. You will see why God put man, a spiritual being, in flesh similar to an animal's. He knew the spirit of Adam would not overcome the flesh! He did not intend it to. He intended for you to try to overcome in your own strength, become defeated and discouraged, and embrace His strength. "Power perfected in weakness!" It was the will of God (the mind and heart of God) that you be defeated and discover His strength. Beautiful! We see again how nothing is out of control, all is done in His wisdom, and His goal is the revelation of Christ in you, the hope of glory. The right choice is to give up, trust God, and abide. Then you will pray, read, and love when needed. Simple! Our God has done it all!

DAY 338
The Sin Of Presumption, Part I

*And seeing at a distance a fig tree in leaf, He went to
see if perhaps He would find anything on it; and when He
came to it, He found nothing but leaves, for it was not the
season for figs. And He answered and said to it,
"May no one ever eat fruit from you again!"
And His disciples were listening.*

—MARK 11:13, 14

He sees a fig tree, finds no figs, for it is not the season
for figs, and the tree is cursed for not having fruit out of
season. That seems odd, but perhaps not so odd in the
context of things. It is springtime, there is an orchard, and
none of the trees have leafed out, save one tree that is early.
Why would one tree have leaves this early? A fig tree is the
only tree that cannot fool man, for the flower and the fruit
are one. An apple tree can be full of blossoms and yet not
yield a single apple. Not so with the fig. Jesus examines the
tree and discovers that though it stands out and above its
brothers, it is nothing more than a hypocrite. It looks so
mature and better than the rest, but it is all just show. "I
see men as trees," said the blind man on the way to being
cured. So did Jesus, in the sense that He cursed the fig tree
and went directly to the temple to do the same with men
who had put themselves above others, even though they
had no fruit.

DAY 339
The Sin Of Presumption, Part II

Peter answered Him and said, "Lord, if it is You,
command me to come to You on the water." And He said,
"Come!" And Peter got out of the boat, and walked on
the water and came toward Jesus. But seeing the wind, he
became afraid, and beginning to sink, he cried out, saying,
"Lord, save me!" And immediately Jesus stretched out His
hand and took hold of him, and said to him, "O you of
little faith, why did you doubt?"

—MATTHEW 14:28-31

Why did Peter assume that Jesus wanted him to walk
on water? What made Peter think he was to participate in
the spectacular? Why is Peter making Jesus prove Himself?
Well, here is the awesome thing about choice: a person can
have what he wants. If he wants to be "like" Jesus, He will
let him try. Jesus was already going to Peter. Why did Peter
want to go to Him? What was in it for Peter? Jesus comes
to us; He has started the journey, and He will get to us.
In every other religion it is man working his way to God.
But we know that Jesus comes to us, and if we break the
order, we drown. No man has the power, the system, or
even the faith for the journey to Jesus, Who is the greatest.
We cannot find Him. As the greatest, He must make the
journey to us. Our doubt and lack of faith will always be
revealed, so I believe it is better to acknowledge our doubt
and little faith and let Him come to us. He will find us; He
found the disciples in the midst of the storm.

DAY 340
The Source Of a Decision:
Fear Or the Loss Of Peace

*Nebuchadnezzar the king to all the peoples, nations, and
men of every language that live in all the earth: "May your
peace abound! It has seemed good to me to declare the signs
and wonders which the Most High God has done for me.
How great are His signs and how mighty are His wonders!
His kingdom is an everlasting kingdom and
His dominion is from generation to generation."*

—DANIEL 4:1-3

A condition called buyer's remorse can arise after
purchasing something like an automobile and then
wondering the next day if the right thing were done.
If the doubt lingers long enough, it will turn into fear.
Sometimes this is a valid experience. Many find they
have been pressured into making a purchase they later
regret; they actually did make a bad decision. However,
the problem is that an emotion like buyer's remorse can
have at its source fear or a lack of peace, and both will
feel the same way. When I purchased my house (the best
investment I ever made), I was filled with fear. "How will
I make the payments? What if I lose the house?" I had the
peace of God when I bought the house, but the enemy
and my humanity (wanting to be a success at playing God)
attempted to prompt me to surrender my peace to the
situation. Fear began directing me rather than the peace of

God. I can have fear and the peace of God at the same time; I just need to recognize the difference. I must ask myself, "Was God leading me? Did I not lift the situation up to Him? Isn't it impossible to lead sheep that are not moving? Isn't it His job to take me to the right place?" Then I can see that my decision was made in peace and I cannot let fear drive me, even if the situation does not work out as I thought it should. For example, what if I lose my job and cannot make the house payments? That does not mean I was not listening on the day He led me to buy it. Some will say this is a cop-out. Well, amen. We Christians are the only ones allowed a cop-out, because our God causes all things to work together for the good.

Christians have made mistakes and at times been bad witnesses of the Truth, but they are the only positive in a negative world. Again, the world takes one of its own who is a .5% success, puts him under a magnifying glass, and tries to make it look as if he were a 100% success without Christ. I have been accused of tearing down the accomplishments of non-Christians. Well, amen. I do not do it by way of judgment, but to prove the point that these people were not the successes without Christ we were led to believe they were. Also, those who accuse me of this do the very same thing with anyone and everything Christian. I do not buy it. Without Christ's life in man, we would be in the dark ages. Think, too, about how Christians are the only ones whose belief system allows for them to take criticism. Try to criticize a Muslim, Hindu, Buddhist, or a Communist and see how far it goes. It will not be heard or accepted. Since Christians are the ones who listen, they get the majority of complaints directed toward them. Watchdog groups in the world make more noise about a single instance of discrimination within a Christian country than it does a wholesale slaughter in a non-Christian country. Why? The Christian has a higher standard, that being the behavior of Christ. The Christian is sensitive toward others because he is cognizant of having received mercy, and he will show it in return. The problem is that the world is constantly making an appeal to the wrong people. Christ and His family simply are not messing up the world, as alleged.

DAY 341
The Spiritual Leader?

But do not be called Rabbi; for One is your Teacher, and you are all brothers. And do not call anyone on earth your father; for One is your Father, He who is in heaven. And do not be called leaders; for One is your Leader, that is, Christ. But the greatest among you shall be your servant.

 —MATTHEW 23:8-11

Jesus, the Head of the Church, is the individual believer's spiritual head. When standing before God to give an account to the Head, Christ, I do not believe anyone would be justified in telling Him, "Jesus, I was not following You because my husband (or my pastor) was not leading spiritually." We are a corporate body and a corporate family; it is simply the Way of things. Being the head of a household—the husband—or the head of the church—the pastor—is organizational in nature for

God. I understand it perfectly well from a management standpoint. One bad leader is better than five attempting to lead at the same time. However, a woman ought to realize that her covenant with Christ will always override the one with her husband. Men and women alike are ultimately accountable to God for their personal, spiritual life.

I do not know when people started using the phrase, "spiritual leader, spiritual head," in reference to a husband or a pastor. Often the husband and pastor are carnal, and women are waiting around for a carnal person to become a "spiritual leader"; that makes no sense to me. Also, what about the woman with an unbelieving husband; is she in an impossible place when it comes to following Jesus? Also, many wives press their husbands to be more spiritual (I hear of it all the time). Then there is the pressure on the husband to begin to perform for the wife and come under a microscope, for the wife's spiritual condition is said to rest on the husband's changing. It puts the wife's spiritual growth in the hand of another, again something I cannot find in Scripture. Then, too, any husband not responding to the pressure is perceived as having moved out of a personal relationship with Christ. The same could be said of the Christian Religion; often the pastor is carnal, but it does not excuse those in the congregation from having a vibrant and meaningful relationship to Christ. I remember the time my grandfather came to the realization that his pastor was anti-Christ, and he promptly went to the church building and told them to take his name off the "church" registry.

Christ is the Head and therefore the One who directs the body, since the head is the source of the body. However, the head does not have the power to make the body agree with it; the body must willingly agree with the head. In the same way, the Church is organizational, given leaders, and there are requirements; however, the individual members do not have to follow. A true leader does not take choice away from those in the body; a leader's responsibility is to lead, and whether he is followed or not is due to a choice made individually by the members. In a sense, a true leader is not recruiting but leading, and people fall in behind because of their choice. This is also true in the family. There is often heard a cry among husbands that their wife does not follow. Actually, more often than not I find out the men are not leading. The husband is responsible to God for leading, but no wife is to be arm-twisted or Bible-thumped to follow. It is the wife's responsibility, by choice, to follow or not. The two are not connected. The command to the husband is to be the head, the leader. If he looks around and sees no one following, he must continue to lead, and so be it. The wife chooses if she wants to follow the Lord in letting her husband lead, and in so doing, she has relieved herself of all the arguments concerning how her husband is not a fit leader. If the wife chooses not to follow and vies for the headship herself, in this case also the husband is not to be excused or deterred from leading. "And whatever you do in word or deed, do all in the name of the Lord Jesus, giving thanks through Him to God the Father" (Colossians 3:17).

DAY 342
The Teeter-Totter Syndrome

*For the mind set on the flesh is death, but the mind set on
the Spirit is life and peace, because the mind set on the flesh
is hostile toward God; for it does not subject itself to
the law of God, for it is not even able to do so.*

—ROMANS 8:6, 7

One of the diagrams I use is of a corral with black horses
and white horses. The point in the diagram is that if the
gate is left open, both colors of horses will escape. If we
open the door to the flesh, the unrighteous and the self-
righteous flesh will both come running to escape and express
themselves. Self-righteousness will lead to unrighteousness;
hence, the rampant growth of immorality among the self-
righteous. The converse is also true. It has taken me years to
see it, but when I put my mind on autopilot, before I know
it I am thinking of mistakes I have made and giving myself
a sound beating over failures, especially in my relationships
with others. I go over what could have been said to help
more, and blah, blah, blah. However, here is what I
noticed. Within minutes of thinking about what I might
have said, I will be thinking about how someone offended
me. Within minutes of thinking about a failure, I will be
thinking about another's failure. This understanding has
brought me to a place of what I believe is a healthy fear and
a deeper understanding of what the Bible says: "Finally,
brethren, whatever is true, whatever is honorable, whatever

is right, whatever is pure, whatever is lovely, whatever is of good repute, if there is any excellence and if anything worthy of praise, let your mind dwell on these things" (Philippians 4:8). Today, the moment I start to think about my failures, stupidity, embarrassments, offenses, or those of others, I immediately have a check in my spirit, heart, and mind that says, "If you go there, you will hang yourself by ending up in self-hatred. If you go there, you will be self- or man-centered, not Christ-centered." I immediately stop myself and move to Him. The freedom is something I have never experienced before. I am not being positive for the sake of being positive, which is shallow. I am merely setting my mind on the things above as I recognize I have been given the mind of Christ and that is where my mind belongs.

DAY 343
The Wooden Judge

Woe to you, scribes and Pharisees, hypocrites, because you travel around on sea and land to make one proselyte; and when he becomes one, you make him twice as much a son of hell as yourselves.

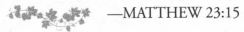

—MATTHEW 23:15

An exhibit in a museum in Peru displays some of the artifacts from an inquisition that took place there. One is a large wooden statue of Jesus. It seems the doctrinal judge would sit beside the statue, which had ropes running from the head, down its back, and under the judge's table. The accused would come and make their case to the wooden Jesus, having been led to believe Jesus was hearing each case. However, the judge was listening; if he thought a person was theologically correct, he pulled the ropes in such a way as to nod the head up and down to indicate Jesus' approval. If the judge did not like what he heard, he would pull the ropes to move the statue's head from right to left, signaling disapproval. In this case the person was executed. What a good illustration of a Pharisee. Today we still have the theological judges prepared for us to make the case for what we believe to them, and they do it under the guise of Jesus. They are "defenders of the faith," yes, but whose faith? Not the faith of Jesus but their own narrow faith. Romans 14:4, "Who are you to judge the servant of another? To his own master he stands or falls; and he will stand, for the Lord is able to make him stand."

Personally, I am no longer going to make my case to a judge's wooden Jesus. If I must make a case, I will make it to the Lord. David, when given the option of making his case to man or to God, quickly chose God (II Samuel 24:14), for at least with God there is compassion and mercy. The Pharisee will never show mercy. Hebrews 4:16, "Therefore let us draw near with confidence to the throne of grace, so that we may receive mercy and find grace to help in time of need."

DAY 344
Theological Differences

You search the Scriptures because you think
that in them you have eternal life;
it is these that bear witness of Me.

—JOHN 5:39

Over the years I have grown away from theological debates, understanding that unity could not come through the agreement of a creed or doctrine, but rather from agreement on whom we recognize and trust, Him in whom we believe. Out of that awareness has come the revelation of the Bible's purpose as being to testify about Jesus. As long as that premise is maintained, believers can have "growth discussions" on a variety of topics, for the underlying question will always be, "How does this passage testify to Christ?" The Bible is misused when it is quoted not to testify to Jesus but rather to testify to an individual's belief system. To say it another way, when the Bible is testifying to itself or to the thinking of an individual rather than to the living Word, Scripture becomes a source of division, pride, and dead doctrinal disputes.

DAY 345
Think On These Things, Part I

As you therefore have received Christ Jesus the Lord, so walk in Him, having been firmly rooted and now being built up in Him and established in your faith, just as you were instructed, and overflowing with gratitude. See to it that no one takes you captive through philosophy and empty deception, according to the tradition of men, according to the elementary principles of the world, rather than according to Christ. For in Him all the fullness of Deity dwells in bodily form, and in Him you have been made complete, and He is the head over all rule and authority.

—COLOSSIANS 2:6-10

Man is controlled through lies and philosophy; we actually know very few facts, and much of our thinking is covertly controlled. We need truth, not philosophy, control, or lies. The truth is Jesus, and once we walk in Him, we are no longer echoes of the fleshly desires of man. As we walk in Him, we gain control, not over governments, systems, or political parties, but of the only things we really can control with certainty. We cannot change the philosophies or the governments that exude them, but we can have control over ourselves. Jesus, Truth, brings freedom the rest of the world simply does not have. Christians have the potential to focus on the things most important: love, joy, peace, patience, kindness, goodness, faithfulness, gentleness, self-control; against such things there is no law. The world has no choice over anything other than which philosophy will deceive the people next. In the Book of The Revelation it is made clear what the end will be, and no amount of choice will stop the coming of the Lord. World issues are not anything over which we have choice. The real freedom Truth brings is the ability to choose to love the people who cut in front of us on the interstate, to wave at the neighbor who is more comfortable being hated, to be patient with a fallen world, to show kindness to those bound in self and sin, to be faithful to the one we love, to laugh (really laugh), to have the peace we receive from looking to Him, and to look to Him before we sin.

I do not want to control the world, for as I attempt it, I will find myself controlled by it. I only desire to have self-control by the power of the Spirit, which successfully operates in a communist, capitalist, kingdom, dictatorship, or socialist setting. The control I have in the Spirit is just as effective in a monastery, prison, or penthouse.

DAY 346
Think On These Things, Part II

See to it that no one takes you captive through philosophy and empty deception, according to the tradition of men, according to the elementary principles of the world, rather than according to Christ.

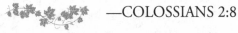

—COLOSSIANS 2:8

A dear friend told me of belonging to the Communist party in South America. He had worked himself through the ranks until one day he was invited to an upper-level party meeting. Upon entering the room he was overcome with the opulence of the facilities, the food, and even the maid service. To his credit, he confronted the leader and told him he was a phony, and he was immediately expelled. He had been deceived, but so are many in a capitalistic society. The philosophies we hold dear are only reality as they remain in the spoken realm; once they move from words to action, we find they lose power and give way to the flesh of man. Communism to the extreme is capitalism (just one big company), and capitalism to the extreme is communism (just one big company). All systems are filled with lofty philosophies of words in order that the participants not become discouraged and quit supporting the flesh of man that created them. India is full of millionaires and philosophies about why the poor are poor. Swiss banks are filled with assets from African millionaires that have some very lofty words for the person in the village who has no water or medical treatment. American politicians have spoken of their great societal strides of late, and yet I fear for my daughter walking from classroom to car.

The motive behind philosophy is to bring someone ELSE into subjection to MY thinking for MY advantage and MY comfort. Therefore, philosophy is not truth but limited understanding of how others could act to make my life better. It is the observation from one pair of shoes (mine) on how the world is, how it should be, and what someone else could do to change it. Philosophy is built, ultimately, on lies. Certainly it does not call for my sacrifice of taking up the cross of Christ.

DAY 347
This Is My Testimony

"How beautiful are the feet of those who bring good news of good things!" However, they did not all heed the good news; for Isaiah says, "Lord, who has believed our report?" So faith comes from hearing, and hearing by the word of Christ.

—ROMANS 10:15-17

"This is my testimony!" What a powerful thing to utter those words. "This is my testimony." It is so important to have a testimony, for it has to do with what the living Christ has done for us. It comes from meeting Him and is what gives us the greatest conviction. Nothing will shake us from our testimony. "One thing I do know, that though I was blind, now I see" (John 9:25). The fact that Jesus Christ is spoken of and reported about in a book is not sufficient proof even though the book is the Bible; this proof must be found in our own hearts. In our hearts we each must find Him, and then we will understand that He is our Savior. None of us should proclaim Him because we have read about Him; we should proclaim Him because we have met Him.

DAY 348
Thoughts To Ponder

Whatever you do, work at it with all your heart,
as working for the Lord, not for men.

—COLOSSIANS 3:23 [NIV]

We must first be salt before we can be light. Salt works in the unseen, while light is seen by all. Many desire to be light first! Be content to be salt. That is, do a little thing as though it were big, and God will allow you to do a big thing as though it were little.

One day I was waiting for a rental car. I sat beside a recently retired man, and together we watched with amazement two wallpaper hangers in another room. The man observed how hard the men were working and commented that they must own the business, for no one else these days would work that hard. As the men came out, one of them recognized me, and we began to talk. The retired man asked if they owned the business. Both responded, "No." Later I said, "Well, that explains their hard work; both are Christians." What a wonderful testimony is doing our work as unto the Lord.

DAY 349
Three Things Not Taught In Seminary

Under these circumstances, after so many thousands of people had gathered together that they were stepping on one another, He began saying to His disciples first of all, "Beware of the leaven of the Pharisees, which is hypocrisy. But there is nothing covered up that will not be revealed, and hidden that will not be known. Accordingly, whatever you have said in the dark will be heard in the light, and what you have whispered in the inner rooms will be proclaimed upon the housetops."

 —LUKE 12:1-3

There are at least three critical omissions from what we are told by schools of ministry. The first thing they neglect to say is that students will leave Bible college, seminary, or a general course of study with a judgmental attitude. It is inevitable! Why? "Knowledge makes arrogant, but love edifies" (I Corinthians 8:1). Generally, courses of study are built upon the premise that people change through knowledge. The one who knows the most has left the realm of the mere human; in short, knowledge will make one superior, placing him on the throne to look down on others. Once placed there, the believer cannot help but judge the ignorant. I get a sick feeling when I think back to my days in Bible college and graduate school. As though on a throne passing judgment on all of Christendom, we students would discuss what we knew that others did not, what we comprehended that others should be doing, and then we even mocked those in the body of Christ for their ignorance of basic theology. Comments ran rampant. "Elders are so stupid; do they not understand the basic requirements for the Church?" "Could anyone be so stupid as to think such things about the Holy Spirit?" "Oh, I cannot agree with the likes of those who have such bad theology." In a survey it was discovered that the weakest churches within a denomination were those within a twenty-five mile radius of the Bible college or seminary!

The second omission is even more critical. The Bible student is not warned that the standard of knowledge he has been led to set for others cannot be kept by himself. The student knows more than he has ever known, but he lives out proportionately less; even the very youngest Christian knows more than he is capable of doing. Knowledge in the student just plain outdistances his ability to do. Since the student set the standard and judges others without mercy, he cannot, in his failure, find mercy for himself. The reputation he made for himself was based on knowledge and cannot be lived up to. In the end, criticism of others turns to self-criticism and self-hatred. The student becomes exhausted and determines that it is much easier to live in the flesh than to strive to meet his own standards. Generally speaking, at this point the Bible college or seminary could be rebuked for false advertising, for while the brochures state as fact without hesitation, "We are making godly men for the equipping of the Church," the reality is they have created someone who feels "twice fit for hell."

However, all is not lost, for God causes all things to work together for good. Omissions one and two are prerequisites to the third exclusion: The student is not informed that knowledge does not come with power. Simply defined as knowledge without power, law is what the scholar has come under, a harsh master with no compassion for failure. The Christian life is something not one of us can live. There is no provision for believers to live the Christian life in our own strength. We must have a power other than our own. From the apprentice to the weathered saint, all of us must abide in Christ. This secret the student is finally ready to receive; the life he has wanted to live through knowledge is now living in him and through him without his effort. This discovery of Christ within brings another revelation. It really was not easier to live in the flesh. In fact, it was a struggle. The scholar had wondered why his participation in deeds of the flesh he had always enjoyed prior to his accepting Christ now always brought emptiness and a forced participation. With Christ as his life, all sin is now unnatural. The end result is a pupil God created, one of compassion, not judgmental or boastful, understanding power in weakness, and able to equip the Church for every good deed.

DAY 350
Time, For God

*For whom He foreknew, He also predestined to become
conformed to the image of His Son, that He might be the
firstborn among many brethren.*

—ROMANS 8:29

*For Christ also died for sins once for all, the just for the
unjust, in order that He might bring us to God,
having been put to death in the flesh, but made alive
in the spirit; in which also He went and made
proclamation to the spirits now in prison.*

 —I PETER 3:18 & 19

It is interesting to think about how God is not in time,
but time is in God. He is in the yesterday, the today, and
the tomorrow. This is why God is never in a hurry, since
He has no place to go. All along He has already been in
the future. He is not worrying over us, for He has been
in our future and sees how glorious it is. I was thinking,
too, how at the death of Christ on the cross, He stepped
out of time and entered eternity. From man's perspective,
Jesus was gone for three days; but in exiting time (where a
thousand years is like a day for the Lord) and stepping back
into eternity, we basically have no concept of what all He
might have accomplished, because we cannot impose time
on eternity. We know that in eternity He took all those
who would have believed from the past and all those who
would believe in the future and crucified them with Him

in a point in time (Galatians 2:20, Romans 6:6). If that is true, then when He was preaching to those held captive outside of time and in eternity (He descended before He ascended), He was actually preaching to all of mankind. Therefore, He was preaching to all who would believe and all who would not. This would mean I was there in eternity, and it was in eternity that I believed in Him. Once born, at a point in my time on earth I confirmed a decision I had already made in eternity. One proof of this is the fact that the day I believed in Jesus, it was not a strange experience but more of a homecoming. In my spirit I knew this was the place I always belonged, and I know all of us who made the same decision experienced the same recognition of belonging in Christ.

DAY 351
To Obey Is Better Than Sacrifice

And Samuel said, "Has the LORD as much delight in burnt offerings and sacrifices as in obeying the voice of the LORD? Behold, to obey is better than sacrifice and to heed than the fat of rams."

—I SAMUEL 15:22

To obey is better than sacrifice, one of the strongest proclamations made in the Old Testament. How did Samuel come to that conclusion? Did he one day wake up with the thought, did God speak it to him, or was it through experience? I believe it was the latter, that life itself taught Samuel this simple and profound truth.

The enemy loves the guilt that comes from sin. Sin is never the issue with the enemy. When we sin, the course of action is quite clear in I John 1:9, "If we confess our sins, He is faithful and righteous to forgive us our sins and to cleanse us from all unrighteousness." After confession there should be rejoicing. I can remember walking, praying, and confessing one evening. As I confessed I felt what was like a hand on my shoulder. Continuing my walk, a still small voice whispered, "Good, now get on; I will take care of everything!" There was a real lightness in my spirit, the lightness that should come after confession. However, the enemy steals our joy. After confession he whispers, "Oh, yes, you are forgiven but are you forgetting something? CONSEQUENCES! God forgives, yes, but the consequences are there for a lifetime." At this point, there is no joy, only the invitation for fear to enter our life.

Let me ask a question: Where is Jesus in all of this? Confession is to bring the focus off ourselves and onto Him. Satan is making sure self is still the focus. But listen, either God forgives or He does not! Anytime our children come to us and ask for forgiveness, we make every effort to block all consequences. Confession of their weakness and stupidity puts all our resources behind them. Well, what about God? Does He not do the same, only more so and much better? When we confess, God works to remove the consequences! He even cleanses us from all unrighteousness! Praise the Lord!

DAY 352
Toil In the Dark

Now when evening came, His disciples went down to the sea, and after getting into a boat, they started to cross the sea to Capernaum. It had already become dark, and Jesus had not yet come to them. The sea began to be stirred up because a strong wind was blowing. Then, when they had rowed about three or four miles, they saw Jesus walking on the sea and drawing near to the boat; and they were frightened. But He said to them, "It is I; do not be afraid." So they were willing to receive Him into the boat, and immediately the boat was at the land to which they were going.

—JOHN 6:16-21

Tertullian said, "The soul is naturally Christian." Was he right? I believe so, for only when we see a man accept Christ is his soul fulfilled and happy. To be an unbeliever is to live in a very unnatural state, to feel disjointed, empty, lacking something, longing for others to fill the vacuum, lost, and very unhappy. To avoid Christianity is to avoid happiness and set oneself on a course of self-destruction.

To live without Christ moment by moment is to toil in the dark. Much of mankind is toiling in the dark with their eyes on themselves and self-effort. In this condition they are lost, frantic, and within the grasp of death. Not until our eyes are set on Jesus do we find ourselves immediately filled with all we desire. We find our true selves there. Why does man insist on looking away from Jesus? What is his fear? The fear is that He will ask the impossible: to lose ourselves, to lose those lesser things we have determined will make us happy! Yet we are sad in this state! We fear the loss of our precious little something, though it has not brought happiness.

"On that day, let not the one who is on the housetop and whose goods are in the house go down to take them away; and likewise let not the one who is in the field turn back. Remember Lot's wife. Whoever seeks to keep his life shall lose it, and whoever loses his life shall preserve it." –Luke 17:31-33

DAY 353
Too Much Talk Of Sin

If we confess our sins, He is faithful and righteous to forgive us our sins and to cleanse us from all unrighteousness.

—I JOHN 1:9

Christians talk too much about sin, and I can think of three major disadvantages to making sin the believers' focus. First, "the mind set on the flesh is death, but the mind set on the Spirit is life and peace" (Rom. 8:6). "How shall we who died to sin still live in it?" (Rom. 6:2) Pastor Ray Andrews, Australia, told of visiting a church and listening to the pastor explain a terrible problem with sexual immorality among the young people. Ray asked what his sermon topics had typically been, and the pastor revealed that for over a year he had been preaching against fornication. Ray explained how what is preached would constantly be on the minds of the young people, and if it were sin, in the end the sin would increase. Ray's approach was to get the minds of the young people on Christ, where it would be difficult to plot and carry out the sin.

When I must make a major purchase, I obsessively look for all the information on the product. I cannot stand to make a poor purchasing decision and find something better in quality or price the next day. You can imagine what happens when it is time to replace an automobile; I read and talk, read and talk, and read and talk, until my poor wife is just plain sick of the conversation. After three or four days of listening to my obsession, she will just get up and walk away when she hears my voice. Her forbearance for three or four days is truly gracious and remarkable; however, she just gets sick of the topic and refuses to enter in.

Consider, then, when making sin the believers' focus, there arises a distinct disadvantage, which is that Christians will talk to God too much about their sins. When a believer sins, at the point of conviction the sin is to be confessed; afterward the believer is to move on. God has made clear in Scripture the fact that we are forgiven, but unbelief causes the Christian to keep confessing, wanting a sign of forgiveness. I get tired of hearing a believer repeatedly report on a sin committed; therefore, I can just imagine how weary God is of the whole thing. God is no longer talking about our past sin, because Christ's death on the cross took care of it. If we want to keep talking about it, we will only be talking to ourselves.

DAY 354
Total Commitment

We love, because He first loved us.
—I JOHN 4:19

This is My commandment, that you love one another, just as I have loved you. Greater love has no one than this, that one lay down his life for his friends.

—JOHN 15:12, 13

Why does the lack of commitment toward us on the part of others upset us so? Why can we so easily spiral into depression when we realize others really do not care, refuse to listen, and do not hold us in the midst of our emotional pain? We may even have thoughts of running, suicide, or self-pity; we may succumb to bitterness. We want total commitment; we want others to feel our pain, to hurt with us, to cry when we do, and to stop living if we do not know how to live. A harsh reality is that the majority do not care about another's plight, and the level of concern toward a depressed person seems to decline in proportion to the length of time the depression lasts. Many committed to help at the beginning grow weary with the passing of time and want to get on with their own lives. This realization causes a deeper depression. The fact is that the relatives do not want to hear from the homeless person, and whether or not this person eats tonight will not change the vacation plans.

As I often mention, nearly every issue in the Christian life is like a coin with two sides: legitimate and illegitimate. The illegitimate side is that we are not gods. Others are not to serve us; we are to be the servants. The life of Christ in us is one of giving, not expecting returns. If we have looked to others for significance and care, we have, in a large measure, received the misery we deserve. Depression can become addictive in consuming so much of life that we would not know how to live without it. Many stomp their feet in frustration over their depression, which involves the feet in plenty of movement, but the primary movement in which our feet are to be involved is taking us forward, putting one foot in front of the other to move out of depression and self-centeredness.

Often I am told that what I teach is simple and only works for a little while. However, if it works for a little while, it can work for a lifetime. The problem is that we stop working! We stop recognizing and receiving His daily presence and work in our lives. This is the work we must do. Too many are not fighting the good fight.

Imagine sitting in your house when the door bursts open and a bear rushes in to attack you. It would be quite normal to panic, get depressed, and even become angry as the bear is killing you and all others refuse to help. That makes sense. However, it makes no sense to sit in a chair, get depressed, panic, become angry, and then get into your car and drive around looking for bears; that is crazy. Yet you do just that if when your feet hit the floor in the morning and you feel worthless, unwanted, unlovable, like a failure, stupid, and depressed, you proceed to spend the day looking for events to prove the feelings. That is crazy. The more you allow lying emotions to control, the sicker you feel; the more you want others to do something, the more you examine yourself and your surroundings for what is wrong, and the more miserable you become. It takes three to five years to walk out of lying emotions. When will you start? When will you put one foot in front of the other? The longer you wait the harder it is! Spiritual laziness and torture are one and the same. You need not punish a cancer for being one; a cancer is its own punishment. So, too, is spiritual laziness.

The legitimate side of yearning for total commitment is that it is a natural desire of man. We are created to have someone totally committed to us. Listen to love songs, read the articles on love, listen to those who are looking for the perfect mate, read the lonely-hearts column in the local paper, and all will confirm man's great need for the total commitment of another, a need closely related to our need for security, love, acceptance, and assurance. We have a gnawing awareness of our need for daily help. We are made to receive water and food and become quite testy when they are denied; it is foolish to say man does not require them. The same is true of total commitment. It is a legitimate need. We are created beings, not self-sufficient gods. We need the assurance that someone greater than us is committed to us. If not, we will never enter the divine rest taught from Genesis to The Revelation. We discover that lack of total commitment shakes the foundation of our being, causing fears, worry, anxiety, and depression. When we consider the legitimate need, we wonder who could fill the shoes of the one who must commit to us. The person must be there at all times, hug us when we are not huggable, forgive, love, witness repeated failures yet not get sick of us, listen, have a healing touch, provide, encourage when we are weak, relate to our difficulties, express compassion, and care about every little detail of life.

Jesus is the Way! Every other way is not the Way! He is totally committed to you. He more than fills the bill. Please do a study in your concordance on the following phrases: "I will," "I do," "I help," "I redeem," "I love," "I overcome," "He Himself will," "He warned," "He forgives," and "He remembers no more." He is committed to you totally, and you love Him. There is no room for discouragement, disappointment in others, or the gnawing feeling of emptiness, for you have a God!

We talk much about the need of the disciple to be totally committed, but this is not possible until we have found out our Lord is committed to us. In His total commitment to us we find the fulfillment of another great need in man: the need we ourselves have to be totally committed to someone. We now find total commitment easy, enjoyable, and without burden. We love because He first loved us.

DAY 355
Turn Your Toes Out

Then He was saying to them all, "If anyone wishes to come after Me, he must deny himself and take up his cross daily and follow Me."

—LUKE 9:23

It is known that when competing in the rodeo, a rider of wild bulls and horses must rake the animal by pointing the toes out and the spurs in. This gives a better ride, more points, and, in the end, more money. A good friend in his youth had fallen on hard times; he was a rodeo champion but had not won for several weeks. He decided to send a telegram to his father asking for financial aid: "To Dad, from Billy. Emergency. Help needed. No food, out of money, need finances immediately. Not winning." Two hours later he received this reply: "To Billy, my beloved son. Turn your toes out. Your loving father." Billy was being reminded that when life is not working, he must return to the basics.

When we are feeling defeated, like everyone is against us and blaming us, no one cares or gives us the understanding and acceptance we need, when we find it too difficult to love and forgive—in short, when life is not working—we, too, must return to the basics. We are told the cross of Christ must be taken up daily. All who were with Jesus when He said this fully understood what He meant. The Romans made a man carry his own cross as a testimony that the death received was the death deserved. Our attitude is to be that everything we know of our crucified self will be denied daily. The old life cannot help, but the new one is more than a conqueror. If we expect to turn to the old life to make things go better, we get the misery we deserve. Fix our gaze on Jesus, take a moment to pray, turn to Psalm 139, listen to what God says, take up the cross that gives everyone the right to offend, and once again we find riches. We never lose life at the mountaintop; we lose life in forgetting the basics.

DAY 356
Unbeliever's Sin Versus Believer's Sin

*On the contrary you should rather forgive
and comfort him, lest somehow such a one be
overwhelmed by excessive sorrow.*

—II CORINTHIANS 2:7

*Let no one say when he is tempted, "I am being tempted
by God"; for God cannot be tempted by evil,
and He Himself does not tempt anyone.*

—JAMES 1:13

It must be said from the beginning that sin is a result of man's action and therefore not something created by God. God is the author of man and man is the author of sin. Now I want to look at this thing called sin. A Christian cannot sin in the same way a non-Christian does, and here is why. Sin and punishment are one. When we invite sin into our life, the LIFE that holds us together (Col. 1:1-15) withdraws and the absence of LIFE is death. If I take the punishment out of sin, do I still have sin? The unbeliever will sin and experience punishment (death where there once was LIFE), but Christ has taken the punishment out of sin for the believer. The believer merely must confess, for the blood of Jesus has cleansed and continues to cleanse him. Therefore, the believer will sin and not be punished, for Christ became his and every other believer's punishment on the cross. This gives sin a new meaning and a different purpose in the believer's life as opposed to the unbeliever's. If sin brings punishment to the unbeliever, what does sin do for the believer?

Imagine sin like cars with no steering wheels, headed for instantaneous wrecks. People are on the wrong road in out-of-control vehicles, and each day the trips are repeated, ending in constant punishment and death. Now sin is also like a train, but unlike a car without a steering wheel, it has tracks leading to a sure destination at the end. We are not to be traveling in sin, either the car or the train. However, only the believer can crawl aboard the sin train, which does not go out of control but heads on tracks to its destination determined by God. The Bible is the greatest encyclopedia of failures in the world. We see over and over again how saints riding the sin train ended up understanding the grace, love, mercy, forgiveness, and goodness of God. Most of the Bible would never have been written if the people of God had not been on the sin train, and yet God had his own destination for them and used the track to get them there. I want to write a book called, "Why This Place?" Why earth? Why man? Why sin? Why failure? Well, it all puts us on the sin train, but there is a God-determined destination for the believer that is redemptive; the unbeliever does not have this and is not allowing God to be redemptive.

Another example is the caterpillar and the butterfly. Both have the same DNA, but they are not the same. The Caterpillar is trapped in a tomb of his own making and lives in darkness. The butterfly is free and yet tossed back and forth by the smallest breeze. Again, the unbeliever is like the caterpillar; sin has trapped him in complete darkness, and he is easily captured or crushed. The believer is like the butterfly, and when he sins he is tossed back and forth by every little move in the atmosphere, and yet somehow he can travel across a continent. The wind against which the butterfly fights is actually taking him to a God-determined destination.

God is using sin in the believers' lives to take them to a revelation of Him. To echo Paul, we definitely are not teaching that we should sin so grace will abound. However, "where sin increased, grace abounded all the more" (Rm. 5:20). If this is not true and God cannot use our failures and be redemptive, then what is the option? We can look at our own lives for the witness and test it. Sin brought us to Christ when as unbelievers we got sick of the car wrecks! Then it has been sin used by Him to reveal who He really is and the "why" of obedience: to make us happy. God is fighting nothing and using everything.

DAY 357
Unreal Expectations

*Because the mind set on the flesh is hostile toward God;
for it does not subject itself to the law of God,
for it is not even able to do so; and those
who are in the flesh cannot please God.*

 —ROMANS 8:7 & 8

Generally in much of the East a person's mate and vocation are chosen for him. Therefore, the expectation of what marriage and vocation can add to the quality of life is very low. People there tend to turn to spiritual things (often wrong spirits), the one place where there is no ceiling and a bit of a feeling of freedom. In the West, where the individual can choose a mate and vocation, there exists a very unreal expectation of what marriage and career can give. In fact, those are expected to give what they cannot give in a way totally different from God's perspective of what marriage and work will accomplish in a person. Remember that the events of earth, passing through His hands, are preparing us for heaven, where there will be no marriage or vocations. In short, He is using our marriage and vocations to prepare us for something greater than what is often portrayed. Man looks for job satisfaction or marital bliss, but God gives the perfect place for the revelation of Christ.

Our first discovery as we travel through life is that marriage and vocations do not give LIFE, and second, we learn we cannot live for man. Third, we become aware of our self-centeredness; fourth, it is apparent we are easily offended. Fifth, and most importantly, it is obvious we are weak in our ability to love, to be faithful, to be content, or to have peace. Most hate to acknowledge it, but here is a simple secret: Admit where you are and you can leave where you are. Admit to God your feelings of being trapped, your supply of love for your mate has run out, you are sick of being used or abused, and you are still looking for life where LIFE cannot be found. Then simply ask Him to come.

A man told me of an experience he had when he said, "All guilt for my failures fell off me in just one moment when I realized I was a bound man." You see, Abraham received the promise of God, and the first thing he did was look at himself, consider himself as good as dead when it came to fulfilling the promise, and trust God to accomplish what he could not do. Have you realized that you are bound, so apart from Him you can do nothing? If God is to get all the glory then God is to do all the work. If I hired you to do a job and then handcuffed you to a tree, what would you think? Yet the day you believed in Jesus, before you could imitate Him, God crucified you to a tree. He is expecting nothing out of you. He knew what you would be at your worst, and still He chose you. You are feeling weak. Do not do anything except admit you are bound and ask Him what He is planning on doing. Get your attention away from self and the whole situation. Choose Jesus. Do not make your first choice the promise to change; make your first choice Jesus. As He flows through you to your mate, your experience will be something about which the most romantic novelists or moviemakers have yet to tell!

Do you enjoy music? You are enjoying the efforts of another as you let it flow in and around you. You do nothing but enjoy others' discipline. In the same way Jesus must flow through you while you, just as relaxed, enjoy the fruit of His work. Beautiful!

DAY 358
Verbal Beating

For our citizenship is in heaven, from which also we eagerly wait for a Savior, the Lord Jesus Christ.

—PHILIPPIANS 3:20

Once I was sitting with my brother in a small market in the Amazon region, eating a piece of cashew fruit, when an elderly Indian woman came up and started cursing me in her language. Startled, I looked up and said that I spoke English and did not understand. That bit of information did not deter her one bit as the verbal assault continued. As soon as possible, we walked away. My brother commented on how the woman was really mad at me. I stated that if I had been able to understand her, I might be apologetic, offended, upset, or vexed by the whole experience, but as it was, I simply did not care; it had no impact on or significance for me. It was easy to walk away and simply say, "Bless you."

As believers, our citizenship is in heaven. It is the language of heaven that we understand, the language of love. Any other language we simply do not understand, respond to, listen to, or traffic in. There is the language of the world filled with competitiveness, control, abuse, judgment, vindictiveness, hatred, outbursts, and slander. This language will only confuse us if we try to sort it out, for it is a form of communication alien to us. Recently I listened to an interview with a man who had regular conversations with space aliens. He sounded quite mad as he deciphered the messages. Believers sound equally mad when describing and deciphering what a carnal mate, unbelieving employer, parent, or child has said, and then what they said back, and again what was said, and so on. It does not even matter, since everyone involved left the conversation immaculately unchanged, distorting and hearing only what each one wanted to.

We are not to respond to the words of the world but to the condition of the world. Likewise, we are not to respond to the message of carnal believers but only to their condition. Love moves past words directly to the heart of humanity.

Regardless of what is said, it is good to remember that our citizenship and language come from heaven.

DAY 359
Wanting the Will Of God

Trials have come so that your faith—of greater worth than gold—may be proved genuine and may result in praise, glory and honor when Jesus Christ is revealed.

—I PETER 1:7 [NIV]

Blessed is the man who perseveres under trial, because when he has stood the test, he will receive the crown of life that God has promised to those who love him.

—JAMES 1:12 [NIV]

For years we have prayed, "Thy will be done on earth as it is in heaven." Yet when His will treads on self-will, we do not want it. His will is what we perfectly need. When it is His will for us to be disrespected, ignored, not comforted, rebuked, abused, or offended, do we rebel against it? Do we know that this, also, is His will?

We are very narrow in our thinking concerning the will of God when we think it only includes things we deem and define to be good. If the neighborhood bully continued to beat up our children, even killing one, and we as parents had the power, right, and authority to send the bully away, would we? God created Satan and could disassemble him. One day God will throw him in a lake of fire. Why is He waiting? Think about it. Why does He not destroy this bully? Is God permitting him for a very good reason? We are often guilty of fighting what God has permitted. In the wisdom of God, could it be the will of God? I am not saying that God created evil or sin, for they are results. However, He knew they would be the results. I do not know the mind of God, but I trust the will of God. If it is His will for me to have an enemy and live in a body of flesh, then I am prepared to accept it.

There is the story of the Korean fish market. One seller always had live, fresh fish; everyone else sold only dead fish. He sold more than anyone else. One day the secret was discovered. In his tank he kept a catfish, the enemy of all the other fish. They would swim around, staying alive and fresh, because their enemy harassed them. Well, amen.

DAY 360
We Are a Voice

I am the voice of one calling in the desert,
"Make straight the way for the Lord."
 —JOHN 1:23 [NIV]

I remember playing dress-up as a child; I would be a cowboy, an adult, or an army officer, and then I would pretend to become a voice in that particular bunch. Adults can continue to dress up as environmentalists, hippies, radicals, intellectuals, activists, religious personalities, political conservatives or liberals, and they leave their places of abode to pretend, simply echoing what they have heard from the world. In this case, they dress, act, and talk to avoid life and the real world, which is proof that what they believe does not even work in the real world. Again, they become an echo, not a voice espousing original convictions. Many have come to conclusions vicariously through the experiences of others. Some—and I hate to say it—develop echoes from watching television sit-coms, movies, and talk shows (shudder)! The world prefers an echo to a voice, followers to leaders, a bland average to a shining light. There is an echo that allows one to become a voice in the world, not a follower or one pretending at life, but one having real, original life in living color with a voice that does not withdraw from the world but takes it. John the Baptist was just such a man.

Christ is in us. When we communicate the life within, we are not echoes but actual voices. Christ is life. He created us, everything is held together by Him, He lives in us, we are His workmanship, we are His righteousness, and we are not imitations. We are each one uniquely His voice. Just as the Father expressed Himself through the Son and the Son was not an echo, the Son desires to express Himself through His people. As we allow this, we are not echoes, for we are voices. We are not imitating Christ; we are participating in His life. We are the branches grafted in, receiving the life of the Son which has become our life. Colossians 3:4, "When Christ, who is our life, is revealed, then you also will be revealed with Him in glory." The only way to be a voice—to pull away from the bunch, to stop pretending, to live life in its fullness—is to abide in Him.

DAY 361
What Brings the People
Must Keep the People

*Do you not yet understand or remember the five loaves of
the five thousand, and how many baskets you took up?*

—MATTHEW 16:9

A man was telling me about a slow leak in his truck
tire. He wanted to get as far down the road as possible,
because he did not have a spare tire. He explained that
his grandfather had told him a secret, "When you have
a slow leak, drive as fast as you can. This will cause more
wheel rotations, and when the part of the tire with the
hole hits the pavement, the pressure will not let the air
escape. Just drive flat out, and you can go longer before the
flat completely stops you." I thought that was interesting
but wondered what it had to do with our seminar. Then,
with a crestfallen countenance, the man looked at me and
said, "I am flat as a pastor and a believer. I have seen there
was a leak in the church, and my approach was to speed
up, introduce as many new programs as possible, keep the
people busy and distracted, and thus ignore the leak. It
did not work, and I am flat and exhausted. Today I have
seen the leak's essence: I had forgotten to proclaim Jesus,
forgotten to determine to make Him known." That I did
understand.

We must be careful as we work in the church, for what
attracts the people will be what is needed to keep the

people. I have seen so many burnt-out believers. Jesus fed the multitude, and when He was not feeding them, they crucified Him. He was feeding their flesh, and their flesh grew.

Imagine two pastors, both with the same message. One attracts the people with videos, music, games, a magnificent facility, miracles, healings, comfort, cappuccino machines, the spectacular, strong personalities, and bribes of a variety of forms. The other attracts with the simple message that a believer is the temple of God, the Holy Spirit will bring about the life of Christ naturally in him, and Jesus can be the source of his heart to bring life to his spirit, soul, body, and the world around him; though in the world there will be trouble, Jesus has overcome the world. The first pastor now needs a football field to accommodate the audience and enough room for motorcycles to jump over him while he speaks or a flagpole from the top of which he has promised to eat pie if everyone in the youth group brings a friend. The other pastor just keeps talking about Jesus and has fifty people attending; they take back to their daily lives and jobs a great secret: Jesus is in them. One must ask what has really attracted the people, because what attracts the people is what will keep them.

I find it interesting that overall attendance in church is decreasing but increasing in the mega-church. What does one have that the other does not? It is a slippery slope and a great temptation when we see the mega-club degrade Christianity to the folly of the flesh that attracts people. Once that has occurred, the only way to keep the people from shifting to another mega-club with more appeal to the flesh is to keep upping the fleshly appeal in the existing club. It is throat-cutting, because flesh begets flesh, and appealing to the flesh of man will ultimately create more flesh. What an ambiance for the church of Jesus Christ!

Take a walk in the woods. Life is something that comes naturally, without effort. If people are attracted by Jesus, then lifting up Jesus will keep the people. The goal is not keeping them coming for any reason but for Him and His glory. It is easy and relaxing. I spoke to a large group in a remote area of Nepal. The pastors came at the break, saying, "We did not know that if God gets the glory, He does the work. Everything we have heard from the U.S. involved a program we needed to do. Preaching Christ has taken a second place."

Yes, and there is one more thing: When did the men of God begin to look to the world for the secret of success? There was a time when the Church led the world. It is as though there is a worldly parade and the Christian club stands on the curb analyzing what has attracted people to join in. Next, the Christians jump to the back of the parade, dressing, imitating, and offering what those with a darkened mind at the front have dreamed up for the masses. They put something of a Christian twist to it, believing that those at the front of the parade will look back and want to be led by the new followers. A club in the Midwest used its budget to buy shot glasses and hand them out to every bar in town for free. The bar owners were asked to serve the whiskey in the glasses, so that when the patron drank the last swig, he would see the message painted on the bottom, "Give our church a shot," along with the address. This kind of thing is hailed as cutting edge. A group of prostitutes for Jesus is said to be going on the streets and sleeping with men before giving them a Bible and inviting them to church. When questioned, they said what so many say, "How else are you going to reach these men? They will not come to church." I want to encourage all of you reading this that Jesus is enough, and if you want to shake the world, you do not have to become like it to be heard. The world knows a contrast when it sees one. We are not joining the world's parade. People attracted to Jesus need only hear talk about Him. That type of fellowship will not ever go flat.

DAY 362
What Do You See?

Now when the attendant of the man of God had risen early and gone out, behold, an army with horses and chariots was circling the city. And his servant said to him, "Alas, my master! What shall we do?" So he answered, "Do not fear, for those who are with us are more than those who are with them." Then Elisha prayed and said, "O LORD, I pray, open his eyes that he may see." And the LORD opened the servant's eyes and he saw; and behold, the mountain was full of horses and chariots of fire all around Elisha.

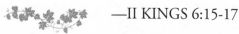 —II KINGS 6:15-17

What do you see? This may be the most important question you must answer in the next few years. Like you, I receive notes from friends who have lost their jobs, had their wages reduced, or in some other way endured a loss. When that pressure is heaped on top of what already existed in family life through needs, relationship hiccups, and an increasingly decadent, anti-God world environment, it is easy to lose hope and slip into despair. Often when discipling I hear a plethora of comments that reveal what is seen.

"I am in the wrong place to find a relationship."

"There is simply no one hiring."

"We have had the same trouble for years in our marriage, and it is not going to change."

"I have tried everything with my son, and he continues on his own way."

"I am just tired of being run over."

"I have been depressed for years."

You get the point. We, like the servant of Elisha, only see the circumstance and not the God who is always behind the circumstance. If we could recognize our God behind the events, we could rest in this moment and not let our emotions and thoughts race ahead to the worst possible outcome, letting events yet to happen determine our lack of joy and peace today. Remember how one saying of a "Praise God" before knowing the outcome of a situation is worth a thousand expressions of "Praise God" after the situation.

In these times believers must draw upon their history with God. We do have a history with Him. Has He ever left us? Has He ever forsaken us? Have we starved, to date? Have we ever not had shelter? "I have been young and now I am old, yet I have not seen the righteous forsaken or his descendants begging bread" (Psalm 37:25). I would be lying to say there were not times in my life when I had lost hope, and in those times my one problem merely multiplied into many more. Hope is the incubator for life.

To lose it is to lose life. We are not of those who are "having no hope and without God in the world" (Ephesians 2:12). When I have been in the place of hopelessness, I have prayed for God's opening of my eyes to see Him all around me. He is there; He shows no partiality and is in the middle of our circumstances.

Often I have seen believers in a pit; it would be inaccurate to say they are not! They are! The best advice does not encourage those for whom all options appear to be gone. I simply ask them to invite Jesus into the pit with them, because He takes responsibility for everything into which we invite Him. "Casting all your anxiety upon Him, because He cares for you . . . and after you have suffered for a little while, the God of all grace, who called you to His eternal glory in Christ, will Himself perfect, confirm, strengthen, and establish you" (I Peter 5:7 & 10).

DAY 363
What He Creates, He Maintains

Now to Him who is able to keep you from stumbling, and to make you stand in the presence of His glory blameless with great joy, to the only God our Savior, through Jesus Christ our Lord, be glory, majesty, dominion and authority, before all time and now and forever. Amen.

—JUDE 24, 25

I have a relationship with Christ because He has kept it alive. I find great joy in that fact. I will tell you a secret: I pray because He put me in places where I had no choice but to pray. I trust Him because He saw to it there was no other option. I have gone to bed depressed and arose in the morning full of hope, because His mercies are new every morning. It is all about Him. I like the old man who, after recounting everything Jesus had done for him, was asked the following question, "But don't we have to do something?" The man pondered and then proclaimed, "Yes, there is something we must do. We must sing hymns of praise!" How right he was. Jesus keeps me from stumbling; self-will and determination do not. Jesus continually brings me into the glory of God, where a great light heals and brings joy. Really, there is not that much a believer has to do besides maintaining focus on Him, for He does the work.

Jesus was the most transparent man ever to live; to look at Him was to look at the Father. One day the disciples, looking at the window named Jesus, said, "Show us the Father!" A voice came from beyond the window, from the One who lived through Jesus, saying, "Have I been with you this long and still you do not know Me?" His goal for us is to become transparent so others might see the One who lives in us. He is in charge of this task, and all we need do is agree with it. "Jesus, it is my heart's desire to have the revelation of Christ in me."

DAY 364
What Is the Real Difference In a Christian Life Versus the Unbeliever's Life?

Peace I leave with you; My peace I give to you; not as the world gives, do I give to you. Let not your heart be troubled, nor let it be fearful.

—JOHN 14:27

But a Pharisee named Gamaliel, a teacher of the law, who was honored by all the people, stood up in the Sanhedrin and ordered that the men be put outside for a little while. Then he addressed them: "Men of Israel, consider carefully what you intend to do to these men. Some time ago Theudas appeared, claiming to be somebody, and about four hundred men rallied to him. He was killed, all his followers were dispersed, and it all came to nothing. After him, Judas the Galilean appeared in the days of the census and led a band of people in revolt. He too was killed, and all his followers were scattered. Therefore, in the present case I advise you: Leave these men alone! Let them go! For if their purpose or activity is of human origin, it will fail. But if it is from God, you will not be able to stop these men; you will only find yourselves fighting against God."

—ACTS 5:34-39 [NIV]

Before the observations are presented in this article, I want to establish a disclaimer of sorts, some thoughts to help clarify what I am not saying. Remember that there are always good hearts at bad meetings. Also, I have met men of God who do minister in huge churches because they are preaching Christ. Another point is that the flesh of man works constantly to turn the Christian Faith (what Jesus does for us) into the Christian Religion (what man can do). Also, keep in mind that sometimes—if not often—the first move we see can be something of God, but the copycat versions are generally a one-off (rarely is God doing something in the U.S. that applies to a village in Africa, with the exception of consistently lifting up Jesus). God's dealing with an individual can be outside of our box of theology and yet easily within His bounds. David was leaping and dancing before the people and the Lord; some watching would have surely thought the cheese had slid off the cracker, but David's actions were acceptable to God.

Having said all of that in preparation and as a foundation, in my nearly four decades as a believer there have been many waves come and go through the Church, washing the believers out to sea. For those "seduced"—many willingly—by the teaching, these waves have often waylaid them years. Most waves scream, "Jesus is not enough!" Interestingly, when these "spiritual" tsunamis hit there is generally havoc in the aftermath. I can remember when some called the deeds of the flesh "demons" and were constantly casting them out, the "spiritual umbrella" movement, the outpouring of laughter, the touching movement, the passive "ask Jesus to tell you" ministry, prophets proclaiming vague assessments of a crowd, the "demand of God movement" (shout and demand what you want until He gives it to you), healing of the memories, inner healing, and myriad baptized-psychology solutions. Of course, there is the "multiply your riches by giving to me" movement, and more. Where are they now? Though all of these waves were presented as absolutes, they have disappeared and were therefore, according to Scripture, man-powered activities. I suppose they had to leave, because something man-driven appeals to the flesh, and flesh will always want more and need variety, something different. In time we will see the prosperity movement and the mega church go the way of the waves that came before them to make room for something else. Many are struggling now in those movements because of the "economy." Interesting, because if it were God-driven and not man-driven, the "economy" would have nothing to do with the problem. Well, amen. I read a secular quote refuting the prosperity gospel because there was no evidence indicating those who believe in God were any less likely to lose their jobs, homes, or retirement funds in a financial downturn. Another article opined about how the prosperity gospel betrayed our faith's legacy of sacrifice and social justice. My point is this: The successful and blest Christian life is being defined improperly all the time. Many are insecure in their faith, so they crave some kind of spiritual experience for validation. This makes them easy prey for the promise of something spectacular, special, unique, secretive, and exclusive to them and their group. If someone were to say God allowed him to walk on water, that person could write a book, be invited to public meetings, and generally make a fairly good living, when the response to such an experience should be, "Yes, and your point? How does the experience help us?" Generally, the hearers are left craving a similar experience for themselves, again for validation. The speaker might not have known what he was doing, but he was setting a standard of "special" acceptance by God if they will but become some of the "special elect."

Well, the benefit of being a child of God is great. Jesus said we would be hated by the world. Paul recounts the struggles of the early believers by saying they were "pressed down." James makes it clear there are trials in our walk. Now we are getting the nut back on the bolt, because we do not hear these things very often! Read Hebrews, Chapter 11, and see what the life of a saint looks like. From beginning to end, the New Testament supports these claims in a variety of places. As you let the experience of those who have come before witness to what the Christian life is, you may discover that your life is more in line with the reality of the Christian life than those believers craving validation from the miraculous or monetary gain. Matthew 12:39, "He answered, 'A wicked and adulterous generation asks for a miraculous sign! But none will be given it except the sign of the prophet Jonah.'"

The purpose of life on earth is not comfort before going to heaven to be even more comfortable, having left behind all the uncomfortable people who encroached on our comfort. The purpose of life on earth is to discover Jesus. Remember, He was driven into the wilderness before His great temptation. What a great place, the wilderness! Nothing is there to stimulate the body or soul, so only a spiritual life could be pursued. In that dry and desolate place, His food was coming via the Spirit. He was not given happiness but joy; there were no grand thoughts, only revelation, no big plans, but rather the will of God, nothing spectacular, but instead the peace of God. At the end of the forty days of being filled with the things of God, the temptations were easily cast aside for what they really were: an attempt by the enemy for Jesus to validate Himself to God and man, when God had already validated Him for forty days with His peace.

Most believers would not be encouraged at being validated by oppression on all sides, but I would ask, "Hasn't He kept you? Didn't He bring you out of the darkness and into His light? Didn't you discover that living through health problems, family crises, a death, or financial distress was not nearly as frightening as you thought it would be when viewing it from a distance? Once actually entering the situation, you found Him there to carry you, like in Daniel where the fellows walked in the fiery furnace with the One and not even the smell of smoke was on them. With Jesus, your situation was not as frightening as you thought it might be." I want those who are in the middle of oppression to remember they, too, will come through.

The difference between a believer's life and an unbeliever's life is not to be expressed in the things of the world or the miraculous; the difference is that believers have peace. Yes, our emotions may be upside down when discovering what a child is up to, but be quiet for a moment and let the peace of God rule in our hearts. We have many of the same problems as unbelievers, and yet they have no peace, no one to carry them through, no hope, no confidence, no faith, no assurance, and no comfort. The things that separate the believer and the unbeliever are not of the world, because we both have bodies of flesh; what separates the believer from the unbeliever are things that cannot be seen. Often I have said to an unbeliever, "Let me shake your hand, because I would have crumbled under your circumstances without Jesus." Of course, he secretly is crumbling. Jesus is keeping the believer, pruning, revealing Himself, filling daily life with LIFE, and permitting a need so He can meet it. It is a wonderful life. The believer is in school, and upon graduation he will understand how the Way on earth was the perfect Way for the child of God.

DAY 365
Why Open the Bible?

You search the Scriptures because you think that in them you have eternal life, and it is these that testify about Me.

—JOHN 5:39

Often I have believers tell of their conflicts and adverse situations which made them turn to the Bible in search of something that would move directly to the heart and touch them, but they found nothing. Has that ever been your experience? You are in need, confused, lacking direction, and upon opening the Bible, you do not find the needed comfort. Perhaps in desperation you have thrown down the Bible in hopes it would open to a suitable passage to bring the needed relief. No doubt there have been times when the Lord used this method to minister to your need, but more often than not the Bible probably fell open to an obscure passage recounting the lineage of some other desperate soul.

Why, when the knowledge of the "word" is proclaimed as the cure-all, do so many find nothing when they are in times of need? Do they have a wrong heart? Why are arguments over doctrines not resolved through study of the Scriptures? Is Scripture not clear on baptism, gifts of the Spirit, and predestination? When a church is splitting and the Scriptural list of right and wrong is presented, why does the division continue to grow? Why in the midst of great temptation does the person who has the whole Bible memorized succumb? Is it because he does not read and meditate upon it with a right heart? If the Bible does not give comfort because the heart is not right, then we must conclude that heart condition is actually greater than the Bible. But isn't the Bible greater than anything man can do or manufacture?

Deep within the heart is a gnawing, all-consuming emptiness felt within the most successful to the most destitute person. I heard one popular celebrity announce he had experienced many miserable days within the past year, but then he challenged the audience to pick out those days, boasting in the great job he did of covering them up. Most people are perplexed by the emptiness within, the feeling of things just not being right or fulfilling, or things peculiarly out of sync. Often the emptiness is not discussed, but the endless methods to fix it certainly are. On the negative side we observe with wonder the world's perversion of sex, the self-centeredness in marriages, the destruction wrought by drugs, and children feeling hopeless enough to consider suicide as a viable option. On the more positive track we notice such things as obsession with the pain felt by all living things without an accompanying poverty of spirit that would allow the people to make sacrifices to help the living; these things, too, are attempts to fill the vacuum. Underlying the positive and negative attempts to fill the void is the ever-present gnawing that something is wrong. According to statistics (if they can be believed), nearly 50 million Americans are depressed, another 20 million suffer from attention deficit disorder, anxiety claims another 30 million, and on and on until in the end, when all statistics are added up, one must conclude that the average person has at least three definable problems. Why?

I have often commented that Christianity is the only religion the world supports; if something is not Christian, it is not natural. As we abide in Him, even the very flowers encourage us along our way. Man needs the relationship with God that comes through Jesus Christ. The gnawing spot in the heart of man, the emptiness causing many of our physical and psychological problems, is in the place where Christ's life belongs. Before their fall, Adam and Eve had the bodies and souls of men but spirits in touch with God. What completes the creation of man today is a new, reborn spirit, the very spirit and life of Christ. He was the firstborn of a new creation, a new man. Man must have a relationship with God to be complete! Understanding the creation and need of man, as well as God's desire for man, will answer many questions. Many are sidetracked, believing the purpose of our creation is holiness, faithfulness, obedience, knowledge of the Bible, proper behavior, lovingkindness, or even self-denial. These are all results of the relationship, not the cause.

The Bible is not the answer book; its purpose is to point us to THE LORD WHO IS THE ANSWER. Nothing will be allowed to substitute for a relationship with Him, and anything outside of Him is nothing. Within the relationship caused and allowed by the Son of God, the Book is beautiful and full of knowledge able to move the eighteen inches from head to heart, and we know experientially that "all Scripture is inspired by God and profitable for teaching, for reproof, for correction, for training in righteousness" (II Timothy 3:16).

DAY 366
Working For An
Unethical Employer

And some tax collectors also came to be baptized, and they said to him, "Teacher, what shall we do?" And he said to them, "Collect no more than what you have been ordered to." And some soldiers were questioning him, saying, "And what about us, what shall we do?" And he said to them, "Do not take money from anyone by force, or accuse anyone falsely, and be content with your wages."

—LUKE 3:12-14

Many times the believer working for an unbeliever has a sense of being trapped. Let's be realistic, many in business are unethical. As believers we can find ourselves working for a company and not agreeing with its techniques for the acquisition of or its usage of monies. We disagree with the questionable morality of the executives, the social causes supported, and what is so eloquently portrayed as technical truth. What is a believer to do, take a stand and quit the company? Many believe so, and if you are one of those, I have a challenge: Find out what the board of directors of the telephone, utility, and city are doing with the money you pay. To be consistent, then, shut off your electricity! You will soon find your lifestyle in bondage to the sin of others.

Paul made the same point in I Corinthians 5:9-13. "I wrote you in my letter not to associate with immoral people; I did not at all mean with the immoral people of this world, or with the covetous and swindlers, or with idolaters, for then you would have to go out of the world. But actually, I wrote to you not to associate with any so-called brother if he is an immoral person, or covetous, or an idolater, or a reviler, or a drunkard, or a swindler—not even to eat with such a one. For what have I to do with judging outsiders? Do you not judge those who are within the church? But those who are outside, God judges."

In the Luke passage John the Baptist is talking to groups of men working for unethical employers. It was not right for those in authority to raise taxes to such levels; it was simply legalized theft, which to this day takes place in many parts of the world when carnal men of greed in authority get together, make up a tax, call it legal, and keep all the money. Who would like to be a believer in charge of collecting such a tax? The men John the Baptist was addressing were just such men. It is no wonder they say, "Teacher, what shall we do?" He gives the answer. Do not use force, do not lie, and do not get into the mindset of your unethical employer. I have been in business and told to do things I did not think were right. I simply followed the above and let the judgment fall on the head of the one(s) who commanded it.

DAY 367
Working Your Way Out Of God

He who overcomes will thus be clothed in white garments;
and I will not erase his name from the book of life,
and I will confess his name before
My Father and before His angels.

—REVELATION 3:5

With my ever-increasing age I have noticed the strength of my eyeglasses having to be changed frequently. When I increase lens intensity, I can see things I was missing. I believe it to be true of my spiritual eyes, as well. As I have gotten older, God keeps giving me new glasses with which I can see things I previously did not notice. With new spiritual glasses come many changes. I still shudder when I think of Bible School and wearing the glasses of superiority because of what I knew, leading to disdain for those "ignorant" of God's Word, which was constantly proclaimed. After all, we were becoming "Theologians." With the glasses I have had for some time, I see the folly of that and have repented of my former attitudes. To think a man will "know" God! My, it is so much nicer to bask in the beauty of this fact: I am known by God.

Well, back to my present prescription. Jesus holds all things together (Colossians 1:15-17; John 1:1-3; Ephesians 4:6; Acts 17:28). He is the Life holding all life together. We all exist in His Life; we are all connected to Him and totally dependent on Him for our existence. Therefore, we are in the Book of Life. The problem is that man lives by Him but refuses to recognize Him. What if God has given us seventy years (plus or minus) to either acknowledge He is our life or to work our way out of the Book of Life? Names are not put in the Book of Life but taken out. So if a man, held together by Life and in the Book of Life, refuses to acknowledge that Life, he has the attitude of actually working his way out of Life during his years on earth. Finally, at death, such a person gets the desire of his heart. His lifetime was spent working his way out of Life, and now for eternity God gives what he wanted and fought for and removes his name from the book of Life. I am amazed at how hard this type of man works to get out of Life. Jesus holds him together, and yet the man hates Him with a passion and is anti-Christ in all he does. He goes to the grave as a God-hater. God, on the other hand, strives to keep him in Life; His sun shines on him, He provides for him, He heals him over and over, He blesses him, He sent His own Son for him, and yet the man wants away from Him, out of the Book of Life. God is doing His utmost to keep the man, who in turn is struggling to be free. Recognizing Jesus is so easy, and in so doing, one will never have his name taken out of the Book of Life. Working one's way out of God is so, so, so very difficult. Amen.